7/17/13
$61.00

ELECTRONIC AMERICA

ISSN 1554-4397

ELECTRONIC AMERICA

Stephen Meyer

INFORMATION PLUS® REFERENCE SERIES
Formerly Published by Information Plus, Wylie, Texas

GALE
CENGAGE Learning·

Detroit • New York • San Francisco • New Haven, Conn • Waterville, Maine • London

Electronic America

Stephen Meyer

Kepos Media, Inc.: Paula Kepos and Janice Jorgensen, Series Editors

Project Editors: Kathleen J. Edgar, Elizabeth Manar, Kimberley McGrath

Rights Acquisition and Management: Robyn Young

Composition: Evi Abou-El-Seoud, Mary Beth Trimper

Manufacturing: Rita Wimberley

Gale
27500 Drake Rd.
Farmington Hills, MI 48331-3535

ISBN-13: 978-0-7876-5103-9 (set)
ISBN-13: 978-1-4144-8137-1

ISBN-10: 0-7876-5103-6 (set)
ISBN-10: 1-4144-8137-3

ISSN 1554-4397

This title is also available as an e-book.
ISBN-13: 978-1-5730-2285-9 (set)
ISBN-10: 1-5730-2285-3 (set)
Contact your Gale sales representative for ordering information.

Printed in the United States of America
1 2 3 4 5   17 16 15 14 13

TABLE OF CONTENTS

The rise of social networking, cloud computing, Twitter, and other advances in online communication are investigated. The integration of electronics and information technologies into American cars and household appliances and utilities is also studied, as are developments in robotics.

PREFACE

Electronic America is part of the *Information Plus Reference Series*. The purpose of each volume of the series is to present the latest facts on a topic of pressing concern in modern American life. These topics include the most controversial and studied social issues of the 21st century: abortion, capital punishment, care for the elderly, crime, the environment, gambling, health care, immigration, minorities, national security, social welfare, women, youth, and many more. Even though this series is written especially for high school and undergraduate students, it is an excellent resource for anyone in need of factual information on current affairs.

By presenting the facts, it is the intention of Gale, Cengage Learning to provide its readers with everything they need to reach an informed opinion on current issues. To that end, there is a particular emphasis in this series on the presentation of scientific studies, surveys, and statistics. These data are generally presented in the form of tables, charts, and other graphics placed within the text of each book. Every graphic is directly referred to and carefully explained in the text. The source of each graphic is presented within the graphic itself. The data used in these graphics are drawn from the most reputable and reliable sources, such as from the various branches of the U.S. government and from private organizations and associations. Every effort has been made to secure the most recent information available. Readers should bear in mind that many major studies take years to conduct and that additional years often pass before the data from these studies are made available to the public. Therefore, in many cases the most recent information available in 2013 is dated from 2010 or 2011. Older statistics are sometimes presented as well, if they are landmark studies or of particular interest and no more-recent information exists.

Although statistics are a major focus of the *Information Plus Reference Series*, they are by no means its only content. Each book also presents the widely held positions and important ideas that shape how the book's subject is discussed in the United States. These positions are explained in detail and, where possible, in the words of their proponents. Some of the other material to be found in these books includes historical background, descriptions of major events related to the subject, relevant laws and court cases, and examples of how these issues play out in American life. Some books also feature primary documents or have pro and con debate sections that provide the words and opinions of prominent Americans on both sides of a controversial topic. All material is presented in an evenhanded and unbiased manner; readers will never be encouraged to accept one view of an issue over another.

HOW TO USE THIS BOOK

During the late 20th and early 21st centuries the United States was transformed by the rapid development and adoption of new electronic devices, programs, and other technologies. Computers, cell phones, CD-ROMs, cable television, e-mail, MP3s, DVDs, viruses, robots, spam, peer-to-peer networks, and massively multiplayer online role-playing games were in limited use in 1980, if they existed at all. By 2013 they had all become more common, and many were ubiquitous. Their effect on the United States, and on the world, has been profound. New types of industries developed to produce and make use of these technologies. Existing businesses used them to become more efficient. New technologies also opened the door to new kinds of crime and criminals, and with them a need for changes in U.S. government and law enforcement. Last but not least, average Americans found that these technologies made it increasingly easy for them to communicate and find information, as well as to enjoy themselves, to be frustrated, or even to be victimized, in new and different ways.

Electronic America consists of nine chapters and three appendixes. Each chapter is devoted to a particular aspect of the changes in the United States brought about by high technology and its applications. For a summary of the information that is covered in each chapter, please see the synopses that are provided in the Table of Contents.

Chapters generally begin with an overview of the basic facts and background information on the chapter's topic, then proceed to examine subtopics of particular interest. For example, Chapter 2: Developments in Telecommunications begins with an assessment of the ways that e-mail and cell phones have transformed the ways Americans communicate in the 21st century. The chapter provides a history of e-mail technology, from its early development as part of the U.S. Department of Defense's ARPANET to its integration into the everyday life of most individuals and businesses by the late 1990s, while also investigating some of the nuisances (such as spam) involved with maintaining an e-mail account. Chapter 2 also examines other forms of electronic communication that have become popular in the 21st century, notably instant messaging and voice over Internet protocol. The chapter proceeds to survey the history of cell phones, analyzing the technology behind their development, the establishment of government standards aimed at creating a national cell phone network, and the emergence of mobile devices as an integral aspect of everyday life. Chapter 2 considers a number of hazards that are associated with cell phone use, including distracted driving and the technology's potential negative impact on the human brain, before concluding with a discussion of fourth-generation wireless service in the early 21st century. Readers can find their way through a chapter by looking for the section and subsection headings, which are clearly set off from the text. They can also refer to the book's extensive Index, if they already know what they are looking for.

Statistical Information

The tables and figures featured throughout *Electronic America* will be of particular use to readers in learning about this topic. These tables and figures represent an extensive collection of the most recent and valuable statistics on new technology and its impact on the United States—for example, graphics cover how many Americans use the Internet, how they use it, and how usage differs depending on demographic characteristics; enrollment in distance learning programs by type of institution; and the percent of American households victimized by identity theft. Gale, Cengage Learning believes that making this information available to readers is the most important way to fulfill the goal of this book: to help readers understand the issues and controversies surrounding new technologies in the United States and reach their own conclusions.

Each table or figure has a unique identifier appearing above it, for ease of identification and reference. Titles for the tables and figures explain their purpose. At the end of each table or figure, the original source of the data is provided.

To help readers understand these often complicated statistics, all tables and figures are explained in the text. References in the text direct readers to the relevant statistics. Furthermore, the contents of all tables and figures

are fully indexed. Please see the opening section of the Index at the back of this volume for a description of how to find tables and figures within it.

Appendixes

Besides the main body text and images, *Electronic America* has three appendixes. The first is the Important Names and Addresses directory. Here, readers will find contact information for a number of government and private organizations that can provide further information on computers and high technology. The second appendix is the Resources section, which can also assist readers in conducting their own research. In this section, the author and editors of *Electronic America* describe some of the sources that were most useful during the compilation of this book. The final appendix is the Index. It has been greatly expanded from previous editions and should make it even easier to find specific topics in this book.

ADVISORY BOARD CONTRIBUTIONS

The staff of Information Plus would like to extend its heartfelt appreciation to the Information Plus Advisory Board. This dedicated group of media professionals provides feedback on the series on an ongoing basis. Their comments allow the editorial staff who work on the project to continually make the series better and more user-friendly. The staff's top priority is to produce the highest-quality and most useful books possible, and the Information Plus Advisory Board's contributions to this process are invaluable.

The members of the Information Plus Advisory Board are:

- Kathleen R. Bonn, Librarian, Newbury Park High School, Newbury Park, California

- Madelyn Garner, Librarian, San Jacinto College, North Campus, Houston, Texas

- Anne Oxenrider, Media Specialist, Dundee High School, Dundee, Michigan

- Charles R. Rodgers, Director of Libraries, Pasco-Hernando Community College, Dade City, Florida

- James N. Zitzelsberger, Library Media Department Chairman, Oshkosh West High School, Oshkosh, Wisconsin

COMMENTS AND SUGGESTIONS

The editors of the *Information Plus Reference Series* welcome your feedback on *Electronic America*. Please direct all correspondence to:

Editors
Information Plus Reference Series
27500 Drake Rd.
Farmington Hills, MI 48331-3535

CHAPTER 1
THE INTERNET AND THE ELECTRONIC AGE

The Internet was a Cold War military project. It was designed for purposes of military communication in a United States devastated by a Soviet nuclear strike.... When I look at the Internet—that paragon of cyberspace today—I see something astounding and delightful. It's as if some grim fallout shelter had burst open and a full-scale Mardi Gras parade had come out.

—Bruce Sterling, in "Literary Freeware—Not for Commercial Use" (with William Gibson), *Speeches to the National Academy of Sciences Convocation on Technology and Education*, Washington, D.C., May 10, 1993

Since the 1980s electronics and communications technologies have become integrated into nearly every aspect of American life, transforming the ways in which people shop, find information, work, and communicate with one another. The speed with which these new technologies have proliferated through U.S. homes and offices is nothing short of astounding. Cell phones, which were once novelties occupying the front seat of a car, can now be found in the pockets of many 10-year-olds. Computers and the Internet, once only accessible to those who worked in government installations, large corporations, and academic institutions, are present in most American homes.

Jennifer Cheeseman Day, Alex Janus, and Jessica Davis of the U.S. Census Bureau report in *Computer and Internet Use in the United States: 2003* (October 2005, http://www.census.gov/prod/2005pubs/p23-208.pdf) that in 1984 only 8.2% of U.S. households had computers. By 2003 the number of homes with computers had increased to 61.8%. The Census Bureau (July 2012, http://www.census.gov/hhes/computer/files/2010/table1C.xls) indicates that by October 2010, 91.7 million (76.7%) out of 119.5 million American households owned some form of personal computer (PC). Meanwhile, the number of Americans who used the Internet also grew sharply during this period. Figure 1.1 shows the steady increase in Internet use among adults between 1995 and 2012. Only 14% of American adults used the Internet in 1995; by 2012 that figure had risen to 85%. According to Internet World

Stats, in "Usage and Population Statistics" (June 30, 2011, http://www.internetworldstats.com/stats14.htm), 245.2 million Americans had access to the Internet as of June 2012.

Since its inception, the Internet has reduced the time needed to complete dozens of mundane tasks, such as finding directions, writing personal correspondence, and conducting financial transactions. Because of these conveniences, online Americans continue to use the Internet more each year. A poll conducted by the Gallup Organization in December 2010 found that 50% of Internet users reported spending more than an hour per day online in 2010. (See Table 1.1.) In 2002 only 26% of American Internet users spent that much time online. Figure 1.2 reveals shifts in Internet usage by age group between 2004 and 2011. The number of Internet users rose substantially across all age demographics during this period. The largest percentage increase occurred in the 18- to 29-year-old age group, from 80% in 2004 to 94% in 2011. The 12- to 17-year-old age group had the most active Internet users throughout this span, rising from 87% in 2004 to 95% in 2011.

Even though the development of technology has affected most people in a positive way, significant pitfalls have developed as well. Typically, underprivileged groups have been left at a bigger disadvantage because the most innovative technologies have been embraced faster by the well educated and wealthy. The Internet and computer databases have also made fraud much easier. The number of cases of identity theft in the United States has skyrocketed. Each day thieves steal hundreds, if not thousands, of Social Security and credit card numbers by simply surfing the Internet or by sending out fraudulent e-mails. The Federal Trade Commission (FTC) reports in "FTC Releases Top Complaint Categories for 2011" (February 28, 2012, http://www.ftc.gov/opa/2012/02/2011complaints.shtm) that it received 279,156 identity theft complaints in 2011. This

FIGURE 1.1

Percentage of adults online, 1995–2012

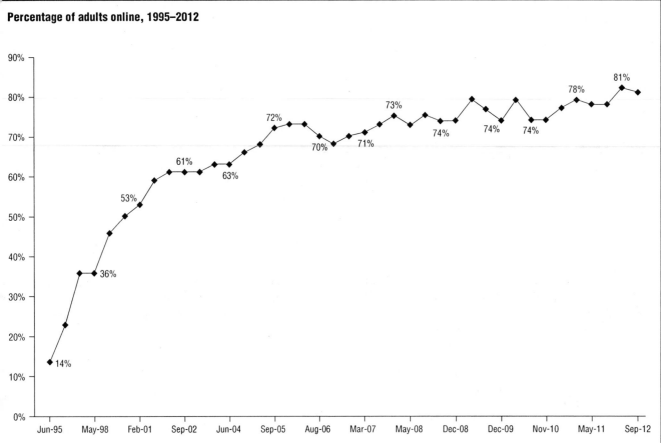

SOURCE: "Internet Adoption, 1995–2012," in *Trend Data*, Pew Internet & American Life Project, August 2012, http://pewinternet.org/Trend-Data-%28 Adults%29/Internet-Adoption.aspx (accessed September 24, 2012). Used by permission of the Pew Internet & American Life Project, which bears no responsibility for the interpretations presented or conclusions reached based on analysis of the data.

TABLE 1.1

Amount of time poll respondents spent on the Internet, 2002–10

HOW MUCH TIME, IF AT ALL, DO YOU PERSONALLY SPEND USING THE INTERNET—MORE THAN AN HOUR A DAY, UP TO ONE HOUR A DAY, A FEW TIMES A WEEK, A FEW TIMES A MONTH OR LESS, OR NEVER?

	More than an hour	Up to one hour	A few times a week	A few times a month or less	Never	No opinion
	%	%	%	%	%	%
2010 Dec 10–12	50	18	11	5	16	*
2008 Dec 4–7	48	17	12	5	18	*
2007 Dec 6–9	43	17	11	7	23	*
2006 Dec 11–14	37	19	13	8	24	*
2005 Dec 5–8	33	18	13	9	27	*
2004 Dec 5–8	32	16	19	8	25	*
2003 Dec 11–14	27	20	15	10	27	1
2002 Dec 5–8	26	16	18	12	28	*

*Less than 0.5%

SOURCE: "How much time, if at all, do you personally spend using the Internet—more than an hour a day, up to one hour a day, a few times a week, a few times a month or less, or never?" in *Computers and the Internet*, The Gallup Organization, 2012, http://www.gallup.com/poll/1591/Computers-Internet.aspx (accessed September 24, 2012) Copyright © 2012 by Gallup, Inc. All rights reserved. The content is used with permission; however, Gallup retains all rights of republication.

figure accounted for 15% of the 1.8 million total consumer complaints the FTC received that year, the most of any type of complaint. (An extended discussion of technology and crime is presented in Chapter 4.)

Another problem that continues to confront owners of computers and mobile devices is the number of viruses, worms, botnets, and Trojan horses making their way around the Internet. Viruses are programs or codes

FIGURE 1.2

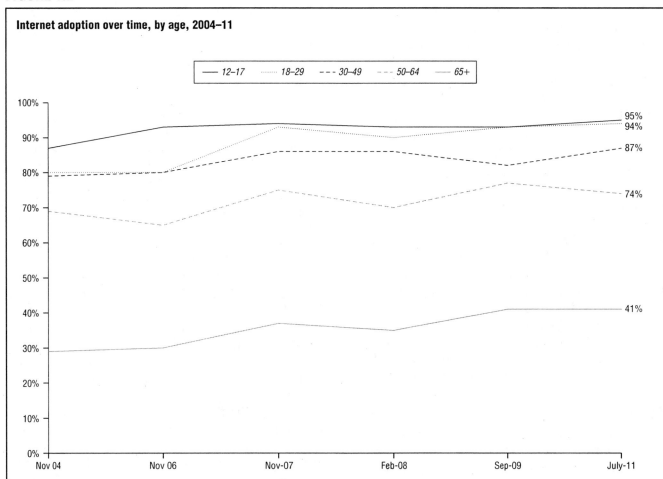

Internet adoption over time, by age, 2004–11

— 12–17   ·········· 18–29   – – – 30–49   – · – 50–64   —— 65+

95%
94%
87%
74%
41%

Nov 04   Nov 06   Nov-07   Feb-08   Sep-09   July-11

SOURCE: Amanda Lenhart et al., "Internet Adoption over Time by Teens and Adults," in *Teens, Kindness and Cruelty on Social Network Sites*, Pew Internet & American Life Project, November 2011, http://pewinternet.org/~/media//Files/Reports/2011/PIP_Teens_Kindness_Cruelty_SNS_Report_Nov_2011_FINAL_110711.pdf (accessed October 8, 2012). Used by permission of the Pew Internet & American Life Project, which bears no responsibility for the interpretations presented or conclusions reached based on analysis of the data.

that "infect" computers by secretly infiltrating systems and interfering with proper functioning; worms are destructive codes that copy themselves over and over on a computer or network; robot networks, or botnets, are groups of computers that have been invaded by a malignant software that is controlled by a hacker or other outside source, effectively transforming the infected computers into "zombies" or "drones"; and Trojan horses are software programs or files that seem legitimate yet act maliciously on the computer or secretly provide access to information contained on the computer to outsiders. Collectively, these invasive programs are often referred to as malicious software, or malware. Not only do viruses, worms, and hackers cost time and energy from their victims, but they also put valuable information at risk. Kaspersky Lab, a leading antivirus software firm, reports in "It Threat Evolution: Q3 2012" (November 1, 2012, http://www.securelist.com/en/analysis/204792250/IT_Threat_Evolution_Q3_2012) that it "detected and neutralized" 1.3 billion online security threats during the third quarter of 2012.

In addition, mobile phones are also susceptible to virus attacks. In October 2004 the first mobile phone virus was detected in Southeast Asia. The virus, known as Cabir, infects mobile phone software and can be used to steal information from mobile phone address books. Since that time other viruses have been identified that target mobile devices, particularly smart phones and those with enhanced web and data capabilities. In some cases the viruses caused mobile phones to send mass text messages using a service that charged the sender a high fee for each message. Others erased stored data, disabled functions, or automatically routed phone calls through high-priced communications providers.

Despite such difficulties, technological innovation showed no sign of slowing down. In 2012 more and more Americans were carrying powerful portable computers in the form of BlackBerries, iPhones, Androids, and other handheld devices, and trends toward wireless fidelity (Wi-Fi) connectivity, touch-screen functioning, voice-recognition software, and alternative power sources continued. One development expected to become commonplace is technology through which price tags at the grocery store will give off radio signals that automatically register the merchandise on a credit card when the buyer leaves the market. Meanwhile, robotic appliances are becoming available that automate some of the more tedious domestic chores, including lawn mowing, vacuuming, and cleaning gutters.

HISTORY OF THE INTERNET

At the center of the information technology and electronics revolution lies the Internet. Many believe the Internet had its origins on October 4, 1957, when the Soviet Union launched the *Sputnik 1* satellite into orbit with a military rocket. The news of *Sputnik 1*, a beeping steel sphere a little bigger in diameter than a basketball, sent the U.S. military into a frenzy. At the time, the United States and the Soviet Union were engaged in what became known as the Cold War (1947–1991), a period of sustained military buildup and ideological conflict. Americans were fearful that Soviet satellite technology could be used to spy on the United States or to launch missile attacks on U.S. targets. Technological superiority, the one advantage the United States thought it had over the Soviets, now seemed tenuous.

In response, the U.S. government formed the Advanced Research Projects Agency (ARPA) within the U.S. Department of Defense in 1958. The central mission of this new agency was to develop state-of-the-art technology to stay well ahead of the Soviet Union. One of the first projects on ARPA's agenda was to create a system by which ARPA operational bases could communicate with one another and their contractors via computer. The agency wanted the system to be resilient enough to survive a nuclear attack.

Joseph Carl Robnett Licklider (1915–1990), a scientist at the Massachusetts Institute of Technology (MIT), was appointed to oversee the computer research program at ARPA in 1962. He conferred with some of the leading researchers in networking technology at the time, including Leonard Kleinrock (1934–), then an MIT graduate student, and Lawrence Roberts (1937–). Their solution, first published in 1967, was a nationwide network of ARPA computers known as ARPANET. In this network a user on any computer terminal in the network would be able to send a message to multiple users at other computer terminals. If any one computer was knocked out in a nuclear attack, the remaining stations could still communicate with each other.

For this network to function properly, the researchers established that the computers would first have to break down information into discrete packets. These packets were then to be sent along high-speed phone lines and reassembled upon reaching their destination at another computer. At the time, telephone conversations traveled across dedicated telephone wires in one long stream of data from one user to another like a single train traveling along a track. Even though this was adequate for chatting with far-off relatives, it did not work well when one computer attempted to send data to several other computers on the network. By packetizing data, the information became more flexible. Much like cars on a highway, the packets could be routed easily to multiple computers. If one packet of information went bad during transmission, it did not disrupt the stream of data transmitting from one computer to another and could easily be resent. Packets could also carry information about themselves and where they were going, they could be compressed for speed, and they could be encrypted for security purposes.

After two years of engineering the parts needed for ARPANET, ARPA researchers set up the first four computer centers in the network. They were located at the University of California, Los Angeles (UCLA), Stanford Research Institute, the University of California, Santa Barbara, and the University of Utah. Between these nodes, AT&T had laid down telephone lines that were capable of transmitting data at 50 kilobytes per second. (Memory circuits are measured according to the base-two, or binary, number system. A kilobyte is equal to 2^{10} bytes, or 1,024 bytes.) The first test of the system commenced on October 29, 1969, when Charles S. Kline at UCLA tried logging into the Stanford system. On encountering the letter *g* in the word *login*, the system crashed. Recalling the event 40 years later in the article "Internet a Teenager at 40" (*Sydney Morning Herald*, October 26, 2009), Kleinrock noted, "So, the first message was 'Lo' as in 'Lo and behold.' ... We couldn't have a better, more succinct first message."

A Loose Affiliation of Networks

Eventually, the researchers at UCLA worked out the problems, and two years later ARPANET was fully functional and had 15 nodes linked to it. Figure 1.3 shows ARPANET in September 1971. Throughout the early and mid-1970s the development of networking technologies progressed slowly. Raymond Tomlinson (1941–) invented the first e-mail program in 1971 to send typed messages across the network, and a year later the first computer-to-computer chat took place at UCLA. In 1973 Robert Metcalfe (1946–) of Xerox Corporation developed Ethernet to connect computers and printers in a large organization. Three years later at AT&T Bell Labs, Michael E. Lesk (1945–) put together the program Unix-to-Unix-copy protocol (UUCP) that allowed Unix computers, which were typically used by academics, to communicate with one another over the phone lines.

Technological developments such as these allowed people and organizations that were not connected into ARPANET to set up networks of their own by the early 1980s.

FIGURE 1.3

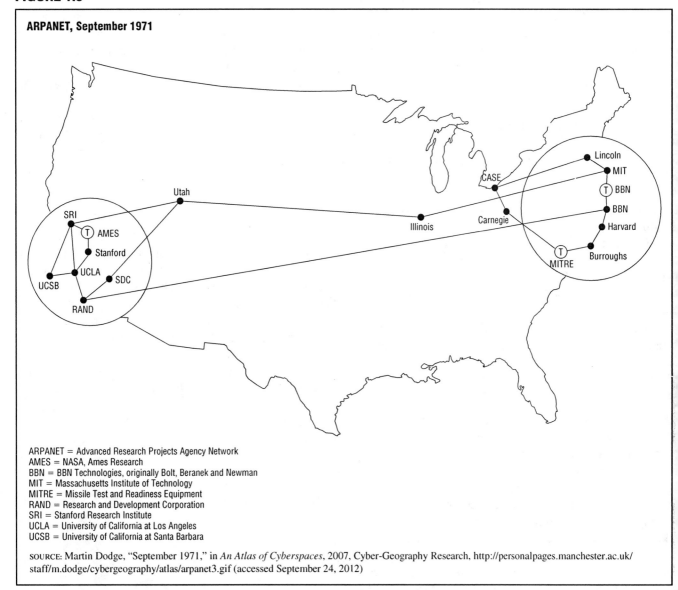

ARPANET, September 1971

ARPANET = Advanced Research Projects Agency Network
AMES = NASA, Ames Research
BBN = BBN Technologies, originally Bolt, Beranek and Newman
MIT = Massachusetts Institute of Technology
MITRE = Missile Test and Readiness Equipment
RAND = Research and Development Corporation
SRI = Stanford Research Institute
UCLA = University of California at Los Angeles
UCSB = University of California at Santa Barbara

SOURCE: Martin Dodge, "September 1971," in *An Atlas of Cyberspaces*, 2007, Cyber-Geography Research, http://personalpages.manchester.ac.uk/staff/m.dodge/cybergeography/atlas/arpanet3.gif (accessed September 24, 2012)

One of the largest of these was the Computer Science Network, which was established by a number of universities with help from the National Science Foundation (NSF). These universities recognized the advantages in resource sharing and communication that ARPANET provided the Ivy League and West Coast schools and wanted to develop similar capabilities. Another network known as Usenet was initially established to connect researchers at Duke University and the University of North Carolina, and it eventually spread throughout the country. The Because It's Time Network (BITNET) was formed to connect computers in the City University of New York system. Most of these smaller networks used standard telephone lines to operate. They were set up primarily to transfer scientific data, share computing resources, post items on bulletin boards, and provide e-mail.

One major problem was that these different networks could not readily communicate with one another. Each network used different methods to identify the computers within the network. A computer in one network could not recognize the computers in different networks, and information packets sent out from one network could not navigate the other networks. The situation would be analogous to a state in the United States having its own unique postal address system that no mail carriers outside of that state could understand.

During the 1970s the engineers Vinton Gray Cerf (1943–) and Robert E. Kahn (1938–) devised the Transmission Control Program and the Internet Protocol (TCP/IP). This suite of programs created a universal address system that could be installed on any existing network. Once installed, the machines on the network could recognize and send information to a machine on any other network, provided they also had TCP/IP. In 1983 ARPANET was split into military and civilian sections, both of which adopted TCP/IP. Many consider the adoption of TCP/IP by ARPANET to be the event that gave birth to the Internet. To this day, each machine on the Internet has a unique IP address that identifies that machine on a network. Servers typically have permanent IP numbers assigned to them, whereas most PCs are given a different number by an Internet service provider (ISP) each time the user begins a new session.

In the year the Internet was born, home computing was still in its infancy. The Commodore 64 had just made its debut, sporting a 1 megahertz microprocessor and 64 kilobytes of random access memory. Relatively few people owned home computers in 1983. Most of them used their machines for basic business applications, such as word processing and spreadsheets, and for playing games. Home users did not have direct access to the Internet. Low-speed modems were widely available by the mid- to late 1980s, and people could dial directly into servers that were owned by CompuServe, Quantum Computer Services (later to be renamed America Online and then simply AOL), and Prodigy. These services allowed people to post messages, go into chat rooms, play games, or send and receive e-mail. However, none of these services were linked to the Internet, and e-mails could only be sent among people subscribing to the same service.

The only people who could surf the Internet freely were those who had access to powerful mainframe computers, most of which were owned by universities, the government, and large corporations. The Internet was an uninviting place during the early 1980s. Users connecting to the Internet had to know exactly what they were looking for to get it. To reach another computer or server on the Internet, users had to key in the IP address for that computer, which consisted of a string of up to 12 numbers, such as 69.32.146.63. To navigate a server, a computer operator had to type in computer code on a prompt line and sift through cryptic directories. There were no web browsers, colorful Internet pages, or search engines.

By 1984 the dedicated name server (DNS), developed by the University of Wisconsin, was introduced, making the Internet somewhat more user-friendly. A DNS is a computer server on the Internet with a database that pairs domain names with IP addresses, giving people the ability to type in a name instead of a multidigit number to reach an Internet destination. Modern Internet browsers contact one of many DNSs each time an address, such as http://www.google.com/, is entered into the address bar. Most ISPs have a DNS that contains the names and IP address numbers of widely used sites. Once the browser makes the request from a DNS, the name server sends back the IP address number, which for Google is 209.85.225.105. The Internet browser then uses this IP address number to access the site (Google in this case).

Along with these name servers, a dedicated name system was also put into place so that no two names would be the same. Domain names with a minimum of two levels were established. The top level designated the country or economic sector a computer was in (e.g., .com or .gov), and a unique second-level domain name designated the organization itself (e.g., National Aeronautics and Space Administration [NASA] or Google). The Information Sciences Institute was put in charge of managing the root DNS in 1985 for all domains to make sure that no two were alike and to track who was registered for what name. Some of the first domain names to be registered were symbolics.com, mit.edu, think.com, and berkeley.edu.

A Major Expansion during the Mid-1980s

In 1986 Internet use expanded exponentially when the NSF installed new supercomputers and a new backbone for the U.S. Internet service, giving rise to the NSFNet. By 2008 ISPs and cable companies typically had their own backbones, which were all tied into one another. When a home user connects to the Internet via phone, digital subscriber line, satellite link, or cable, the signal is directed to a bank of modems called a point of presence (POP) that is owned by the service provider. (See Figure 1.4.) Each POP from each service provider, be it AOL or Comcast or one of many others, feeds into a network access point (NAP). These NAPs are connected to one another via backbones that consist of bundles,

FIGURE 1.4

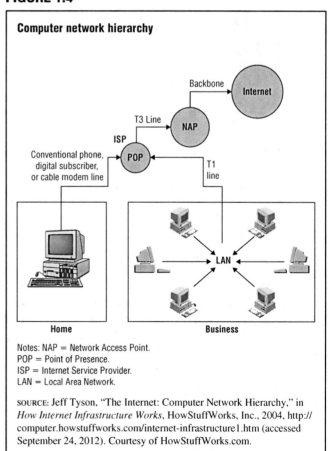

Computer network hierarchy

Notes: NAP = Network Access Point.
POP = Point of Presence.
ISP = Internet Service Provider.
LAN = Local Area Network.

SOURCE: Jeff Tyson, "The Internet: Computer Network Hierarchy," in *How Internet Infrastructure Works*, HowStuffWorks, Inc., 2004, http://computer.howstuffworks.com/internet-infrastructure1.htm (accessed September 24, 2012). Courtesy of HowStuffWorks.com.

or trunks, of fiber-optic cables that carry cross-country transmissions. The first NSF-funded backbone consisted of 56-kilobytes-per-second wire to connect the access points. The wire was laid down by AT&T. The NSF also provided five supercomputers to route traffic between the NAPs and bundles. In 1988 the NSF upgraded the NSFNet when it installed supercomputers that could handle 1.5 gigabytes of traffic per second and fiber-optic line that could transfer information at 1.5 megabytes per second. (Computers process the long lines of complex computer code in small quantities known as bytes. Each byte consists of a string of eight ones and zeros that can be used to represent binary numbers from 0 to 255. In binary, which is a base-two number system, 1 is 00000001, 2 is 00000010, 3 is 00000011, and so on up to 255, which is represented as 11111111. A thousand bytes equal a kilobyte, a million bytes equal a megabyte, and a billion bytes equal a gigabyte.)

The creation of the NSFNet ended the transmission bottlenecks that existed in the early Internet. The network also provided access for most major research institutions and universities. Academic departments and government agencies across the country jumped at the chance to set up servers and share information with their colleagues. Richard T. Griffiths notes in *History of the Internet, Internet for Historians* (October 11, 2002, http://www.let.leide nuniv.nl/history/ivh/frame_theorie.html) that from 1986 to 1987 the number of hosts (machines with a distinct IP address) on the Internet jumped from 5,000 to 28,000.

The NSF strictly prohibited the use of its site for commercial purposes. Even though such a rule seemed harsh, it had the intended consequence of fostering the development of private Internet providers. In 1987 the UUNET became the first commercial Internet provider, offering service to Unix computers. Three years later, in 1990, The World—the first commercial provider of dial-up access—began operating, and computer scientists at McGill University in Montreal, Quebec, invented Archie, the first Internet search engine for finding computer files.

An Internet for Everyone

In 1991 Tim Berners-Lee (1955–) of the Conseil Européen pour la Recherche Nucléaire (CERN; European Organization for Nuclear Research), which is located in Switzerland, introduced the three technologies that would give rise to the World Wide Web. The first of Berners-Lee's technologies was the web browser, a program that allowed a user to jump from one server computer on the Internet to another. The second was the hypertext markup language (HTML), which was a programming language for creating web pages with links to other web pages and graphics. The third was the hypertext transfer protocol (HTTP), a command used by the browser to retrieve the HTML information contained on the server's website. In concert, these three innovations led to the World Wide Web as it became known during the early 21st century. On his server, Berners-Lee created the first website at CERN in 1990. Even though this site is no longer active, an early screen shot of Berners-Lee's web browser may be accessed at http://info.cern.ch/NextBrowser.html. As the technology spread, many more web servers and sites quickly came into being. Sam Nurmi, the founder of the website troubleshooting company Pingdom, states in "Internet 2011 by the Numbers" (January 17, 2012, http://royal.pingdom.com/2012/01/17/internet-2011-in-numbers/) that by December 2011 there were approximately 555 million websites on the Internet; 300 million of the sites had been created that year.

With Berners-Lee's invention, people were no longer required to use complex computer codes or sift through cryptic directories to retrieve information from other computers on the Internet. To reach a server with a website, a user simply types in the name of a server along with the HTTP command (e.g., http://www.google.com/) into the address bar of his or her browser. The browser then contacts a DNS server to get the IP address of the server. Once the browser connects with the website, the browser then sends out the HTTP command. The HTTP tells the server to send the browser the HTML code for the specified website. On receiving the HTML code, the browser deciphers the code and simply displays the web page on the user's computer (e.g., Google's home page).

At the same time that these strides were being made in establishing the Internet, the U.S. government took a more active role in its development. In 1991 Senator Albert Gore Jr. (1948–; D-TN) introduced the U.S. High Performance Computing Act into Congress. The act set aside more than $2 billion for further research into computing and to improve the infrastructure of the Internet. Even though most of it was earmarked for large agencies such as the NSF and NASA, some of the funds were placed into the hands of independent software developers.

Marc Andreessen (1971?–) developed the Mosaic X web browser in 1993 using a federal grant received through this act. The browser was one of the first commercial browsers to employ the HTML program language and HTTP, and it became the first browser to be embraced by the general public. It was easy to set up, simple to use, and backed by a full customer support staff. It displayed images in an attractive way and contained many of the standard features used on present-day web browsers, such as the address prompt and Back and Forward buttons. Tens of thousands of copies of Mosaic X were sold.

Once Mosaic X became popular, more and more websites employing HTML and HTTP were posted. According to Robert H. Zakon, in *Hobbes' Internet Timeline 10.2* (December 30, 2011, http://www.zakon.org/robert/internet/timeline/), in June 1994 there were 2,738 web servers, by June 1995 there were an estimated 23,500 servers, and by

June 1996 there were an estimated 252,000 servers. Zakon indicates that the growth in hosts, or computers with a unique IP address, during the same period reflected an increase from 3.2 million in July 1994, to 6.6 million in July 1995, to 12.9 million in July 1996.

The web was growing at such a rapid rate that the NSF created the Internet Network Information Center (InterNIC) as an agency to handle domain names. InterNIC contracted with Network Solutions to handle domain registration. By 1995 the companies that ran the older dial-up services for home users, such as CompuServe, AOL, and Prodigy, brought their clients to the Internet and offered Internet service for all. Internet network providers, such as MCI and Qwest, began laying fiber-optic cables and communications networks at a breakneck pace. Advertising appeared on the web for the first time (the first banner being for the alcoholic beverage Zima), e-shopping appeared on the Internet, and many companies such as Netscape went public. In the following years the Internet gained a firm foothold in American life. As of July 2012, the nonprofit Internet Systems Consortium (http://www.isc.org/solutions/survey/history) estimated the number of Internet hosts at 908.6 million.

DIGITAL DIVIDE

Even though the Internet swept into U.S. households at a faster rate than almost any other technology, many people were still not connected to the Internet well after the turn of the 21st century. Table 1.2, which reflects poll data from the Pew Internet and American Life Project (Pew/Internet), shows computer and Internet adoption among American adults between 2002 and 2012 and indicates that as of May 2008, 73% of American adults classified themselves as Internet users; by February 2012 this figure had risen to 80%, an increase of seven percentage points. Table 1.3 shows the demographic differences between those connected to the Internet and those who were not. The biggest discrepancies were in age, income, and educational attainment. For example, 96% of respondents aged 18 to 29 years were Internet users in August 2012; by comparison, only 58% of seniors aged 65 years and older went online. Table 1.3 also reveals that those in typically disadvantaged demographics had the least exposure to the Internet. Seventy-five percent of adults living in households earning less than $30,000 per year went online in 2012, compared with 99% of adults living in households earning $75,000 or more per year.

TABLE 1.2

Computer and Internet use by adults, selected years 2002–12

Activity label	Notes a change in wording over time	Mar–May-02	Feb-04	Feb–Apr-06	May-08	May-10	Feb-12
Q5 Asked of all respondents	**Use a computer**	69%	73%	75%	74%	77%	
	Men	71%	73%	76%	74%	78%	
	Women	68%	72%	74%	74%	76%	
	Whites	70%	73%	76%	75%	79%	
	Blacks	61%	62%	65%	65%	72%	
	Hispanics	70%	75%	79%	77%	74%	
	18–29	83%	86%	88%	90%	89%	
	30–49	80%	85%	86%	86%	86%	
	50–64	66%	71%	76%	70%	78%	
	65+	23%	30%	36%	35%	42%	
Q6 Asked of all respondents	**Use the Internet**	58%	63%	73%	73%	79%	80%
	Men	60%	65%	74%	73%	79%	81%
	Women	56%	61%	71%	73%	79%	79%
	Whites	60%	64%	73%	75%	80%	83%
	Blacks	45%	46%	61%	59%	71%	71%
	Hispanics	54%	63%	76%	80%	82%	71%
	18–29	74%	77%	88%	90%	95%	94%
	30–49	67%	74%	84%	85%	87%	88%
	50–64	52%	58%	71%	70%	78%	79%
	65+	18%	23%	32%	35%	42%	48%
Q7 Asked of internet users	**Used the Internet yesterday**	57%	55%	66%	70%	78%	82%
	Men	60%	57%	68%	72%	78%	82%
	Women	55%	53%	64%	68%	77%	82%
	Whites	59%	59%	68%	71%	78%	84%
	Blacks	41%	35%	55%	65%	77%	68%
	Hispanics	53%	41%	66%	61%	74%	75%
	18–29	53%	51%	66%	72%	82%	89%
	30–49	58%	58%	69%	74%	81%	85%
	50–64	61%	55%	63%	65%	72%	74%
	65+	62%	59%	59%	56%	68%	70%

SOURCE: Adapted from "Usage over Time," in *Trend Data*, Pew Internet & American Life Project, 2012, http://pewinternet.org/Static-Pages/Trend-Data-%28Adults%29/Usage-Over-Time.aspx (accessed September 24, 2012). Used by permission of the Pew Internet & American Life Project, which bears no responsibility for the interpretations presented or conclusions reached based on analysis of the data.

TABLE 1.3

Demographics of Internet users, August 2012

	% who use the Internet
All adults	85
Men	85
Women	85
Race/ethnicity	
White, non-Hispanic	86
Black, non-Hispanic	86
Hispanic (English- and Spanish-speaking)	80
Age	
18–29	96
30–49	93
50–64	85
65+	58
Household income	
Less than $30,000/yr	75
$30,000–$49,999	90
$50,000–$74,999	93
$75,000+	99
Educational attainment	
No high school diploma	61
High school graduate	80
Some college	94
College+	97

SOURCE: "Demographics of Internet Users," in *Trend Data*, Pew Internet & American Life Project, August 2012, http://pewinternet.org/Trend-Data-%28Adults%29/Whos-Online.aspx (accessed September 24, 2012). Used by permission of the Pew Internet & American Life Project, which bears no responsibility for the interpretations presented or conclusions reached based on analysis of the data.

A divide exists as well between those with faster, broadband connectivity and those with older equipment and slow connection speeds. For example, the overall number of Americans with access to broadband rose dramatically between 2000 and 2012. In 2000 only 3% of adults went online via broadband, compared with 34% who accessed the Internet with a dial-up connection. (See Figure 1.5.) By 2012 the percentage of adults with broadband access had risen to 66%, whereas those using dial-up had dropped to only 3%. Still, research reveals significant demographic differences between broadband users. As Table 1.4 shows, 76% of adults aged 18 to 29 years accessed the Internet via broadband in 2011, compared with only 30% of adults aged 65 years and older. On racial and ethnic lines, non-Hispanic whites (66%) were more likely than Hispanics (51%) or non-Hispanic African-Americans (49%) to go online using a broadband connection.

Wealth and Education

Wealth lies at the heart of this digital divide and has for more than a decade. Table 1.4 reveals a significant gap in broadband Internet use between low-income and high-income households. It also proves that education plays an important role in determining whether or not an adult is more or less likely to go online via a high-speed connection. For example, 85% of respondents with a college degree had broadband service in their home in 2011, whereas only 22% of respondents who had not completed high school used broadband to access the Internet at home.

Differences also exist in how varying income groups use the Internet. As shown in Table 1.5, 90% of adults with an annual household income of $75,000 or more shopped online in 2011, compared with only 51% adults with an annual household income of less than $30,000. A similar discrepancy existed in online banking activities, with those earning $75,000 or more per year (80%) being almost twice as likely to bank online than those making less than $30,000 per year (42%). Interestingly, social media activities were comparable between the two groups. Sixty-eight percent of adults earning less than $30,000 per year used social networking sites in 2011, compared with 66% of those earning $75,000 or more per year.

Americans with high levels of education use the Internet in much the same way as those with high incomes. Table 1.5 demonstrates a sizable gap in certain online activities between adults with a college education and those who never completed high school. For example, 87% of respondents with a college degree shopped online in 2011, compared with only 33% of those without a high school diploma. Considerable differences also exist between adults who have finished high school and those who have not. Sixty-nine percent of adults without a high school diploma used e-mail in 2011, whereas among adults who have completed high school, the figure rose to 87%.

Age

Age is another factor that plays a major role in how people use the Internet. Adults aged 65 years and older were the most likely to use the Internet to conduct a search (87%) or use e-mail (86%) in 2011. (See Table 1.5.) In contrast, only 29% of seniors used the Internet to engage in social networking activities. Younger Internet users are far more likely to use social media. In 2011, 87% of adults aged 18 to 29 years visited social networking sites. This rate was 19 percentage points higher than that found among adults aged 30 to 49 years, 68% of whom engaged in social networking online.

However, it is reasonable to expect that these percentages will change significantly over time, as new generations become retirees. Young and middle-aged Internet users are expected to continue using the Internet at the same volume they do today and may even spend more time online during their retirement. Indeed, by 2012 there were signs that the Internet age gap was narrowing. Table 1.2 shows shifts in Internet use among various age groups between 2002 and 2012. In March–May 2002, 74% of adults aged 18 to 29 years used the Internet, the largest

FIGURE 1.5

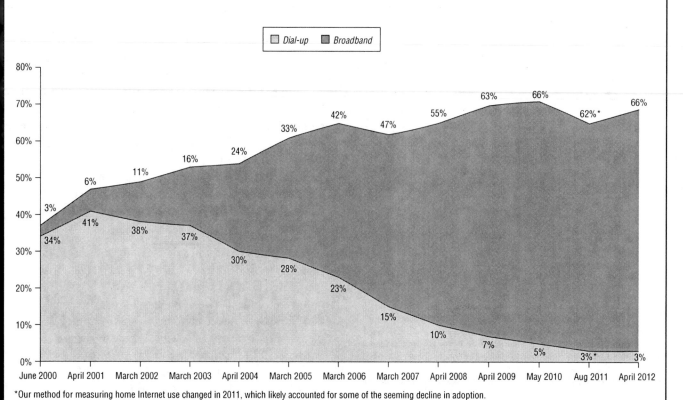

Percentage of adults who access the Internet via dial-up or broadband, 2000–12

% of American adults who access the Internet at home via dial-up or broadband, over time. As of April 2012, 66% of American adults age 18+ have a high-speed broadband connection at home.

*Our method for measuring home Internet use changed in 2011, which likely accounted for some of the seeming decline in adoption.

SOURCE: "Broadband and Dial-up Adoption, 2000–2012," in *Trend Data*, Pew Internet & American Life Project, 2012, http://pewinternet.org/Static-Pages/ Trend-Data-%28Adults%29/Home-Broadband-Adoption.aspx (accessed September 24, 2012). Used by permission of the Pew Internet & American Life Project, which bears no responsibility for the interpretations presented or conclusions reached based on analysis of the data.

proportion of any age group; among adults aged 65 years and older the figure was only 18%. Even though the number of online adults in both age groups grew considerably over the next decade, the largest proportional increase occurred among seniors aged 65 years and older. As Table 1.2 shows, 48% of adults over the age of 65 years were using the Internet in February 2012— an increase of 167% when compared with March– May 2002.

Race and Ethnicity

Variations in Internet usage between different races and ethnicities—while not as dramatic as differences between education and income groups—remained noticeable in 2011. In general, Hispanic Internet users lagged behind non-Hispanic whites and non-Hispanic African-Americans in most types of online activities. For example, only 59% of online Hispanics purchased a product over the Internet in 2011, compared with 73% of non-Hispanic whites and 74% of non-Hispanic African-Americans. (See Table 1.5.) A similar gap existed between Hispanics and other ethnic groups when it came to online

banking. However, Hispanics (67%) were more likely than non-Hispanic whites (63%) to visit social networking sites, while non-Hispanic African-Americans (70%) were the most prevalent social media users in 2011. The years between 2000 and 2012 witnessed sharp increases in Internet usage among all ethnic groups. The most noticeable growth occurred among African-Americans. As Table 1.2 reveals, only 45% of African-Americans went online in March–May 2002, compared with 54% of Hispanics and 60% of whites. By 2012 the proportion of African-American Internet users equaled that of Hispanics. According to Table 1.2, 71% each of African-Americans and Hispanics went online in February 2012. However, in February 2012 Hispanics (75%) were more likely than African-Americans (68%) to have used the Internet within the previous day.

Research reveals stark differences in online activities within the Hispanic community itself. In "The Latino Digital Divide: The Native Born versus the Foreign Born" (July 28, 2010, http://www.pewhispanic.org/2010/07/28/ the-latino-digital-divide-the-native-born-versus-the-foreign-born/), Gretchen Livingston of the Pew Hispanic Center reports that native-born Hispanics are far more likely to go

TABLE 1.4

Broadband users by selected characteristics, 2011

	% who access the Internet via broadband at home
All adults (age 18+)	**62%**
Men	65
Women	59
Race/ethnicity	
White, non-Hispanic	66
Black, non-Hispanic	49*
Hispanic (English- and Spanish-speaking)	51*
Age	
18–29	76
30–49	70
50–64	60
65+	30
Household income	
Less than $30,000/yr	41
$30,000–$49,999	66
$50,000–$74,999	81
$75,000+	89
Educational attainment	
No high school diploma	22
High school graduate	52
Some college	73
College+	85

*All differences are statistically significant except for those between the rows designated with an asterisk.

Note: Population = 2,260 adults age 18 and older, including 916 interviews conducted by cell phone. Interviews were conducted in both English and Spanish.

SOURCE: Kathryn Zickuhr and Aaron Smith, "Home Broadband Demographics," in *Digital Differences*, Pew Internet & American Life Project, April 13, 2012, http://pewinternet.org/Reports/2012/Digital-differences/Overview/Digital-differences.aspx (accessed September 25, 2012). Used by permission of the Pew Internet & American Life Project, which bears no responsibility for the interpretations presented or conclusions reached based on analysis of the data.

online than Hispanics born outside the United States. In 2009, 85% of U.S.-born Hispanics aged 16 years and older were Internet users, whereas only 51% of foreign-born Hispanics in the same age group went online. Language also plays a significant role in determining Internet habits. In 2009, 87% of Hispanics who predominantly spoke English used the Internet, compared with 77% of bilingual Hispanics and 35% of Hispanics who primarily spoke Spanish. Furthermore, Livingston notes that there was a negligible difference between second-generation (84%) and third-generation and higher (87%) U.S.-born Hispanics who went online.

Gender

Differences in gender were not so apparent when looking at the number of overall users in 2011. Eighty-five percent of adult males went online, as did 85% of women. (See Table 1.3.) The real differences came in how the two genders used the Internet. As Table 1.5 shows, in 2011 men (65%) were more likely than women (57%) to conduct banking activities over the Internet. In contrast, women were more likely than men to shop online (74% versus 69%), use social networking sites (66% versus 63%), and use e-mail (93% versus 89%).

Broadband Access by Region

Internet usage in the United States also diverges according to region. According to Kim Severson, in "Digital Age Is Slow to Arrive in Rural America" (*New York Times*, February 17, 2011), a 2011 U.S. Department of Commerce study revealed that 70% of urban households had access to broadband Internet service, compared with 60% of rural households. Indeed, Severson notes that expanding high-speed Internet access to less-populated areas of the country was a key priority of the Obama administration, which designated $7.2 billion in stimulus funds to extend broadband service to rural America. Brian Depew of the Center for Rural Affairs in Lyons, Nebraska, viewed the president's initiative as vital to the development of the United States' rural areas, describing broadband as a "critical utility" in the 21st century. For Depew, the importance of broadband was not limited to economic factors. "You often hear people talk about broadband from a business development perspective, but it's much more significant than that," he said to Severson. "This is about whether rural communities are going to participate in our democratic society. If you don't have effective broadband, you are cut out of things that are really core to who we are as a country."

In *Broadband Internet Access and the Digital Divide: Federal Assistance Programs* (September 7, 2012, http://www.fas.org/sgp/crs/misc/RL30719.pdf), Lennard G. Kruger and Angele A. Gilroy of the Congressional Research Service provide a comprehensive breakdown of broadband access throughout the United States. The researchers indicate that 6% of the U.S. population was unable to access broadband service in 2012. In urban and other nonrural areas, only 1.8% of Americans were unable to go online via a broadband connection; in stark contrast, 23.7% of rural Americans had no access to high-speed Internet. By a considerable margin, West Virginia had the highest proportion of residents without broadband access, at 45.9%; other states with a high percentage of residents without broadband were Montana (26.7%), South Dakota (21.1%), and Oklahoma (16.2%). On the opposite end of the spectrum, the most comprehensive broadband network in 2012 was in Rhode Island, where 99.8% of the population had access to high-speed Internet, followed by New Jersey (99.3%), Massachusetts (99%), and New York (98.7%).

THE FUTURE OF COMPUTING AND THE INTERNET

For many, the Internet has become an essential part of everyday life, and people increasingly want to be able to log on to the Internet from any location, in private or public spaces. It is therefore not surprising that more

TABLE 1.5

Demographic differences in online activities, May and August 2011

Date of survey	Search May 2011	Email Aug 2011	Buy a product May 2011	Use social network sites Aug 2011	Bank online May 2011
All adults	92%	91%	71%	64%	61%
Men	93	89	69	63	65
Women	91	93	74	66	57
Race/ethnicity					
White, non-Hispanic	93	92	73	63	62
Black, non-Hispanic	91	88	74	70	67
Hispanic (English- and Spanish-speaking)	87	86	59	67	52
Age					
18–29	96	91	70	87	61
30–49	91	93	73	68	68
50–64	91	90	76	49	59
65+	87	86	56	29	44
Household income					
Less than $30,000/yr	90	85	51	68	42
$30,000–$49,999	91	93	77	65	65
$50,000–$74,999	93	94	80	61	74
$75,000+	98	97	90	66	80
Educational attainment					
No high school diploma	81	69	33	63	32
High school graduate	88	87	59	60	47
Some college	94	95	74	73	66
College+	96	97	87	63	74

Note: Interviews were conducted landline and cell phone, in both English and Spanish.

SOURCE: Kathryn Zickuhr and Aaron Smith, "Online Activities, by Demographics," in *Digital Differences*, Pew Internet & American Life Project, April 13, 2012, http://pewinternet.org/Reports/2012/Digital-differences/Overview/Digital-differences.aspx (accessed October 4, 2012). Used by permission of the Pew Internet & American Life Project, which bears no responsibility for the interpretations presented or conclusions reached based on analysis of the data.

Americans are turning to wireless technologies. In *Generations and Their Gadgets* (February 3, 2011, http://www.pewinternet.org/~/media//Files/Reports/2011/PIP_Generations_and_Gadgets.pdf), Kathryn Zickuhr of Pew/Internet finds that 52% of American adults owned laptop computers in 2010, compared with 59% who owned desktop computers. Younger adults were the most likely to use laptops rather than desktop computers. According to Zickuhr, 70% of adults between the ages of 18 and 34 years owned laptops in 2010, compared with 57% who owned desktops. As smart phones, tablet computers, and other mobile devices gain popularity, more and more adults are accessing the Internet using a wireless connection. As Table 1.6 shows, 63% of adults were using either a laptop or cell phone to access the Internet in 2011. The highest numbers of wireless users were found among younger adults. Eighty-eight percent of adults aged 18 to 29 years went online with a laptop or cell phone in 2011, compared with 76% of adults aged 30 to 49 years, 53% of adults aged 50 to 64 years, and 21% of adults aged 65 years and older. As with other technologies, wealth and educational attainment also play a role in determining wireless Internet use. Eighty-six percent of adults with annual household incomes of $75,000 or higher used wireless Internet, compared with 50% of adults with annual household incomes of less than $30,000. Adults with a college degree or higher (82%) were also more likely than adults who had never completed high school (36%) to go online with a wireless connection.

Improvements in cell phone technology were instrumental in the rapid growth of wireless Internet activity. Table 1.7 shows the increase in cell phone Internet use between April 2009 and April 2012. During this period the number of cell phone owners who went online using their phones rose from 31% to 55%, which was an increase of 24 percentage points. The most significant increase was in the 25- to 34-year-old age demographic, where cell phone Internet use grew from 43% in 2009 to 80% in 2012. As Table 1.7 reveals, non-Hispanic African-Americans (64%) were the most likely to use their cell phones to go online in 2012, followed by Hispanics (63%) and non-Hispanic whites (52%). Urban adults (62%) were considerably more likely than those living in rural areas (44%) to access the Internet with their phones, while a far higher number of adults with college degrees (64%) used their phones to go online than those who never completed high school (45%).

Tablet computers, notably the iPad, also played a key role in the rise of wireless computing during these years. According to Zickuhr, only 4% of adults used a tablet

TABLE 1.6

Mobile Internet users by selected characteristics, 2011

	% who go online wirelessly
All adults (age 18+)	**63%**
Men	67
Women	59
Age	
18–29	88
30–49	76
50–64	53
65+	21
Race/ethnicity	
White, non-Hispanic	63*
Black, non-Hispanic	62*
Hispanic (English- and Spanish-speaking)	63*
Household income	
Less than $30,000/yr	50
$30,000–$49,999	64
$50,000–$74,999	75
$75,000+	86
Educational attainment	
No high school diploma	36
High school graduate	53
Some college	72
College+	82

*All differences are statistically significant except for those between the rows designated with an asterisk.
Note: Population = 2,260 adults age 18 and older, including 916 interviews conducted by cell phone. Interviews were conducted in both English and Spanish.

SOURCE: Kathryn Zickuhr and Aaron Smith, "Home Broadband Demographics," in *Digital Differences*, Pew Internet & American Life Project, April 13, 2012, http://pewinternet.org/Reports/2012/Digital-differences/Overview/Digital-differences.aspx (accessed September 25, 2012). Used by permission of the Pew Internet & American Life Project, which bears no responsibility for the interpretations presented or conclusions reached based on analysis of the data.

TABLE 1.7

Percentage of cell phone owners who use their cell phones to access the Internet, by selected characteristics, 2009–2012

% of cell owners within each group who use the Internet or email on their cell phone

	April 2009	April 2012	Change
All cell owners	**31%**	**55%**	**+24 percentage points**
Gender			
Men	35	57	+22
Women	27	54	+28
Age			
18–24	45	75	+30
25–34	43	80	+37
35–44	38	68	+30
45–54	28	53	+25
55–64	17	30	+13
65+	7	16	+9
Race/ethnicity			
White, non-Hispanic	27	52	+25
Black, non-Hispanic	44	64	+20
Hispanic	44	63	+19
Household income			
Less than $30,000	26	50	+24
$30,000–$49,999	31	52	+21
$50,000–$74,999	29	60	+31
$75,000+	43	69	+26
Education level			
Less than high school	28	45	+17
High school graduate	24	49	+25
Some college	35	57	+22
College+	36	64	+28
Geographic location			
Urban	30	62	+32
Suburban	25	56	+31
Rural	17	44	+27

SOURCE: Aaron Smith, "Changes in Cell Phone Internet Use by Demographic, 2009–2012," in *17% of Cell Phone Owners Do Most of Their Browsing on Their Phone, Rather Than a Computer or Other Device*, Pew Internet & American Life Project, June 26, 2012, http://www.pewinternet.org/~/media//Files/Reports/2012/PIP_Cell_Phone_Internet_Access.pdf (accessed September 25, 2012). Used by permission of the Pew Internet & American Life Project, which bears no responsibility for the interpretations presented or conclusions reached based on analysis of the data.

computer to access the Internet in 2010. Lee Rainie of Pew/Internet reveals in "25% of American Adults Own Tablet Computers" (October 4, 2012, http://www.pewinternet.org/~/media//Files/Reports/2012/PIP_TabletOwnership_August2012.pdf) that by 2012 a quarter of all American adults owned a tablet computer. Rainie notes that wealth and education were key factors in determining whether or not someone owned an iPad or similar device. Among adults earning $75,000 or more per year, 47% owned tablet computers, and 41% of college graduates were tablet owners. By comparison, only 10% of adults who made less than $30,000 per year and 7% of adults without a high school diploma owned a tablet computer in 2012.

In "PC Is Dead. Cloud Computing, Mobile Devices Taking Over" (*Christian Science Monitor*, June 8, 2011), Chad Brooks suggests that the popularity of tablet devices, combined with the proliferation of online data storage systems, or "cloud computing," might signal the end of the traditional desktop computer. "We don't need PCs anymore," Brooks quoted technology expert John Quain as saying. "They are dead." Indeed, as tablet ownership saw a dramatic increase, desktop computer sales declined

in the United States. According to Gartner, Inc., in the press release "Gartner Says Worldwide PC Shipments Grew 1.9 Percent in First Quarter of 2012" (April 11, 2012, http://www.gartner.com/it/page.jsp?id=1981717), PC sales in the United States fell 3.5% between the first quarter in 2011 and the first quarter in 2012, from 16.1 million units to 15.5 million units.

The number of wireless hotspots has risen in response to increasing demand. The advertising network JiWire, which compiles an industry directory, indicates that the number of wireless Internet hotspots in the world surpassed the 100,000 mark in early 2006. According to JiWire (November 26, 2012, http://v4.jiwire.com/search-hotspot-locations.htm), there were 819,968 wireless Internet locations in 145 countries in November 2012. South Korea had the largest number of wireless hotspots in the world, with 186,759, followed by the United Kingdom (182,086) and the United States (133,688). Within the United States, Brooklyn, New York (2,114); Bronx, New York (1,857); Philadelphia, Pennsylvania (1,627); and New York City (1,621) were the cities with the largest number of Wi-Fi hotspots in 2012.

Increasing Mobile Connectivity

As wireless devices grow in popularity, several emerging technologies allow people to access high-speed Internet on their laptops wherever they go. Worldwide interoperability for microwave access (WiMAX) uses base-station transmitters much like those in a mobile phone network. Any laptop computer that is equipped with a WiMAX receiver should be able to instantly log on to one of these stations and receive high-speed Internet access up to 30 miles (48 km) away. The WiMax Forum indicates in "WiMax Forum Newsletter" (August 2010, http://www .wimaxforum.org/sites/wimaxforum.org/files/page/2010/ 08/wmf_newsletter_08-2010.pdf) that by July 2010 WiMAX capability had expanded to 593 networks in 149 countries worldwide.

One of the most popular technologies on the market during the first decade of the 21st century was high-speed third-generation (3G) cell phone service. First introduced in the United States in 2003, 3G service allows cell phones to receive and send signals that contain much more information than standard cellular phone signals, enabling 3G cell phone users to access the Internet at speeds approaching those of a cable modem. This high connection speed also enables 3G cell phone users to download various applications (commonly known as "apps") such as games, videos, online tools, and websites. As wireless technology advanced, 3G phones were capable of offering data transmission speeds of between 400 and 4,000 kilobytes per second (Kbps).

By 2010 most major cellular operators in the United States were offering 3G service to their customers, and devices such as the BlackBerry, the Apple 3G iPhone, and Samsung Instinct were making multifunction smart phones relatively affordable. Proving consumer demand for such products, the Apple 3G iPhone, which combined 3G phone, Internet, personal data, and music capabilities in one device, sold more than a million units in three days following its release in July 2008. Following the success of the iPhone, a number of other 3G portable wireless devices were introduced, including the iPod Touch and the iPad from Apple Inc., the Droid from Motorola Inc., and the Zune from Microsoft Corporation.

During this period a new wireless technology, known as long-term evolution (LTE), or fourth generation (4G), was beginning to emerge, with the promise of even faster connection speeds for consumers. Launched as an initiative by the International Telecommunications Union (ITU) in March 2008, the development of a new global 4G standard,

offering connection speeds of between 100 megabytes and 1 gigabyte per second, became the top priority of telecommunications companies worldwide. With connection speeds that were expected to exceed those offered by 3G devices, 4G promised to enable cell phone users to stream much more advanced forms of data, such as live television broadcasts, interactive games, and other multimedia applications at a much faster rate. However, as companies became eager to sell 4G products to consumers, the ITU's efforts to establish universal 4G standards became a low priority for cell phone carriers and the organization abandoned the initiative. As a result, several of the first phones to be marketed as 4G were actually no faster than their 3G predecessors. In "3G vs. 4G: What's the Difference?" (*PC Mag*, February 24, 2012), Sascha Segan notes that by 2012 so many 4G technologies had emerged that the term had become "almost meaningless." Still, as 4G-LTE networks continued to expand throughout the United States, it was clear that 4G would eventually supersede 3G as the industry standard. In anticipation of this shift, Apple released its iPhone 5, the first iPhone to be compatible with 4G-LTE networks, in September 2012.

Internet2

In the long term, however, the future of the Internet will likely be the Internet2. Internet2 is not a new Internet, but a collaboration of dozens of academic institutions and corporations working together to develop technologies that will be integrated into the Internet. One project the consortium began testing in 2008 was version six of the Internet protocol (IPv6). By 2012 the number of computers, cell phones, and other devices using the Internet had grown exponentially. Each time one of these devices logs on to the Internet, it requires its own address. Until 2012, these devices all operated within version four of the Internet protocol (IPv4), which only allowed for a little more than 4 billion addresses. As the number of new IP addresses continued to rise, IPv4 would eventually prove insufficient to accommodate all users. IPv6 introduced a new Internet address system that would allow for trillions upon trillions of new addresses. With such a network, Americans would be able to watch high-definition television via the Internet, teleconference with associates and family at any time, and easily access entire libraries of music and books online.

In June 2011 a number of companies and institutions, including Google, Facebook, and the Department of Commerce, participated in World IPv6 Day, an event that was designed to test the functionality of the new Internet protocol. The experiment proved a success, and IPv6 was officially launched on June 6, 2012. Iljitsch van Beijnum reports in "IPv6 on Its Way to Conquer the World after World IPv6 Launch" (ArsTechnica.com, August 1, 2012) that 19 million IPv6 addresses saw activity during the launch, with 71% of the total traffic occurring in the

United States. According to Fahmida Y. Rashid, in "What to Expect for IPv6 Day" (*PC Mag*, June 6, 2012), by the day of the launch 12% of existing Internet networks were compatible with the new protocol. By 2015, 28% of new Internet connections were expected to operate within the IPv6 system. While the existing IPv4 network continued to operate alongside IPv6, by 2012 it seemed clear that the new protocol represented the networking platform of the future.

The Younger Generation of Internet Users

As the Internet became integrated into everyday life, many began raising questions about the ways an information-driven, interconnected world might transform human behavior. Janna Quitney Anderson and Lee Rainie surveyed over 1,000 technology experts concerning the long-term impact of an increasingly online existence on teens and young adults and reported their findings in *Millennials Will Benefit and Suffer Due to Their Hyperconnected Lives* (February 29, 2012, http://www.pewinternet.org/~/media//Files/Reports/2012/PIP_Future_of_Internet_2012_Young _brains_PDF.pdf). According to Anderson and Rainie, most experts agreed that the Internet will ultimately reshape the ways that human beings think, although they differed on whether or not the consequences will ultimately be positive or negative. Fifty-five percent of those surveyed agreed with the assertion that young people will benefit from an increasingly interconnected world, in large part because the Internet will allow them to "search effectively and access collective intelligence." In contrast, 42% of the experts concurred with the notion that the overall effects of multitasking and hyperconnectivity will have "baleful results" on the minds of young people by diminishing their ability to "retain information" and eroding their "deep-thinking capabilities."

In the survey, experts also identified a number of unique skills that young people will potentially develop to navigate the interconnected world, including the capacity to process, evaluate, and recapitulate information effectively, otherwise known as "digital literacy"; the ability to engage in "public problem-solving" or "crowd-sourcing"; and the power to become "strategically future-minded" in addressing society's needs. However, Anderson and Rainie note that many of the experts suggested that having virtually unlimited access to vast amounts of data threatens to transform the very nature of human memory. For example, Anderson and Rainie quote Amber Case of Geoloqi, a geo-locating application firm, who surmised that "memories are becoming hyperlinks to information triggered by keywords and URLs. We are becoming 'persistent paleontologists' of our own external memories, as our brains are storing the keywords to get back to those memories and not the full memories themselves."

CHAPTER 2
DEVELOPMENTS IN TELECOMMUNICATIONS

Communication has undeniably been one of the central motivations behind the technical strides that have taken place since the beginning of the Cold War (1947–1991). The Internet was first conceived as a way of connecting computers for the purpose of communication, and e-mail was the first application to gain acceptance and widespread use on the Internet. When looking at what online activities Americans participate in the most, e-mail is the leading pursuit, along with searching the Internet. In 2011, 91% of online adults used e-mail, and 59% of adult Internet users sent or received e-mails daily. (See Table 2.1 and Table 2.2.) According to the web-monitoring company Pingdom, in "Internet 2011 in Numbers" (January 17, 2012, http://royal .pingdom.com/2012/01/17/internet-2011-in-numbers/), in 2011 there were 3.2 billion e-mail accounts worldwide. Even though e-mail certainly makes communication easier and faster, it also poses a number of challenges, particularly to people in the workplace. Ki Mae Heussner reports in "Tech Stress: How Many Emails Can You Handle a Day?" (ABC News, July 20, 2010) that e-mail presents a unique obstacle to productivity in the 21st century. Citing a conversation with Joanne Cantor, the author of *Conquer CyberOverload: Get More Done, Boost Your Creativity, and Reduce Stress* (2009), Heussner writes, "For people trying to write reports, prepare presentations or complete other tasks that take creativity and strategic thinking, those billions of emails mean billions of interruptions that lead to lower quality work."

E-mail is not the only communications system to flourish, however. Since the early 1980s a second phone system has sprung up across the United States. According to the U.S. Census Bureau (2012, http://www.census.gov/ compendia/statab/2012/tables/12s1149.pdf), the number of cellular phone subscribers in the United States grew from 5.3 million in 1990 to 302.9 million in 2010, an increase of over 5,600%. Meanwhile, the amount of revenue that was brought in by the cellular phone system rose from $4.5 billion to $159.9 billion over this 20-year period. At the same time, the average cost to the consumer declined significantly during this span. Whereas the average cell phone bill was about $81 per month in 1990, it dropped to roughly $47 per month by 2010.

In some ways these new forms of communication have made life easier. Most Americans no longer have to look for a pay phone and search for change when they need to make a phone call away from home. Nor do most travelers have to worry about being stranded on a deserted roadway miles from a phone. Using e-mail and instant messaging, online Americans can now easily stay in touch with anyone in any country around the world. At the same time, however, Americans now have to comb through spam daily, worry about unleashing e-mail viruses, and endure strangers' phone conversations and cell phone ring tones virtually everywhere they go.

E-MAIL

E-mail was the first of these new communications technologies to emerge. Not more than two years after the initial ARPANET test in 1969, Raymond Tomlinson (1941–) of ARPANET created the first e-mail program. Tomlinson developed the idea from a program that had been used on mainframe computers with time-share operating systems. These computers, which were prevalent during the early 1960s, consisted of a number of remote terminals that were all connected to a central host computer, where all the office files and programs were stored. The remote terminals, which were typically spread throughout the office building, were little more than a screen and a keyboard, and the office workers shared the resources of the central computer. Programs were written for these systems wherein people could leave messages for one another within the core computer. Tomlinson simply adapted one of these static internal mail programs into a program that could send messages to other computers on ARPANET. The first mass e-mail Tomlinson

TABLE 2.1

Percentage of adult Internet users who participated in selected activities, 2006–12

	% Internet users who do this	Survey month	Survey date (approximate)
Use a search engine to find information	91	February 2012	2/1/12
Send or read e-mail	91	August 2011	8/1/11
Look for info on a hobby or interest	84	August 2011	8/1/11
Search for a map or driving directions	84	August 2011	8/1/11
Check the weather	81	May 2010	5/1/10
Look for health/medical info[a]	80	September 2010	9/1/10
Look for information online about a service or product you are thinking of buying[b]	78	September 2010	9/1/10
Get news	76	May 2011	5/1/11
Go online just for fun or to pass the time	74	August 2011	8/1/11
Buy a product	71	May 2011	5/1/11
Watch a video on a video-sharing site like YouTube or Vimeo	71	May 2011	5/1/11
Search for info about someone you know or might meet[b]	69	September 2009	9/1/09
Look for "how-to," "do-it-yourself" or repair information	68	August 2011	8/1/11
Visit a local, state or federal government website	67	May 2011	5/1/11
Use an online social networking site like MySpace, Facebook or LinkedIn.com*	66	February 2012	2/1/12
Buy or make a reservation for travel	65	May 2011	5/1/11
Do any banking online	61	May 2011	5/1/11
Look online for news or information about politics[b]	61	August 2011	8/1/11
Look online for info about a job[b]	56	May 2011	5/1/11
Look for information on Wikipedia	53	May 2010	5/1/10
Use online classified ads or sites like Craigslist	53	May 2010	5/1/10
Get news or information about sports[b]	52	January 2010	1/1/10
Take a virtual tour of a location online	52	August 2011	8/1/11
Do any type of research for your job	51	March 2007	3/1/07
Upload photos to a website so you can share them with others online	46	November 2010	11/1/10
Send instant messages	46	December 2010	12/1/10
Pay to access or download digital content online[b]	43	August 2008	8/1/08
Look for info about a place to live[b]	39	August 2006	8/1/06
Download music files to your computer	37	December 2007	12/1/07
Get financial info online, such as stock quotes or mortgage interest rates	37	May 2010	5/1/10
Rate a product, service or person using an online rating system	37	May 2011	5/1/11
Play online games[b]	36	September 2010	9/1/10
Categorize or tag online content like a photo, news story or blog post	33	December 2008	12/1/08
Read someone else's online journal or blog[b]	32	May 2010	5/1/10
Look for religious/spiritual info	32	September 2010	9/1/10
Post a comment or review online about a product you bought or a service you received	32	September 2009	9/1/09
Post comments to an online news group, website, blog or photo site	32	September 2010	9/1/10
Share something online that you created yourself	30	September 2010	9/1/10
Research your family's history or genealogy online[b]	27	September 2009	9/1/09
Download video files to your computer	27	December 2007	12/1/07
Participate in an online auction	26	September 2010	9/1/10
Make a donation to a charity online	25	May 2011	5/1/11
Make a phone call online, using a service such as Skype or Vonage	25	August 2011	8/1/11
Participate in an online discussion, a listserv, or other online group forum that helps people with personal issues or health problems[b]	22	December 2006	12/1/06
Download a podcast so you can listen to it or view it later[b]	21	September 2010	9/1/10
View live images online of a remote location or person, using a webcam	17	September 2009	9/1/09
Use Twitter	15	February 2012	2/1/12
Create or work on web pages or blogs for others, including friends, groups you belong to, or for work	15	September 2009	9/1/09
Take material you find online—like songs, text or images—and remix it into your own artistic creation	15	May 2008	5/1/08
Download or share files using peer-to-peer file-sharing networks, such as BitTorrent or LimeWire	15	August 2006	8/1/06
Sell something online	15	September 2009	9/1/09
Create or work on your own webpage	15	January 2010	1/1/10
Create or work on your own online journal or blog[b]	14	May 2011	5/1/11
Buy or sell stocks, bonds, or mutual funds	11	September 2009	9/1/09
Use an online dating website[b]	8	September 2009	9/1/09
Visit virtual worlds such as Second Life	4	September 2009	9/1/09

[a]Based on a series of questions about specific health topics.
[b]Item wording has changed slightly over time.

SOURCE: "Internet Activities," in *Trend Data*, Pew Internet & American Life Project, 2012, http://pewinternet.org/Static-Pages/Trend-Data-%28Adults%29/Usage-Over-Time.aspx (accessed September 25, 2012). Used by permission of the Pew Internet & American Life Project, which bears no responsibility for the interpretations presented or conclusions reached based on analysis of the data.

sent out with his program was a message to all ARPANET employees telling them that "electronic mail" was now available. He instructed them to address one another using the following convention: "user's log-in name@host computer name." This same convention is still being used.

The first e-mail program was not user-friendly. The e-mails did not have subject lines or date lines, they had to be opened in the order that they were received, and they read as strings of continuous text. Despite these inconveniences, the e-mail application caught on in the

TABLE 2.2

Percentage of adult Internet users who performed selected activities daily, 2006–12

On a typical day, 82% of adult Internet users use the Internet. Here are some of the things that Internet users do on a typical day.

	% of Internet users who report doing this "yesterday"	Survey month	Survey date (approximate)
Use a search engine to find information	59	February 2012	2/1/12
Send or read e-mail	59	August 2011	8/1/11
Use an online social networking site like MySpace, Facebook or LinkedIn.com*	48	February 2012	2/1/12
Get news	45	May 2011	5/1/11
Go online just for fun or to pass the time	44	August 2011	8/1/11
Look for info on a hobby or interest	35	August 2011	8/1/11
Check the weather	34	May 2010	5/1/10
Look online for news or information about politics*	28	August 2011	8/1/11
Look for information online about a service or product you are thinking of buying	28	September 2010	9/1/10
Watch a video on a video-sharing site like YouTube or Vimeo	28	May 2011	5/1/11
Do any banking online	24	May 2011	5/1/11
Do any type of research for your job	23	March 2007	3/1/07
Send instant messages*	18	December 2010	12/1/10
Look for information on Wikipedia	17	May 2010	5/1/10
Search for a map or driving directions	17	August 2011	8/1/11
Get sports scores and info online*	15	August 2006	8/1/06
Play online games*	13	September 2010	9/1/10
Visit a local, state or federal government website*	13	May 2011	5/1/11
Get financial info online, such as stock quotes or mortgage interest rates	12	May 2010	5/1/10
Use online classified ads or sites like Craigslist	11	May 2010	5/1/10
Categorize or tag online content like a photo, news story or blog post	11	September 2010	9/1/10
Look online for info about a job*	11	May 2011	5/1/11
Look for "how-to," "do-it-yourself" or repair information	11	August 2011	8/1/11
Read someone else's online journal or blog*	10	December 2008	12/1/08
Look for health/medical info*	10	May 2011	5/1/11
Pay to access or download digital content online*	10	September 2010	9/1/10
Use Twitter	8	February 2012	2/1/12
Post comments to an online news group, website, blog or photo site	8	September 2009	9/1/09
Search for info about someone you know or might meet	8	August 2008	8/1/08
Download music files to your computer	7	December 2007	12/1/07
Participate in an online discussion, a listserv, or other online group forum that helps people with personal issues or health problems*	7	September 2010	9/1/10
Buy a product	6	May 2011	5/1/11
Take a virtual tour of a location online	6	August 2011	8/1/11
Download video files to your computer	5	December 2007	12/1/07
Look for info about a place to live*	5	August 2006	8/1/06
Upload photos to a website so you can share them with others online	5	August 2006	8/1/06
Look for religious/spiritual info	5	May 2010	5/1/10
Make a phone call online using a service such as Skype or Vonage	4	August 2011	8/1/11
Buy or make a reservation for travel	4	May 2011	5/1/11
Share something online that you created yourself	4	September 2009	9/1/09
Create or work on web pages or blogs for others, including friends, groups you belong to, or for work	4	September 2009	9/1/09
Create or work on your own online journal or blog*	4	May 2011	5/1/11
Rate a product, service or person using an online rating system	4	May 2011	5/1/11
Participate in an online auction	4	May 2010	5/1/10
Post a comment or review online about a product you bought or a service you received	4	September 2010	9/1/10
Create or work on your own webpage	4	May 2011	5/1/11
Download or share files using peer-to-peer file-sharing networks, such as BitTorrent or LimeWire	3	May 2008	5/1/08
Download a podcast so you can listen to it or view it later*	3	May 2010	5/1/10
Take material you find online—like songs, text or images—and remix it into your own artistic creation	2	September 2009	9/1/09
Use an online dating website*	2	September 2009	9/1/09
View live images online of a remote location or person, using a webcam	2	December 2006	12/1/06
Visit virtual worlds such as Second Life	1	September 2009	9/1/09
Research your family's history or genealogy online*	1	September 2009	9/1/09
Sell something online	1	August 2006	8/1/06
Buy or sell stocks, bonds, or mutual funds	1	April 2009	4/1/09
Make a donation to a charity online	1	May 2011	5/1/11

*Item wording has changed slightly over time for the items marked with a single asterisk.

SOURCE: "Daily Internet Activities," in *Trend Data*, Pew Internet & American Life Project, 2012, http://pewinternet.org/Static-Pages/Trend-Data-%28Adults%29/Usage-Over-Time.aspx (accessed September 25, 2012). Used by permission of the Pew Internet & American Life Project, which bears no responsibility for the interpretations presented or conclusions reached based on analysis of the data.

ARPANET community quickly, and the computer scientists in the organization worked out most of the kinks. Within several years users could list messages by subject and date, delete selected messages, and forward messages to other users. E-mail soon became the most popular application for the busy researchers working at ARPANET.

When communicating by e-mail, they did not have to worry about the formalities or the long delays inherent in letter writing. Unlike a phone conversation, no time was wasted on small talk, and a copy of the communication could be retained. People could also send e-mails to one another at any time of day or night. By the late 1970s e-mail discussion groups had formed within the ARPANET community. Two of the more popular discussion groups were a science-fiction group and a group that discussed the potential future social impacts of e-mail.

During the late 1970s and early 1980s other networks began to develop, such as Usenet and Because It's Time Network (BITNET), which consisted of mainframe computers that were connected to one another over telephone lines. The central purpose of these networks was to connect universities and government agencies that were not on ARPANET. Some of these networks, such as Usenet, were set up for the express purpose of sending e-mail and posting messages on newsgroups. Usenet consisted of computers of various sizes all over the country. A relatively small number of large, powerful computers formed the backbone of the network, and many smaller computers logged on to the network through the larger ones. For example, to send an e-mail from Indiana to South Carolina a person on a small computer in Indiana would first dial into and post an e-mail onto the nearest large computer. The person operating the large computer in Indiana would then pass the e-mail via modem along with other messages from the region to all the other large computers in the network, including those in South Carolina. When the recipient of the e-mail in South Carolina logged into the network through the nearest large computer, the e-mail would then automatically be downloaded to his or her smaller computer.

By the late 1980s e-mail was commercially available for home users to a limited extent. Companies such as Quantum Computer Services (now known as AOL) and Prodigy set up chat rooms and e-mail services that could be enjoyed by people with home computers. Quantum Link, for example, was a service compatible with the Commodore 64 computer. Home users dialed into local Quantum Link mainframes, which were located in most major cities around the country. The mainframes were interconnected via open phone lines, so that anyone using the service could e-mail or chat with anyone else logged onto the service across the country. A member, however, could not contact someone on another commercial service or on the much larger Internet.

E-mail Becomes Widespread

The development of the National Science Foundation Internet and the standardization of Internet protocols during the mid-1980s brought most of the smaller academic networks such as BITNET together, allowing people throughout academia and government agencies to communicate with one another via e-mail. The invention of the World Wide Web, the Mosaic X web browser, and the widespread use of more powerful personal computers allowed home users access to Internet e-mail by the early 1990s. In 1994 AOL (known at the time as America Online) began offering people a limited service on the web with the ability to send and receive e-mail. Within a year, all the established dial-up services such as CompuServe and Prodigy moved their e-mail subscribers onto the larger Internet.

Since the mid-1990s e-mail has become the most used application on the Internet. In "Americans Going Online...Explosive Growth, Uncertain Destinations" (October 16, 1995, http://www.people-press.org/1995/10/16/americans-going-online-explosive-growth-uncertain-destinations/), the Pew Research Center reports that 12 million adult Americans were regular users of e-mail in June 1995 (with "regular user" defined as one who checked e-mail at least once per week). Since that time e-mail use has skyrocketed. As Table 2.3 shows, e-mail use reached an all-time high in May 2010, when 94% of online adults were e-mail users and 62% sent and received e-mails daily. E-mail use actually dipped slightly in 2011, largely due to the increasing popularity of other platforms for online communication, notably instant messaging and social networking sites such as Facebook. Still, with 91% of adults sending and receiving e-mails in 2011—and 59% using it daily—e-mail remained the most prevalent form of online communication. Most people said e-mail helped them maintain relationships with friends, communicate better on their job, and interact more effectively with local governments.

Who Uses E-mail?

The Pew Internet and American Life Project (Pew/Internet) reveals in "Usage over Time" (2012, http://pewinternet.org/Static-Pages/Trend-Data-%28Adults%29/Usage-Over-Time.aspx) that e-mail use remains fairly consistent over a range of demographic groups. In 2011, 91% of adults aged 18 to 29 years sent and received e-mail, and 93% of online adults aged 30 to 49 years reported doing so. Those aged 65 years and older embraced e-mail nearly as much as any other age group, with 86% of online seniors sending or receiving e-mail. E-mail is by far the Internet activity that seniors engage in more than any other. Slight differences were also noted along racial lines, with 86% of online English-speaking Hispanics using e-mail in 2011, compared with 88% of African-Americans and 92% of whites on the Internet.

Spam

By far one of the biggest problems facing e-mail in the early 21st century is spam, which is generally defined as unsolicited e-mail sent in bulk. Even though different organizations gauge the number of e-mails sent worldwide

TABLE 2.3

Email use by adults, selected years 2002–11

Activity label		Mar–May-02	Feb-04	Feb–Apr-06	May-08	May-10	Aug-11
Asked of all Internet users	Please tell me if you ever do any of the following when you go online…						
ACT01	Do you ever… Send or read email	93%	91%			94%	91%
	Men	92%	89%			93%	89%
	Women	94%	93%			94%	93%
	Whites	94%	92%			94%	92%
	Blacks	90%	85%			92%	88%
	Hispanics	90%	92%			92%	86%
	18–29	92%	89%			96%	91%
	30–49	94%	92%			94%	93%
	50–64	94%	90%			92%	90%
	65+	93%	94%			89%	86%
ACT01-Y	Yesterday, did you? Send or read email	50%	48%			62%	59%
	Men	52%	49%			61%	57%
	Women	48%	47%			63%	61%
	Whites	53%	51%			64%	62%
	Blacks	35%	29%			62%	48%
	Hispanics	42%	36%			55%	49%
	18–29	46%	45%			62%	59%
	30–49	51%	50%			67%	61%
	50–64	56%	47%			60%	60%
	65+	51%	52%			55%	48%

SOURCE: Adapted from "Usage over Time," in *Trend Data*, Pew Internet & American Life Project, 2012, http://pewinternet.org/Static-Pages/Trend-Data-%28Adults%29/Usage-Over-Time.aspx (accessed September 25, 2012). Used by permission of the Pew Internet & American Life Project, which bears no responsibility for the interpretations presented or conclusions reached based on analysis of the data.

differently, most agree that the vast majority of them are spam. In "Spam Evolution 2011" (March 1, 2012, http://www.securelist.com/en/analysis/204792219/Kaspersky_Security_Bulletin_Spam_Evolution_2011), Kaspersky Lab, a leading antivirus software firm, indicates that the problem reached its peak in 2009, when over 85% of all e-mails were spam. By 2011 this percentage had dropped to 80.3%, due in part to international law enforcement efforts that were aimed at curtailing the activities of botnet operations. In "Spam in September 2012" (October 24, 2012, http://www.securelist.com/en/analysis/204792249/Spam_in_September_2012), Kaspersky charts a further decline for the month of August 2012, when the proportion of spam dropped to 70.2% of all e-mails, before rising slightly to 72.5% in September 2012. According to Kaspersky, China was responsible for more than a quarter (26.4%) of all spam-generated e-mail in September 2012, the most of any country; the United States was the second-largest distributor, accounting for 12.5% of all spam e-mails. Interestingly, as the percentage of spam e-mails witnessed an overall decline between 2009 and 2011, the prevalence of malware e-mail attachments increased, rising from just under 1% of all e-mails in 2009 to 3.4% of all e-mails in September 2012.

The Spamhaus Project, an organization that tracks and works to eliminate spam, estimates in "The World's Worst Spammers" (November 30, 2012, http://www.spamhaus.org/statistics/spammers/) that in 2012 approximately 80% of the world's spam was being generated by a group of roughly 100 spam operations known as "spam gangs."

On average, these gangs consisted of between one and five individual spammers; the total number of individual spammers was estimated to be between 300 and 400. In November 2012 one of the worst offenders was a long-running spam gang known as Canadian Pharmacy. Believed to be based in Ukraine, Canadian Pharmacy generated tens of millions of spam e-mail messages every day, primarily through botnets. According to Spamhaus, in "The World's Worst Spam Producing Countries" (November 30, 2012, http://www.spamhaus.org/statistics/countries/), in November 2012 there were 3,094 high-volume spammers active in the United States alone. Indeed, the United States was the country of origin for the largest number of spammers, about two and a half times the number of the second-ranked country, China (1,260). Other countries with major spam operations in November 2012 included the Russian Federation (920), the United Kingdom (526), Ukraine (378), Japan (364), Brazil (361), Turkey (337), France (312), and India (308).

ANTISPAM LEGISLATION. As early as 2003 many people worried that spam was reaching epidemic proportions and was on the verge of making e-mail an impractical means of communication. In response to the growing concerns, the federal government attempted to limit spam, when, on January 1, 2004, the Controlling the Assault of Non-solicited Pornography and Marketing Act (CAN-SPAM Act) of 2003 went into effect. Enforced by the Federal Trade Commission (FTC) and the states' attorneys general, this act lays out a number of provisions that commercial e-mail senders must follow. One provision states that commercial e-mail senders must clearly identify unsolicited e-mail as solicitations or advertisements for products and services. Commercial e-mail senders must also provide a way for the recipient of the mail to opt out of receiving any more e-mails from them, and all e-mails must contain a legitimate address and use honest subject lines. Even though these provisions address the issue of spam in the United States, enforcement has been difficult. Creating a false identity on the Internet is easy, and once spammers know they are being tracked, they can easily relocate their operations to a different state or country.

In the face of this seemingly unstoppable nuisance, Internet Service Providers (ISPs), along with web security firms, developed new technologies that were aimed at reducing the volume of spam being dumped in people's in-boxes. In *Spam Summit: The Next Generation of Threats and Solutions* (November 2007, http://www.ftc .gov/os/2007/12/071220spamsummitreport.pdf), the FTC's Division of Marketing Practices reports that approximately two-thirds of e-mail users used some form of spam-filtering software. In a study published in the report, researchers found that two web-based ISPs were able to block the majority of spam e-mails through the use of filtering software; one ISP succeeded in blocking 92% of all spam e-mails, and the other managed to filter 68% of spam.

Still, in 2012 the problem of spam remained a fact of life among Internet users. Even though consumers typically object to spam, entrepreneurs recognize the potential profit in sending out unsolicited messages. Issuing spam costs next to nothing per message sent. Even if only 1% of people respond to a spam attack, be it for a legitimate digital cable filter or a fraudulent credit card scam, the spammer stands to make a lot of money or bring in a lot of credit card numbers. As long as a small percentage of the population responds to spam, it is potentially profitable. Bringing this number down to zero would likely be impossible. In the end, spam may just become another form of white noise that has to be endured in the modern world.

INSTANT MESSAGING

Instant messaging (IM) is a tool that allows people to communicate via text messages in near real time over the Internet and is typically available on personal computers and on selected cell phones. In "Usage over Time," Pew/Internet indicates that in November 2010, 48% of Internet users had contacted someone via IM, which was up 10 percentage points from November 2008. According to the Radicati Group, Inc. (November 15, 2012, http://www .radicati.com/?p=8417), a technology market research company, the number of IM accounts worldwide was expected to top 2.7 billion by the end of 2012.

IM provides people some unique advantages that other communication devices do not. Most IM applications are compact in size and easy to access, making IM easy to use while taking part in other activities. In *How Americans Use Instant Messaging* (September 1, 2004, http://www.pewinternet.org/~/media//Files/Reports/2004/ PIP_Instantmessage_Report.pdf.pdf), Eulynn Shiu and Amanda Lenhart of Pew/Internet report that in 2004, 32% of adult Americans said they were multitasking almost every time when they used IM. IM also has a clandestine aspect to it. A person can type a message without anyone knowing what he or she is doing. Nearly a quarter (24%) of all IM users said they used IM to converse with someone they were in close proximity to— typically because a class or meeting was in progress.

Like most forms of communication technology, IM evolved rapidly in the 21st century. According to the AOL–Associated Press survey "AP-AOL Instant Messaging Trends Survey Reveals Popularity of Mobile Instant Messaging" (November 15, 2007, http://www.businesswire .com/news/home/20071115005196/en/AP-AOL-Instant-Mes saging-Trends-Survey-Reveals-Popularity), by 2007 roughly a quarter (24%) of IM users had begun to send and receive instant messages from their cell phones. Over the next five years the number of mobile IM users rose rapidly, driven largely by the increasing popularity of smart phone devices. Analysys Mason reports in the press release "IPhone Users Account for 80% of the Heaviest Smartphone Data Users" (May 30, 2012, http://www.analysys mason.com/About-Us/News/Press-releases1/consumer-smartphone-usage-May2012/?bp=%252fNews%252f) that by 2012, 45% of smart phone owners used some form of IM service on their phone.

During this period IM began diversifying into new platforms. In April 2008 the popular social networking site Facebook introduced Facebook Chat, a communication tool that enabled users to initiate instant conversations with other people within their personal networks. In February 2010 Facebook reached an agreement with AOL to integrate their IM services, enabling users to communicate between the two IM platforms. Even as other messaging tools such as texting and Twitter were gaining popularity by decade's end, IM remained a vital form of rapid communication for many Internet users. Teens remained particularly likely to use IM services as a regular means of communicating and socializing online. Amanda Lenhart of Pew/American reveals in *Teens, Smartphones & Texting* (March 19, 2012, http://pewinternet .org/~/media//Files/Reports/2012/PIP_Teens_Smartphones _and_Texting.pdf) that 50% of teens exchanged instant messages at least once a week in 2011; an even higher proportion (66%) communicated via messaging services on social networking sites. (See Figure 2.1.) At the same time, social networking became a popular mode of communication among adult Internet users. As Table 2.4 shows, 83% of adult Facebook users sent private

FIGURE 2.1

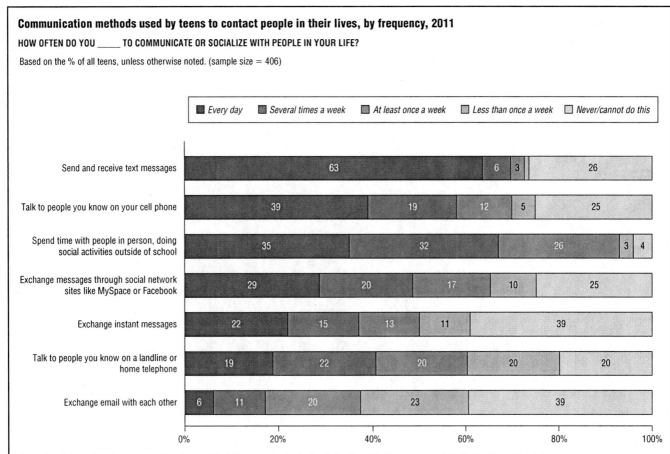

Communication methods used by teens to contact people in their lives, by frequency, 2011

HOW OFTEN DO YOU _____ TO COMMUNICATE OR SOCIALIZE WITH PEOPLE IN YOUR LIFE?

Based on the % of all teens, unless otherwise noted. (sample size = 406)

Legend: ■ Every day ■ Several times a week ■ At least once a week □ Less than once a week □ Never/cannot do this

Method	Every day	Several times a week	At least once a week	Less than once a week	Never/cannot do this
Send and receive text messages	63		6	3	26
Talk to people you know on your cell phone	39	19	12	5	25
Spend time with people in person, doing social activities outside of school	35	32	26	3	4
Exchange messages through social network sites like MySpace or Facebook	29	20	17	10	25
Exchange instant messages	22	15	13	11	39
Talk to people you know on a landline or home telephone	19	22	20	20	20
Exchange email with each other	6	11	20	23	39

Notes: Population = 799 for teens 12–17 and parents, including oversample of minority families. Interviews were conducted in English and Spanish.

SOURCE: Amanda Lenhart, "How Often Do You—to Communicate or Socialize with People in Your Lives?" in *Teens, Smartphones & Texting*, Pew Internet & American Life Project, March 19, 2012, http://pewinternet.org/~/media//Files/Reports/2012/PIP_Teens_Smartphones_and_Texting.pdf (accessed September 25, 2012). Used by permission of the Pew Internet & American Life Project, which bears no responsibility for the interpretations presented or conclusions reached based on analysis of the data.

TABLE 2.4

Frequency with which social networking users send private messages via Facebook, by age, 2010

	All SNS users	Age 18–22	Age 23–35	Age 36–49	Age 50–65	Age 65+
Several times a day	4%	2%	5%	4%	4%	0%
About once per day	7%	11%	7%	5%	5%	2%
3–5 days per week	8%	7%	10%	10%	6%	2%
1–2 days per week	19%	24%	23%	13%	16%	14%
Every few weeks	21%	16%	25%	21%	20%	15%
Less often	24%	21%	22%	22%	30%	30%
Never	19%	18%	9%	25%	20%	38%
N (weighted)	940	154	309	236	184	57

Notes: SNS = social network site. Survey conducted on landline and cell phone. Population for full sample = 2,255 and margin of error is +/−2.3 percentage points. Population for Facebook users = 877 and margin of error is +/−3.6 percentage points.

SOURCE: Keith N. Hampton et al., "Frequency of Sending Private Messages on Facebook by Age," in *Social Networking Sites and Our Lives*, Pew Internet & American Life Project, June 16, 2011, http://www.pewinternet.org/~/media//Files/Reports/2011/ PIP%20-%20Social%20networking%20sites%20and%20 our%20lives.pdf (accessed October 8, 2012). Used by permission of the Pew Internet & American Life Project, which bears no responsibility for the interpretations presented or conclusions reached based on analysis of the data.

messages via the social networking site in 2010. Male Facebook users (82%) were slightly more likely to use the site's private messaging system than female Facebook users (81%). (See Figure 2.2.)

VOICE OVER INTERNET PROTOCOL

Another type of Internet communications technology is voice over Internet protocol (VoIP). VoIP is an application that allows the user to make phone calls over the Internet.

FIGURE 2.2

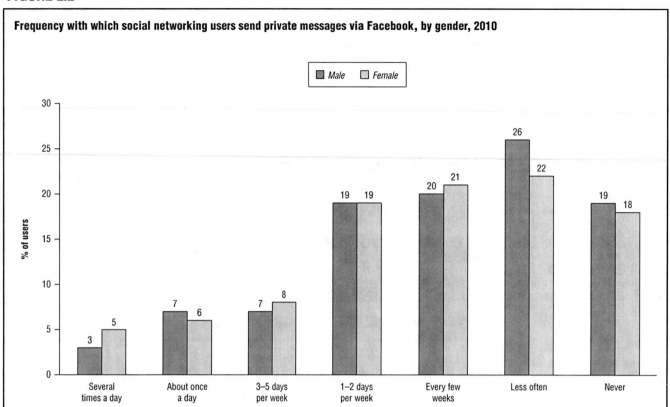

Frequency with which social networking users send private messages via Facebook, by gender, 2010

■ Male □ Female

Notes: Survey conducted on landline and cell phones. Population for full sample = 2,255 and margin of error is +/−2.3 percentage points. Population for Facebook users = 877 and margin of error is +/−3.6 percentage points.

SOURCE: Keith N. Hampton et al., "Frequency of Sending Private Messages on Facebook by Sex," in *Social Networking Sites and Our Lives*, Pew Internet & American Life Project, June 16, 2011, http://www.pewinternet.org/~/media//Files/Reports/2011/PIP%20-%20Social%20networking%20sites%20and%20our%20lives.pdf (accessed October 8, 2012). Used by permission of the Pew Internet & American Life Project, which bears no responsibility for the interpretations presented or conclusions reached based on analysis of the data.

The user attaches the phone to an adapter that sits between the phone and the computer. When a call is in progress, the adapter breaks down the voice stream into data packets and sends them over the Internet just like e-mail to the user's destination. (Regular phone conversations typically travel as streams of continuous data over a dedicated phone line that connects two people directly.) If the person on the other end of the call is also equipped with VoIP, then the entire conversation is treated by the Internet as nothing more than an instant message or e-mail. If the person using VoIP dials to a traditional phone, then the call must be converted into a continuous voice stream by a telecommunications company before the call reaches its destination.

During the early part of the 21st century VoIP began gaining widespread acceptance among consumers. According to Pew/Internet and the New Millennium Research Council (June 30, 2004, http://www.newmillenniumresearch.org/news/pewvoip_coverage.html), by 2004, 34 million Americans (27% of Internet users) had heard of VoIP, and nearly 14 million (11%) had used VoIP at some point during their life. The marketing research firm TeleGeography indicates in the press release "US VoIP Gains Mean RBOC Pain" (May 19, 2008, http://www.telegeography.com/press/press-releases/2008/05/19/us-voip-gains-mean-rboc-pain/index.html) that "by the first quarter of 2008, 16.3 million consumer VoIP lines were in service, representing 13.8 percent of all U.S. households, and 27 percent of broadband households." This reflected growth of 758% since 2005, when 1.9 million households had subscribed to VoIP. In *24% of Internet Users Have Made Phone Calls Online* (May 30, 2011, http://www.pewinternet.org/~/media//Files/Reports/2011/PIP_Internet%20phone%20calls.pdf), Lee Rainie of Pew/Internet reports that roughly one out of four (24%) online adults in the United States made phone calls over the Internet in 2011, up from 8% in 2007. Rainie also reveals that roughly 5% of all Internet users engage in an online call on any given day. Meanwhile, the number of Americans using VoIP technology on their mobile devices also saw a substantial increase. Rebtel, a VoIP provider, notes in "New Rebtel Mobile Device Survey Shows that 20 Million American Smartphone Owners Spend Approx. $37.8 Billion Annually on International Calls" (August 16, 2012, http://www.rebtel.com/) that by 2012, 35% of American adults who owned both a smart phone and tablet had a VoIP application on at least one of their devices. VoIP technology also found massive growth potential in the business world. In "VoIP Adoption: More and More Companies Say 'Yes'" (May 12, 2011, http://www.windstreambusiness.com/blog/2011/05/voip-adoption-more-and-more-companies-say-yes), Terry O'Brian indicates that by 2011, 31% of all business phone lines in the United States used VoIP technology. This figure was expected to rise to 66.5% by 2015.

MOBILE PHONES

The cell phone is the only information technology adopted since the mid-1980s that has outpaced the Internet in terms of use. The development of the modern cell phone began during the mid-1940s, nearly 20 years before scientists even conceived of an Internet. In St. Louis, Missouri, the Bell System introduced the first commercial radio-telephone service that could connect to the national phone system. The radio-telephone, which was typically mounted under the front dashboard of a car or truck, received incoming telephone calls via radio waves that were transmitted from a large tower planted on a downtown building. A bell rang and a light went off on the radio-telephone to signify an incoming call. When the person using the radio-telephone answered, his or her side of the conversation was transmitted to one of several receiving stations around the city that were all open to the same frequencies. Both the incoming and outgoing signals were relayed through a switchboard and routed into the national phone system. From its inception in 1946, this system had a number of limitations. Calls had to be routed through a live switchboard operator, both parties involved in a conversation could not talk at once, and only three conversations could take place citywide at any given time because of bandwidth restrictions.

History and Development

D. H. Ring at Bell Laboratories first posited the idea for the modern mobile cellular phone network in 1947 in an internal memorandum. The memo proposed a system that would overcome many of the flaws inherent in the Bell radio-telephone. The plan called for a network of low-powered cellular towers that could receive and transmit telephone calls via radio waves to and from mobile phones. Each tower would have a 3-mile (4.8-km) broadcast radius. As the user of the mobile phone traveled across these cells, the call would be automatically routed from one tower to the next and the phone would switch frequencies. Because of a limited number of frequencies available in the spectrum, towers that were out of range of one another were to send and receive radio signals of the same frequency. That way two people who were 3 miles apart or more could carry on separate conversations using the same frequency without interfering with each other's reception.

To implement this vision on a large scale and make a profit, AT&T (the successor to Bell Labs) required more frequencies on the radio spectrum than the Federal Communications Commission (FCC) then allowed for two-way radio communications. The radio spectrum is essentially a long ribbon of frequencies that stretch from 3 kilohertz (kHz) to 300 gigahertz. Only one device in an area, be it a radio station or a television station, can use a particular part of this ribbon to broadcast or else interference will arise. The FCC regulates what type of devices can operate over various sections of the radio spectrum. Cell phones generally take up a large part of each spectrum because each cell phone requires two signals at two different frequencies—one signal for the incoming signal and one for the outgoing signal. With the limits the FCC imposed in 1947, only 23 cellular phone conversations could take place in a metropolitan area equipped with Bell Lab's proposed cellular system. When AT&T approached the FCC and asked for additional room on the radio spectrum, the FCC granted AT&T only a fraction of the space requested.

Over the next 20 years, mobile phone technology advanced slowly. In 1948 the Richmond Radiotelephone Company implemented the first automated radio-telephone service that did not require a live switchboard operator. In 1964 the Bell System rolled out the Improved Mobile Telephone Service to replace its aging radio-telephone network. This system allowed for both people to talk at once during a call. The bandwidth that each phone occupied on the radio spectrum was narrowed, so more people in a city could use it.

Technological Developments after 1960

AT&T once again approached the FCC in 1958, this time asking for 75 megahertz (MHz) of spectrum located in the 800 MHz range of the radio spectrum. At the time, hardly anyone in the United States employed this part of the spectrum for broadcasting. The FCC did not review the proposal until 1968. It considered the request for two years and made a tentative decision to let AT&T use that part of the spectrum for two-way radio in 1970. Meanwhile, the Bell System, Motorola, and several other companies began engineering the technologies that were necessary for the cell phone network. In 1969 the Bell System installed the first working cell phone system aboard a train. The system consisted of a set of pay phones placed on the Metroliner trains that ran between New York City and Washington, D.C. Cell phone towers were set up along the track. As the train sped along, telephone conversations were routed from tower to tower just as described in the 1947 Bell Labs proposal. Four years after this first cellular phone went into use, Martin Cooper (1928–) of Motorola Inc. developed the first personal, handheld cellular phone. Motorola erected a single prototype cellular tower in New York City to test the phone. Cooper made his first call to his rival at Bell Labs, who was attempting to create a similar device.

In 1978 the FCC allowed AT&T to test an analog cellular telephone service. AT&T chose Chicago, Illinois, as one of the trial cities and set up 10 cellular towers, which covered 21,000 square miles (54,000 sq km) of the Chicago metropolitan area. Customers who wanted to use the service leased large, car-mounted telephones. The trial run was a success, and Ameritech, the regional Bell in metropolitan Chicago, launched the first commercial cellular service in the United States in 1983. (Other cell phone services had already begun operating in Europe, Asia, and the Middle East.) Two months after Ameritech began service, Cellular One offered service in the Washington-Baltimore area. Most people had car-mounted phones that occupied the middle of the front seat of a car. The alternatives were large portable phones that were so big they had to be carried around in a suitcase. At first, the cellular systems being put in place were not compatible with one another, and roaming outside of the calling area was not a possibility.

During the late 1980s the Telecommunications Industry Association established some basic standards for cell phone companies. The standards paved the way for a continuous, cross-country network that everyone could use regardless of which company was providing the service (oftentimes with extra roaming charges). The first standard was for analog phones. Analog phones process signals in much the same way as car radios or traditional phones do. When a person speaks into the cell phone, the microphone turns the signal into a continuous stream of electrical impulses, which travels out from the phone's antennae and to the cellular tower. Both the outgoing signals and the incoming signals on modern analog phones were each allowed 30 kHz of space on the radio wave spectrum.

Modern Cell Phone Networks

The Census Bureau (2012, http://www.census.gov/compendia/statab/2012/tables/12s1149.pdf) indicates that by 1990 the number of people using cell phones increased dramatically to 5.3 million subscribers. With the analog standard and the frequency limitations imposed by the FCC, less than 60 people in each network were able to use one cellular tower at once. If the number of cell phone subscriptions continued to increase at its then-current rate, then cell phone companies would soon require new technologies that allowed more cell phone conversations to take place in a given area. The cell phone companies' solution was to adopt digital technology.

A digital signal is a signal that is broken down into impulses representing ones and zeros. When a digital cell phone receives a digital signal, a chip inside the phone known as a digital signal processor (DSP) reads these ones and zeros and then constructs an analog signal that travels to the phone's speaker. Conversely, the DSP also processes the analog signal coming from the phone's microphone, converting it into ones and zeros, before sending

the signal to a cell tower. By breaking down the signal into ones and zeros, more telephone calls can be handled by one-frequency cell phone towers. The process is analogous to breaking down and cutting up boxes to allow more to fit inside a trash can. The first digital system widely used by the cell phone companies was the time division multiple access (TDMA) method. Figure 2.3 and Figure 2.4 show the difference between the older, frequency division multiple access (FDMA) used for analog phones and TDMA. FDMA requires each phone to use a different frequency. TDMA allows three cell phone conversations to be contained in the same 30-kHz-wide band that holds only one analog conversation. By the early 1990s cellular companies were erecting digital cellular towers enabled with TDMA across the country.

Meanwhile, the TDMA systems were looking as if they might hit capacity. In response, the FCC auctioned off more frequency bands in the radio wave spectrum between the 1850 MHz and 1900 MHz range. Services set up on these bands were known as personal communications services (PCS). PCS networks were designed for handheld mobile phones instead of car phones and had smaller cells than the original cellular network. The PCS networks also employed a newer technology known as code division multiple access (CDMA). CDMA could pack up to 10 calls into one frequency band. (See Figure 2.5.)

FIGURE 2.3

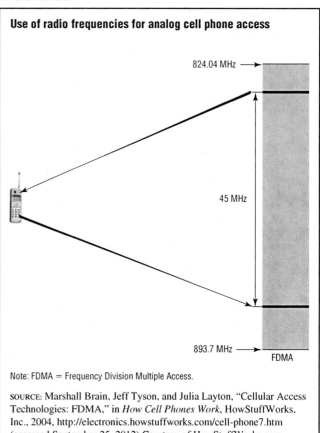

Use of radio frequencies for analog cell phone access

824.04 MHz

45 MHz

893.7 MHz

FDMA

Note: FDMA = Frequency Division Multiple Access.

SOURCE: Marshall Brain, Jeff Tyson, and Julia Layton, "Cellular Access Technologies: FDMA," in *How Cell Phones Work*, HowStuffWorks, Inc., 2004, http://electronics.howstuffworks.com/cell-phone7.htm (accessed September 25, 2012) Courtesy of HowStuffWorks.com.

FIGURE 2.4

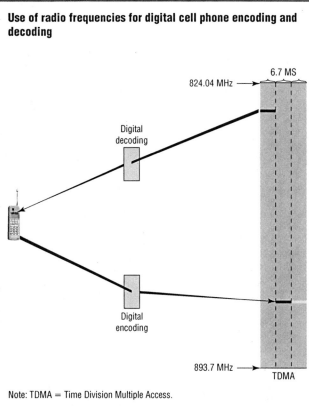

Use of radio frequencies for digital cell phone encoding and decoding

6.7 MS

824.04 MHz →

Digital decoding

Digital encoding

893.7 MHz →

TDMA

Note: TDMA = Time Division Multiple Access.

SOURCE: Marshall Brain, Jeff Tyson, and Julia Layton, "Cellular Access Technologies: TDMA," in *How Cell Phones Work*, HowStuffWorks, Inc., 2004, http://electronics.howstuffworks.com/cell-phone7.htm (accessed September 25, 2012) Courtesy of HowStuffWorks.com.

FIGURE 2.5

Use of radio frequencies for code division multiple access

1850MHz →

Digital decoding

Digital decoding

1990MHz →

CDMA

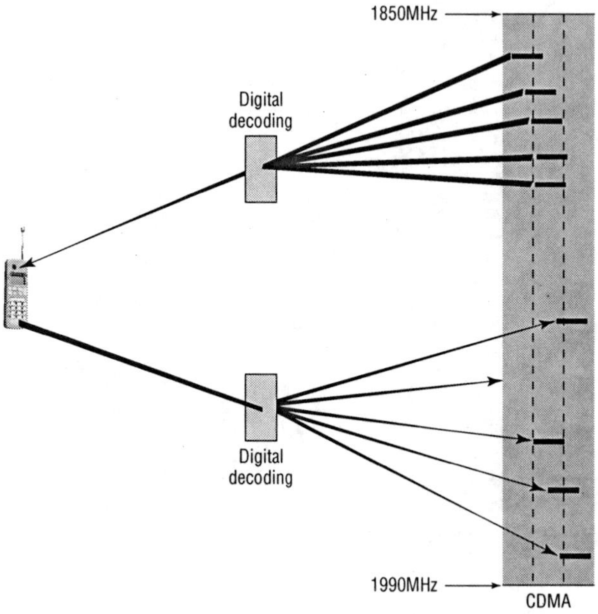

Note: CDMA = Code Division Multiple Access

SOURCE: Marshall Brain, Jeff Tyson, and Julia Layton, "Cellular Access Technologies: CDMA," in *How Cell Phones Work*, HowStuffWorks, Inc., 2004, http://electronics.howstuffworks.com/cell-phone7.htm (accessed September 25, 2012). Courtesy of HowStuffWorks.com.

With so many bands available, cell phone companies introduced a multitude of standard features into their phones, such as the ability to send instant messages, surf the web, play games, send e-mail, and check the identity of callers.

For both adults and teens, by the beginning of the 21st century cell phones had become an integral part of their daily lives. By 2010, 85% of all adults owned cell phones. (See Figure 2.6.) Younger adults were the most likely to own cell phones; 95% of respondents aged 18 to 34 years and 92% of those aged 35 to 46 years owned mobile phones in 2010. Meanwhile, cell phone ownership was also prevalent among teens during the second decade of the 21st century. According to Table 2.5, 77% of all teens aged 12 to 17 years owned a cell phone by 2011. Cell phone ownership rose considerably as teens grew older; 87% of teens aged 14 to 17 years owned a cell phone, compared with 57% of those aged 12 to 13 years. Family income was among the most significant factor in determining cell phone ownership among American teens. As Table 2.5 reveals, 91% of teens living in a household that earned $75,000 or more per year owned a cell phone in 2011, whereas only 62% of teens with household incomes below $30,000 per year owned a cell phone.

As cell phone ownership increased, use of landline phones dropped steadily among teens. Figure 2.7 shows the frequency with which teens talked to their friends on landline phones between November 2006 and July 2011. In 2006, 39% of teens talked to their friends every day over a landline, whereas only 8% never used a landline to communicate with friends. Less than five years later these figures were nearly reversed; only 14% of teens talked to their friends over a landline daily, whereas 31% never used a landline phone. Meanwhile, as Figure 2.8 reveals, the number of teens who did not use a cell phone fell steadily during the same period, from 41% who never spoke to friends on a cell phone in 2006, to 28% in 2011.

Texting and Other Nonvoice Applications

Interestingly, the number of teens who talked to their friends on a cell phone every day actually dropped between 2009 and 2011, from 38% to 26%. (See Figure 2.8.) This decline was likely related to the increasing popularity of texting among teens. As Figure 2.9 shows, 49% of teens texted their friends daily in 2011. Indeed, of the diverse features that were available on cell phones in the early 21st century, texting was arguably one of the most popular. According to Figure 2.1, more teens engaged in texting on a daily basis in 2011 than in any other form of communication or social activity outside of school. Also, the number of texts that teens sent and received on an average day also increased between 2009 and 2011. For example,

FIGURE 2.6

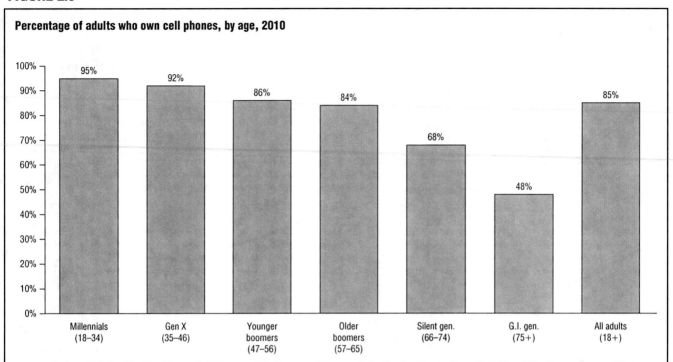

Percentage of adults who own cell phones, by age, 2010

SOURCE: Kathryn Zickuhr, "Do You Have a Cell Phone, or Blackberry or iPhone or Other Device That Is Also a Cell Phone?" in *Generations and Their Gadgets*, Pew Internet & American Life Project, February 3, 2011, http://www.pewinternet.org/~/media//Files/Reports/2011/PIP_Generations_and_Gadgets.pdf (accessed October 8, 2012). Used by permission of the Pew Internet & American Life Project, which bears no responsibility for the interpretations presented or conclusions reached based on analysis of the data.

18% of teens sent between 21 and 50 texts on an average day in 2009, whereas in 2011 this percentage had increased to 20%. (See Figure 2.10.) Concerning teens who sent over 200 texts on an average day, this percentage increased from 15% in 2009 to 18% in 2011.

Between 2009 and 2012 an increasing number of cell phone owners were using their mobile devices to access the Internet. In 2009, 31% of adult cell phone owners went online using their phone; by 2012 this figure had risen to 55%, an increase of 24 percentage points. (See Table 1.7 in Chapter 1.) Cell phone owners aged 25 to 34 years (80%) were the most likely to access the Internet with their phone, while non-Hispanic African-Americans (64%) were more likely than Hispanics (63%) or non-Hispanic whites (52%) to use their cell phone to go online. As Table 2.6 shows, in 2012 cell phones were the primary means of accessing the Internet for 31% of all cell phone owners. Non-Hispanic African-Americans (51%) were the most likely to conduct the majority of their online activities using their phone, whereas non-Hispanic whites (24%) were the least likely to go online using their phone. Among cell phone owners who used their phone as their primary means of going online, 38% cited convenience as their principal reason for doing so. (See Table 2.7.)

To a large extent, the increase in mobile Internet use was driven by the growth of smart phone ownership in

the United States. As Table 2.8 shows, the percentage of American adults who owned smart phones grew from 35% in May 2011 to 46% in February 2012, an increase of 11 percentage points in just over half a year. In 2011, 25% of smart phone owners used their phones as their primary means of accessing the Internet. (See Table 2.9.)

Issues and Concerns

DISTRACTED DRIVING. Even though cell phones have brought a great deal of convenience to modern society, they have become a source of trouble as well. Many believe that cell phones contribute to automobile accidents because drivers cannot concentrate on the road appropriately while speaking on a cell phone. Indeed, cell phone use while driving has become a central aspect of everyday life. As Table 2.10 shows, in 2010 a majority of adults (61%) admitted to having talked on a cell phone while driving; among cell phone users, this proportion rose to 75%. Texting was far less prevalent, with just over a quarter (27%) of all adults admitting to having sent or received texts while driving; among texters, however, this figure rose to almost half (47%). At the same time, 44% of adults stated that they had been in a situation in which a driver's use of a cell phone had made them feel endangered.

Scientific studies show that talking on a cell phone seriously impairs the ability of most adults to operate a

TABLE 2.5

Percentage of teens who own cell phones, by selected characteristics, 2011

All teens (sample size = 799)	77%
Gender	
Boys (sample size = 391)	76
Girls (sample size = 408)	78
Age	
12–13 (sample size = 225)	57[a]
14–17 (sample size = 574)	87[a]
Race/ethnicity	
White, non-Hispanic (sample size = 442)	81[a]
Black, non-Hispanic (sample size = 123)	72
Hispanic (English- and Spanish-speaking) (sample size = 172)	63[a]
Household income	
Less than $30,000 (sample size = 192)	62
$30,000–$49,999 (sample size = 111)	75
$50,000–$74,999 (sample size = 119)	72
$75,000+ (sample size = 304)	91[b]
Education level of parents	
Less than high school (sample size = 89)	47[b]
High school graduate (sample size = 171)	82
Some college (sample size = 179)	79
College+ (sample size = 357)	82
Community type	
Urban (sample size = 279)	69[a]
Suburban (sample size = 397)	83[a]
Rural (sample size = 96)	73

[a]Indicates statistically significant difference between rows.
[b]Indicates a data point that is significant with regards to all other data points in the row section.
Notes: Sample size = 799 teens ages 12–17 and a parent or guardian. Interviews were conducted in English and Spanish on landlines and cell phones.

SOURCE: Amanda Lenhart, "Who Has a Cell Phone?" in *Teens, Smartphones & Texting*, Pew Internet & American Life Project, March 19, 2012, http://pewinternet.org/~/media//Files/Reports/2012/PIP_Teens_Smartphones_and_Texting.pdf (accessed September 25, 2012). Used by permission of the Pew Internet & American Life Project, which bears no responsibility for the interpretations presented or conclusions reached based on analysis of the data.

vehicle. In "Supertaskers: Profiles in Extraordinary Multitasking Ability" (*Psychonomic Bulletin & Review*, vol. 17, no. 4, 2010), James M. Watson and David L. Strayer of the University of Utah demonstrate that only 2.5% of the population have the innate ability to drive a car safely while using a cell phone. The study also shows that the vast majority (97.5%) of people took 20% longer to apply the brakes when talking on a cell phone while driving. The National Safety Council estimates in *Understanding the Distracted Brain: Why Driving While Using Hands-Free Cell Phones Is Risky Behavior* (March 2010, http://www.fnal.gov/pub/traffic_safety/files/NSC%20White%20Paper%20-%20Distracted%20Driving%203-10.pdf) that cell phone use while driving plays a role in more than 25% of all highway traffic accidents.

As of 2012, Congress continued to debate whether or not to institute a nationwide ban on handheld cell phone use in automobiles, but many states already had laws in place. Table 2.11 indicates which states had adopted cell phone driving laws as of 2012. As can be seen, 10 states and the District of Columbia had statewide bans on the use of handheld devices while driving. In addition, 39 states and the District of Columbia banned drivers from text-messaging while behind the wheel; 32 states and the District of Columbia banned cell phones for drivers with learner permits or provisional licenses; and 19 states and the District of Columbia prohibited the use of cell phones by school bus drivers carrying passengers.

USE BY CHILDREN. As cell phone makers add features such as Internet access and video games, many believe cell phones are becoming a bigger distraction and a source of potential trouble for children. Laura Willard reports in "Cell Phone Safety Tips for Kids, Tweens and Teens" (January 30, 2012, http://www.sheknows.com/parenting/articles/947333/cell-phone-safety-tips-for-kids-tweens-and-teens) that in 2012 nearly a quarter (22%) of children aged six to nine years owned a cell phone; among children aged 10 to 14 years the percentage rose to 60%. As mobile Internet capability becomes more widespread, young people are accessing increasingly large amounts of data on their cell phone. In "New Mobile Obsession: U.S. Teens Triple Data Usage" (December 15, 2011, http://blog.nielsen.com/nielsenwire/online_mobile/new-mobile-obsession-u-s-teens-triple-data-usage/), the Nielsen Company reveals that between the third quarter of 2010 and the third quarter of 2011 the average monthly mobile data usage among teens aged 13 to 17 years rose from 90 megabytes to 321 megabytes, an increase of 256%. Nielsen also reports that the highest data consumption occurred within the 25- to 34-year-old demographic, which used an average of 578 megabytes of data per month during the third quarter of 2011.

In the face of this trend, many school districts throughout the country have banned the use of phones during school hours, citing the disruptive nature of phones as well as the potential use of phones for cheating and for taking inappropriate photographs, among other reasons. Parents and students disagree, however, claiming that it is a violation of students' rights to prohibit them from carrying a cell phone while at school. After the Columbine High School massacre in Colorado, and following the September 11, 2001, terrorist attacks on the United States in New York City and Washington, D.C., many parents consider cell phones a crucial communication tool and an integral part of a family emergency plan. In New York City, where a legal battle raged regarding cell phones in public schools, a court upheld the ban in 2008, affecting 1.1 million students. Jennifer Medina reports in "Court Upholds School Cellphone Ban" (*New York Times*, April 22, 2008) that "the court ruled squarely in favor of the city, stating that: 'Nothing about the cell phone policy forbids or prevents parents and their children from communicating with each other before or after school.'"

FIGURE 2.7

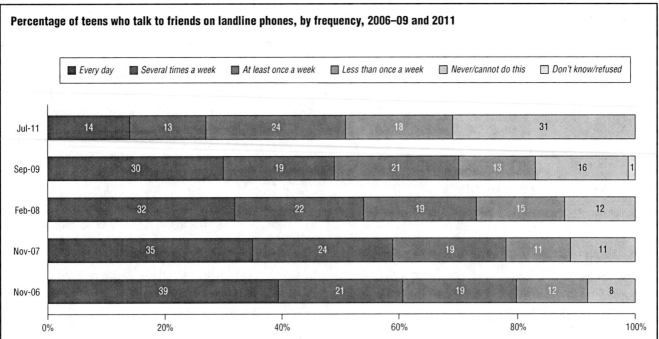

Percentage of teens who talk to friends on landline phones, by frequency, 2006–09 and 2011

| | Every day | Several times a week | At least once a week | Less than once a week | Never/cannot do this | Don't know/refused |

Notes: Sample size = 799 teens 12–17 and a parent or guardian. Interviews were conducted in English and Spanish, by landline and cell phone.

SOURCE: Amanda Lenhart, "How Often Do You Talk to Friends on a Landline Phone?" in *Teens, Smartphones & Texting*, Pew Internet & American Life Project, March 19, 2012, http://pewinternet.org/~/media//Files/Reports/2012/PIP_Teens_Smartphones_and_Texting.pdf (accessed September 25, 2012). Used by permission of the Pew Internet & American Life Project, which bears no responsibility for the interpretations presented or conclusions reached based on analysis of the data.

FIGURE 2.8

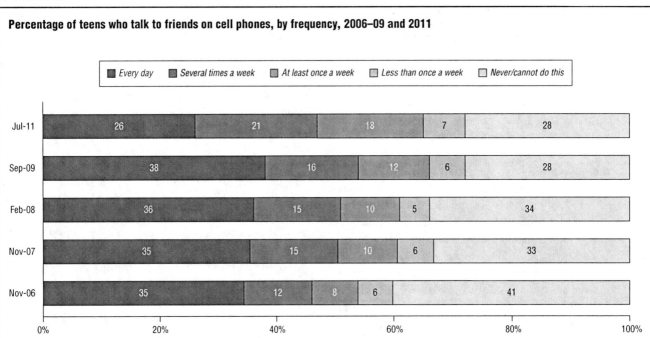

Percentage of teens who talk to friends on cell phones, by frequency, 2006–09 and 2011

| | Every day | Several times a week | At least once a week | Less than once a week | Never/cannot do this |

Notes: Sample size = 799 teens 12–17 and a parent or guardian. Interviews were conducted in English and Spanish, by landline and cell phone.

SOURCE: Amanda Lenhart, "How Often Do You Talk to Friends on Your Cell Phone?" in *Teens, Smartphones & Texting*, Pew Internet & American Life Project, March 19, 2012, http://pewinternet.org/~/media//Files/Reports/2012/PIP_Teens_Smartphones_and_Texting.pdf (accessed September 25, 2012). Used by permission of the Pew Internet & American Life Project, which bears no responsibility for the interpretations presented or conclusions reached based on analysis of the data.

FIGURE 2.9

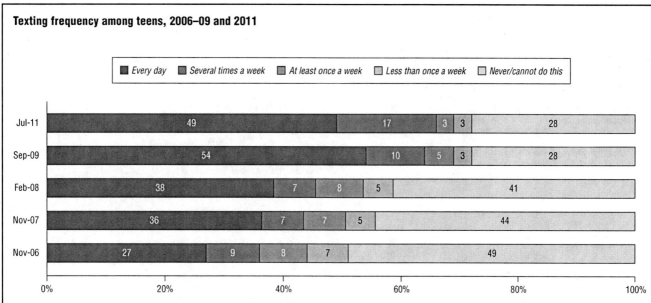

Texting frequency among teens, 2006–09 and 2011

Legend: ■ Every day ■ Several times a week ■ At least once a week □ Less than once a week □ Never/cannot do this

Date	Every day	Several times a week	At least once a week	Less than once a week	Never/cannot do this
Jul-11	49	17	3	3	28
Sep-09	54	10	5	3	28
Feb-08	38	7	8	5	41
Nov-07	36	7	7	5	44
Nov-06	27	9	8	7	49

Notes: Sample size = 799 teens 12–17 and a parent or guardian. Interviews were conducted in English and Spanish, by landline and cell phone.

SOURCE: Amanda Lenhart, "The Number of Teens Who Text Daily with Friends Has Not Changed Significantly since 2009," in *Teens, Smartphones & Texting,* Pew Internet & American Life Project, March 19, 2012, http://pewinternet.org/~/media//Files/Reports/2012/PIP_Teens_Smartphones_and_Texting.pdf (accessed September 25, 2012). Used by permission of the Pew Internet & American Life Project, which bears no responsibility for the interpretations presented or conclusions reached based on analysis of the data.

FIGURE 2.10

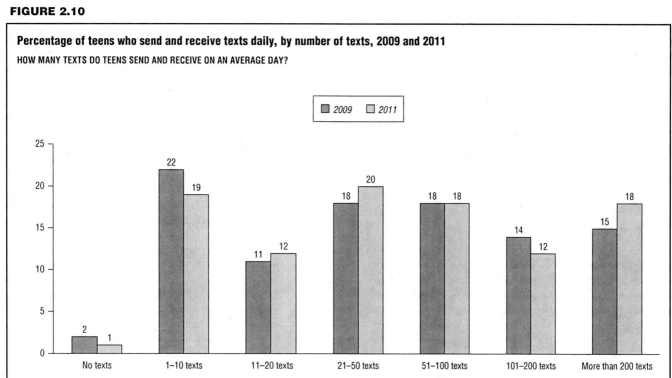

Percentage of teens who send and receive texts daily, by number of texts, 2009 and 2011

HOW MANY TEXTS DO TEENS SEND AND RECEIVE ON AN AVERAGE DAY?

Legend: ■ 2009 □ 2011

Number of texts	2009	2011
No texts	2	1
1–10 texts	22	19
11–20 texts	11	12
21–50 texts	18	20
51–100 texts	18	18
101–200 texts	14	12
More than 200 texts	15	18

Notes: Sample size = 799 teens 12–17 and a parent or guardian. Interviews were conducted in English and Spanish, by landline and cell phone.

SOURCE: Amanda Lenhart, "How Many Texts Do Teens Send and Receive on an Average Day?" in *Teens, Smartphones & Texting*, Pew Internet & American Life Project, March 19, 2012, http://pewinternet.org/~/media//Files/Reports/2012/PIP_Teens_Smartphones_and_Texting.pdf (accessed September 25, 2012). Used by permission of the Pew Internet & American Life Project, which bears no responsibility for the interpretations presented or conclusions reached based on analysis of the data.

TABLE 2.6

Percentage of cell phone owners who use their cell phones as primary means of accessing the Internet, by selected characteristics, 2012

WHICH CELL INTERNET USERS GO ONLINE MOSTLY USING THEIR PHONES?

55% of cell owners use the Internet or email on their phones, and 31% of these cell Internet users go online MOSTLY using their cell phone instead of some other device. (Example of how to read this chart: 45% of cell Internet users ages 18–29 go online mostly using their phone, rather than some other device)

Total for cell Internet users (sample size = 929)	**31%**
Gender	
Men (sample size = 469)	29
Women (sample size = 460)	32
Age	
18–29 (sample size = 260)	45**
30–49 (sample size = 383)	29*
50+ (sample size = 274)	11
Race/ethnicity	
White, non-Hispanic (sample size = 601)	24
Black, non-Hispanic (sample size = 137)	51*
Hispanic (sample size = 115)	42*
Household income	
Less than $30,000 (sample size = 173)	43*
$30,000–$49,999 (sample size = 138)	36*
$50,000–$74,999 (sample size = 136)	24
$75,000+ (sample size = 341)	21
Education level	
High school graduate or less (sample size = 278)	39*
Some college (sample size = 234)	38*
College+ (sample size = 412)	16
Geographic location	
Urban (sample size = 291)	33
Suburban (sample size = 481)	28
Rural (sample size = 118)	32

*Represents significant difference compared with non-starred rows in group.
**Represents significant difference compared with all other rows in group.

SOURCE: Aaron Smith, "Which Cell Internet Users Go Online *Mostly* Using Their Phones?" in *17% of Cell Phone Owners Do Most of Their Browsing on Their Phone, Rather Than a Computer or Other Device*, Pew Internet & American Life Project, June 26, 2012, http://www.pewinternet.org/~/media//Files/Reports/2012/PIP_Cell_Phone_Internet_Access.pdf (accessed September 25, 2012). Used by permission of the Pew Internet & American Life Project, which bears no responsibility for the interpretations presented or conclusions reached based on analysis of the data.

TABLE 2.7

Reasons adult cell phone owners who use their phones as primary means of accessing the Internet do so, 2012

17% of adult cell phone owners say that they go online mostly using their cell phone instead of some other device; these are the factors they cite as their MAIN reason for doing so.

Cell phone is more convenient	38%
Cell phone is always with me	23
Mostly do basic activities online	7
Don't have a computer at home	6
Cell phone is easier to use than a computer	6
Use phone for work, or to go online while at work	4
Only have Internet access on phone/no Internet at home	4
Speed/phone is faster than computer	2
Someone else is usually using computer	1
Other	6
Don't know/refuse	3
Summary of reasons	
Convenience/availability (is more convenient + is always with me + speed/faster)	64%
Usage (mostly do basic online activities + easier to use + use for/at work + someone else usually on computer)	18
Access (don't have computer + no other Internet access)	10

SOURCE: Aaron Smith, "Main Reasons for Going Online Mostly Using Cell Phone," in *17% of Cell Phone Owners Do Most of Their Browsing on Their Phone, Rather Than a Computer or Other Device*, Pew Internet & American Life Project, June 26, 2012, http://www.pewinternet.org/~/media//Files/Reports/2012/PIP_Cell_Phone_Internet_Access.pdf (accessed September 25, 2012). Used by permission of the Pew Internet & American Life Project, which bears no responsibility for the interpretations presented or conclusions reached based on analysis of the data.

Most parents have mixed feelings regarding the increasing centrality of mobile phones and the Internet to their children's daily lives. Table 2.12 shows various positive and negative attitudes among parents toward teen cell phone use in 2011. A high percentage of parents felt these technologies offer their teens a good way to access information (88%) or maintain contact with family and friends (88%), and roughly two-thirds (67%) believed cell phones and the Internet provide their teens with a positive means of learning to becoming independent. However, more than four-fifths (81%) of parents feared that increased cell phone and Internet access threatened to expose their teens to inappropriate content, while a similar proportion (80%) expressed concern about the negative ways that teens acted toward each other over the Internet or on their cell phone.

HEALTH RISKS. Finally, health concerns associated with cell phone use have also been identified. In the landmark study "Nerve Cell Damage in Mammalian Brain after Exposure to Microwaves from GSM Mobile Phones" (*Environmental Health Perspectives*, vol. 111, no. 7, June 2003), Leif G. Salford et al. found that cell phone radiation causes brain damage in rats. The researchers mounted a cell phone to the side of the rats' cage for two hours per day for 50 days to emulate the amount of exposure that is received by a habitual cell phone user. The rats' brains showed significant blood vessel leakage as well as areas of damaged neurons. Other studies followed but were inconclusive. However, the University of Pittsburgh Cancer Institute warns in "The Case for Precaution in the Use of Cell Phones" (July 22, 2008, http://www.upci.upmc.edu/news/pdf/The-Case-for-Precaution-in-Cell-Phone-Use.pdf) that:

> Electromagnetic fields generated by cell phones should be considered a potential human health risk. Sufficient time has not elapsed in order for us to have conclusive data on the biological effects of cell phones and other cordless phones—a technology that is now universal.

> Studies in humans do not indicate that cell phones are safe, nor do they yet clearly show that they are dangerous. But, growing evidence indicates that we should reduce exposures, while research continues on this important question.

TABLE 2.8

Growth in smart phone ownership by selected characteristics, May 2011 and February 2012

	May 2011	Feb. 2012
All adults (age 18+)	35%	46%
Men	39	49
Women	31	44
Race/ethnicity		
White, non-Hispanic	30	45
Black, non-Hispanic	44	49
Hispanic (English- and Spanish-speaking)	44	49
Age		
18–29	52	66
30–49	45	59
50–64	24	34
65+	11	13
Household income		
Less than $30,000/yr	22	34
$30,000–$49,999	40	46
$50,000–$74,999	38	49
$75,000+	59	68
Education level		
No high school diploma	18	25
High school graduate	27	39
Some college	38	52
College+	48	60
Geographic location		
Urban	38	50
Suburban	38	46
Rural	21	34

Notes: "Smart phone ownership" includes those who say their phone is a smart phone, or who describe their phone as running on the Android, Blackberry, iPhone, Palm or Windows platforms. For 2011 data, sample size = 2,277 adults age 18 and older, including 755 interviews conducted on respondent's cell phone. For 2012 data, sample size = 2,253 adults and survey includes 901 cell phone interviews. Both 2011 and 2012 data include Spanish-language interviews.

SOURCE: Kathryn Zickuhr and Aaron Smith, "Smartphone Ownership Demographics," in *Digital Differences*, Pew Internet & American Life Project, April 13, 2012, http://pewinternet.org/Reports/2012/Digital-differences/Overview/Digital-differences.aspx (accessed September 25, 2012). Used by permission of the Pew Internet & American Life Project, which bears no responsibility for the interpretations presented or conclusions reached based on analysis of the data.

TABLE 2.9

Percentage of smart phone users who primarily use their phones to go online, by selected characteristics, 2011

	% who go online mostly using their cell phone
All smartphone owners (age 18+, n = 688)	25%
Men (sample size = 349)	24
Women (sample size = 339)	26
Race/ethnicity	
White, non-Hispanic (sample size = 417)	17
Black/Hispanic (sample size = 206)	38
Age	
18–29 (sample size = 177)	42
30–49 (sample size = 256)	21
50+ (sample size = 240)	10
Household income	
Less than $30,000/yr (sample size = 131)	40
$30,000–$49,999 (sample size = 118)	29
$50,000+ (sample size = 334)	17
Education level	
High school graduate (sample size = 169)	33
Some college (sample size = 171)	27
College+ (sample size = 308)	13

Notes: Sample size = 2,277 adult Internet users ages 18 and older, including 755 cell phone interviews. Interviews were conducted in English and Spanish.

SOURCE: Kathryn Zickuhr and Aaron Smith, "The Demographics of Smartphone Users Who Go Online Mostly Using Their Cell Phone (May 2011)," in *Digital Differences*, Pew Internet & American Life Project, April 13, 2012, http://pewinternet.org/Reports/2012/Digital-differences/Overview/Digital-differences.aspx (accessed September 25, 2012). Used by permission of the Pew Internet & American Life Project, which bears no responsibility for the interpretations presented or conclusions reached based on analysis of the data.

TABLE 2.10

Selected cell phone distractions experienced by adults, 2010

[In percent]

	All adults	Cell users	Texters
Been in a car when the driver was sending or reading text messages on their cell phone	49	54	65
Been in a car when the driver used a cell phone in a way that put themselves or others in danger	44	47	54
Talked on a cell phone while driving	61	75	84
Sent or read a text message while driving	27	33	47
Physically bumped into another person or object because you were distracted by talking or texting on your phone	14	17	22

SOURCE: Mary Madden and Lee Rainie, "Adults and Cell Phone Distractions," in *Adults and Cell Phone Distractions*, Pew Internet & American Life Project, June 18, 2010, http://www.pewinternet.org/~/media//Files/Reports/2010/PIP_Cell_Distractions.pdf (accessed September 25, 2012). Used by permission of the Pew Internet & American Life Project, which bears no responsibility for the interpretations presented or conclusions reached based on analysis of the data.

The institute emphasizes that children are particularly at risk because their brains are still developing and suggests that children should not use mobile phones except in emergencies. Nevertheless, other studies find no evidence of human health risks related to cell phone use. In "No Evidence Linking Cell Phone Use to Risk of Brain Tumors" (May 2010, http://www.fda.gov/downloads/ForConsumers/ConsumerUpdates/UCM212306.pdf), the U.S. Food and Drug Administration (FDA), citing findings released by the World Health Organization, indicates that no specific health risks related to cell phone use have been identified. However, the FDA also states that scientific research on the subject is still "ongoing."

DEVELOPMENTS IN COMMUNICATIONS TECHNOLOGY

The Census Bureau (2012, http://www.census.gov/compendia/statab/2012/tables/12s1149.pdf) notes that by 2010 there were 302.9 million cell phone subscribers in the United States, and they were connecting with each other and with the Internet at an unprecedented rate. Consumers quickly adopted mobile technologies and began demanding that more and more functions be

TABLE 2.11

State cell phone and texting laws, September 2012

State	Handheld ban	All cell phone ban		Text messaging ban			Crash data
		School bus drivers	Novice drivers	All drivers	School bus drivers	Novice drivers	
Alabama			16, or 17 w/ intermediate license <6 months (primary)	Yes (primary)	Covered under all driver ban		
Alaska				Yes (primary)	Covered under all driver ban		Yes
Arizona		Yes (primary)					
Arkansas[a]	18–20 years old (primary)	Yes (primary)	<18 (secondary)	Yes (primary)	Covered under all driver ban		Yes
California	Yes (primary)	Yes (primary)	<18 (secondary)	Yes (primary)	Covered under all driver ban		Yes
Colorado			<18 (primary)	Yes (primary)	Covered under all driver ban		Yes
Connecticut	Yes (primary)	Yes (primary)	<18 (primary)	Yes (primary)	Covered under all driver ban		
Delaware	Yes (primary)	Yes (primary)	Learner or intermediate license (primary)	Yes (primary)	Covered under all driver ban		Yes
D.C.	Yes (primary)	Yes (primary)	Learners permit (primary)	Yes (primary)	Covered under all driver ban		Yes
Florida							Yes
Georgia		Yes (primary)	<18 (primary)	Yes (primary)	Covered under all driver ban		Yes
Guam	Yes (primary)			Yes (primary)	Covered under all driver ban		
Hawaii[b]	See footnote						
Idaho[c]				Yes (primary)	Covered under all driver ban		See footnote
Illinois[d]	See footnote	Yes (primary)	<19 (primary)	Yes (primary)	Covered under all driver ban		Yes
Indiana			<18 (primary)	Yes (primary)	Covered under all driver ban		Yes
Iowa			Restricted or intermediate license (primary)	Yes (secondary)	Covered under all driver ban		Yes
Kansas			Learner or intermediate license (primary)	Yes (primary)	Covered under all driver ban		Yes
Kentucky		Yes (primary)	<18 (primary)	Yes (primary)	Covered under all driver ban		
Louisiana	Learner or intermediate license (regardless of age)	Yes (primary)	1st year of license (primary for <18)	Yes (primary)	Covered under all driver ban		Yes
Maine			<18 (primary)	Yes (primary)	Covered under all driver ban		Yes
Maryland	Yes (secondary)		<18 w/ learner or provisional license (secondary)	Yes (primary)	Covered under all driver ban		Yes
Massachusetts		Yes (primary)	<18 (primary)	Yes (primary)	Covered under all driver ban		Yes
Michigan[e]			See footnote	Yes (primary)	Covered under all driver ban		Yes
Minnesota	Yes (primary)		<18 w/ learner or provisional license (primary)	Yes (primary)	Covered under all driver ban		Yes
Mississippi		Yes (primary)			Yes (primary)	Learner or provisional license (primary)	
Missouri						≤21 (primary)	
Montana							Yes
Nebraska			<18 w/ learner or intermediate license (secondary)	Yes (secondary)	Covered under all driver ban		Yes
Nevada	Yes (primary)			Yes (primary)	Covered under all driver ban		Yes
New Hampshire[f]				Yes (primary)	Covered under all driver ban		
New Jersey	Yes (primary)	Yes (primary)	Permit or provisional license (primary)	Yes (primary)	Covered under all driver ban		Yes
New Mexico	In state vehicles		Learner or provisional license (primary)			Learner or provisional license (primary)	Yes

TABLE 2.11

State cell phone and texting laws, September 2012 [CONTINUED]

State	Handheld ban	All cell phone ban		Text messaging ban			Crash data
		School bus drivers	Novice drivers	All drivers	School bus drivers	Novice drivers	
New York	Yes (primary)			Yes (primary)	Covered under all driver ban		Yes
North Carolina		Yes (primary)	<18 (primary)	Yes (primary)	Covered under all driver ban		
North Dakota			<18 (primary)	Yes (primary)	Covered under all driver ban		Yes
Ohio			<18 (primary)	Yes (secondary)	Covered under all driver ban		
Oklahoma	Learner or intermediate license (primary)	Yes (primary)			Yes (primary)	Learner or intermediate license (primary)	Yes
Oregon	Yes (primary)		<18 (primary)	Yes (primary)	Covered under all driver ban		Yes
Pennsylvania				Yes (primary)	Covered under all driver ban		Yes
Rhode Island		Yes (primary)	<18 (primary)	Yes (primary)	Covered under all driver ban		Yes
South Carolina[g]							See footnote
South Dakota							Yes
Tennessee		Yes (primary)	Learner or intermediate license (primary)	Yes (primary)	Covered under all driver ban		Yes
Texas[h]		Yes, w/ passenger ≤17 (primary)	Intermediate license, 1st 12 mos. (primary)		Yes, w/ passenger ≤17 (primary)	Intermediate license, 1st 12 mos. (primary)	Yes
Utah[i]	See footnote			Yes (primary)	Covered under all driver ban		Yes
Vermont			<18 (primary)	Yes (primary)	Covered under all driver ban		
Virgin Islands	Yes			Yes	Covered under all driver ban		Yes
Virginia		Yes (primary)	<18 (secondary)	Yes (secondary)	Covered under all driver ban (primary)	Covered under all driver ban	Yes
Washington	Yes (primary)		Learner or intermediate license (primary)	Yes (primary)	Covered under all driver ban		Yes
West Virginia	Yes (secondary until 7/1/13)		<18 w/ learner or intermediate license (primary)	Yes (primary)	Covered under all driver ban		
Wisconsin			Learner or intermediate license (primary) (eff. 11/1/12)	Yes (primary)	Covered under all driver ban		
Wyoming				Yes (primary)	Covered under all driver ban		Yes
Total states	**10 + D.C.** Guam, Virgin Islands Primary (8 + D.C., Guam) Secondary (2)	**19 + D.C.** All primary	**32 + D.C.** Primary (27 + D.C.) Secondary (5)	**39 + D.C.,** Guam, Virgin Islands Primary (35 + D.C., Guam) Secondary (4)	**3** All primary	**5** All primary	**35 + D.C.,** Virgin Islands

[a]Arkansas also bans the use of handheld cell phones while driving in a school zone or in a highway construction zone. This law is secondarily enforced.
[b]Hawaii does not have a state law banning the use of handheld cell phones. However, all of the state's counties have enacted distracted driving ordinances.
[c]Idaho has a "Distraction in/on Vehicle (List)" attribute as part of its Contributing Circumstances element, and officers are supposed to list the distractions in the narrative.
[d]Illinois bans the use of handheld cell phones while driving in a school zone or in a highway construction zone.
[e]In Michigan, teens with probationary licenses whose cell phone usage contributes to a traffic crash or ticket may not use a cell phone while driving.
[f]Dealt with as a distracted driving issue; New Hampshire enacted a comprehensive distracted driving law.
[g]South Carolina has a Distracted/inattention attribute under Contributing Factors.
[h]Texas has banned the use of hand-held phones and texting in school zones.
[i]Utah's law defines careless driving as committing a moving violation (other than speeding) while distracted by use of a handheld cellphone or other activities not related to driving.

SOURCE: "Cell Phone and Texting Laws," in *State Highway Safety Laws & Funding*, Governors Highway Safety Association, September 2012, http://www.ghsa.org/html/stateinfo/laws/cellphone_laws.html (accessed September 25, 2012)

integrated into portable devices. As of 2012, many people were using iPhones and other personal digital assistants and smart phones that combine Internet, computer, and cellular technologies. These devices are wireless and handheld, and they can download e-mail on the web by dialing into a cell phone network and then connecting to the Internet. Such devices also have personal organizer capabilities, including an address book and planner, and they can surf the web.

High-speed fourth-generation (4G) cell phone service, the newest generation of wireless technology, allows for even more integration of Internet technologies into cell phones. Because it is an advanced form of CDMA, 4G allows more people to share a broader bandwidth of frequencies on the current cell phone networks. Cell phone providers installed software known as high-speed downlink packet access into cell phone base stations. This software increased the amount of data that could flow through cell

TABLE 2.12

Parental attitudes concerning the impact of cell phones and the Internet on their children, 2011

POSITIVE IMPACTS: THE % OF PARENTS OF TEEN CELL OR INTERNET USERS WHO RATE THE JOB OF THE INTERNET AND CELL PHONES THIS WAY...

	Excellent	Good	Total saying positive impact	Fair	Poor	Total saying not positive impact
Connecting your child to information	48%	40%	88%	9%	2%	11%
Connecting your child to friends and family	40%	48%	88%	9%	3%	11%
Helping your child be more independent	21%	46%	67%	22%	8%	31%

NEGATIVE IMPACTS: THE % OF PARENTS OF TEEN CELL OR INTERNET USERS WHO SAY THEY ARE CONCERNED ABOUT THESE ISSUES...

	Very concerned	Somewhat concerned	Total citing concerns about negative impact	Not too concerned	Not at all concerned	Total saying they have little concern
Your child's exposure to inappropriate content through the Internet or cell phones	47%	34%	81%	9%	9%	19%
How teens in general treat each other online or on their cell phones	45%	35%	80%	10%	9%	19%
Your child's Internet or cell phone use taking time away from face-to-face interactions with friends or family	31%	33%	63%	20%	16%	36%

Notes: Population = 799 for parents, including oversample of minority families. Interviews were conducted in English and Spanish. Data in this chart based on parents of teen cell phone or Internet users.

SOURCE: Amanda Lenhart et al., "Parents' Feelings about the Impact of the Internet and Cell Phones on their Kids," in *Teens, Kindness and Cruelty on Social Network Sites*, Pew Internet & American Life Project, November 2011, http://pewinternet.org/~/media//Files/Reports/2011/PIP_Teens_Kindness_Cruelty_SNS_Report_Nov_2011_FINAL_110711.pdf (accessed October 8, 2012). Used by permission of the Pew Internet & American Life Project, which bears no responsibility for the interpretations presented or conclusions reached based on analysis of the data.

phone networks and boosted Internet connection speeds to over 1 megabyte per second. With such high-speed access, more people began using their cell phones to download and play video files, watch newscasts, and shop online. By 2012 a number of telecommunications companies had introduced 4G mobile wireless products, many of them offering connection speeds of up to 1 gigabyte per second. Continued development of smaller electronics and display screens will bring even higher quality cameras, video games systems, and web cameras to cell phones.

CHAPTER 3
INFORMATION TECHNOLOGY AND U.S. BUSINESS

The desire of U.S. corporations to make money fueled the proliferation of electronics and communications technologies during the 1980s and 1990s. High-technology (high-tech) companies such as Microsoft, Apple, and Intel strove to create affordable computers, Internet technologies, cell phones, and a variety of electronics-based products for use in the office and at home. A huge market segment, commonly referred to as the information technology (IT) industry, developed around the production of these new technologies and included the manufacture of computers and electronic products, software publishing, data processing services, advanced telecommunications, and computer systems design. Matt Bodimeade reports in "Global Information Technology Market" (September 13, 2012, http://www.companiesandmarkets.com/Market Insight/Information-Technology/Global-Information-Tech nology-Market/NI5265) that the global market for the IT sector was expected to reach $3.6 trillion in 2011, a 5.6% increase over 2010 figures. Indeed, many analysts predicted similar growth for the industry heading into the second decade of the 21st century. Citing a report compiled by the technology market research company Tech-Navio, the article "Global IT Market 2011–2015" (April 2012, http://www.researchandmarkets.com/reports/2121358/global_it_market_20112015) indicates that the global IT market is estimated to grow at a rate of 5.9% annually between 2011 and 2015.

As information technologies spread through U.S. offices and corporations, they also transformed other industries outside of the IT sector. In the financial industries, innovations such as interconnected bank networks and electronic bill pay greatly reduced the number of paper checks in circulation daily. The retail industry discovered a new way to sell merchandise. The U.S. Census Bureau notes in *E-Stats* (May 10, 2012, http://www.census.gov/econ/estats/2010/2010reportfinal.pdf) that by 2010, $169 billion in retail sales were conducted over the Internet annually. Furthermore, e-commerce manufacturing shipments in

2010 amounted to nearly $2.3 trillion. (See Table 3.1.) During the second quarter of 2011, e-commerce retail sales totaled $47.6 billion; during the second quarter of 2012 online retail sales reached $54.8 billion, an increase of 15.3% over the same period the previous year. (See Table 3.2.)

The economic impact of IT reverberated well beyond those industries that sold goods on the Internet, however. Every industry from trucking to real estate to health care to manufacturing incorporated new technologies that helped make doing business more efficient and affordable. Entire medical and law libraries were replaced by online databases that could be searched in minutes. Retail inventories, which used to be counted by hand, were linked directly to barcode scans taken at cash registers, a process that ultimately made ordering stock more efficient and reduced expensive storage costs. Bookkeeping and accounting, which was once an arduous task completed in thick, paper ledgers, was done in a fraction of the time and at a fraction of the cost using computer accounting software.

However, IT did not have a positive effect on all businesses. For example, travel agencies saw an enormous drop in revenue because many people began making their own travel arrangements using online reservations sites. The growth in online bookings led to a 40% drop in the number of travel agency jobs in the United States between 1999 and 2011. In *Occupational Employment and Wage Estimates* (May 2011, http://www.bls.gov/oes/2011/may/oes_nat.htm), the U.S. Department of Labor's Bureau of Labor Statistics (BLS) states that 67,490 travel agents were employed in 2011, compared with 111,130 in 1999. The ease with which the typical consumer could make travel arrangements online was largely responsible for this decline. The Pew Internet & American Life Project (Pew/Internet) reports in *Usage over Time* (2012, http://pewinternet.org/Static-Pages/Tr

TABLE 3.1

Total and e-commerce shipments, sales, and revenues, 2000–10

[Estimates are based on data from the 2010 Annual Survey of Manufactures, 2007 Economic Census—Manufacturing, 2010 Annual Wholesale Trade Survey, 2010 Annual Retail Trade Survey, and 2010 Service Annual Survey. Shipments, sales, and revenues are shown in millions of dollars]

		Value of—			
	Manufacturing	Merchant wholesale trade sales[a]		Retail trade	Selected services
Item	shipments[a]	Excluding MSBOs[b]	Including MSBOs[b]	sales[c]	revenues[d]
2010					
Total	4,916,647	4,132,327	5,773,411	3,841,530	11,066,928
E-commerce	2,283,412	833,019	1,421,790	168,965	255,008
Percent of total	46.4	20.2	24.6	4.4	2.3
2009					
Total	4,419,501	3,699,214	5,157,837	3,627,628	10,776,635
E-commerce	1,891,533	757,752	1,269,069	145,260	239,250
Percent of total	42.8	20.5	24.6	4.0	2.2
2008					
Total	5,468,093	4,431,775	6,148,518	3,946,406	NA
E-commerce	2,170,818	767,817	1,353,164	142,297	NA
Percent of total	39.7	17.3	22.0	3.6	NA
2007					
Total	5,338,307	4,174,286	5,888,989	3,999,256	NA
E-commerce	1,879,424	749,607	1,346,308	138,108	NA
Percent of total	35.2	18.0	22.9	3.5	NA
2006					
Total	5,015,553	3,930,123	5,626,482	3,874,085	NA
E-commerce	1,566,799	688,824	1,280,625	115,075	NA
Percent of total	31.2	17.5	22.8	3.0	NA
2005					
Total	4,742,076	3,613,384	5,255,388	3,690,162	NA
E-commerce	1,343,852	630,153	1,219,257	92,964	NA
Percent of total	28.3	17.4	23.2	2.5	NA
2004					
Total	4,308,971	3,316,409	4,846,078	3,473,568	NA
E-commerce	996,174	515,159	1,063,166	74,212	NA
Percent of total	23.1	15.5	21.9	2.1	NA
2003					
Total	4,015,081	2,971,817	4,371,004	3,262,978	NA
E-commerce	842,666	454,511	960,755	58,255	NA
Percent of total	21.0	15.3	22.0	1.8	NA
2002					
Total	3,920,632	2,835,528	4,162,169	3,128,552	NA
E-commerce	751,985	382,254	873,180	45,249	NA
Percent of total	19.2	13.5	21.0	1.4	NA
2001					
Total	3,970,500	2,785,152	NA	3,062,267	NA
E-commerce	724,228	332,551	NA	34,608	NA
Percent of total	18.2	11.9	NA	1.1	NA
2000					
Total	4,208,582	2,814,554	NA	2,983,275	NA
E-commerce	755,807	280,492	NA	27,761	NA
Percent of total	18.0	10.0	NA	0.9	NA

NA = Not available.

Note: Estimates are not adjusted for price changes and are subject to revision.

MSBO = Manufacturers' Sales Branches and Offices.

[a]Estimates include data only for businesses with paid employees.

[b]Manufacturers' Sales Branches and Offices.

[c]Estimates include data for businesses with or without paid employees.

[d]Includes NAICS 22 (Utilities), NAICS 4849y (Transportation and warehousing), NAICS 51 (Information), NAICS 52 (Finance and insurance), NAICS 53 (Real estate and rental and leasing), NAICS 54 (Selected professional, scientific, and technical services), NAICS 56 (Administrative and support and waste management and remediation services), NAICS 61 (Educational services), NAICS 62 (Health care and social assistance), NAICS 71 (Arts, entertainment, and recreation services), NAICS 72 (Accommodation and food services), and NAICS 81 (Selected other services). Estimates include data for businesses with paid employees except for Accomodation and Food Services, which also includes businesses without paid employees.

SOURCE: "Table 7. Summary of U.S. Shipments, Sales, Revenues, and E-commerce: 2000–2010," in *E-Stats: 2010 E-Commerce Multi-sector Data Tables*, U.S. Department of Commerce, U.S. Census Bureau, May 10, 2012, http://www.census.gov/econ/estats/2010/table7.xls (accessed September 25, 2012)

TABLE 3.2

Estimated quarterly U.S. retail sales, total and E-commerce, 2011–12

[Estimates are based on data from the Monthly Retail Trade Survey and administrative records.]

Quarter	Retail sales (millions of dollars)		E-commerce as a percent of total	Percent change from prior quarter		Percent change from same quarter a year ago	
	Total	E-commerce		Total	E-commerce	Total	E-commerce
Adjusted							
2nd quarter 2012ᵖ	1,076,934	54,842	5.1	−0.4	3.3	4.3	15.3
1st quarter 2012ʳ	1,081,347	53,091	4.9	1.5	2.9	6.4	15.3
4th quarter 2011	1,065,030	51,575	4.8	2.0	6.2	7.5	15.1
3rd quarter 2011	1,044,075	48,564	4.7	1.1	2.1	8.9	12.8
2nd quarter 2011ʳ	1,032,271	47,575	4.6	1.5	3.3	8.4	15.7
Not adjusted							
2nd quarter 2012ᵖ	1,092,727	51,181	4.7	6.1	1.8	4.3	15.1
1st quarter 2012ʳ	1,029,472	50,295	4.9	−7.5	−18.6	7.9	15.4
4th quarter 2011	1,112,422	61,765	5.6	6.9	37.6	7.2	15.8
3rd quarter 2011	1,040,438	44,876	4.3	−0.7	0.9	8.7	12.3
2nd quarter 2011	1,047,396	44,473	4.2	9.8	2.1	8.4	15.5

ᵖPreliminary estimate.
ʳRevised estimate.
Notes: E-commerce sales are sales of goods and services where an order is placed by the buyer or price and terms of sale are negotiated over an Internet, extranet, Electronic Data Interchange (EDI) network, electronic mail, or other online system. Payment may or may not be made online.
Estimates are adjusted for seasonal variation, but not for price changes. Total sales estimates are also adjusted for trading-day differences and moving holidays.

SOURCE: "Table 1. Estimated Quarterly U.S. Retail Sales: Total and E-commerce," in *Quarterly Retail E-commerce Sales: 2nd Quarter 2010*, U.S. Department of Commerce, U.S. Census Bureau, August 16, 2012, http://www.census.gov/retail/mrts/www/data/pdf/ec_current.pdf (accessed September 25, 2012)

---

end-Data-%28Adults%29/Usage-Over-Time.aspx) that 36% of adults made travel reservations online in 2000. By 2011 this number had risen to 65%.

IT INDUSTRY

Even though IT has been around since International Business Machines (IBM) began mass-producing computers in the early 1950s, it did not become a large part of the U.S. economy until the 1990s. A number of high-tech companies, such as Microsoft and Dell, had positioned themselves as the commercial leaders in Internet, personal computer, and cell phone technologies during the 1980s. When use of the World Wide Web became common in 1994 and the price of electronics began to drop, Americans flocked to these technologies. Revenues in the high-tech industry as a whole increased at a rate not seen in any industry since the postwar boom of the 1950s. Microsoft reported sales of $140 million in 1985. Ten years later its revenues had increased to $6 billion. Cisco Systems, the leading commercial maker of Internet routers and switches, grew at an even faster rate. Between 1990 and 2001 the company's revenues grew from $69 million to $22 billion. Dell, the top seller of home computers in the U.S. market in 2009, saw sales increase from $300 million in 1989 to $61.5 billion in fiscal year (FY) 2011.

The growth of these companies along with the rest of the IT-producing industries had a tremendous impact on the economy. Table 3.3 shows a list of the types of businesses that make up the IT-producing industries. According to the U.S. Department of Commerce, in *Digital Economy 2003* (December 2003, http://www.esa.doc.gov/sites/default/files/reports/documents/dig_econ_2003.pdf), the IT industries made up roughly 8% to 9% of the U.S. domestic economy between 1996 and 2000.

TABLE 3.3

Information technology-producing industries

Hardware industries

Computers and equipment
Wholesale trade of computers and equipment*
Retail trade of computers and equipment*
Calculating and office machines
Magnetic and optical recording media
Electron tubes
Printed circuit boards
Semiconductors
Passive electronic components
Industrial instruments for measurement
Instruments for measuring electricity
Laboratory analytical instruments

Communications equipment industries

Household audio and video equipment
Telephone and telegraph equipment
Radio and TV communications equipment

Software/services industries

Computer programming
Prepackaged software
Wholesale trade of software*
Retail trade of software*
Computer-integrated system design
Computer processing, data preparation
Information retrieval services
Computer services management
Computer rental and leasing
Computer maintenance and repair
Computer related services, nec

Communications services industries

Telephone and telegraph communications
Cable and other TV services

*Wholesale and retail from computer manufacturer sales from branch offices.

SOURCE: David Henry and Donald Dalton, "Box 1.1. Information Technology Producing Industries," in "Information Technology Producing Industries—Hopeful Signs in 2003," *Digital Economy 2003*, U.S. Department of Commerce, Economics and Statistics Administration, December 2003, http://usinfo.org/enus/economy/technology/docs/DE-Chap1.pdf (accessed October 1, 2012)

However, these industries were responsible for 1.4 percentage points of the nation's 4.6% annual average real gross domestic product (GDP) growth over these years. The GDP is one of the basic yardsticks used to measure the U.S. economy and is defined as the value, or sale price, of all goods that are produced in a country minus the cost of the materials that went into making those goods. In other words, the entire IT industry, which made up a little under one-tenth of the economy, accounted for over one-third of the economic growth. Between 1993 and 2000 employment in the IT industries expanded rapidly as well. IT companies hired people at twice the rate of all private industries and added more than 1.8 million jobs to the workforce in sectors such as software and computer services, computer hardware, and communication services.

End of the IT Boom

Toward the turn of the 21st century many Americans thought the IT boom would continue indefinitely. They invested enormous sums of money in IT and IT-related stocks. From late 1998 to early 2000 the value of Microsoft stocks and Dell stocks doubled; Cisco Systems' stock value quadrupled. The National Association of Securities Dealers Automated Quotation System (NASDAQ), a stock index that tracks the value of many IT stocks, rose from 2,442 on August 10, 1999, to a peak value of 5,132 on Friday, March 10, 2000—one of the largest increases of a major stock index in history. Many Americans invested not only in large, well-established corporations but also in small e-commerce companies such as Pets.com and eToys. Many of these dot-coms were brand-new businesses that had yet to produce any profits. People invested in them in the hope that these dot-coms would enjoy the sort of huge rise in value that made early investors in Dell or Microsoft millionaires.

On Monday, March 13, 2000, the NASDAQ dropped roughly 300 points, from a high of 5,013 to a closing low of 4,706. The index dropped for a couple more days, rebounded to a point close to its all-time high, and then proceeded to fall intermittently for the next two-and-a-half years, finally hitting bottom on October 10, 2002, at 1,108. Other stock indexes, such as the Dow Jones Industrial Average and Standard and Poor's 500, followed this downward trend, ultimately returning to 1998 levels. The stock bubble burst because investors began to fear that many IT and IT-related companies were not living up to expectations and pulled their money out of the market.

The entire nation slipped into a recession. By 2001 numerous dot-coms were out of business, and many established IT companies were beginning to post losses. From 2001 to 2002 Cisco Systems' sales dropped more than $3.4 billion, and Dell's annual earnings dipped by roughly $700 million. The Department of Commerce

explains in *Digital Economy 2003* that the main reason for the slowdown in the IT industries was that the private business sector stopped buying equipment. Throughout the 1990s just about every type of business—from law firms to paper producers to grocery stores to auto shops—was either buying or updating its computers, printers, and networks. Businesses that did not make such investments quickly became outdated and inefficient and did not survive. By the turn of the 21st century many companies outside of the IT industries had already made an initial investment in IT equipment and required only upgrades as hardware needed replacement or as software was updated. In addition, the components that make up the infrastructure for the Internet (fiber-optic cables, routers, and switches) had largely been laid down by the late 1990s, so the need for these components greatly diminished as well.

The industries that produced hardware components and communications equipment were the hardest hit. The overall GDP for these industries dropped 22% in 2000 and 18% in 2001. The Department of Commerce reports that among the most negatively affected industries, semiconductor manufacturing fell from $67.9 billion in 2000 to $44.1 billion in 2001, a 35% decrease. The industries that did reasonably well during this recessionary period were the software and services industries and the communications services industries. Prepackaged software, computer processing, information retrieval services, computer services management, computer maintenance and repair, and other computer-related services all showed modest gains. Even though U.S. businesses as a whole had bought much of their hardware, many still had the need for new software, Internet service, and computer maintenance.

Lost Jobs

To cut their losses in this down market, IT companies began laying off many of the workers they had hired during the 1990s. In *Digital Economy 2003*, the Department of Commerce reveals that roughly 600,000 jobs were shed in the IT industries between 2000 and 2002. This job loss accounted for more than a quarter of all the jobs that were lost during the recession. The rate of job loss in the IT industries was six times that of all private industry. Not surprisingly, the industry that lost the most jobs was computer hardware, from a high of nearly 1.7 million in 2000 to 1.4 million in 2002.

Even though many of the jobs that were lost simply ceased to exist, two additional trends combined to decrease the number of traditional employment positions. The term *outsourcing* refers to work that is contracted to nonemployees such as temporary workers; *offshoring* refers to situations in which the positions are assumed by workers located in another country where wages are cheaper. With the advent of e-mail, the Internet, and low-cost international phone calls, offices separated by continents could be linked through cyberspace. Geography was no longer a predominant concern for many companies. In India, for example, there were large numbers of highly educated people who spoke English, were knowledgeable about computer science, and were more than happy to work for a fraction of the typical U.S. hourly wage. Companies such as Dell moved high-paying technical assistance jobs, low- to midlevel computer programming jobs, and even technical documentation jobs to other countries.

Mark Gongloff reports in "U.S. Jobs Jumping Ship" (CNN.com, January 19, 2004) that over 40% of U.S. companies had either contracted IT services or had run a pilot offshore outsourcing program by mid-2003. Deducing the number of jobs that have moved overseas since 2000, however, is all but impossible. The BLS, the government agency in charge of recording who loses their job and why, only began counting the number of jobs that moved overseas in 2004. In the press release "Extended Mass Layoffs—Second Quarter 2012" (August 9, 2012, http://www.bls.gov/news.release/archives/mslo_08092012.pdf), the BLS notes that during the second quarter of 2012, 7,506 workers lost their jobs due to movement of work, either through reorganization within the company or relocation of the work to another location in the United States or abroad. Roughly 18%

(1,315 workers) of those who lost their jobs through movement of work were affected by out-of-country relocations. These figures dropped considerably during the third quarter of 2012, however, with only 10 out of 3,941 jobs moving overseas. (See Table 3.4.)

IT Becomes a Mature Industry

According to the Department of Commerce, in *Digital Economy 2003*, by 2003 the IT industries showed signs of recovery. The GDP in the IT-producing industries grew 4.8% to $871.9 billion in 2003 as business spending on IT equipment began to accelerate. In the first nine months of 2003 IT spending by the private sector as a whole rose an estimated 2.3% on average. Consumer and household spending on IT equipment, which did not abate as sharply during the recession, grew faster through 2002 and into 2003. In addition, the IT industries did not cut back on research and development during the recession. Consequently, many new products were being developed by the end of the recession. Nevertheless, employment numbers in the IT industries had not recovered significantly by 2003. The Department of Commerce considered these developments taken together to indicate that the IT industries had settled into maturity and predicted that future growth would likely be more modest and less volatile than it was during the 1980s and 1990s.

By 2010 the information, communications, and technology-producing industries reached a gross output

TABLE 3.4

Movement of work actions by type of separation, selected quarters, 2011–12

	Actions*			Separations		
Activities	III 2011	II 2012ʳ	III 2012ᵖ	III 2011	II 2012ʳ	III 2012ᵖ
With separations reported	31	30	21	3,443	3,750	1,585
By location						
Out-of-country relocations	3	3	1	185	1,315	10
Within company	—	3	1	—	1,315	10
Different company	3	—	—	185	—	—
Domestic relocations	28	26	20	3,258	2,360	1,575
Within company	24	26	19	2,520	2,360	1,420
Different company	4	—	1	738	—	155
Unable to assign place of relocation	—	1	—	—	75	—
By company						
Within company	24	29	20	2,520	3,675	1,430
Domestic	24	26	19	2,520	2,360	1,420
Out of country	—	3	1	—	1,315	10
Unable to assign	—	—	—	—	—	—
Different company	7	1	1	923	75	155
Domestic	4	—	1	738	—	155
Out of country	3	—	—	185	—	—
Unable to assign	—	1	—	—	75	—

*Only actions for which separations associated with the movement of work were reported are shown.
ᵖPreliminary.
ʳRevised.
Note: Dash represents zero.

SOURCE: "Table 10. Movement of Work Actions by Type of Separation Where Number of Separations Is Known by Employers, Selected Quarters, 2011 and 2012," in *Extended Mass Layoffs—Third Quarter 2012*, U.S. Department of Labor, Bureau of Labor Statistics, November 8, 2012, http://www.bls.gov/news.release/pdf/mslo.pdf (accessed November 15, 2012)

of $1.2 trillion. (See Table 3.5; gross output equals the value of the industry's total sales and other operating income.) This figure represented growth of 3.4% over the $1.1 trillion in gross output experienced in 2009, and was roughly comparable to the $1.1 trillion the industries generated in 2008, before the global financial crisis caused major declines across all economic sectors. Indeed, in spite of the general economic uncertainty of these years, many high-tech companies such as Google and Apple saw their revenues exceed expectations during this period. Apple reported sales of $108.3 billion in 2011, an increase of 152% compared with the $42.9 billion in revenues the company generated in 2009. Google, which posted sales of $23.7 billion in FY 2009, saw revenues rise to $37.9 billion in 2011, an increase of

60%. Microsoft, which posted revenues of $58.4 billion in 2009, saw sales grow to $69.9 billion for FY 2011, an increase of 20%.

Trends in IT employment during this span also showed signs of the industry's economic rebound. In Table 3.6, the BLS charts a steep rise in IT layoffs between 2007 and 2009. (An extended mass layoff, as defined by the BLS, is one that affects at least 50 individuals from a single employer for a period of at least 31 days; the number of events and of workers affected in mass layoff statistics do not reflect totals for the industry, but are indicative of overall trends.) As Table 3.6 shows, extended mass layoffs in the IT sector swelled from 5,363 in 2007 to 8,259 in 2008, an increase of 54%. The

TABLE 3.5

Gross output by industry, 2008–10

[Billions of dollars]

	2008	2009	2010
All industries	**26,561.9**	**24,568.6**	**25,811.4**
Private industries	23,477.2	21,425.4	22,553.8
Agriculture, forestry, fishing, and hunting	381.6	343.7	371.1
Mining	578.6	353.2	423.8
Utilities	458.2	361.5	366.7
Construction	1,259.6	1,089.5	988.9
Manufacturing	5,328.9	4,365.4	4,832.5
Wholesale trade	1,224	1,027.6	1,231.9
Retail trade	1,271.4	1,198.7	1,335.5
Transportation and warehousing	836.5	712.7	775.9
Information	1,197.6	1,165.8	1,205.7
Publishing industries (includes software)	327.4	310.3	317.8
Motion picture and sound recording industries	102.5	98.1	102.1
Broadcasting and telecommunications	636.7	625.7	644.8
Information and data processing services	130.9	131.7	141
Finance, insurance, real estate, rental, and leasing	4,870.4	4,836.4	4,860.5
Finance and insurance	2,237.7	2,246	2,332.6
Real estate and rental and leasing	2,632.7	2,590.4	2,527.9
Professional and business services	2,649	2,526.9	2,592.6
Professional, scientific, and technical services	1,562.5	1,489.8	1,535.1
Computer systems design and related services	255.9	250.3	271
Management of companies and enterprises	399.8	377.8	406.2
Administrative and waste management services	686.7	659.2	651.4
Educational services, health care, and social assistance	1,853.3	1,936.1	2,015.9
Educational services	224.4	233.2	249.5
Health care and social assistance	1,628.8	1,702.8	1,766.3
Arts, entertainment, recreation, accommodation, and food services	999.1	964.1	996.5
Arts, entertainment, and recreation	229.3	220	225.9
Accommodation and food services	769.8	744.1	770.6
Other services, except government	569	543.9	556.3
Government	3,084.7	3,143.2	3,257.6
Federal	1,040.3	1,091.4	1,157.4
State and local	2,044.5	2,051.7	2,100.3
Addenda:			
Private goods-producing industries[a]	7,548.7	6,151.8	6,616.3
Private services-producing industries[b]	15,928.5	15,273.7	15,937.4
Information-communications-technology-producing industries[c]	1,106.5	1,033.7	1,106.9

[a]Consists of agriculture, forestry, fishing, and hunting; mining; construction; and manufacturing.
[b]Consists of utilities; wholesale trade; retail trade; transportation and warehousing; information; finance, insurance, real estate, rental, and leasing; professional and business services; educational services, health care, and social assistance; arts, entertainment, recreation, accommodation, and food services; and other services, except government.
[c]Consists of computer and electronic products; publishing industries (includes software); information and data processing services; and computer systems design and related services.

SOURCE: Adapted from "Gross Output by Industry," in *Industry Economic Accounts*, U.S. Department of Commerce, Bureau of Economic Analysis, December 31, 2011, http://www.bea.gov/iTable/iTable.cfm?ReqID=5&step=1 (accessed October 1, 2012)

TABLE 3.6

Extended mass layoffs in information technology-producing industries, 1996–2012

Year/quarter	Total extended mass layoffs		Computer hardware[a]		Software and computer services[b]		Communications equipment[c]		Communications services[d]	
	Layoff events	Separations	Layoff events	Separations	Layoff events	Separations	Layoff events	Separations	Layoff events	Separations
1996	4,760	948,122	121	20,598	14	6,982	36	5,857	33	6,612
1997	4,671	947,843	75	13,637	14	1,625	36	3,891	19	3,357
1998	4,859	991,245	178	40,350	16	3,160	38	7,444	28	4,512
1999	4,556	901,451	116	28,745	19	3,581	31	5,310	18	3,930
2000	4,591	915,962	76	19,991	40	6,514	36	7,250	27	4,375
2001	7,375	1,524,832	522	105,343	176	23,235	151	37,423	144	30,869
2002	6,337	1,272,331	318	63,284	127	17,687	121	24,537	180	32,445
2003	6,181	1,216,886	221	36,917	69	9,806	69	11,266	115	22,014
2004	5,010	993,909	94	13,974	44	6,184	21	3,011	82	17,446
2005	4,881	884,661	90	13,971	28	4,952	19	3,612	48	7,779
2006	4,885	935,969	66	16,662	19	1,965	28	5,334	37	5,275
2007	5,363	965,935	91	15,956	18	2,277	22	3,494	25	2,930
2008	8,259	1,516,978	156	31,448	57	7,720	21	3,456	65	10,836
2009	11,824	2,108,202	345	76,908	94	15,791	50	8,126	98	17,672
2010										
First quarter	1,870	314,512	35	6,248	15	1,570	5	1,089	25	6,023
Second quarter	2,008	381,622	24	3,714	14	1,614	9	912	13	1,924
Third quarter	1,370	222,357	24	2,851	7	2,217	6	498	12	1,825
Fourth quarter	1,999	338,643	7	1,019	9	1,345	3	451	15	3,255
Total	7,247	1,257,134	90	13,832	45	6,746	23	2,950	65	13,027
2011										
First quarter	1,490	225,456	14	2,027	14	1,930	4	558	14	2,124
Second quarter	1,810	317,546	11	1,691	18	2,432	7	930	10	7,322
Third quarter	1,393	235,325	12	2,247	12	1,764	3	238	10	3,015
Fourth quarter[r]	1,903	334,383	21	3,857	14	1,635	4	694	6	1,381
Total[r]	6,596	1,112,710	58	9,822	58	7,761	18	2,420	40	13,842
2012										
First quarter[r]	1,290	245,901	13	1,978	18	3,331	4	467	8	1,387
Second quarter[p]	1,476	262,848	16	2,956	17	2,269	e	e	8	1,533

Note: Information technology-producing industries are defined by the MLS program using the 2012 version of the North American Industrial Classification System (NAICS). MLS definitions closely follow definitions originally published in Digital Economy 2003 (U.S. Department of Commerce, Economics and Statistics Administration, 2003), which were based on NAICS 2002 industries.

[a]The industries included in this grouping, based on the 2012 NAICS, are: semiconductor machinery manufacturing; other commercial and service machinery mfg.; electronic computer manufacturing; computer storage device manufacturing; other computer peripheral equipment mfg.; bare printed circuit board manufacturing; semiconductors and related device mfg, capacitor, resistor, and inductor mfg.; electronic connector manufacturing; printed circuit assembly manufacturing; other electronic component manufacturing; industrial process variable instruments; electricity and signal testing instruments; analytical laboratory instrument mfg.; computer and software merchant wholesalers; and electronics stores.

[b]The industries included in this grouping, based on the 2012 NAICS, are: software publishers; data processing, hosting and related services; Internet publishing and web search portals; office equipment rental and leasing; custom computer programming services; computer systems design services; computer facilities management services; other computer related services; and computer and office machine repair.

[c]The industries included in this grouping, based on the 2012 NAICS, are: telephone apparatus manufacturing; broadcast and wireless communications equip.; audio and video equipment manufacturing; blank magnetic and optical media mfg.; software and prerecorded media reproducing; and fiber optic cable manufacturing.

[d]The industries included in this grouping, based on the 2012 NAICS, are: wired telecommunications carriers; wireless telecommunications carriers; satellite telecommunications carriers; telecommunications resellers; all other telecommunications; and communication equipment repair.

[e]Data do not meet BLS or state agency disclosure standards.

[p]Preliminary.

[r]Revised.

SOURCE: "Information Technology–Producing Industries: Extended Mass Layoff Events and Separations, Private Nonfarm Sector, 1996–2012," in *Mass Layoff Statistics*, U.S. Department of Labor, Bureau of Labor Statistics, 2012. http://www.bls.gov/mls/mlsprod.htm (accessed October 1, 2012)

industry's employment prospects declined even more sharply in 2009, when 11,824 extended mass layoffs were reported, an increase of 3,565 compared with the previous year. This trend was particularly notable in the computer hardware business, where extended mass layoff events rose from 91 in 2007 to 345 in 2009, an increase of 279%. By decade's end, however, this downward trend began to reverse. After falling to 7,247 in 2010, extended mass layoffs for the IT sector dropped to 6,596 in 2011. Figures for the first half of 2012 revealed even stronger signs of recovery. Extended mass IT layoffs for the first and second quarters of 2012 fell to 2,766, which was a considerable drop from the 3,300 extended mass layoffs the industry recorded for the first two quarters of 2011.

EFFECT OF IT ON U.S. BUSINESSES

The rise of the IT industries, though dramatic, did not affect the U.S. economy nearly as much as the products that these industries produced. Nearly every task in a modern office, regardless of the business, employs some piece of technology that either was not present before the proliferation of IT or was only present in a limited way. These technologies have had a profound effect on both the productivity of businesses and individual employees.

Figure 3.1 charts shifts in productivity in the private, nonfarm business sector between 1947 and 2011. Between 1979 and 1990 the productivity of workers in the United States increased at a rate of 1.4% per year. Between 1990 and 2000, the period in which the Internet became widespread, the productivity of workers rose

FIGURE 3.1

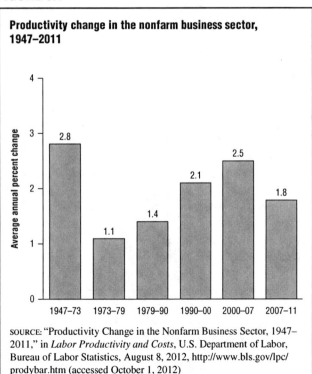

Productivity change in the nonfarm business sector, 1947–2011

SOURCE: "Productivity Change in the Nonfarm Business Sector, 1947–2011," in *Labor Productivity and Costs*, U.S. Department of Labor, Bureau of Labor Statistics, August 8, 2012, http://www.bls.gov/lpc/prodybar.htm (accessed October 1, 2012)

significantly, to 2.1% growth per year. This upward trend continued for the next seven years, as annual productivity rates grew an average of 2.5% between 2000 and 2007, before dropping to 1.8% between 2007 and 2011.

In *Digital Economy 2003*, the Department of Commerce investigates some of the causes behind the sudden rise in worker productivity during the 1990s. To determine if this sudden acceleration in worker productivity was indeed because of the introduction of IT into the workforce, the Department of Commerce separates all private industry into those that were IT intensive, such as finance and retail, and those that were less IT intensive, such as construction. The department reveals that IT-intensive industries, which already had a relatively high worker productivity growth per year, increased in productivity much faster than less IT-intensive industries in 1995. During the recessionary period in 2000 and 2001, the IT-intensive industries' worker productivity did not wane. Conversely, yearly growth in worker productivity in non-IT-intensive industries did not occur before 1995; it then rose 1% per year until 2000 before turning negative. Such results suggest that the introduction of IT into the workplace not only improved worker productivity for the long term but also increased the rate at which it improves.

How IT Has Increased Productivity

The ways in which IT increased productivity and made businesses more profitable are nearly endless. Word processors and desktop publishing software dramatically reduced the time necessary to complete many mundane office tasks, particularly in the communications industry. The reduction of paper filing systems in the workplace reduced corporate storage needs and made document retrieval more efficient. Computer systems in factories allowed manufacturers precise control over production lines, increasing efficiency and thus saving millions of dollars. Interoffice and Internet networks gave corporations daily access to sales numbers and profit margins, enabling them to make faster decisions to increase profitability. For example, if a line of clothing was not selling, a company could see the figures immediately and pull the line from the stores, rather than allow it to take up valuable retail space.

E-COMMERCE

E-commerce, which is simply the sale of goods and services over the Internet, has grown steadily every year since the debut of the World Wide Web in 1991. Even though much attention has been given to online retail, most e-commerce actually occurs in business-to-business transactions. For example, the Census Bureau reports in *E-Stats* that business-to-business transactions accounted for 90% of all e-commerce activity in 2010. The Census Bureau provides a breakdown of e-commerce as a percentage of the value of sales in each industry that did business online in 2010. By far, most e-commerce that year occurred in manufacturing, where shipments ordered online accounted for 46.4% ($2.3 trillion) of the total value of all manufacturing shipments. (See Figure 3.2.) Merchant wholesalers came in second, with e-commerce representing 24.6% ($1.4 trillion) of business, and retail trade finished third, with 4.4% ($169 billion) of all sales originating from e-commerce. Selected services revenues were sales made by a number of sectors in the services industry and include businesses such as travel brokers and online publications. Some 2.3% ($255 billion) of the total revenues generated by the selected services industry came from e-commerce.

Manufacturers are companies that take raw materials and parts and manufacture products that are used by other businesses or individuals. For instance, a soft drink company typically buys its cans from a manufacturer that makes the cans from raw aluminum. Dell buys computer components from dozens of manufacturers around the world to assemble its computers. The reason so many manufacturers use the Internet to conduct business transactions is that the Internet cuts costs and streamlines the processes that are involved in buying and selling

manufactured goods. E-commerce allows the buyer to compare competitors' prices, reduces the costs of writing up and sending paper purchase orders and invoices, maintains an electronic copy of each sale, and decreases the time it takes for the goods to reach the buyer. The value of manufactured goods shipped through e-commerce rose 20.7% between 2009 and 2010, nearly twice the growth rate of 11.2% for total manufacturing shipments. (See Table 3.7.) By far, primary metal manufacturing enjoyed the largest boost in e-commerce sales, rising from $68.2 billion in 2009 to $105.7 billion in 2010, an increase of 55.1%. Only the printing and related support activities, apparel manufacturing, and furniture and related product manufacturing sectors saw a decline in e-commerce shipments during this span, falling 0.5%, 1.9%, and 2.5%, respectively, between 2009 and 2010.

Merchant wholesale trade sales made up the second-largest block of e-commerce transactions in 2010. Wholesalers act as a mediator between manufacturers and retailers. Wholesalers typically buy large quantities of goods from a number of manufacturers and then resell these goods in bulk to retail outlets. The wholesalers save the retailers the trouble of contacting each manufacturer themselves. Table 3.8 presents U.S. merchant wholesale trades in 2009 and 2010. Year-over-year wholesale e-commerce increased 12% between 2009 and 2010, which was slightly higher than the 11.9% growth generated by wholesale trades overall. Wholesale e-commerce growth outstripped overall merchant wholesale trades in several key businesses. For example, between 2009 and 2010 e-commerce sales of metals and minerals increased 49.8%, more than double the 22.7% growth rate in overall sales for that sector.

E-Commerce and Retail

Retail sales consist of any product that is sold to an individual customer or company for use. Since the late 1990s nearly every major retailer from AutoZone to Neiman Marcus to Wal-Mart has created a website. Many offer a greater variety of merchandise online than what is available in the store. The growth of such websites has allowed Americans to order just about anything and have it delivered to their front door within days.

The amount of money made from e-commerce in retail increased rapidly from the late 1990s. The Census Bureau explains in *E-Stats Archives* (2012, http://www.census.gov/econ/estats/archives.html) that e-commerce accounted for only 0.2% ($5 billion) of all retail sales in 1998. This percentage more than doubled to 0.5% ($15.6 billion) in 1999 and nearly doubled again to 0.9% ($28.8 billion) in 2000. In 2002 e-commerce represented 1.4% ($44.3 billion) of retail sales. E-commerce revenues nearly quadrupled by 2010, when online transactions accounted for 4.4% ($169 billion) of all retail sales. As Table 3.9 shows, more than half (50.6%, or

FIGURE 3.2

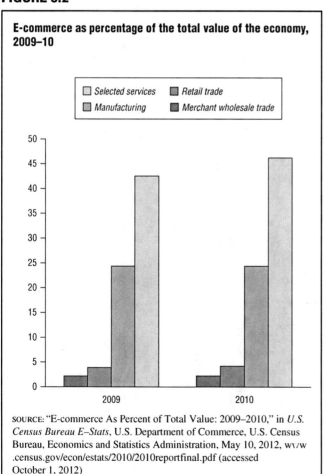

E-commerce as percentage of the total value of the economy, 2009–10

Legend:
- Selected services
- Retail trade
- Manufacturing
- Merchant wholesale trade

SOURCE: "E-commerce As Percent of Total Value: 2009–2010," in *U.S. Census Bureau E–Stats*, U.S. Department of Commerce, U.S. Census Bureau, Economics and Statistics Administration, May 10, 2012, www.census.gov/econ/estats/2010/2010reportfinal.pdf (accessed October 1, 2012)

TABLE 3.7

Total and e-commerce value of manufacturing shipments, 2009–10

[Data are based on the 2010 Annual Survey of Manufactures and 2009 Annual Survey of Manufactures. Value of Shipments are shown in millions of dollars, consequently subsector estimates may not be additive.]

NAICS code	Description	Value of shipments				Y/Y percent change		E-commerce as percent of total shipments		Percent distribution of e-commerce shipments	
		2010		2009							
		Total	E-commerce	Revised total	Revised E-commerce	Total shipments	E-commerce shipments	2010	2009	2010	2009
	Total manufacturing	**4,916,647**	**2,283,412**	**4,419,501**	**1,891,533**	**11.2**	**20.7**	**46.4**	**42.8**	**100.0**	**100.0**
311	Food manufacturing	646,451	292,298	627,185	262,608	3.1	11.3	45.2	41.9	12.8	13.9
312	Beverage and tobacco product manufacturing	131,845	82,128	127,943	77,180	3.0	6.4	62.3	60.3	3.6	4.1
313	Textile mills	29,109	14,876	26,324	12,589	10.6	18.2	51.1	47.8	0.7	0.7
314	Textile product mills	21,818	10,679	21,366	10,019	2.1	6.6	48.9	46.9	0.5	0.5
315	Apparel manufacturing	13,643	5,458	13,909	5,179	−1.9	5.4	40.0	37.2	0.2	0.3
316	Leather and allied product manufacturing	5,049	1,166	4,327	1,102	16.7	5.8	23.1	25.5	0.1	0.1
321	Wood product manufacturing	69,957	19,894	65,000	16,538	7.6	20.3	28.4	25.4	0.9	0.9
322	Paper manufacturing	169,954	79,089	161,636	69,312	5.1	14.1	46.5	42.9	3.5	3.7
323	Printing and related support activities	82,488	29,002	82,919	26,274	−0.5	10.4	35.2	31.7	1.3	1.4
324	Petroleum and coal products manufacturing	627,572	288,470	495,777	219,546	26.6	31.4	46.0	44.3	12.6	11.6
325	Chemical manufacturing	701,230	310,223	624,367	263,587	12.3	17.7	44.2	42.2	13.6	13.9
326	Plastics and rubber products manufacturing	188,583	82,783	171,115	69,935	10.2	18.4	43.9	40.9	3.6	3.7
327	Nonmetallic mineral product manufacturing	90,781	27,711	89,662	24,250	1.2	14.3	30.5	27.0	1.2	1.3
331	Primary metal manufacturing	231,185	105,728	168,927	68,168	36.9	55.1	45.7	40.4	4.6	3.6
332	Fabricated metal product manufacturing	295,187	106,121	280,939	89,201	5.1	19.0	36.0	31.8	4.6	4.7
333	Machinery manufacturing	317,694	147,917	288,006	118,721	10.3	24.6	46.6	41.2	6.5	6.3
334	Computer and electronic product manufacturing	340,683	152,047	320,724	134,103	6.2	13.4	44.6	41.8	6.7	7.1
335	Electrical equipment, appliance, and components	110,993	48,590	105,417	42,354	5.3	14.7	43.8	40.2	2.1	2.2
336	Transportation equipment manufacturing	633,275	409,441	539,921	318,687	17.3	28.5	64.7	59.0	17.9	16.8
337	Furniture and related product manufacturing	58,795	23,203	60,287	20,685	−2.5	12.2	39.5	34.3	1.0	1.1
339	Miscellaneous manufacturing	150,353	46,588	143,749	41,495	4.6	12.3	31.0	28.9	2.0	2.2

Note: Estimates are not adjusted for price changes. Estimates include data only for businesses with paid employees and are subject to revision.

SOURCE: "Table 1. U.S. Manufacturing Shipments—Total and E-commerce Value: 2010 and 2009," in *E-Stats: 2010 E-Commerce Multi-Sector Data Tables*, U.S. Department of Commerce, U.S. Census Bureau, Economics and Statistics Administration, May 10, 2012, http://www.census.gov/econ/estats/2010/table1.xls (accessed October 1, 2012)

TABLE 3.8

Total and e-commerce wholesale trade sales, 2009–10

[Estimates are based on data from the 2010 Annual Wholesale Trade Survey. Sales estimates are shown in millions of dollars, consequently industry group estimates may not be additive.]

NAICS code	Description	Value of sales 2010 Total	Value of sales 2010 E-commerce	Value of sales 2009 Revised total	Value of sales 2009 Revised e-commerce	Y/Y percent change Total sales	Y/Y percent change E-commerce sales	E-commerce as percent of total sales 2010	E-commerce as percent of total sales 2009	Percent distribution of e-commerce sales 2010
42	**Total merchant wholesale trade including MSBOs***	**5,773,411**	**1,421,790**	**5,157,837**	**1,269,069**	**11.9**	**12.0**	**24.6**	**24.6**	**100.0**
423	**Durable goods**	**2,618,197**	**599,286**	**2,306,739**	**499,647**	**13.5**	**19.9**	**22.9**	**21.7**	**42.2**
4231	Motor vehicles and automotive equipment	562,275	282,627	458,834	223,335	22.5	26.5	50.3	48.7	19.9
4232	Furniture and home furnishings	72,022	10,315	70,382	9,796	2.3	5.3	14.3	13.9	0.7
4233	Lumber and other construction material	125,533	10,127	125,224	9,295	0.2	9.0	8.1	7.4	0.7
4234	Professional and commercial equipment and supplies	508,202	139,402	473,326	127,314	7.4	9.5	27.4	26.9	9.8
42343	Computer equipment and supplies	282,450	87,442	254,062	78,367	11.2	11.6	31.0	30.8	6.2
4235	Metals and minerals, excluding petroleum	175,721	21,215	143,205	14,160	22.7	49.8	12.1	9.9	1.5
4236	Electrical goods	447,767	(S)	398,242	55,937	12.4	(S)	(S)	14.0	(S)
4237	Hardware, plumbing and heating equipment	109,862	13,920	105,313	13,058	4.3	6.6	12.7	12.4	1.0
4238	Machinery, equipment and supplies	397,720	31,042	357,634	23,784	11.2	30.5	7.8	6.7	2.2
4239	Miscellaneous durable goods	219,095	23,543	174,579	22,968	25.5	2.5	10.7	13.2	1.7
424	**Nondurable goods**	**3,155,214**	**822,504**	**2,851,098**	**769,422**	**10.7**	**6.9**	**26.1**	**27.0**	**57.8**
4241	Paper and paper products	132,190	28,101	127,297	25,896	3.8	8.5	21.3	20.3	2.0
4242	Drugs, drug proprietaries and druggists' sundries	600,939	399,202	583,863	390,941	2.9	2.1	66.4	67.0	28.1
4243	Apparel, piece goods, and notions	138,767	41,318	129,442	35,421	7.2	16.6	29.8	27.4	2.9
4244	Groceries and related products	705,372	169,165	680,157	158,501	3.7	6.7	24.0	23.3	11.9
4245	Farm-products raw materials	182,756	27,551	164,604	23,512	11.0	17.2	15.1	14.3	1.9
4246	Chemicals and allied products	186,274	(D)	158,071	(D)	17.8	(D)	(D)	(D)	(D)
4247	Petroleum and petroleum products	806,242	12,494	617,116	9,325	30.6	34.0	1.5	1.5	0.9
4248	Beer, wine, and distilled beverages	121,411	(D)	119,745	(D)	1.4	(D)	(D)	(D)	(D)
4249	Miscellaneous nondurable goods	281,263	27,938	270,803	25,714	3.9	8.6	9.9	9.5	2.0

(S) Estimate does not meet publication standards because of high sampling variability (coefficient of variation is greater than 30%) or poor response quality (total quantity response rate is less than 50%).
(D) Denotes an estimate withheld to avoid disclosing data of individual companies; data are included in higher level totals.
Note: Estimates are not adjusted for price changes.
Estimates include data only for businesses with paid employees and are subject to revision.
*Manufacturers' Sales Branches and Offices.

source: "Table 2.0. U.S. Merchant Wholesale Trade Sales, Including Manufacturers' Sales Branches and Offices—Total and E-commerce Sales: 2010 and 2009," in *E-Stats: 2010 E-Commerce Multi-Sector Data Tables*, U.S. Department of Commerce, U.S. Census Bureau, Economics and Statistics Administration, May 10, 2012, http://www.census.gov/econ/estats/2010/table2.0.xls (accessed October 1, 2012)

TABLE 3.9

Total and e-commerce retail sales, 2009–10

[Estimates are based on data from the 2010 Annual Retail Trade Survey. Sales estimates are shown in millions of dollars, consequently industry group estimates may not be additive.]

NAICS code	Description	Value of sales				Y/Y percent change		E-commerce as percent of total sales		Percent distribution of e-commerce sales
		2010		2009						
		Total sales	E-commerce	Revised total sales	Revised e-commerce	Total sales	E-commerce sales	2010	2009	2010
	Total retail trade	**3,841,530**	**168,965**	**3,627,628**	**145,260**	**5.9**	**16.3**	**4.4**	**4.0**	**100.0**
441	Motor vehicles and parts dealers	746,924	20,561	673,531	17,107	10.9	20.2	2.8	2.5	12.2
442	Furniture and home furnishings stores	87,216	(S)	86,111	(S)	1.3	(S)	(S)	(S)	(S)
443	Electronics and appliance stores	99,152	1,049	97,963	894	1.2	17.3	1.1	0.9	0.6
444	Building materials and garden equipment and supplies stores	267,900	555	266,871	477	0.4	16.4	0.2	0.2	0.3
445	Food and beverage stores	581,972	862	568,841	837	2.3	3.0	0.1	0.1	0.5
446	Health and personal care stores	261,190	229	253,150	185	3.2	23.8	0.1	0.1	0.1
447	Gasoline stations	446,150	(ZZ)	389,690	(ZZ)	14.5	(Z)	(Z)	(Z)	(Z)
448	Clothing and clothing accessories stores	213,735	3,469	204,626	2,939	4.5	18.0	1.6	1.4	2.1
451	Sporting goods, hobby, book, and music stores	81,620	2,192	80,890	1,911	0.9	14.7	2.7	2.4	1.3
452	General merchandise stores	607,968	281	591,613	219	2.8	28.3	(Z)	(Z)	0.2
453	Miscellaneous store retailers	106,514	2,504	102,926	2,197	3.5	14.0	2.4	2.1	1.5
454	Nonstore retailers	341,189	135,572	311,416	117,097	9.6	15.8	39.7	37.6	80.2
4541	Electronic shopping and mail-order houses	260,557	131,786	233,530	113,332	11.6	16.3	50.6	48.5	78.0

(S) Estimate does not meet publication standards because of high sampling variability (coefficient of variation is greater than 30%) or poor response quality (total quantity response rate is less than 50%).
(Z) Estimate is less than 0.05%.
(ZZ) Estimate is less than $500,000.
Notes:
Estimates are not adjusted for price changes.
Estimates for 2009 and all previous years were revised to reflect improvements in the coverage of nonemployer businesses (i.e., businesses with no paid employees) that were implemented with the release of the 2009 Nonemployer Statistics.
Estimates include data for businesses with or without paid employees and are subject to revision.

SOURCE: "Table 5. U.S. Retail Trade Sales—Total and E-commerce: 2010 and 2009," in *E-Stats: 2010 E-Commerce Multi-Sector Data Tables*, U.S. Department of Commerce, U.S. Census Bureau, Economics and Statistics Administration, May 10, 2012, http://www.census.gov/econ/estats/2010/table5.xls (accessed October 1, 2012)

$131.8 billion) of all sales revenues for electronic shopping and mail-order houses came from e-commerce transactions in 2010. By comparison, e-commerce accounted for just 0.2% of sales of building materials and garden equipment and supplies stores, which generated only $555 million in revenues from online transactions.

Table 3.10 focuses solely on the electronic shopping and mail-order house segment of retail. Many of the businesses in this category, such as Dell, sell their products primarily online and through catalogs. Others are divisions of larger department stores, such as Nordstrom, and were created to sell the stores' products online. Online sales accounted for 50.6% of overall sales for electronic shopping and mail-order businesses in 2010, up 16.3% from 2009. Regarding individual types of products, 87.9% of the revenues from the sale of music and videos came from online sales in 2010. This represented the highest percentage of online sales for any type of product in this retail segment, followed by books and magazines (82.7%) and electronics and appliances (82.1%). In terms of sheer sales volume, more clothing and accessories ($23.2 billion) were sold online than any other type of product. Indeed, e-commerce had become an important aspect of the Internet for most people. According to Pew/Internet, in *Usage over Time*, 71% of people with an Internet connection in May 2011 had bought something online.

Online Auctions: A New Segment of the Economy

When e-commerce developed during the mid-1990s, many small business owners created modest commercial websites, hoping to sell their wares. However, Internet fraud and the propagation of questionable websites made people reluctant to give personal information to unknown vendors on the web. Smaller vendors and buyers needed a common marketplace with rules and regulations to trade goods.

In 1998 Pierre Omidyar (c. 1967–), Jeff Skoll (1965–), and Meg Whitman (1957–) went public with eBay. The company, which was at first an auction site for collectibles such as Beanie Babies, quickly attracted the attention of small business owners. For a modest insertion fee, people could list their products on eBay's website. Buyers then bid on the objects, and when a sale was final, the seller paid eBay a commission of 1.3% to 5% of the item's sale price. The website included payment options that did not require the purchaser to provide credit card information, and it even offered protections against fraud.

The eBay website and its imitators created a whole new economic outlet for small business owners and people who simply wanted to pawn off their used goods. No longer was someone who wanted to sell embroidered pillows relegated to local flea markets. Individual vendors from crafters to high-end car salespeople could reach out to a nationwide audience. Even people with used stuff suddenly had more options than simply giving it to charity or holding a garage sale. eBay (2012, http://www.ebayinc.com/who) notes that in 2011 it had over 100 million active users who bought and sold $68.6 billion worth of merchandise.

Virtual Goods

One of the more unusual industries to develop, due in part to eBay, was the sale of virtual goods, including money and characters from massively multiplayer online role-playing games. Games such as *World of Warcraft* and *EverQuest* place players in virtual worlds with thousands of other people where they can buy virtual property, kill monsters, and collect gold and other valuable virtual artifacts. Some of these online games even provide the player with the option to marry and build houses in a virtual world. Progressing far in these games and obtaining a high level, however, requires hundreds of hours of playtime. As a result, an entire cottage industry developed around the sale of virtual gold and characters on auction sites such as eBay. Typically, a player would buy the game, build up a character and gold, and then sell his or her password to the game to a buyer on eBay, sometimes fetching hundreds of dollars. Such sales represented the first industry that was centered on completely virtual goods. Soon, other sites began trading in virtual currencies, as the online community bought and sold everything from virtual gaming weapons to virtual flowers. Dean Takahashi reports in "Study: Gamers Are Gaga for Virtual Goods" (February 29, 2012, http://venturebeat.com/2012/02/29/study-gamers-are-gaga-for-virtual-goods/) that the U.S. market for virtual goods reached $2.3 billion in 2011. In "Next Wave of Asian Exports to U.S. May Be Virtual Goods" (*New York Times*, October 4, 2012), Malathi Nayak estimates that the U.S. market would grow to $3 billion in 2012 and climb to $6 billion by 2014.

E-Commerce in the Services Industries

The services industries in the United States are enormous and encompass everything from brokerage houses to real estate companies to travel agents to health care. Generally, any business that sells its services or some type of expertise belongs in this category. Of all the industries presented in Figure 3.2, e-commerce revenue made up the smallest percentage of total revenue for the services industries in 2010. In those areas of the services industry where e-commerce has broken through, however, it has created much change.

TRAVEL INDUSTRY. Probably no other type of business in the services sector was affected more by the Internet than travel reservations services. Before the Internet, travelers either combed through travel books and called airlines, hotels, restaurants, and other venues

TABLE 3.10

Total and e-commerce sales of electronic shopping and mail-order houses by merchandise line, 2009–10

[Estimates are based on data from the 2010 Annual Retail Trade Survey. Sales estimates are shown in millions of dollars, consequently merchandise line estimates may not be additive.]

| | Value of sales | | | | Y/Y percent change | | E-commerce as percent of total sales | Percent distribution | |
| | 2010 | | 2009 | | | | | Total sales | E-commerce sales |
Merchandise lines	Total sales	E-commerce sales	Revised total sales	Revised e-commerce	Total sales	E-commerce sales	2010	2010	2010
Total electronic shopping and mail-order houses (NAICS 4541)	**260,557**	**131,786**	**233,530**	**113,332**	**11.6**	**16.3**	**50.6**	**100.0**	**100.0**
Books and magazines	7,536	6,231	6,595	5,186	14.3	20.2	82.7	2.9	4.7
Clothing and clothing accessories (includes footwear)	29,510	23,157	25,931	19,550	13.8	18.5	78.5	11.3	17.6
Computer hardware	24,187	11,421	21,519	10,734	12.4	6.4	47.2	9.3	8.7
Computer software	6,078	3,315	5,621	3,172	8.1	4.5	54.5	2.3	2.5
Drugs, health aids, and beauty aids	78,341	7,220	71,512	6,254	9.5	15.4	9.2	30.1	5.5
Electronics and appliances	21,259	17,462	18,463	14,840	15.1	17.7	82.1	8.2	13.3
Food, beer, and wine	3,819	2,391	3,698	2,242	3.3	6.6	62.6	1.5	1.8
Furniture and home furnishings	15,182	11,882	13,262	9,797	14.5	21.3	78.3	5.8	9.0
Music and videos	6,872	6,042	5,944	5,076	15.6	19.0	87.9	2.6	4.6
Office equipment and supplies	7,190	5,343	7,217	5,449	−0.4	−1.9	74.3	2.8	4.1
Sporting goods	7,785	5,741	7,087	4,897	9.8	17.2	73.7	3.0	4.4
Toys, hobby goods, and games	6,656	4,395	5,866	3,596	13.5	22.2	66.0	2.6	3.3
Other merchandise[a]	32,094	17,048	28,586	14,028	12.3	21.5	53.1	12.3	12.9
Nonmerchandise receipts[b]	14,048	10,138	12,229	8,511	14.9	19.1	72.2	5.4	7.7

Notes:

Estimates are not adjusted for price changes.

Estimates for 2009 and all previous years were revised to reflect improvements in the coverage of nonemployer businesses (i.e., businesses with no paid employees) that were implemented with the release of the 2009 Nonemployer Statistics. For additional information on these improvements and their effect on the nonemployer totals, see the Nonemployer Statistics home page at http://www.census.gov/econ/nonemployer/index.html

Estimates include data for businesses with or without paid employees, are grouped according to merchandise categories used in the Annual Retail Trade Survey, and are subject to revision.

[a]Includes other merchandise such as collectibles, souvenirs, auto parts and accessories, hardware, lawn and garden equipment and supplies, and jewelry.

[b]Includes nonmerchandise receipts such as auction commissions, customer training, customer support, advertising, and shipping and handling.

SOURCE: "Table 6. U.S. Electronic Shopping and Mail-Order Houses (NAICS 4541)—Total and E-commerce Sales by Merchandise Line: 2010 and 2009," in *E-Stats: 2010 E-Commerce Multi-Sector Data Tables*, U.S. Department of Commerce, U.S. Census Bureau, Economics and Statistics Administration, May 10, 2012. http://www.census.gov/econ/estats/2010/table6.xls (accessed October 1, 2012)

one by one, or hired a travel agent to do it for them. When the Internet became widely available, businesses such as Expedia set up websites where anyone could search for rates and make travel reservations with most airlines and hotels. Existing businesses, such as the airlines, developed websites of their own. These Internet innovations made it much easier for travelers to comparison shop and make travel plans on their own. E-commerce made up $8.3 billion (22.5%) of the total revenue ($37 billion) of travel arrangement and reservation services in 2010. (See Table 3.11.) In "U.S. Travel to International Destinations Declined Three Percent in 2011" (July 16, 2012, http:// tinet.ita.doc.gov/outreachpages/download_data_table/ 2011_Outbound_Analysis.pdf), the International Trade Administration of the Department of Commerce notes that 40% of Americans traveling overseas used the Internet to book their trips in 2011, compared with 29% who used travel agents.

As a consequence, many traditional travel agencies have faced tough times since the late 1990s. The BLS indicates in the press release "Occupational Employment and Wages, 2000" (November 14, 2001, http://www.bls .gov/news.release/History/ocwage_11142001.txt) that there were 124,030 travel agents working in the United States in 2000. In the press release "Occupational Employment and Wages—May 2011" (March 27, 2012, http://www.bls.gov/ news.release/pdf/ocwage.pdf), the BLS reveals that by 2011 the number of travel agents had plunged to 67,490. To avoid losing their jobs, many travel agents began offering specialized services that cater to consumers seeking unique travel experiences centered on hobbies, activities, or unusual destinations.

FINANCIAL SERVICES. Another services industry that experienced a great deal of change because of IT was the financial brokerage business. Beginning in the early 1980s many of those who worked in the industry employed powerful computers and networking capabilities to track financial markets in real time and make financial transactions electronically. When the Internet became mainstream, large financial services organizations, such as Fidelity Investments and Charles Schwab, offered brokerage accounts to customers, allowing them to trade stocks online. Customers also had access to many of the research services that were only available to stockbrokers before the introduction of the World Wide Web.

Dave Pettit and Rich Jaroslovsky indicate in *Wall Street Journal Online's Guide to Online Investing: How to Make the Most of the Internet in a Bull or Bear Market* (2002) that in 1996, 1.5 million brokerage accounts existed online; by 2001 this number had increased to 20 million. In *Usage over Time*, Pew/Internet reveals that 11% of Internet users said they bought and sold stocks, bonds, or mutual funds over the Internet in 2009. Even after the collapse of the global financial markets in 2008,

competition among the top online brokerage firms remained fierce. Matt Krantz describes in "As Economy Heals, Online Brokerages Go after Investors" (*USA Today*, January 19, 2010) how several of the large online brokerage firms began slashing their commissions and fees as a way of attracting new investors. According to Krantz, much of the competition for clients was actually between Internet brokerages and traditional full-service firms, as consumers were turning to online investing as a way of reducing their costs. This trend toward discounted online trading eventually caught the attention of the larger investment houses. In July 2010 Merrill Lynch entered the virtual brokerage business with the creation of Merrill Edge, a new online investment account service. J. Alex Tarquinio reports in "Best and Worst Brokers of 2012" (SmartMoney.com, May 16, 2012) that by 2012 many brokerage firms had introduced a wide range of technological tools to attract investors, including cell phone applications (apps) and social media features. For example, TD Ameritrade's Snapstock enabled potential investors to learn a company's ticker symbol by scanning a product's barcode with their phone.

REAL ESTATE SERVICES. The real estate brokerage sector was another services industry that underwent many changes because of the Internet. Before the Internet became widely available, people could only find real estate listings in the newspaper or at a real estate agency. Many websites, such as Realtor.com, began listing thousands of houses for sale in every region of the country. These sites make it possible for people in Virginia, for example, to get a feel for real estate properties and prices in Alaska, Wyoming, or even their own neighborhood. The National Association of Realtors reports in "Traffic Notes" (http://www.realtor .org/sites/default/files/reports/2012/nar-website-traffic- stats-2012-10.pdf) that Internet traffic on its site reached 10.9 million unique visitors in October 2012.

The Internet has also become a valuable tool for real estate brokers and agents. According to J. Barlow Herget, in "Internet Now an Indispensable Tool for Veteran Realtors Who Were once Skeptical" (NewsObserver.com, July 14, 2012), e-mail and mobile phones enable realtors to maintain contact with a wider range of prospective homeowners, including those who live out of state or even overseas. Meanwhile, the Internet empowers consumers to identify desirable properties on their own, allowing real estate agents to streamline the home viewing process. Herget quotes Phyllis Brookshire of Allen Tate Realtors in Charlotte, North Carolina, as saying, "The Internet is an agent's best partner if they learn how to use it. You absolutely have to have it."

M-Commerce

As more Americans own handheld devices, retailers are beginning to explore ways to reach consumers

TABLE 3.11

Total and e-commerce revenue, selected services, 2009–10

[Except where indicated, estimates are based on data from the 2010 Service Annual Survey. Revenue estimates are shown in millions of dollars, consequently industry group estimates may not be additive. Select estimates have been adjusted using results of the 2007 Economic Census.]

NAICS code	Description	Value of revenue				Y/Y percent change		E-commerce as percent of total revenue		Percent distribution of e-commerce revenue
		2010		2009						
		Total	E-commerce	Revised total	Revised e-commerce	Total revenue	E-commerce revenue	2010	2009	2010
	Total for selected services industries[a]	**11,066,928**	**255,008**	**10,776,635**	**239,250**	**2.7**	**6.6**	**2.3**	**2.2**	**100.0**
22	**Utilities**[b]	**501,658**	**1,089**	**477,637**	**923**	**5.0**	**18.0**	**0.2**	**0.2**	**0.4**
2211	Electric power generation, transmission, and distribution	380,686	985	360,824	832	5.5	18.4	0.3	0.2	0.4
4849y	**Transportation and warehousing**[c]	**640,168**	**51,610**	**595,200**	**52,028**	**7.6**	**-0.8**	**8.1**	**8.7**	**20.2**
4849x	Selected transportation and warehousing[d]	290,483	7,021	272,847	6,774	6.5	3.6	2.4	2.5	2.8
481	Air transportation	135,140	35,421	124,090	34,847	8.9	1.6	26.2	28.1	13.9
483	Water transportation	32,161	2,802	29,999	5,197	7.2	-46.1	8.7	17.3	1.1
484	Truck transportation	194,616	6,772	180,460	6,579	7.8	2.9	3.5	3.6	2.7
485	Transit and ground passenger transportation	25,441	(S)	26,211	219	-2.9	(S)	(S)	0.8	(S)
486	Pipeline transportation	31,043	278	28,649	284	8.4	-2.1	0.9	1.0	0.1
487	Scenic and sightseeing transportation	2,205	214	2,076	188	6.2	13.8	9.7	9.1	0.1
488	Support activities for transportation	123,695	5,124	111,328	4,519	11.1	13.4	4.1	4.1	2.0
492	Couriers and messengers	71,622	(S)	69,849	(S)	2.5	(S)	(S)	(S)	(S)
493	Warehousing and storage	24,245	(S)	22,538	(S)	7.6	(S)	(S)	(S)	(S)
51	**Information**	**1,110,225**	**55,335**	**1,074,959**	**53,872**	**3.3**	**2.7**	**5.0**	**5.0**	**21.7**
511	Publishing industries (except Internet)	265,718	22,174	264,194	20,908	0.6	6.1	8.3	7.9	8.7
517	Telecommunications	507,533	(S)	495,062	6,169	2.5	(S)	(S)	1.2	(S)
51811	Internet service providers and web search portals	30,426	6,486	29,105	7,061	4.5	-8.1	21.3	24.3	2.5
52	**Finance and insurance**[e]	**3,345,367**	**50,824**	**3,372,587**	**46,048**	**-0.8**	**10.4**	**1.5**	**1.4**	**19.9**
5223	Activities related to credit intermediation	77,351	7,207	70,006	5,645	10.5	27.7	9.3	8.1	2.8
523x	Selected finance[f]	474,570	12,892	472,659	12,583	0.4	2.5	2.7	2.7	5.1
5231	Securities and commodity contracts intermediation and brokerage	284,557	11,687	295,424	11,987	-3.7	-2.5	4.1	4.1	4.6
53	**Real estate and rental and leasing**	**356,013**	**12,559**	**349,597**	**12,256**	**1.8**	**2.5**	**3.5**	**3.5**	**4.9**
532	Rental and leasing services	111,250	9,503	110,223	9,576	0.9	-0.8	8.5	8.7	3.7
54	**Selected professional, scientific, and technical services**[g]	**1,304,872**	**25,406**	**1,258,045**	**23,532**	**3.7**	**8.0**	**1.9**	**1.9**	**10.0**
5415	Computer systems design and related services	283,790	5,682	260,466	5,147	9.0	10.4	2.0	2.0	2.2
56	**Administrative and support and waste management and remediation services**	**636,388**	**19,176**	**595,620**	**17,395**	**6.8**	**10.2**	**3.0**	**2.9**	**7.5**
5615	Travel arrangement and reservation services	36,997	8,307	33,863	7,656	9.3	8.5	22.5	22.6	3.3
61	**Educational services**[h]	**49,491**	**3,775**	**45,152**	**3,397**	**9.6**	**11.1**	**7.6**	**7.5**	**1.5**
62	**Health care and social assistance**	**1,917,183**	**3,229**	**1,842,674**	**1,350**	**4.0**	**139.2**	**0.2**	**0.1**	**1.3**
71	**Arts, entertainment, and recreation**	**191,982**	**4,618**	**188,158**	**4,158**	**2.0**	**11.1**	**2.4**	**2.2**	**1.8**
72	**Accommodation and food services**[i]	**629,268**	**18,620**	**613,086**	**16,655**	**2.6**	**11.8**	**3.0**	**2.7**	**7.3**
81	**Selected other services**[j]	**384,313**	**8,767**	**363,920**	**7,636**	**5.6**	**14.8**	**2.3**	**2.1**	**3.4**
811	Repair and maintenance	131,468	974	128,212	920	2.5	5.9	0.7	0.7	0.4
813	Religious, grantmaking, civic, professional, and similar organizations	170,069	5,448	154,317	4,826	10.2	12.9	3.2	3.1	2.1

TABLE 3.11

Total and e-commerce revenue, selected services, 2009–10 [CONTINUED]

[Except where indicated, estimates are based on data from the 2010 Service Annual Survey. Revenue estimates are shown in millions of dollars, consequently industry group estimates may not be additive. Select estimates have been adjusted using results of the 2007 Economic Census.]

(S) Estimate does not meet publication standards because of high sampling variability (coefficient of variation is greater than 30%) or poor response quality (total quantity response rate is less than 50%).

(Z) Estimate is less than 0.05%

Note: Estimates are not adjusted for price changes.

Estimates are subject to revision and include data only for businesses with paid employees except for Accommodation and Food Services, which also includes businesses without paid employees.

[a]Includes NAICS 22 (Utilities), NAICS 4849y (Transportation and warehousing), NAICS 51 (Information), NAICS 52 (Finance and insurance), NAICS 53 (Real estate and rental and leasing), NAICS 54 (Selected professional, scientific, and technical services), NAICS 56 (Administrative and support and waste management and remediation services), NAICS 61 (Educational services), NAICS 62 (Health care and social assistance), NAICS 71 (Arts, entertainment, and recreation), NAICS 72 (Accommodation and food services), and NAICS 81 (Selected other services).

[b]Excludes government owned utilities.

[c]Excludes NAICS 482 (Rail transportation) and NAICS 491 (Postal service).

[d]Excludes NAICS 481 (Air transportation), NAICS 482 (Rail transportation), NAICS 483 (Water transportation), NAICS 485 (Transit and ground passenger transportation), NAICS 486 (Pipeline transportation), NAICS 487 (Scenic and sightseeing transportation), NAICS 488 (Support activities for transportation), and NAICS 491 (Postal service).

[e]Excludes NAICS 525 (Funds, trusts, and other financial vehicles).

[f]Excludes NAICS 5232 (Securities and commodity exchanges), NAICS 52391 (Miscellaneous intermediation), and NAICS 52399 (All other financial investment activities).

[g]Excludes NAICS 54112 (Offices of notaries).

[h]Excludes NAICS 6111 (Elementary and secondary schools), NAICS 6112 (Junior colleges), and NAICS 6113 (Colleges, universities, and professional schools).

[i]Estimates are based on data from the 2010 Annual Retail Trade Survey.

[j]Excludes NAICS 81311 (Religious organizations), NAICS 81393 (Labor unions and similar labor organizations), NAICS 81394 (Political organizations), and NAICS 814 (Private households).

SOURCE: "Table 4. U.S. Selected Services Revenue—Total and E-commerce: 2010 and 2009," in *E-Stats: 2010 E-Commerce Multi-Sector Data Tables*, U.S. Department of Commerce, U.S. Census Bureau, Economics and Statistics Administration, May 10, 2012, http://www.census.gov/econ/estats/2010/table4.xls (accessed October 1, 2012)

through mobile wireless technology. This emerging trend, known as mobile commerce (m-commerce), has become a vital mode of communication between sellers and consumers in the 21st century. The technology firm Cognizant reveals in "Retail Mobility: Navigating the 21st Century Gold Rush" (2012, http://www.cognizant .com/insights/perspectives/retail-mobility-navigating-the-21st-century-gold-rush) that in 2011, 83% of the nation's top retailers had launched at least one app for mobile phones. Of these, 67% had implemented a platform for mobile web service (access to the Internet via a handheld mobile device), 66% had developed apps for iPhones, and 49% had installed platforms for Android phones. These apps enabled customers to perform a range of tasks using their phone, including locating retail outlets, finding information about sales, and contacting customer support. Cognizant finds that even as mobile retail capability became more prevalent in 2011, only a minority of retailers managed to optimize their apps to take full advantage of available technology. For example, only 36% of mobile retailers had developed platforms for all three mobile devices, thereby expanding their potential customer base. Cognizant also notes that few retailers had integrated their mobile services with social media platforms. In 2011 only 31% of mobile web retail apps and 29% of iPhone apps enabled customers to share product information over Facebook.

Meanwhile, mobile shopping continues to attract increasingly large numbers of American shoppers. According to the mobile marketing firm SnapHop, in "Mobile Marketing Statistics 2012" (2012, https://snaphop.com/2012-mobile-marketing-statistics/), 52% of American cell phone owners used their mobile device to find product information while shopping in 2011. An even larger proportion (79%) of smart phone owners used their phone to help make shopping decisions; of these, 74% ultimately made a purchase.

IT AND CURRENCY

IT has not only changed how people pay for merchandise but also how people make and receive payments in general. Credit cards, debit cards, electronic bank transfers, and online banking have eliminated much of the need to carry cash and personal checks. In "The Future of Banking in America: The Effect on U.S. Banking of Payment System Changes" (*FDIC Banking Review*, vol. 16, no. 2, 2004), Neil B. Murphy of Virginia Commonwealth University reports that 88% of households in the United States used some form of electronic payment in 2001. The National Automatic Clearing House Association (NACHA) notes in "ACH Payment Volume Exceeds 20.2 Billion in 2011" (April 12, 2012, https://www.nacha.org/node/1130) that the Automated Clearing House processed more than 20.2 billion electronic payment transactions in 2011, with an overall value of $33.9 trillion.

The advantages of a cashless system are undeniable. With credit and debit cards people always have buying power at their disposal, they can make purchases instantly, and they can access and transfer money online. Banks and businesses are no longer required to spend money moving paper bills and checks all over the country. Furthermore, store owners do not have to worry about the security risks that are inherent with keeping large amounts of cash on hand. At the same time, electronic financial transactions have a positive impact on the environment. According to PayItGreen, in "Frequently Asked Questions" (2012, http://payitgreen.org/consumer/FAQ.aspx), the average household could save up to 6 pounds (3 kg) of paper and 23 pounds (10 kg) of wood and reduce carbon emissions by 29 pounds (13 kg) annually by conducting all their financial activities online.

Credit and Debit Cards

In the 21st century credit and debit cards have become the predominant mode of payment for the majority of American consumers. By enabling individuals to make an array of purchases with a single piece of plastic, credit and debit cards bring unprecedented convenience to a range of financial transactions, from shopping at retail outlets to paying bills over the phone. Furthermore, credit and debit card accounts allow individuals to track their spending over the Internet, providing them with a range of new tools designed to help them manage their spending more easily and efficiently.

However, the ubiquity of credit and debit cards has also created unique risks for 21st-century consumers. For one, credit and debit cards provide potential thieves with relatively easy access to an individual's sensitive personal and financial information, leading to dramatic increases in the number of unauthorized purchases and identity theft. (See Chapter 4.) Also, credit card companies and banks charge transaction fees for credit and debit card purchases, which imposes additional expenses on merchants and retailers. David Lazarus reports in "Hidden from View, Credit Card 'Swipe Fees' May Still Raise Prices" (*Los Angeles Times*, July 17, 2012) that these additional costs are sometimes passed down to consumers, usually in the form of higher prices. "A lot of merchants will consider it a cost of doing business and will raise all their prices," the consumer advocate Linda Sherry told Lazarus. "Consumers won't know if this is for the processing fees or not." Furthermore, the ease of using credit and debit cards makes it challenging for some consumers to manage their money effectively. Ben Woolsey and Matt Schulz report in "Credit Card Statistics, Industry Facts, Debt Statistics" (2012, http://www.creditcards.com/credit-card-news/credit-card-industry-facts-personal-debt-statistics-1276.php) that revolving debt (debt that changes from month to month, based on consumer purchases and payments) in the United States topped $793.1 billion in 2011; 98% of this amount was credit card debt. That same year, 50.2 million American households owed money on their credit cards, with an average debt of $15,799.

CREDIT CARDS. The most firmly established of these electronic payment methods is the credit card. Diners Club issued the first general-purpose credit card in 1950. This credit card allowed restaurant patrons in Manhattan to charge a meal at any restaurant that participated in the program. Even though credit card use has increased almost every year since then, credit card transactions took place entirely on paper at first, which kept some people away. During the 1980s a computerized, networked credit card system was put into place using modems and other networking technologies. The result was that credit card use skyrocketed. Murphy estimates that in 2004 there were more than 1.2 billion credit cards in the United States. A little under half (551.9 million) of these cards were issued directly by retailers under a private label (e.g., Banana Republic or JC Penney). The rest were issued by banks or as travel and entertainment cards. Murphy reports that between 1997 and 2001 the number of credit card transactions grew from 12.9 billion to 17 billion. In *The 2010 Federal Reserve Payments Study: Noncash Payment Trends in the United States: 2006–2009* (April 5, 2011, https://www.frbservices.org/files/communications/pdf/research/2010_payments_study.pdf), the Federal Reserve System determines that 21.6 billion general-purpose credit card transactions, with a total value of $1.9 trillion, were processed in the United States in 2009. Of these transactions, 43.7% were for payments of $25 or less.

According to the Census Bureau (2012, http://www.census.gov/compendia/statab/2012/tables/12s1188.pdf), approximately 1.2 billion credit cards were active in the United States in 2009, and that number was projected to decrease by roughly 78 million in 2012. As to annual spending, $1.9 trillion was charged to credit cards in 2009 and was projected to increase to $2.4 trillion in 2012. Meanwhile, overall consumer credit card debt was expected to dip slightly during this period, from $886 billion in 2009 to $870 billion in 2012.

DEBIT CARDS. Since their introduction to the U.S. market during the 1980s, debit cards have also become a popular method of payment for many Americans. Debit cards remove existing money from a money market or bank account when used, unlike credit cards, which are effectively making loans to their users. A debit card user does not owe money after the transaction, but must have sufficient funds in his or her account to cover the transaction.

Debit cards grew out of the automated teller machine (ATM) system that became widespread during the early 1980s. The first U.S. ATM was a Chemical Bank cash dispenser that went into operation in Long Island, New York, in 1969. The American Bankers Association reports in *2012 ABA Media Guide: Addressing the Nation's Banking Issues* (2012, http://www.aba.com/aba/documents/MediaGuide/ABAMediaGuide2012.pdf) that in 2009 there were approximately 401,500 ATMs in the United States. According to Woolsey and Schulz, there were 521 million debit cards in circulation by the end of 2011. Of these, 392 million were issued by Visa, and the remaining 129 million were issued by MasterCard.

Some ATM networks, which were originally constructed to allow bank cards access to ATMs at multiple banks, expanded their networks to grocery stores and select mainstream retail stores such as Wal-Mart. Customers could then use their ATM cards to buy groceries or merchandise at the register without first having to withdraw cash from a machine. When this debit card system appeared as if it might become widely used, Visa and MasterCard responded by opening their extensive networks to banks and debit card users. Since 1995 the use of debit cards has grown at a rapid pace. According to Murphy, between 1995 and 2001 the percentage of American households using a debit card grew from 17.6% to 47%. In 1995 there were 1.4 billion debit card transactions, and by 2000 the number of transactions had increased to 8.3 billion. The Census Bureau (2012, http://www.census.gov/compendia/statab/2012/tables/12s1188.pdf) reveals that the total number of debit card transactions reached 38.5 billion in 2009 and was projected to climb to 52.6 billion in 2012. The total purchase volume of debit cards was also expected to rise significantly during this period, from $1.4 trillion in 2009 to $2.1 trillion in 2012.

Electronic Transfer of Money

Another type of paperless monetary transaction that has grown in popularity is the electronic transfer of money, formally known as the automated clearinghouse (ACH) system. Electronic transfer is an electronic form of the checking system. When making an ACH transaction, the person or business with the checking account provides the account and routing number to another party along with the authorization to wire money directly into or out of an account. For the most part, large corporations employ this method of payment and receipt more extensively than individual households. Murphy notes that 97% of large corporations used the ACH system extensively in 2002, largely for business-to-business transactions involving substantial amounts of money.

Individuals who use the ACH system typically do so to receive regular salary or Social Security payments and to make regular monthly payments. According to the Social Security Administration (http://www.ssa.gov/deposit/GIS/data/Reports/T2StateSum.htm), in December 2012, 94.8% of Social Security recipients received their payments through direct deposit.

Many Americans also file their tax returns and receive refunds through an electronic payment method. The Internal Revenue Service (June 8, 2012, http://www.irs.gov/uac/Filing-Season-Statistics-for-Week-Ending-June-8,-2012) states that through June 2012, 113.1 million (82%) out of 137.2 million 2011 tax returns had been filed electronically. Meanwhile, the government paid $234.6 billion out of a total of $282.8 billion in tax refunds through direct deposit.

As electronic transfers have become more common, the number of paper checks written by Americans has steadily declined. According to the Federal Reserve, in *2010 Federal Reserve Payments Study*, Americans wrote 24.5 billion checks in 2009, a 7.1% decrease from the 30.5 billion checks written in 2006. During this same period, the debit card surpassed the personal check as the most prevalent form of noncash payment in the United States. In 2009 the largest percentage of checks were those written by consumers to businesses (44.3%), followed by business-to-business check payments (27.1%) and business-to-consumer checks (18.3%).

Because the cost of creating, mailing, and handling so many paper checks is enormous, the U.S. government has made efforts to reduce the number of paper checks in the system. Early in 2003 the Federal Reserve reduced what it charges banks for processing electronic transfers and raised the prices it charges banks for processing paper checks. Then in October 2003 Congress passed and President George W. Bush (1946–) signed the Check Truncation Act, which went into effect in October 2004. Under the Check Truncation Act banks are no longer required to hold onto the original paper checks they receive. Instead, when a payee deposits a check in a bank, the bank makes a digital copy of the check and shreds the original. The bank then simply wires the payer's bank for the money, avoiding the postage and processing involved in sending the actual check to the payer's bank. If the payer needs a copy of the check, the stored digital image can be printed.

WILL AMERICANS ABANDON THE BANK?

Dennis Jacobe of the Gallup Organization reports in *Banking Customers Still Love Bricks and Mortar* (June 10, 2003, http://www.gallup.com/poll/8593/Banking-Customers-Still-Love-Bricks-Mortar.aspx) that in 2003 Americans wanted both the option of banking electronically and of visiting their local bank branch. Because of the high costs of hiring tellers and leasing branch space, banks have encouraged the use of electronic banking among customers as a whole. The banks' efforts appear to be working. In March 2000 only 7% of Americans reported any experience with online banking, and by 2003, 29% of Americans said they banked online from home at least once a month. In *Usage over Time*, Pew/

Internet reports that in March 2000, 17% of Internet users reported that they had banked online at some time. In January 2005 this percentage had increased to 44%. By May 2011 more than three-fifths (61%) of Internet users did their banking online.

Even though Americans have taken advantage of online banking, debit cards, and ATM services, most still make regular trips to a bank branch location. Jacobe notes that in March 2000, 87% of respondents said they were bank customers and 78% said they used the bank once per week; in 2003, 83% of Americans still visited their bank once per month on average and 29% visited the bank four to five times per month. Between 2000 and 2003 the frequency of visits appeared to have gone down, but the number of banking customers did not change. Overall, Jacobe concludes that seeing a teller face to face was still important to Americans in 2003. Indeed, in-person banking actually increased as the decade progressed. According to the Census Bureau (July 2009, http://www.census.gov/compendia/statab/2010/tables/10s1148.pdf), 78% of households continued to conduct at least some banking in person in 2004; by 2007, this figure had risen to 85%.

ANTITRUST LITIGATION

Throughout U.S. history, technological innovation has tended to give rise to the formation of monopolies. Those companies that create a widespread demand and a standard for new technologies often become the only producer of that technology, shutting down further competition in that industry. Since the passage of the Sherman Antitrust Act in 1890, companies in the private sector have been forbidden from blocking competitors from entering the market. If a company grows large enough and powerful enough to keep competitors out of the market and become a monopoly, then the U.S. Department of Justice (DOJ) typically intervenes and either reaches a settlement with the company or files an antitrust suit and takes the company to court. The U.S. government takes the stance that monopolies reduce competition, which hinders economic progress and innovation. Even though this law may appear easy to understand, the courts and the DOJ have to weigh a number of factors before breaking up a monopoly, including the negative effects the ruling may have on consumers.

In 1998 the DOJ and the attorneys general of 20 states filed an antitrust suit against Microsoft Corporation. Along with other charges, the government claimed that Microsoft violated antitrust law when it integrated its Internet Explorer web browser software with Windows. At the time, Windows was the only operating system widely available for the personal computer (PC). When Microsoft integrated Internet Explorer and Windows, other web browsers such as Netscape could not compete.

The DOJ maintained that this act created unfair competition for those other companies that made browsers for PC systems. Microsoft officials claimed that Internet Explorer was now part of Windows and that separating the two would destroy the most current versions of the operating system and years of development on their part.

In November 1999 Judge Thomas Penfield Jackson (1937–) of the U.S. District Court presented a preliminary ruling, which asserted that Microsoft did have a monopoly with its PC operating system and that the monopoly prevented fair competition among companies that made software for personal computers. Five months later, in April 2000, Judge Jackson gave his final ruling, ordering that Microsoft should be split into two separate units: one that would produce the operating system and one that would produce other software components such as Internet Explorer.

Microsoft immediately appealed, and the case went to the federal appeals court under Judge Colleen Kollar-Kotelly (1943–). In the midst of the judicial review, the White House administration changed, and the DOJ, now led by John D. Ashcroft (1942–), came to an agreement with Microsoft that did not involve the breakup of the company. However, several of the states continued to battle the software giant in court. In November 2002 Judge Kollar-Kotelly ruled that the company should not be broken up and should follow the agreement laid down by the DOJ and accepted by the attorneys general of Illinois, Kentucky, Louisiana, Maryland, Michigan, New York, North Carolina, Ohio, and Wisconsin. Additional remedies proposed by California, Connecticut, the District of Columbia, Iowa, Florida, Kansas, Massachusetts, Minnesota, Utah, and West Virginia were dismissed. The agreement required Microsoft to take a number of steps that would allow competitors to once again compete in the market. Among these provisions, Microsoft was required to give computer makers the option of removing Internet Explorer and other Microsoft programs that run on top of the Windows operating system. Microsoft was also forced to reveal details about the Windows operating system that would allow makers of other software to better integrate software with Windows.

In a series of reports that are issued at roughly three-month intervals, the DOJ (http://www.usdoj.gov/atr/cases/ms_index.htm) updates Microsoft's progress in complying with the terms of the final judgment in the case. Each report covers progress toward goals such as sharing technical documentation, providing feedback to software developers, promoting data portability, and supporting interoperability among systems. In *Joint Status Report on Microsoft's Compliance with the Final Judgments* (April 22, 2011, http://www.justice.gov/atr/cases/f270200/270210.pdf), the DOJ explains that as of April 15, 2011, there were still 837 technical documentation issues awaiting resolution from Microsoft.

While the DOJ awaited a resolution of the Microsoft antitrust case, other high-profile tech companies came under scrutiny for allegedly monopolistic business practices. In "IBM Hits Back at 'Mainframe Monopoly' Accusations" (*Information Age*, March 15, 2010), Daniel Shane reports that in 2010 the Indian Council for Research on International Economic Relations filed a report claiming that IBM had attempted to assert monopoly control over India's computer mainframe business sector. Two years later, Google found itself the target of a European Union investigation, amid charges that the company had violated European antitrust law. Indeed, Susan P. Crawford notes in "Is Google a Monopoly? Wrong Question" (Bloomberg.com, July 8, 2012) that in 2012 Google accounted for 80% of all search engine traffic on the European continent. As both the IBM and Google cases illustrate, the era of economic globalization not only offered new opportunities for American tech companies to extend their reach into overseas markets but also introduced a range of potential new legal obstacles to overseas expansion.

CHAPTER 4
TECHNOLOGY AND CRIME

New technologies almost always introduce new problems into a society. The information technology that became widespread during the 1980s and 1990s is no exception. The advent of online shopping and the increased use of electronic currency have given rise to an identity theft epidemic. The digitization of music, movies, television, and the printed word has led to widespread intellectual property theft and losses of millions of dollars for the entertainment industry.

High-technology (high-tech) crime—also known as cybercrime, web crime, computer crime, netcrime, and electronic crime (e-crime)—has grown ever more common in the 21st century. The Federal Bureau of Investigation's (FBI's) Internet Crime Complaint Center (IC3) reports in its *2011 Internet Crime Report* (2012, http://www.ic3.gov/media/annualreport/2011_ic3report.pdf) that 314,246 cybercrime incidents were reported to the IC3 in 2011, a 3.4% rise over 2010, when the center received 303,809 complaints. In addition, the Federal Trade Commission (FTC) estimates that Americans lost $1.52 billion to identity theft and other Internet scams in 2011 ("Americans Reported $1.52 Bln in Fraud Complaints in 2011: FTC" (February 28, 2012, http://www.reuters.com/article/2012/02/28/us-consumer-fraud-idUSTRE81R1RT20120228). As more people become dependent on information technology, Internet crimes will likely continue to grow more common, in some part because they do not require a face-to-face confrontation with the victim.

IDENTITY THEFT

The FTC has the responsibility of tracking identity theft and consumer fraud in the United States. Each year the FTC gathers consumer complaints of fraud and identity theft and logs them into its Consumer Sentinel database. In 2011 more reports of identity theft found their way to its Consumer Sentinel database than any other single type of fraud complaint. (See Table 4.1.) Simply put, identity theft is the theft of an individual's personal information such as a telephone number, address, credit card number, or Social Security number. Thieves use this information to buy things, set up false credit card and cell phone accounts, or perpetrate other crimes. With a victim's Social Security number, address, and phone number, a thief can apply for credit cards in the victim's name and proceed to run up the limits on these cards. Such a crime leaves the victim's credit report in shambles, making it difficult to apply for loans or additional cards in the future.

In some instances, identity theft is perpetrated on a massive scale by sophisticated criminal networks. One of the most extensive identity theft cases was broken in 2008, when federal prosecutors brought indictments against 11 individuals accused of operating an international identity theft ring. According to the press release "Retail Hacking Ring Charged for Stealing and Distributing Credit and Debit Card Numbers from Major U.S. Retailers" (August 5, 2008, http://www.usdoj.gov/opa/pr/2008/August/08-ag-689.html), between 2006 and 2008 the 11 defendants in the case stole an estimated 40 million credit and debit card numbers from patrons of retail chains throughout the United States. According to DOJ allegations, the accused defendants hacked into the wireless computer networks of TJX Companies, BJ's Wholesale Club, OfficeMax, Boston Market, Barnes & Noble, Sports Authority, Forever 21, and DSW to install "sniffer" programs that capture customers' account information. Once in possession of the credit and debit card numbers, the conspirators used them to encode the magnetic strips of blank cards, or else sold them to other criminals. As the Department of Justice reports in "Leader of Hacking Ring Sentenced for Massive Identity Thefts from Payment Processor and U.S. Retail Networks" (March 26, 2010, http://www.justice.gov/opa/pr/2010/March/10-crm-329.html), the ringleader of the scam, Albert Gonzalez, was eventually convicted on multiple charges, including aggravated identity theft, and sentenced to 20 years in prison.

Another high-profile case, dubbed Operation Swiper, was exposed in October 2011. As Julia Greenberg reports in "111 Indicted in One of Largest Identity-Theft Cases in the U.S." (October 7, 2011, http://www.ibtimes.com/111-indicted-one-largest-identity-theft-cases-us-322083), the ringleaders of the scam recruited bank tellers, restaurant employees, and retail associates throughout the New York City borough of Queens to steal credit card information from customers. One of the four principal organizers of the operation, Amar Singh, was eventually sentenced to up to 10 2/3 years in prison for his role in the scam, according to Allie Compton of the Huffington Post ("Largest ID Theft Case in U.S. History: Amar Singh and Wife, Neha Punjani-Singh, Plead Guilty to Massive Fraud," August 7, 2012, http://www.huffingtonpost.com/2012/08/07/largest-id-theft-in-history_n_1751241.html).

Since the 1980s credit card companies and other financial institutions have made obtaining a credit card or setting up a financial account much easier. Because of the convenience of debit and credit cards, nearly every brick-and-mortar store, website, and catalog now accepts them, often with no proof of identification. Consequently, identity theft is not difficult, and it continues to grow. In its *Consumer Sentinel Network Data Book for January–December 2011* (February 2012, http://ftc.gov/sentinel/reports/sentinel-annual-reports/sentinel-cy2011.pdf), the FTC reports that in 2011 it received roughly 1.8 million cybercrime complaints. Of these, 15% were related to identity theft. (See Figure 4.1.)

Table 4.2 reflects reported incidents of identity theft by state. California had the highest number of complaints in the country in 2011, with 38,607. Florida topped the list with the highest rate of reported cases of identity theft per capita, registering 178.7 complaints per 100,000 population. The FTC notes that if the District of Columbia were included among the states listed in Table 4.2, then it would be second with a rate of 166 identity theft victimization reports per 100,000 population. Georgia (120 per 100,000 population) and California (103.6) also experienced rates higher than 100 complaints per 100,000 population. North

TABLE 4.1

Top consumer fraud complaints reported to the Consumer Sentinel Network, 2011

Rank	Category	No. of complaints	Percentages*
1	Identity theft	279,156	15%
2	Debt collection	180,928	10%
3	Prizes, sweepstakes and lotteries	100,208	6%
4	Shop-at-home and catalog sales	98,306	5%
5	Banks and lenders	89,341	5%
6	Internet services	81,805	5%
7	Auto related complaints	77,435	4%
8	Impostor scams	73,281	4%
9	Telephone and mobile services	70,024	4%
10	Advance-fee loans and credit protection/repair	47,414	3%
11	Foreign money offers and counterfeit check scams	43,101	2%
12	Health care	38,246	2%
13	Mortgage foreclosure relief and debt management	38,140	2%
14	Credit cards	37,932	2%
15	Television and electronic media	37,404	2%
16	Business opportunities, employment agencies and work-at-home plans	36,111	2%
17	Internet auction	35,926	2%
18	Travel, vacations and timeshare plans	32,736	2%
19	Credit bureaus, information furnishers and report users	30,203	2%
20	Magazines and books	21,636	1%
21	Office supplies and services	15,917	1%
22	Computer equipment and software	13,435	1%
23	Home repair, improvement and products	13,020	1%
24	Grants	12,823	1%
25	Real estate	8,763	<1%
26	Investment related complaints	7,657	<1%
27	Charitable solicitations	3,474	<1%
28	Clothing, textiles and jewelry	3,358	<1%
29	Education	3,164	<1%
30	Buyers' clubs	2,660	<1%

*Percentages are based on the total number of Consumer Sentinel Network (CSN) complaints (1,813,080) received by the Federal Trade Commission (FTC) between January 1 and December 31, 2001. Ten percent (187,442) of the total CSN complaints received by the FTC were coded Other.

SOURCE: "Consumer Sentinel Network Complaint Categories, January 1–December 31, 2011," in *Consumer Sentinel Network Data Book for January–December 2011*, Federal Trade Commission, February 2012, http://ftc.gov/sentinel/reports/sentinel-annual-reports/sentinel-cy2011.pdf (accessed October 1, 2012)

FIGURE 4.1

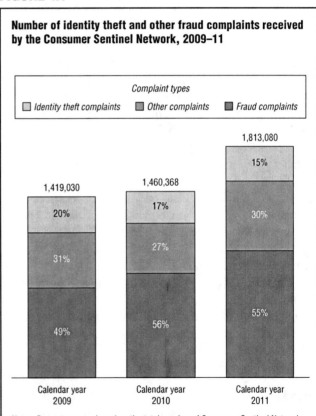

Number of identity theft and other fraud complaints received by the Consumer Sentinel Network, 2009–11

Complaint types
- Identity theft complaints
- Other complaints
- Fraud complaints

Calendar year 2009: 1,419,030 — 20%, 31%, 49%
Calendar year 2010: 1,460,368 — 17%, 27%, 56%
Calendar year 2011: 1,813,080 — 15%, 30%, 55%

Notes: Percentages are based on the total number of Consumer Sentinel Network complaints by calendar year.

SOURCE: "Consumer Sentinel Network Complaint Type Percentages, Calendar Years 2009 through 2011," in *Consumer Sentinel Network Data Book for January–December 2011*, Federal Trade Commission, February 2012, http://ftc.gov/sentinel/reports/sentinel-annual-reports/sentinel-cy2011.pdf (accessed October 1, 2012)

TABLE 4.2

Fraud, identity theft, and other complaints received by the Consumer Sentinel Network, by state, 2011

	Fraud & other complaints				Identity theft complaints		
Rank	Consumer state	Complaints per 100,000 population*	Complaints	Rank	Victim state	Complaints per 100,000 population*	Complaints
1	Colorado	573.7	28,854	1	Florida	178.7	33,595
2	Delaware	552.2	4,958	2	Georgia	120.0	11,625
3	Maryland	547.0	31,581	3	California	103.6	38,607
4	Nevada	530.3	14,320	4	Arizona	98.5	6,296
5	Virginia	527.0	42,165	5	Texas	96.1	24,162
6	Florida	515.1	96,854	6	New York	92.3	17,880
7	Arizona	503.7	32,195	7	Nevada	89.9	2,427
8	Washington	473.4	31,832	8	New Jersey	86.4	7,599
9	Ohio	472.4	54,493	9	Maryland	86.3	4,980
10	New Jersey	452.0	39,737	10	Delaware	83.5	750
11	New Hampshire	451.8	5,948	11	Colorado	82.6	4,156
12	Missouri	448.5	26,863	12	Alabama	82.5	3,942
13	Georgia	447.9	43,395	13	Michigan	82.1	8,119
14	Alaska	440.7	3,130	14	Illinois	80.8	10,361
15	Idaho	433.2	6,790	15	Pennsylvania	79.2	10,061
16	South Carolina	426.3	19,720	16	New Mexico	78.2	1,610
17	Pennsylvania	425.3	54,027	17	Mississippi	74.5	2,210
18	Tennessee	425.3	26,987	18	Washington	72.2	4,853
19	Oregon	423.1	16,208	19	Missouri	71.5	4,282
20	California	418.7	155,986	20	South Carolina	68.5	3,168
21	Hawaii	418.7	5,695	21	Virginia	67.7	5,416
22	Illinois	407.4	52,278	22	Connecticut	67.5	2,413
23	Montana	406.3	4,020	23	Tennessee	67.4	4,275
24	Texas	406.1	102,107	24	Kansas	67.1	1,914
25	Connecticut	404.2	14,447	25	North Carolina	65.9	6,287
26	Alabama	403.9	19,304	26	Ohio	64.8	7,479
27	Wyoming	403.8	2,276	27	Louisiana	64.7	2,934
28	Massachusetts	400.8	26,245	28	Arkansas	63.9	1,862
29	Wisconsin	399.8	22,736	29	Massachusetts	63.0	4,128
30	North Carolina	399.2	38,063	30	Rhode Island	58.3	614
31	Louisiana	397.1	18,000	31	Oregon	58.1	2,226
32	Utah	394.2	10,895	32	Oklahoma	56.4	2,115
33	Kansas	393.4	11,225	33	Indiana	54.8	3,555
34	Indiana	390.1	25,296	34	Utah	54.8	1,514
35	New Mexico	389.6	8,023	35	Minnesota	50.4	2,671
36	New York	387.9	75,163	36	Wyoming	49.7	280
37	Rhode Island	380.4	4,004	37	Wisconsin	48.9	2,782
38	Michigan	374.4	37,007	38	Nebraska	47.6	869
39	Nebraska	373.6	6,824	39	New Hamnshire	46.9	617
40	Vermont	372.0	2,328	40	Alaska	44.5	316
41	Minnesota	371.0	19,679	41	Kentucky	43.6	1,891
42	Kentucky	369.9	16,053	42	Hawaii	42.9	583
43	Oklahoma	359.4	13,481	43	Idaho	42.0	658
44	Arkansas	353.7	10,314	44	Vermont	41.4	259
45	Maine	345.5	4,589	45	Iowa	39.7	1,208
46	Mississippi	323.4	9,595	46	West Virginia	39.4	731
47	West Virginia	323.1	5,987	47	Montana	39.4	390
48	Iowa	315.5	9,611	48	Maine	37.9	503
49	South Dakota	296.6	2,415	49	South Dakota	25.3	206
50	North Dakota	257.5	1,732	50	North Dakota	23.2	156

*Per 100,000 unit of population estimates are based on the 2010 U.S. Census (accessed January 2012 at http://2010.census.gov/2010census/data/). Numbers for the District of Columbia are: Fraud and others = 4,736 complaints and 787.1 complaints per 100,000 population; Identity theft = 999 victims and 166.0 victims per 100,000 population.
Note: In calculating the State and Metropolitan Areas rankings, we excluded nine State-specific data contributors' complaints (the Minnesota Department of Public Safety, the North Carolina Department of Justice, the Tennessee Division of Consumer Affairs, and the Offices of the Attorneys General for Idaho, Michigan, Mississippi, Ohio, Oregon, and Washington).

SOURCE: "Consumer Sentinel Network State Complaint Rates, January 1–December 31, 2011," in *Consumer Sentinel Network Data Book for January–December 2011*, Federal Trade Commission, February 2012, http://ftc.gov/sentinel/reports/sentinel-annual-reports/sentinel-cy2011.pdf (accessed October 1, 2012)

Dakota (23.2) and South Dakota (25.3) had the lowest number of reported victims of identity theft per 100,000 population in 2011.

Criminals perpetrate identity theft in a variety of ways. Figure 4.2 shows the types of identity theft experienced in select years between 2005 and 2010. As Figure 4.2 reveals, existing credit cards consistently account for the highest proportion of identity theft cases in the United States. Among income groups, households earning $75,000 or more per year experienced higher incidences of identity theft in 2010; among geographical locations, suburban households accounted for 4.7 million cases of identity theft in 2010, or more than half of the 8.6 million total cases reported that year. (See Table 4.3.) Of households that suffered a financial loss due to identity theft in 2010, one-quarter (24.6%) reported losing between $100 and $499.

According to the *Consumer Sentinel Network Data Book for January–December 2011*, more than half of those reporting identity theft in calendar years 2009,

FIGURE 4.2

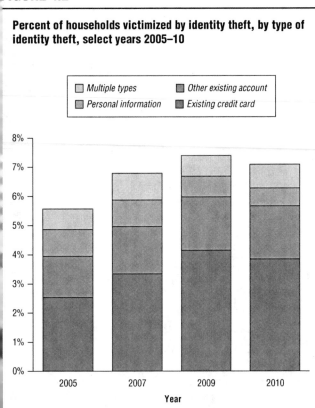

Percent of households victimized by identity theft, by type of identity theft, select years 2005–10

Legend:
- Multiple types
- Personal information
- Other existing account
- Existing credit card

Notes: Annual estimates are not available for 2008 because 6 months of identity theft data were collected.

SOURCE: Lynn Langton, "Figure 1. Percent of Households That Experienced Identity Theft, by Type of Identity Theft, 2005, 2007, 2009, and 2010," in *Identity Theft Reported by Households*, 2005–2010, U.S. Department of Justice, Office of Justice Programs, Bureau of Justice Statistics, November 2011, http://bjs.ojp.usdoj.gov/content/pub/pdf/itrh0510.pdf (accessed November 27, 2012)

2010, and 2011 were over the age of 40. (See Table 4.4; note that total numbers do not coincide with those in Table 4.1 because not all victims reported their age.) In 2011, 23% of complaints came from those between the ages of 50 and 59, and 20% were received from those ages 40 to 49. Between 2010 and 2011, the number of identity theft complaints received from those 19 years old and younger rose by 263%, from 3,143 to 11,423. Complaints from those 70 years old and older, on the other hand, dropped slightly between 2010 and 2011, from 36,491 to 35,686. (See Table 4.4.)

The FTC also provides information on how identity theft victims' information was misused. Fourteen percent of victims suffered credit card fraud in 2011, with 8.4% reporting that new accounts were set up in their name, and 5.8% reporting bogus charges made to their existing accounts. (See Table 4.5.) These figures represented a slight decline from 2010 when 15% of victims experienced credit card fraud. Phone and utilities fraud was reported by 13% of victims in 2011, with 3.1% indicating that imposters set up wireless accounts in their name, and

another 1% claiming that bogus telephone accounts had been established under their personal information. Bank fraud, which was reported by 10% of identity theft victims in 2009 and 2010, fell to 9% in 2011. Bank fraud complaints included unauthorized electronic fund transfers (3.8%), misuse of existing accounts (2.3%), and fraudulent new accounts (2.6%). Loan fraud was reported by 3% of identity theft victims in 2011. Those reporting identity theft crimes to the FTC in 2011 experienced many other types of fraud, including everything from phony child-support claims to property rental fraud. In addition, 13% of identity theft complaints in 2011 included more than one type of fraud.

Identity Theft and the Internet

Identity thieves can operate alone or as part of a large crime organization. They can be someone the victim knows or a complete stranger. They gather personal information in various ways, stealing wallets and checkbooks or going through trash bins outside of homes and businesses to dig out credit card statements, old checkbooks, and receipts. Some pilfer financial statements and other private information from open mailboxes. Since the mid-1990s many thieves have turned to the Internet to steal information.

There are a number of ways in which thieves employ the Internet to retrieve personal information. Tech-savvy crooks will often take the direct method and hack into business and bank servers, and make off with hundreds of credit card numbers. Most identity thieves, however, do not deal in such sophisticated methods. According to Duncan Graham-Rowe, in "Internet Fuels Boom in ID Theft" (*New Scientist*, March 13, 2004), one of the easiest ways to steal identities is simply to use a search engine such as Google. Many people naively post all manner of personal information on home and even office websites, including their Social Security number, date of birth, mother's maiden name, current address, and phone number. Simply typing "driver's license" or "passport" into a search engine yields hundreds of photos of driver's licenses and passports from around the country and the world. Businesses or institutions that keep lists of Social Security and credit card numbers sometimes inadvertently place the information in an insecure location. In "Foreign Hacker Steals 3.6 Million Social Security Numbers from State Department of Revenue" (October 26, 2012, http://www.greenvilleonline.com/article/20121026/NEWS/310260024/Foreign-hacker-steals-3-6-million-Social-Security-numbers-from-state-Department-Revenue), Tim Smith reports that between August and October 2012 a hacker exploited a vulnerability in the South Carolina Revenue Department's database, stealing millions of Social Security and credit card numbers of state residents. As Jennifer Sinco Kelleher reports in "The Trouble with Being Too Social" (*Newsday*, July 22, 2010), even posting

TABLE 4.3

Percent of households victimized by identity theft, by household location, income, and size, 2005 and 2010

Household characteristic	2005 Number	2005 Percent in each category	2010 Number	2010 Percent in each category
Total	6,424,900	5.5%	8,571,900	7.0%
Household income				
Less than $7,500	240,400	4.7%	238,600	5.3%
$7,500–14,999	315,300	3.7	334,500	4.8
$15,000–24,999	455,900	3.9	470,500	4.6
$25,000–34,999	547,500	4.9	616,900	6.0
$35,000–49,999	773,300	5.5	884,700	6.6
$50,000–74,999	1,059,500	6.8	1,152,100	7.9
$75,000 or more	2,050,300	9.5	2,835,300	12.3
Unknown	982,600	3.3	2,039,400	5.1
Location				
Urban	2,037,300	5.8%	3,083,100	7.6%
Suburban	3,526,100	5.9	4,718,500	7.6
Rural	861,400	3.9	770,300	3.9
Number of persons age 12 or older in household				
1	1,519,000	4.2%	2,130,000	5.5%
2–3	4,148,000	5.9	5,468,300	7.5
4–5	677,400	6.8	898,800	8.5
6 or more	80,400	10.8	74,800	8.3

Note: Numbers rounded to nearest hundred.

SOURCE: Lynn Langton, "Table 2. Income, Location, and Size of Households That Experienced Identity Theft, 2005 and 2010," in *Identity Theft Reported by Households, 2005–2010*, U.S. Department of Justice, Office of Justice Programs, Bureau of Justice Statistics, November 2011, http://bjs.ojp.usdoj.gov/content/pub/pdf/itrh0510.pdf (accessed November 27, 2012)

information on a social networking site can be perilous. According to Kelleher, revealing such data as "birth dates, school names, cell phone numbers, [or] hometowns" can all leave an individual vulnerable to identity theft or other forms of Internet fraud. For a patient identity thief, the Internet is a treasure trove.

Another technique thieves use to acquire personal information is known as phishing. Thieves will often send out bogus e-mails to scores of people. Typically, these e-mails will look like authentic e-mails from a prominent Internet service provider or bank. The e-mail will inform the receivers that there is something wrong with their account and that the problem can be fixed by clicking on a hyperlink. When victims click on the link, they are then taken to an official-looking site, where they are asked to provide passwords, Social Security information, and even credit card information. The moment the victims type in their personal information, the thieves have them. Once crooks have a credit card in another person's name, the Internet makes it easy to purchase items. No longer do criminals have to risk being caught using someone else's account in a shopping mall or grocery store.

In response to these threats, federal law enforcement agencies have established unique task forces and initiatives aimed at countering identity theft. As part of its counteroffensive, the government has also placed a high priority on keeping citizens informed about potential risks.

The FBI provides information about cybercrime on its Identity Theft page (2012, http://www.fbi.gov/about-us/investigate/cyber/identity_theft), which contains an overview of law enforcement initiatives targeting Internet fraud, as well as valuable advice on how consumers can identify and avoid online threats. Along these lines, IC3 has created a comprehensive list of "Internet Crime Schemes" (2012, http://www.ic3.gov/crimeschemes.aspx), which contains detailed descriptions of some of the most common online scams. The federal government also maintains an Internet Fraud site (2012, http://www.usa.gov/Citizen/Topics/Internet-Fraud.shtml), which provides a list of resources aimed at helping citizens understand potential Internet threats, while providing information on how to report incidences of identity theft and other online crimes.

Americans' Awareness of Identity Theft

By 2012, as electronic record keeping became more prevalent throughout all sectors of society, identity theft had become a major concern for a large majority of the population. As Judy Greenwald writes in "Consumers Lose Confidence in Companies' Data Protection Efforts: Survey" (September 19, 2011, http://www.businessinsurance.com/article/20110919/NEWS07/110919885?tags=l299l305l340l303), by 2011, 80% of Americans expressed concern about having their medical records transferred online, out of fear of exposing sensitive personal information to potential criminal threats. Furthermore, 16% of Americans asserted that they

TABLE 4.4

Identity theft complaints received by the Consumer Sentinel Network, by victim's age, 2009–11

Consumer age	Calendar year 2009		Calendar year 2010		Calendar year 2011	
	Complaints	Percentages*	Complaints	Percentages*	Complaints	Percentages*
19 and under	3,169	1%	3,143	1%	11,423	2%
20–29	76,294	18%	80,852	17%	73,877	15%
30–39	88,804	21%	92,634	20%	82,723	17%
40–49	103,124	24%	109,567	23%	96,172	20%
50–59	105,062	24%	114,703	24%	108,091	23%
60–69	26,986	6%	31,545	7%	70,678	15%
70 and over	25,596	6%	36,491	8%	35,686	7%
Total reporting age	**429,035**		**468,935**		**478,650**	

*Percentages are based on the total number of consumers reporting their age for CSN fraud complaints each calendar year (CY): CY-2009 = 429,035; CY-2010 = 468,935; and CY-2011 = 478,650. 48% of consumers reported this information during CY-2011, 61% and 58% for CY-2009 and CY-2010, respectively.

SOURCE: "Consumer Sentinel Network Identity Theft Complaints by Consumer Age, Calendar Years 2009 through 2011," in *Consumer Sentinel Network Data Book for January–December 2011*, Federal Trade Commission, February 2012, http://ftc.gov/sentinel/reports/sentinel-annual-reports/sentinel-cy2011.pdf (accessed October 1, 2012)

would terminate all business with a firm or institution that had compromised their personal information due to a data breach. While concerns about online security became increasingly widespread, however, actual incidences of Internet crime continued to impact a small minority of the population. As Lydia Saad of the Gallup Organization reports in *In U.S., 11% of Households Report Computer Crimes, a New High* (December 13, 2010, http://www.gallup.com/poll/145205/New-High-Households-Report-Computer-Crimes.aspx), 11% of Americans were victimized by some form of Internet-related crime in 2010, up from 7% the previous year.

INTERNET FRAUD

Internet fraud takes other forms than identity theft, including auction fraud, phishing schemes, and fund-transfer scams. The FTC notes in *Consumer Sentinel Network Data Book for January–December 2011* that 62% of fraud complainants reported the method used by companies to contact them: 52% were solicited through e-mail, and 16% had initial contact via a website. In comparison, 17% were contacted by phone, and 10% were contacted through surface mail.

In a typical Internet auction scheme, a con artist advertises merchandise on an auction site until a buyer is found. The buyer then sends a payment but receives no merchandise. In 2011 the FTC received 35,926 complaints of Internet auction fraud. (See Table 4.1.) Another type of scheme involves the wire transfer of funds drawn on what turns out to be a bogus check. Typically, a victim receives overpayment for a product or service that they have sold and is instructed to immediately deposit the money and wire a portion to a third party; however, the initial check payment turns out to be false, leaving the victim at a loss.

Even though identity theft and auction fraud make up a sizable proportion of crimes on the Internet, countless other frauds have been perpetrated over the years. These ranged from false merchandise advertised on a phony web page to work-at-home e-mail schemes in which the victim is told to send in money as an initial investment. One of the more famous e-mail scams is the Nigerian letter fraud scam, which has been circulating via traditional mail since the early 1980s. In its electronic form, an e-mail purportedly from a "Nigerian dignitary" informs the victim that he or she has the opportunity to receive vast sums of money currently being held in Nigeria. When the victim responds to the message, he or she is then told that the Nigerian dignitary requires money in advance, usually to bribe government officials, so that the funds can be released and deposited in the victim's account. According to the FTC in the *Consumer Sentinel Network Data Book for January–December 2011*, Nigeria was home to the fourth-highest percentage (2%) of Internet fraud perpetrators in 2011, behind the United States (80%), Canada (4%), and the United Kingdom (4%).

Still other, more elaborate scams were designed to manipulate the stock market. Such scams were particularly effective in the late 1990s during the stock market bubble. The best known of these is the pump-and-dump scam. The criminals invest in a stock that is lightly traded and then trick online investors into buying it. Typically, this involves posting fake documents and press releases on financial websites or sending fake e-mail announcements, telling investors that the company is either about to be bought out or has developed a new, moneymaking product. In other instances scam artists bribe lesser-known stock pundits to tout the lifeless stock. After the stock takes off, the criminals simply sell their holdings, leaving other investors holding the bag as the stock goes back down to sustainable levels.

Each year the IC3 profiles in its annual report several cases that it has helped solve. In the *2011 Internet Crime Report*, the IC3 reports that beginning in July 2007 it

TABLE 4.5

How identity theft victims' information was misused, 2009–11

Government documents or benefits fraud	Percentages		
	CY-2009	CY-2010	CY-2011
Theft subtype			
Tax or wage related fraud	12.7%	15.6%	24.1%
Government benefits applied for/received	1.7%	1.8%	1.5%
Other government documents issued/forged	1.1%	0.9%	0.8%
Driver's license issued/forged	0.9%	0.9%	0.8%
Total	**16%**	**19%**	**27%**
Credit card fraud			
Theft subtype			
New accounts	10.2%	9.0%	8.4%
Existing account	7.0%	6.7%	5.8%
Total	**17%**	**15%**	**14%**
Phone or utilities fraud			
Theft subtype			
Utilities—new accounts	8.3%	9.4%	8.7%
Wireless—new accounts	4.6%	3.7%	3.1%
Telephone—new accounts	2.0%	1.5%	1.0%
Unauthorized charges to existing accounts	0.6%	0.5%	0.5%
Total	**15%**	**14%**	**13%**
Bank fraud			
Theft subtype			
Electronic fund transfer	4.4%	4.8%	3.8%
New accounts	3.1%	3.2%	2.6%
Existing accounts	3.1%	2.8%	2.3%
Total	**10%**	**10%**	**9%**
Employment-related fraud			
Theft subtype			
Employment-related fraud	13%	11%	8%
Loan fraud			
Theft subtype			
Business/personal/student loan	1.8%	1.7%	1.4%
Auto loan/lease	1.2%	1.0%	0.9%
Real estate loan	1.1%	1.0%	0.8%
Total	**4%**	**4%**	**3%**

TABLE 4.5

How identity theft victims' information was misused, 2009–11
[CONTINUED]

Other identity theft	Percentages		
	CY-2009	CY-2010	CY-2011
Theft subtype			
Miscellaneous	8.3%	7.6%	8.5%
Uncertain	9.0%	8.6%	8.1%
Data breach*	—	—	1.7%
Internet/email	1.2%	1.9%	1.6%
Evading the law	1.4%	1.5%	1.2%
Medical	1.3%	1.3%	1.0%
Apartment or house rented	0.7%	0.7%	0.7%
Insurance	0.3%	0.3%	0.3%
Securities/other investments	0.1%	0.1%	0.1%
Property rental fraud	0.1%	0.1%	0.1%
Child support	0.2%	0.2%	0.1%
Magazines	0.2%	0.1%	0.1%
Bankruptcy	0.1%	0.1%	0.1%
Total	**23%**	**22%**	**23%**
Attempted identity theft			
Theft subtype			
Attempted identity theft	6%	7%	7%

CY = Calendar year.
Note: Percentages are based on the total number of CSN identity theft complaints for each calendar year: CY-2009 = 278,385; CY-2010 = 251,105; and CY-2011 = 279,156. Note that 13% of identity theft complaints included more than one type of identity theft in CY-2011; and 12% in CY-2010 and CY-2009.
*Theft Subtype "Data Breach" was added to the database in CY-2011.

SOURCE: "Consumer Sentinel Network Identity Theft Complaints: How Victims' Information Is Misused, Calendar Years 2009 through 2011," in *Consumer Sentinel Network Data Book for January–December 2011*, Federal Trade Commission, February 2012, http://ftc.gov/sentinel/reports/sentinel-annual-reports/sentinel-cy2011.pdf (accessed October 1, 2012)

began receiving complaints about an international scam targeting law firms and involving third-party debt collection. In this type of fraud, criminals approach U.S. law firms via e-mail seeking legal assistance with the wire transfer of a large sum of money. The perpetrators then send the law firms counterfeit checks, requesting that the firms subsequently wire the money in question (minus legal fees) to a third party; in some instances, fake checks were issued for amounts exceeding $100,000. In one high-profile case of this type, a Nigerian man named Emmanuel Ekhator operated a third-party debt collection scam that ultimately defrauded U.S. law firms out of more than $29 million. In August 2011 a Nigerian court ruled to allow Ekhator's extradition to the United States, where he was to stand trial on fraud charges in a U.S. District Court in Pennsylvania.

VIRUSES

The term *computer virus* is often used to refer to all malware (*mal*icious soft*ware*)—that is, programs such as

viruses, worms, and Trojan horses that infect and destroy computer files. Technically speaking, viruses are self-replicating programs that insert themselves into other computer files. The virus is spread when the file is transferred to another computer via the Internet or portable media such as a CD-ROM. The first computer virus was created in 1982, when 15-year-old Rich Skrenta (1967–) wrote Elk Cloner, a virus that attached itself to an Apple DOS 3.3 operating system and spread to other computers by floppy disk.

People have all sorts of reasons for creating and sending viruses. Some viruses are written as pranks. Others are written by political activists or terrorists. Still other viruses are intended to injure specific corporations. Regardless of the virus creators' intentions, the number of viruses infecting the world's computers continues to grow. The first computer worm to attract attention appeared in 1988 and was written by Robert T. Morris (1965–), a graduate student at Cornell University. Worms are self-contained, self-replicating computer programs that spread through the Internet from computer to computer. Unlike viruses, they spread via the Internet under their own power and do not rely on people's actions or files to move from one machine to another. Like viruses, worms can destroy files and take advantage of vulnerabilities in computer programs or operating systems.

A Trojan horse does not self-replicate and is typically disguised as something more innocent, such as an e-mail attachment. When the user opens the e-mail, malicious code is unleashed on the computer. As malware has become more advanced, the distinctions between types of malware have become less obvious. For example, Trojan horses often contain viruses that replicate through computer files. For this reason the term *virus* will be used in this chapter to designate any type of malware, unless otherwise specified.

Viruses behave in a number of different ways. For example, the Netsky virus is typically hidden in an e-mail attachment and is launched when the user opens the attachment. Once active, Netsky sets up its own e-mail protocol, looks for e-mail accounts on the hard drive, and mass-mails itself to these accounts. Another virus named MSBlaster appeared on August 13, 2003, and quickly wormed its way through the Internet, infecting hundreds of thousands of computers in a day through vulnerability in the Windows operating system. Once on a personal computer, the virus instructed the computer to take part in a distributed denial-of-service (DDoS) attack on the Windowsupdate.com website. (A DDoS attack occurs when thousands of computers are used to access a single website, thus making it inaccessible.) Other viruses known as "bombs" lie dormant in a computer until a specific date is registered on the computer's clock. Still other viruses disable any virus removal program on the computer, making the virus difficult to remove.

Computer Emergency Response Team

Two weeks after the Morris worm was let loose on the Internet in November 1988, the Defense Advanced Research Projects Agency formed the Computer Emergency Response Team (CERT) with headquarters at Carnegie Mellon University in Pittsburgh, Pennsylvania. The purpose of the organization is to identify threats to the Internet as a whole. CERT coordinates the actions of the private and public sectors when major Internet incidents occur. Even though CERT does issue alerts on individual viruses that affect home users, it is more concerned with the big picture. The organization provides emergency incident response for network access ports, root dedicated name servers, and other components that make up the Internet's infrastructure. It analyzes virus code to develop solutions that thwart viruses. CERT also coordinates responses to large automated attacks against the Internet, such as the Slammer virus in January 2003, and monitors threats to U.S. government computers in coordination with the U.S. Computer Emergency Readiness Team, which was formed in 2003 by the U.S. Department of Homeland Security (DHS).

For many years CERT published a list of vulnerabilities reported to it. Vulnerabilities are weaknesses in computer and Internet software that hackers and virus makers exploit to cause trouble. As the organization reports on its website (February 12, 2009, http://www.cert.org/stats/), between 1999 and 2002 the number of major vulnerabilities reported in Internet and computer systems shot up 890%, from 417 to 4,129. Between 2002 and 2004 the number of vulnerabilities decreased some, and then increased again by 58%, from 3,780 in 2004 to 5,990 in 2005. After rising dramatically to 8,064 in 2006, 2007 saw a slight decline to 7,236. Over the first three quarters of 2008, however, the organization tracked 6,058 vulnerabilities, putting it on a pace to exceed the 2006 total by the end of the year. These numbers seem to suggest that even as software designers and computer manufacturers were becoming better at identifying vulnerabilities, computer hackers and criminals were also stepping up their attacks. In addition, as the complexity of computers and the Internet increases, more vulnerabilities are likely to appear.

In 2008 the Internet security researcher Dan Kaminsky (1978?–) discovered a vulnerability in the design of the domain name system (DNS). The security breach allowed criminals to attack the system and reroute Internet traffic to imposter websites, with users completely unaware that they had been directed to fraudulent sites. How it worked was fairly simple. Each time an address such as http://www.google.com/ is entered into the address bar of an Internet browser, the browser contacts one of many domain name servers distributed on the Internet. Once the browser makes the request from the DNS, the name server sends back the corresponding address number, which for Google is 209.85.225.147. The Internet browser then uses this numeric address to access the site (Google in this case). Each domain name server has a cache that stores widely used sites' names and numeric addresses for a limited time. The vulnerability, known as "cache poisoning," worked by substituting a vandal-controlled Internet address for the one normally linked with a well-known domain name. For a name not stored in its cache, a name server forwards the request to other name servers on the network until it finds the address or one very similar. The attack allowed criminals to flood the DNS with requests that would ensure that their site addresses were stored and distributed rather than the legitimate ones.

In March 2008 experts in Internet security met secretly at Microsoft Corporation headquarters in Redmond, Washington, to discuss the problem and determine a plan of action. They did not reveal the vulnerability to the public until patches were available to fix the situation in July 2008. As reported by Stuart Corner in *iTWire* (August 5, 2008, http://www.itwire.com/business-it-news/security/19850-major-dns-flaw-details-likely-to-be-revealed-at-black-hat), Kaminsky explained the effectiveness of the patch in his blog at DoxPara Research:

> After the attack: A bad guy has a one in 65,000 chance of stealing your Internet connection, and he can try a couple thousand times a second.

After the patch: A bad guy has a one in a couple hundred million, or even a couple billion chance of stealing your Internet connection. He can still try to do so a couple thousand times a second, but it's going to make *a lot* of noise.

In spite of the proven success of the DNS patch, computer security breaches remain a constant threat in the second decade of the 21st century. Indeed, as Matthew J. Schwartz reports in "10 Security Trends to Watch in 2012" (January 17, 2012, http://www.informationweek.com/security/vulnerabilities/10-security-trends-to-watch-in-2012/232400392), by 2012 most companies had come to view security breaches as an inevitable side effect of doing business in the information age, therefore shifting the emphasis of their data protection efforts to the rapid detection, identification, and blocking of cyber threats. At the same time, the growth of mobile data and social networking platforms provided hackers and other criminals with new ways to exploit the online vulnerabilities of both businesses and individuals. Furthermore, as Internet security firm Sophos describes in its *Security Threat Report 2012* (2012, http://www.sophos.com/en-us/medialibrary/PDFs/other/SophosSecurityThreatReport2012.pdf), 2011 saw a sharp rise in politically-motivated security breaches, as "hacktivist" groups such as Anonymous and LulzSec began to target government agencies, defense firms, and other powerful entities with the aim of disrupting the economic and political status quo.

E-CRIME AND ORGANIZATIONS

Except for computer viruses, e-crimes that affect individuals, such as auction fraud or identity theft, are usually different from the e-crimes that affect businesses. Most large organizations are concerned about hackers entering into their servers or dissatisfied employees sabotaging their computer network. In *2011 Cybersecurity Watch Survey: Organizations Need More Skilled Cyber Professionals to Stay Secure* (January 31, 2011, www.cert.org/archive/pdf/CyberSecuritySurvey2011.pdf), CERT provides a detailed picture of how e-crimes affect companies in the United States. The survey polled more than 600 organizations of all sizes and asked them about the problems they faced with regard to computer crimes between August 2009 and July 2010. According to the survey, 28% of respondents reported experiencing an increase in the number of attacks between 2009 and 2010, while 19% claimed to have not been the target of any online criminal activity during the same period. The survey also showed that concern over attacks by foreign entities had doubled from 5% in CERT's 2010 report to 10% in the *2011 Cybersecurity Watch Survey*.

In its *2010/2011 Computer Crime and Security Survey* (December 2, 2010, https://cours.etsmtl.ca/log619/documents/divers/CSIsurvey2010.pdf), the Computer Security Institute (CSI) presents similar findings to CERT's *2011 Cybersecurity Watch Survey*. Robert Richardson of the CSI lists in *2010/2011*

Computer Crime and Security Survey (2011, https://cours.etsmtl.ca/log619/documents/divers/CSIsurvey2010.pdf) multiple e-crimes that plagued survey respondents between 2005 and 2010. Malware infection topped the list in 2010, affecting 67.1% of survey respondents, up from 50% in 2008. One-third (33.5%) of survey respondents reported the theft of mobile devices or laptop computers. One-quarter (24.8%) of companies indicated they had suffered incidences of insider abuse of web access; 8.7% were victims of financial fraud, down from 19.5% in 2009. According to Patrick Béhar, Laurent Colombani, and Sophie Krishnan of Bain & Company, Inc., in *Publishing in the Digital Era* (2011, http://www.bain.com/bainweb/PDFs/cms/Public/BB_Publishing_in_the_digital_era.pdf), a number of threat categories became more prevalent between 2009 and 2010. For example, attacks by botnets or zombie computers affected 23% of respondents in 2009; by 2010 the percentage of companies attacked by botnets had risen to 29%. The researchers also note that there was a rise in phishing scams between 2009 (34%) and 2010 (39%). In 2009 CSI began keeping data on the use of social networking sites as a means of infiltrating a company's security system. According to Béhar, Colombani, and Krishnan, the proportion of organizations that suffered breaches of their social networking sites actually declined between 2009 and 2010, from 7% to 5%.

INTELLECTUAL PROPERTY THEFT

Intellectual property, which includes copyrighted material such as games, software, and movies, is a huge part of the U.S. economy. These industries are important to the economy and to the people employed in them, and financial profit is critical for those who create music, video games, books, or software. As such, the issue of intellectual property theft is of vital importance to the federal government. In a speech delivered on March 11, 2010, at the Export-Import Bank's Annual Conference (http://www.whitehouse.gov/omb/intellectualproperty/quotes/), President Barack Obama (1961–) asserted that the goal of his administration was

> to aggressively protect our intellectual property. Our single greatest asset is the innovation and the ingenuity and creativity of the American people. It is essential to our prosperity and it will only become more so in this century. But it's only a competitive advantage if our companies know that someone else can't just steal that idea and duplicate it with cheaper inputs and labor. There's nothing wrong with other people using our technologies, we welcome it—we just want to make sure that it's licensed, and that American businesses are getting paid appropriately.

In "A Statistical Analysis of Trade Secret Litigation in Federal Courts" (*Gonzaga Law Review*, vol. 45, no. 1, 2009/10), David S. Almeling et al. report that the net worth of intellectual property in the United States came to roughly $5 trillion, or nearly one-half of the total value of the economy. According to the *2010 Joint Strategic Plan on Intellectual Property Enforcement* (June 2010, http://www.whitehouse.gov/sites/default/files/omb/assets/intellectualproperty/intellectualproperty_strategic_plan.pdf), industries that rely on copyrighted material for their revenues make vital contributions to the domestic economy. For example, in 2007 the U.S. software industry accounted for $261 billion of gross domestic product (GDP; the total value of all goods produced in a country minus the cost of the materials that went into making those goods); the Motion Picture Association of America (MPAA), meanwhile, generated $15.7 billion in tax revenues in 2008. Citing a report created by the Institute for Policy Innovation (IPI) in 2007, the *2010 Joint Strategic Plan* states that copyright violations against the software and entertainment industries cost the U.S. economy approximately $58 billion in total output, 373,375 jobs, $16.3 billion in wages, and $2.6 billion in total tax revenues each year.

Intellectual property theft has posed perhaps the greatest single threat to the copyright industries since the 1990s. In the mid-1980s pirating software and entertainment media on a large enough scale to make a profit demanded a large initial investment and a huge time commitment. For example, pirating movies required large banks of video cassette recorders (VCRs) along with hundreds of blank tapes. Copies of the movie were typically of much lower quality than the original, and national copyright laws made storing, selling, and distributing the bulky tapes difficult. As a result, most pirated copies of movies, music, games, or software were copied and distributed overseas in countries where copyright law was nonexistent or not enforced.

Technological advances during the 1990s put an end to many of the hassles faced by intellectual property thieves. The Internet, along with powerful computers and the conversion of nearly every type of media into digital form, made copying and distributing intellectual property easy even within the United States. Once a thief finds a way around the copyright protection that exists on the digitized copyrighted material, the computer provides an easy way to store the material. Because digital media do not degrade when copied, the thief can produce perfect duplicates. Distribution of the media to any country in the world is easily accomplished over the Internet using peer-to-peer (P2P) networks or file transfer protocol (FTP) sites, which employ standard file copying protocols to upload and download files on a server.

The explosion in illegal content-sharing over the Internet seemed to pose a serious threat to creative industries that depended on copyrighted material for their revenues, particularly the Recording Industry Association of America (RIAA) and the MPAA. As Figure 4.3 shows, music industry revenues fell by roughly 50% during the first decade of the 21st century. Even consistent growth in digital music downloads and music streaming services were unable to compensate for the steep decline in sales

FIGURE 4.3

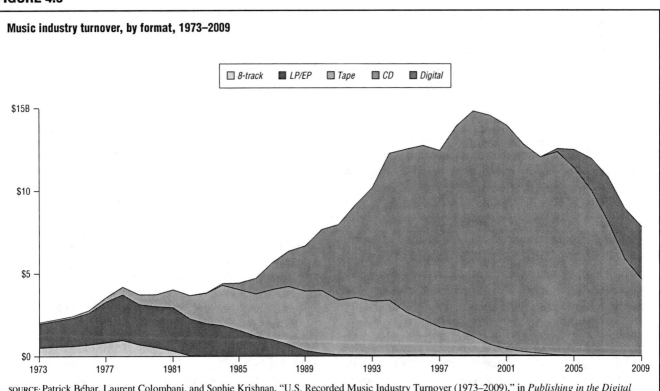

Music industry turnover, by format, 1973–2009

SOURCE: Patrick Béhar, Laurent Colombani, and Sophie Krishnan, "U.S. Recorded Music Industry Turnover (1973–2009)," in *Publishing in the Digital Era*, Bain & Company, Inc., 2011, http://www.bain.com/bainweb/PDFs/cms/Public/BB_Publishing_in_the_digital_era.pdf (accessed October 1, 2012)

of physical music formats. Indeed, while digital sales were expected to grow by $1.3 billion between 2011 and 2012, physical sales were projected to decrease by $1.9 billion, a net loss of $0.6 billion. (See Figure 4.4.) Still, the steady rise in digital sales offered promise for the future of the music industry. As Jim Jansen reports in *65% of Internet Users Have Paid for Online Content* (December 30, 2010, http://www.pewinternet.org/~/media//Files/Reports/2010/PIP-Paying-for-Online-Content_final.pdf), roughly two-thirds (65%) of Internet adults paid for some form of online content in 2010; one-third (33%) paid for music online. In its *Digital Music Report 2012* (2012, http://www.ifpi.org/content/library/DMR2012.pdf), the International Federation of the Phonographic Industry (IFPI) states that digital formats accounted for more than half (52%) of all U.S. music sales in 2011. Overall, sales rose from $4.8 billion to $5.2 billion between 2010 and 2011, an 8% increase.

Creative Industries Fight Copyright Violators

One of the biggest threats to music industry profitability has been peer-to-peer networks. In the late 1990s peer-to-peer networks were created to connect music lovers around the world. Napster was the largest of these, with tens of millions of users at its peak. Napster, like all peer-to-peer networks, did not contain any music on its own website.

Instead, Napster tracked the songs and albums its members had on their individual computers. By logging into the central server of the network owned by Napster, members could first locate what music files were available on the network and then proceed to download the music from another member's computer. From the industry point of view, the problem with peer-to-peer networks was that once an album made it on to the network, millions of people suddenly had access to it for free.

Less than a year after the Napster website opened, the RIAA filed a case against Napster in U.S. federal district court on December 6, 1999. The RIAA represented most major recording labels and claimed that Napster infringed on the companies' copyrights. The court sided with the RIAA. Napster appealed the ruling, but in September 2001 it settled with the RIAA by paying $26 million for copyright infringement. Before the case was settled, the Napster creator Shawn Fanning (1980–) sold Napster to Bertelsmann, a huge German media conglomerate. Bertelsmann dismantled the file-sharing network and constructed a database of songs that could be downloaded for a fee, part of which goes to pay the record company royalties.

The court's ruling against the practice of open music file-sharing meant that the RIAA and other organizations

FIGURE 4.4

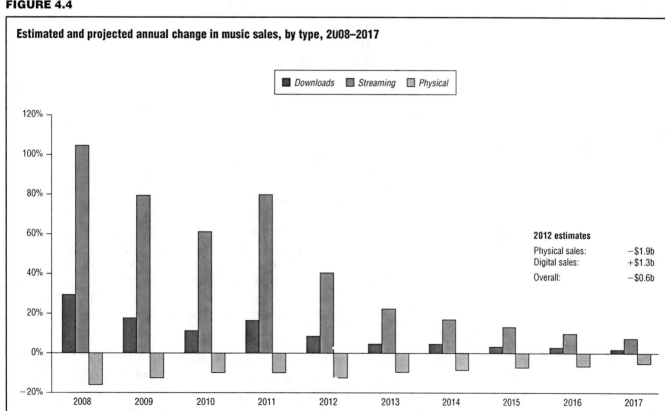

Estimated and projected annual change in music sales, by type, 2008–2017

2012 estimates
Physical sales: −$1.9b
Digital sales: +$1.3b
Overall: −$0.6b

SOURCE: Felix Richter, "Estimated Annual Change in Global Music Revenues, by Type (in %)," in *Streaming Boom Can't Offset Decline in Physical Music Sales*, Statista, August 20, 2012, http://www.statista.com/markets/14/topic/111/music-audio/chart/551/estimated-annual-change-in-global-music-revenues/ (accessed October 1, 2012)

could continue to sue peer-to-peer networks that allowed the sharing of copyrighted material for free. However, while the RIAA was suing Napster, a new problem arose. Networks began popping up that did not have a clearly defined center of operations. For example, the Kazaa and Gnutella networks had no central server to let members know who on the network had which songs. Instead, each member of the network installed a program that allowed him or her to see the individual music libraries of others on the network. Michael Desmond estimates in "Sneaky Sharing" (*PC World*, September 2, 2004, http://www .pcworld.com/article/117637/sneaky_sharing.html) that despite music industry attempts to curb illegal file sharing, users were developing new techniques for acquiring music as sales dropped from an all-time high of $14.6 billion in 2000 to $11.9 billion in 2003, which was well after the original Napster was shut down.

In late 2003 the RIAA began to go after individual file-swappers. Lee Rainie et al. of Pew/Internet report in *Data Memo: The Impact of Recording Industry Suits against Music File Swappers* (January 2004, http://www.pewinternet .org/~/media/Files/Reports/2004/PIP_File_Swapping_Memo _0104 .pdf.pdf) that the RIAA filed 382 lawsuits in 2003 against individual illegal music file swappers, most of whom quickly settled their cases for between $2,500 and $10,000.

On January 27, 2005, the RIAA announced 717 new lawsuits against individual file-swappers. Six months later, the U.S. Supreme Court made a landmark decision in favor of the movie and music industries. In *Metro-Goldwyn-Mayer Studios v. Grokster* (545 U.S. 913 [2005]), the court unanimously ruled that businesses that encourage others to steal intellectual property are liable for their customers' illegal actions. Because companies such as Grokster developed their technology almost solely for the purpose of swapping music and video files illegally, they likely were in violation of the ruling.

Inspired by the music industry's success, the MPAA also took steps to prevent piracy. Usually, the most damaging instances of piracy in the motion picture business occur when bootleggers digitally record movies in theaters as they watch the films. The bootleggers then transfer the recorded movies via the Internet to buyers, who then offer the movies on the Internet or make copies on a digital video disc and sell them in foreign countries. In "It's Curtains for Video Pirates" (*New Scientist*, August 14, 2004), Barry Fox explains that the Warner cinema chain began handing out night-vision goggles to some employees in California to look for these bootleggers during premiers. In 2004 the MPAA began working with the high-tech engineering firm Cinea in Reston, Virginia, to develop imaging techniques that would prevent digital camcorders from recording movies in theaters. One technique involved altering the frame rate in movies so that the film would move out of synchronization with most digital

camcorders' refresh rate, resulting in a copy of the movie that shudders when played. Finally, in November 2004 the MPAA announced that it, too, would be prosecuting individuals who used peer-to-peer networks to view movies. The organization filed 250 lawsuits in 2005 against individuals who downloaded movies. The MPAA also prosecuted websites such as isoHunt.com (http://isohunt.com/) and Torrentspy.com (http://www.torrentspy.com/) that directed visitors to places on the web where movies could be downloaded free of charge. As a result of these lawsuits, by 2012 Torrentspy.com had been permanently shut down, and isoHunt.com offered restricted service to U.S. users in compliance with court rulings.

Even with the success of these measures, however, online piracy remained a persistent problem for the entertainment industry. As the MPAA asserts in the press release "MPAA Statement on Strong Showing of Support for Stop Online Piracy Act" (December 16, 2011, http://www.mpaa .org/resources/5a0a212e-c86b-4e9a-abf1-2734a15862cd .pdf), U.S. losses due to content theft came to $58 billion in 2011. The MPAA urged members of Congress to pass a new law, the Stop Online Piracy Act (SOPA), as a means of cracking down on copyright infringement. Introduced in Congress in October 2011 by Representative Lamar Smith (1947–; R-TX), SOPA was referred to the House Subcommittee on Intellectual Property, Competition, and the Internet in December 2011. No further action had been taken as of December 2012.

DOJ Begins to Crack Down

Most litigation over copyright law is conducted in civil courts where individual citizens and organizations sue one another. If the defendant is found guilty, such as in the *RIAA v. Napster* case, then the defendant typically has to pay money to the plaintiff. In a criminal case the defendant serves jail or probationary time if found guilty. The DOJ is in charge of prosecuting criminal cases against people and organizations that violate national copyright laws. The DOJ also has specialized units based in cities where high-tech theft is common. These units are known as the Computer Hacking and Intellectual Property (CHIP) units, and they identify and help prosecute intellectual-property suspects. Most of these investigations involve international copyright crime organizations or individuals who make tens of thousands of dollars stealing intellectual property.

Responding to the increased threats to intellectual property brought on by new media, the U.S. attorney general, John D. Ashcroft (1942–), created the DOJ's Task Force on Intellectual Property in March 2004. The task force was assigned to examine the entire range of intellectual property theft from counterfeit automotive parts to the theft of trade secrets to copyright infractions in the entertainment industry. In October 2004 the task force published *Report of the Department of Justice's Task Force on Intellectual Property* (http://www.justice.gov/olp/ip_task_force_report.pdf), which included its recommendations on how to address the rise in intellectual property theft. The task force recommended that five additional specialized CHIP units be placed in areas rife with intellectual property theft and that more FBI agents be put on intellectual property theft cases. The task force also believed that more aggressive measures should be taken against crime organizations and individuals who infringe on copyrights. More specifically, the task force suggested that Congress pass an act making it illegal for people to post copyrighted material they do not own on the Internet.

In 2005 President George W. Bush (1946–) signed the Family Entertainment Copyright Act into law. Under this act any attempt to record a movie in a theater can result in federal prosecution, fines, and up to three years in prison. A similar sentence can be given to anyone who distributes a creative work that is intended for commercial distribution but has not been released, such as a video game or movie that is still in production. Since the passing of the act, a number of people have been prosecuted by the DOJ for violating the law (although most litigation still takes place in civil courts). Manuel Sandoval, a 70-year-old retired painter from Los Angeles, was the first person to be convicted under the new act in April 2006. He was caught recording the matinee showing of *The Legend of Zorro* in Los Angeles in October 2005. Table 4.6 shows the number of intellectual property crimes investigated and

prosecuted by the U.S. Attorney General's Office between 2007 and 2011. These figures represent crimes such as trafficking in counterfeit labels for audio recordings and copies of motion pictures; criminal infringement of copyright, including unlawful reproduction or distribution of copyrighted works; producing and distributing sounds and images of live musical performances without the consent of the performers; and trafficking in counterfeit goods or services. As Table 4.6 shows, the number of filed intellectual property theft cases peaked at 200 in 2007, before dropping to 150 in 2009 and 158 in 2010 and 2011.

Even with the number of prosecuted cases declining, copyright infringement remains a major concern of the federal government. As reported by the DOJ in the *2010 Joint Strategic Plan on Intellectual Property Enforcement*, in February 2010 the DOJ established a "revitalized DOJ Task Force on Intellectual Property." Two months later, the DOJ assigned 20 new FBI special agents, along with 15 new assistant U.S. attorneys, to investigate and prosecute cases involving intellectual property theft.

In the ensuing years, the prosecution of intellectual property crimes reached global proportions, requiring the collaboration of law enforcement agencies from across the world. One high-profile case emerged in January 2012, when authorities in New Zealand, working with the U.S. Department of Justice, arrested Kim Schmitz (alias Kim Dotcom), founder of the popular file-sharing site Megaupload, on charges of copyright infringement. In "Feds Shutter Megaupload, Arrest

TABLE 4.6

Intellectual property crimes investigated and prosecuted by the U.S. Department of Justice, fiscal years (FY) 2007–11

	All districts—all statutes				
	Fiscal years				
	2007	2008	2009	2010	2011
Referrals and cases					
Number of investigative matters received	368	303	243	343	330
Number of defendants	561	467	404	543	481
Number of cases filed	200	179	150	158	158
Number of defendants	268	239	203	239	203
Number of cases resolved/terminated	177	174	175	152	135
Number of defendants	278	270	230	212	206
Disposition of defendants in concluded cases					
Number of defendants who pleaded guilty	240	220	198	185	178
Number of defendants who were tried and found guilty	10	8	5	7	13
Number of defendants against whom charges were dismissed	15	26	21	14	11
Number of defendants acquitted	1	8	2	2	1
Other terminated defendants	12	8	4	4	3
Prison sentencing for convicted defendants (# represents defendants)					
No imprisonment	129	101	114	114	92
1 to 12 months imprisonment	44	46	31	33	26
13 to 24 months	33	39	27	25	31
25 to 36 months	18	20	6	9	15
37 to 60 months	11	19	17	7	21
61+ months	15	3	8	4	6

SOURCE: "Title 18. United States Code, Sections 2318, 2319, 2319A, 2320 or Title 17, United States Code, Section 506," in *FY 2011 Performance and Accountability Report*, U.S. Department of Justice, November 2011, http://www.justice.gov/ag/annualreports/pr2011/par2011.pdf (accessed October 1, 2012)

Executives" (January 19, 2012, http://www.wired.com/threatlevel/2012/01/megaupload-indicted-shuttered/), David Kravets reports at the time Megaupload accounted for 4% of all traffic on the Internet, receiving roughly 50 million visits per day.

Still, some experts began to question whether lawsuits or prosecutions were having any real impact on deterring intellectual property theft. As Mary Madden of Pew/Internet reports in *The State of Music Online: Ten Years after Napster* (June 15, 2009, http://www.pewinternet.org/~/media//Files/Reports/2009/The-State-of-Music-Online_-Ten-Years-After-Napster.pdf), by 2008 the RIAA began to scale back its litigation against violators, as it became increasingly clear that the lawsuits were doing little to stem the flow of material circulating illegally on the Internet. Indeed, the report reveals that the number of personal computers that had at least one P2P application grew from roughly 184 million in 2006 to more than 200 million in 2008. Clearly, file sharing was only increasing in popularity. Some observers believed that this trend signaled a larger movement toward a radically different economic model. In "Free! Why $0.00 Is the Future of Business" (*Wired*, February 25, 2008, http://www.wired.com/techbiz/it/magazine/16-03/ff_free?currentPage=all), Chris Anderson sparked fierce debate when he argued that providing free content was the best way for industries to attract consumers willing to pay for premium content and service. At about this time, music-streaming services such as Last.fm and Pandora, which offered consumers unlimited access to online music libraries for a monthly fee, began to compete with iTunes and other sites that sold music files. As illegal content-sharing continued unabated, innovative approaches to generating revenue were beginning to emerge.

In spite of the claims of the MPAA and other creative industries concerning lost revenues, it also remains unclear to what extent piracy exerts a negative impact on the economy. In *Intellectual Property: Observations on Efforts to Quantify the Economic Effects of Counterfeit and Pirated Goods* (April 2010, http://www.gao.gov/new.items/d10423.pdf), the Government Accountability Office (GAO) questions the assumption that there is a one-to-one relationship (or substitution rate) between pirated materials and lost sales, as the various creative industries have insisted over the years. In other words, if an individual downloads an illegal copy of an album that retails for $15, it does not actually represent a $15 loss for the music industry, according to the GAO report. Citing a survey by Rafael Rob and Joel Waldfogel titled "Piracy on the High C's: Music Downloading, Sales Displacement, and Social Welfare in a Sample of College Students" (*Journal of Law and Economics*, April 2006), the GAO asserts that for every five illegal music downloads, one legitimate music sale is lost. At the same time,

the survey finds that the average college student values pirated music between one-third and one-half less than he or she values music that is purchased. In many cases, the report suggests, a consumer has no intention of purchasing the music they have downloaded, regardless of whether or not it is available for free. The GAO concludes its report by stating that "it is difficult, if not impossible, to quantify the net effect of counterfeiting and piracy on the economy as a whole," in large part because relatively few studies investigating the positive effects of piracy have emerged.

Many outside observers have also challenged the accuracy of the economic losses claimed by the MPAA in its December 2011 press release. In "Cato Institute Digs into MPAA's Own Research to Show That SOPA Wouldn't Save a Single Net Job" (January 4, 2012, http://www.techdirt.com/articles/20120104/04545217274/cato-institute-digs-into-mpaas-own-research-to-show-that-sopa-wouldnt-save-single-net-job.shtml), Mike Masnick cites a Cato Institute report arguing that actual losses suffered by the entertainment industry in 2011 likely totaled only $446 million—less than 1% of the $58 billion originally claimed by the MPAA. During this time, privacy advocates began to express serious concern over granting the entertainment industry and other major corporations greater power to control Internet content, claiming that such a development posed a grave threat to the rights of individual citizens. As Kravets reports in "Megaupload Case Has Far-Reaching Implications for Cloud-Data Ownership Rights" (November 7, 2012, http://www.wired.com/threatlevel/2012/11/megaupload-data-what-to-do/), in the wake of Kim Dotcom's arrest, U.S. prosecutors blocked all traffic to the Megaupload site, preventing millions of users from accessing content they legally owned. As concerns over Internet freedom spread, opposition to proposed regulations such as SOPA became more vocal. Indeed, as David Lieberman reports in "Congress Puts Anti-Piracy Bill on Hold" (January 20, 2012, http://www.deadline.com/2012/01/senate-postpones-vote-on-anti-piracy-protect-ip-act/), widespread public outcry against SOPA ultimately forced Senate Majority Leader Harry Reid (D-NV; 1939–) to postpone a vote on the bill indefinitely, while members of Congress worked to address ways to protect the privacy rights of Internet users.

CHILD PORNOGRAPHY AND OTHER INTERNET-RELATED CRIMES

Unlike any other technology in human history, the Internet has enabled individuals to communicate with unprecedented speed and frequency. One of the downsides of the Internet's ability to help people share information more easily, however, is that it also provides criminals and other predators with a powerful weapon to use against potential victims. One area of major concern to law enforcement officials is the proliferation of child pornography on the Internet. As Table 4.7 shows, between March 10 and December 31, 1998, the National Center for Missing & Exploited Children (NCMEC) received 3,175 reports of child pornography through its CyberTipline, an online reporting system; by comparison, between January 1 and November 30, 2011, the Cyber-Tipline received 267,468 reports of child pornography. Between March 1998 and November 2011, the organization received a total of 1,151,419 reports of child pornography, as well as 54,729 reports of online enticements. (See Table 4.8.) Online enticements are cases in which a predator uses the Internet to "identify, and then coerce, their victims to engage in illegal sex acts."

Technological innovations have also created avenues for new forms of online criminal behavior. One disturbing new trend that emerged with the increasingly widespread popularity of wireless handheld devices was called sexting. Sexting is defined as the practice through which individuals share sexually suggestive images of each other via text message. As Amanda Lenhart of Pew/Internet reports in *Teens and Sexting* (December 15, 2009, http://pewresearch.org/assets/pdf/teens-and-sexting.pdf), among teens aged 12 to 17 who own cell phones, 15% have received nude or seminude images from someone they know in a text message, and 4% admit to having sent sexually suggestive images of themselves.

One website that has come under increasing criticism for abetting criminal behavior in recent years is Craigslist. In addition to providing online classified ads for such things as apartment rentals and sales of goods, Craigslist also allows users to post listings for services. While most of these listings are legitimate, they can also make it easier for online predators to attract victims. In one notable case (August 15, 2010, http://www.boston.com/news/local/breaking_news/2010/08/accused_craigsl_2.html), Boston University Medical School student Philip Markoff (1986–2010) was arrested in April 2009 for the murder of Julissa Brisman (1983–2009), a masseuse whom Markoff had contacted through the website's adult services section. Dubbed the "Craigslist Killer," Markoff killed himself in his jail cell in August 2010, before standing trial for the murder. In the wake of these and other incidents, law enforcement officials urged Craigslist to shut down its adult services listings altogether. As Evan Hansen reports in "Censored! Craigslist Adult Services Banned in U.S." (*Wired*, September 4, 2010, http://www.wired.com/epicenter/2010/09/censored-craigslist-adult-services-blocked-in-u-s/), the website's adult services listings often served as a cover for prostitution and other forms of illegal sex-trafficking. Craigslist resisted opposition to its policy on adult listings for years, largely for financial reasons. As Hansen reports, the adult services section accounted for roughly 30% of the company's total revenue in 2010. Still, negative publicity and increased pressure from state attorneys continued to plague the online classifieds site, and in September 2010 Craigslist abruptly discontinued its adult services listings, replacing it with a black bar reading "Censored."

HIGH-TECH LAW ENFORCEMENT

Criminals have not been the only ones taking advantage of high tech. Since the 1980s new technologies have provided law enforcement with myriad resources to combat crime and protect citizens. Video cameras have helped tremendously in identifying thieves who rob automated teller machines, banks, and convenience stores. Wiretaps and surveillance equipment have allowed law

TABLE 4.7

Comparison of CyberTipline reports, March 30–December 31, 1998 and January 1–November 30, 2011, by category

Type of report	1998 reports (Mar. 10–Dec. 31)	2011 reports (Jan. 1–Nov. 30)
Child pornography (possession, manufacture and distribution)	3,175	267,468
Child prostitution	142	1,563
Child sex tourism	79	244
Child sexual molestation (not in the family)	365	1,718
Online enticement of children for sexual acts	707	3,306
Unsolicited obscene material sent to a child	NA[a]	453
Misleading domain name	NA[b]	406
Misleading words or digital images on the Internet	NA[c]	1,558
Submitted without incident type	92	3
Total reports	**4,560**	**276,719**

[a]This category was added in 2002 to reflect reports received.
[b]This category was added in 2004 to reflect reports received.
[c]This category was added in 2008.

SOURCE: "Comparison of CyberTipline Reports for 1998 and 2011," in *Google Technology Makes Reporting Child Sexual Exploitation Easier*, National Center for Missing and Exploited Children, December 28, 2011, http://www.missingkids.com/missingkids/servlet/NewsEventServlet?LanguageCountry=en_US&PageId=4604 (accessed October 8, 2011)

TABLE 4.8

Total CyberTipline reports, 1998–2011

Type of incident	To date
Child pornography	1,151,419
Child prostitution	10,928
Child sex tourism	3,869
Child sexual molestation (not in family)	20,689
Online enticement of children for sexual acts	54,729
Unsolicited obscene material sent to a child	9,289
Misleading domain name	10,197
Misleading words or digital images on the Internet	7,266
Submitted without incident type	865
Total number of reports	**1,269,251**

source: "Total Number of CyberTipline Reports through November 30, 2011," in *Google Technology Makes Reporting Child Sexual Exploitation Easier*, National Center for Missing and Exploited Children, December 28, 2011, http://www.missingkids.com/missingkids/servlet/NewsEventServlet?LanguageCountry=en_US&PageId=4604 (accessed October 8, 2011)

enforcement officials to catch criminals without putting themselves in harm's way. However, the biggest boon to law enforcement by far has been the increased access law enforcement officers have had to information. During the 1970s, for example, if a law enforcement officer in New York wanted the records of a criminal in California, he or she would have to call a police station in California and have the information read over the phone. Computer databases and communications technologies have connected law enforcement offices and provided them easy access to criminal records across the country. In 1995 the FBI launched Law Enforcement Online, or LEO (http://www.fbi.gov/about-us/cjis/leo), an online communication and data system that enables law enforcement agencies from around the world to exchange information about criminal investigations. Originally comprising just 20 members using a dial-up network, by 2012 LEO had more than 100,000 participants worldwide. At the same time, phone networks and portable computers have also given the police the ability to access criminal records and information on license plates and license holders from within the patrol car. Electronic credit and debit card networks, bank machines, and rental car records have all provided law enforcement with easily accessible, real-time information on where criminals have been and where they are going.

Communications technologies have also allowed law enforcement agencies to inform communities of terrorism, kidnapping, or other criminal activity to bring the perpetrators to justice. America's Missing: Broadcast Emergency Response (AMBER) Plan is named after nine-year-old Amber Hagerman (1986–1996), who was kidnapped and murdered in Arlington, Texas, in 1996. After her murder Texas instituted the first statewide AMBER Plan in 1999. Since that time the program has been introduced by the DOJ into the 49 other states. When an AMBER Alert is issued, the regional Emergency Alert System is used to tell the public about the missing child. Programs on television and radio stations are interrupted and followed by pertinent information about the abduction. All law enforcement officers are put on alert, and digital emergency signs above the highways tell people on the freeway where to receive more information about the abduction. The DOJ's AMBER Alert statistics (2012, http://www.amberalert.gov/statistics.htm) indicate that as of December 2012, 595 children had been recovered as a result of the plan. In the *National Center for Missing and Exploited Children 2011 AMBER Alert Report* (2012, http://www.amberalert.gov/pdfs/11_amber_report.pdf), the NCMEC analyzes the effectiveness of AMBER Alert broadcasts. In nearly three-quarters (71%) of cases in which children were safely recovered in 2011, either a law enforcement official or another individual recognized the vehicle described in an AMBER Alert (50%), or else an individual contacted authorities after recognizing either the child or the abductor after hearing an AMBER Alert broadcast (21%).

In the meantime, the continually-evolving nature of online threats posed arguably the biggest challenge to law enforcement agencies in the 21st century. As Dawn Kawamato reports in "The Top Ten Looming Computer Security Threats of 2012" (January 3, 2012, http://www.dailyfinance.com/2012/01/03/the-top-10-looming-computer-security-threats-of-2012/), criminals had developed increasingly sophisticated modes of launching online attacks by 2012, while developing the capacity to inflict extensive damage onto both public and private computer systems. Some of the biggest emerging threats included attacks on industrial systems, hacktivist activities targeting government agencies and other public entities, and "cyber warfare" between antagonistic nations. (See Chapter 7, "Information Technology and Government.")

CHAPTER 5
ELECTRONICS, THE INTERNET, AND ENTERTAINMENT MEDIA

For many Americans, new technologies simply mean new toys. Almost every advancement in consumer technology since the 1980s has in some way been tied to entertainment. In *Statistical Abstract of the United States: 2011* (2011, http://www.census.gov/compendia/statab/2011/tables/11s1130.pdf), the U.S. Census Bureau examines the amount of money Americans spent between 2003 and 2008 for media content, which included pay-television subscriptions, video games, home video, and music. On average, Americans aged 12 years and older spent $882.02 on all media in 2008, which was $142.27 more than they spent in 2003, a 19.2% increase. In general, media usage also increased during this span. In 2008 the average American aged 12 and older watched 1,693 hours of television, compared with 1,548 in 2003. During this period, however, broadcast television saw an 8.7% decline in viewership, from 701 hours per person in 2003 to 640 in 2008; at the same time, viewing of cable and satellite television services grew from 847 hours per person in 2003 to 1,053 in 2008, a 24.3% increase.

Even though television was still the media outlet of choice in 2012, Americans have been rapidly turning to new forms of entertainment made available by the Internet and other technologies. According to "Trend Data" compiled by the Pew Internet & American Life Project (Pew/Internet; 2012, http://www.pewinternet.org/Static-Pages/Trend-Data-%28Adults%29/Online-Activites-Total.aspx), as of August 2011, 74% of American adults who used the Internet had surfed websites for fun. In 2012, 91% reported they had gone online to use a search engine, 69% had visited a social networking site such as Facebook or Google Plus, and 16% had read or posted text on Twitter.

ELECTRONIC GAMING

Once considered the pastime of children and socially challenged adults, video and computer games now represent a major form of entertainment in the United States. Video games, also known as console and arcade games, are played using a computer that is specifically designed to play games. By contrast, computer games are just one type of program that can be run on standard personal computers. The difference between the two types of games is in how they are accessed, not necessarily in their content. Many games can be played using either a video game system or a computer. Thus, the terms *video game* and *computer game* are sometimes used interchangeably. According to Kathryn Zickuhr of Pew/Internet (February 3, 2011, http://www.pewinternet.org/~/media//Files/Reports/2011/PIP_Generations_and_Gadgets.pdf), 63% of adults between the ages of 18 and 46 owned gaming consoles in 2010. (See Figure 5.1.) In *Essential Facts about the Video Gaming Industry* (2012, http://www.theesa.com/facts/pdfs/ESA_EF_2012.pdf), the Entertainment Software Association (ESA) reports that the average American household owned at least one personal computer, gaming console, or smart phone in 2012. Of households that owned PCs, consoles, smart phones, handheld gaming devices, or wireless gaming devices, 70% played games on their consoles, 65% played on their PCs, and 38% played on their smart phones. Indeed, during this time games designed for mobile devices steadily grew in popularity, particularly among younger adults. As Zickuhr reports, 57% of cell phone users between the ages of 18 and 34 used their mobile phones to play video games in 2010.

On the whole, parents view video games as having a positive impact on the lives of their children. According to the ESA in *Essential Facts about the Video Gaming Industry*, more than half (52%) of parents considered video games "a positive part of their children's lives" in 2012. Of these, 66% believed that video games provided their children with mental or intellectual stimulation, 61% viewed video games as a valuable way of spending family time, and 59% saw video games as an important means of encouraging children to socialize with friends. In general, gaming had become increasingly social by 2012. As the ESA reports, 62% of all

FIGURE 5.1

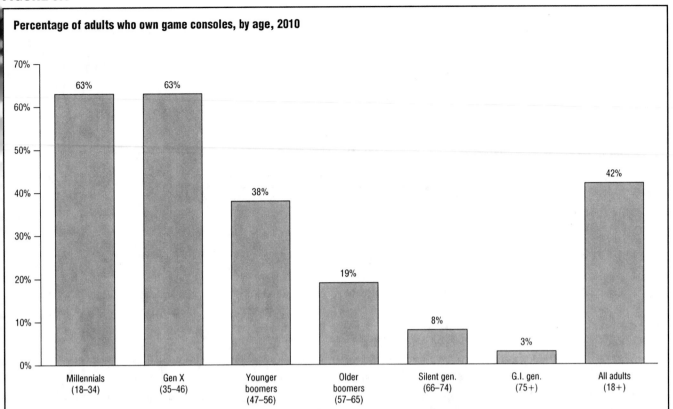

Percentage of adults who own game consoles, by age, 2010

SOURCE: Kathryn Zickuhr, "Do You Own a Game Console, Like an Xbox or Play Station?" in *Generations and Their Gadgets*, Pew Internet & American Life Project, February 3, 2011, http://www.pewinternet.org/~/media//Files/Reports/2011/PIP_Generations_and_Gadgets.pdf (accessed October 8, 2012). Used by permission of the Pew Internet & American Life Project, which bears no responsibility for the interpretations presented or conclusions reached based on analysis of the data.

gamers participated in games involving other people, either in person or over the Internet.

Rise of Video and Computer Games

Computer and video games are almost as old as computers. Many credit Alexander Shafto Douglas (1921–2010) with creating the first graphics-based computer game at Cambridge University in England in 1952. Part of his doctoral research on human-computer interaction, the game was played on an enormous Electronic Delay Storage Automatic Calculator (EDSAC) computer, which was one of the first computers in existence and was made primarily from rows and rows of vacuum tubes. The EDSAC display screen was a 35-by-16 array of monochromatic dots. The name of Douglas's game was *OXO*, or *Noughts and Crosses*, a human-versus-machine version of tic-tac-toe in which the human player chose the first square. Ten years later, computer games were developed on mainframe computers and eventually on ARPANET, the nationwide network of military defense computers that preceded the Internet.

One of the more popular games that spread to computer mainframes across the United States during the 1960s was *Spacewar! Spacewar!* was created in 1961 by Steve Russell (1937–), Martin Graetz (1935–), and Wayne Wiitanen (1935–) at the Massachusetts Institute of Technology to test the capabilities of the $120,000 Digital Equipment Corporation PDP-1 computer. The game consisted of two low-resolution ships, one shaped like a needle and the other like a wedge, flying around a dot that represented a sun in the middle of the screen. The object was to destroy the other player's ship while maneuvering through the sun's gravitational pull.

In 1971 Nutting Associates released *Computer Space*, the first video game for the general public. *Computer Space*, a direct imitator of *Spacewar!*, was set in a futuristic arcade-style cabinet. Most people considered the game too complicated at the time, so Nutting only made 1,500 units and then stopped production. The next year, however, Atari released *Pong*. In this monochromatic game, a small cube was bounced back and forth between two slightly larger rods controlled by the player(s). The video game was a smash hit, and Atari sold more than 800,000 arcade cabinets. A month earlier, Magnavox released the Odyssey, which was the first home-console video game system that ran on a television set. The Odyssey, which sold for $100 (about $550 in 2012 dollars), had several different games installed on it, all of which involved hitting a pixilated square (or squares) on the screen with rectangles. According to the Atari Museum (2012, http://www.atarimuseum.com/videogames/dedicated/homepong.html), the Atari home version of *Pong* was released in 1975 and sold over 150,000 units during the holiday season alone.

Golden Age of Video Games

Within a year after these initial offerings, video games quickly gained a foothold in the United States. A steady stream of unremarkable cabinet games was released throughout the 1970s. For most of the decade, video games were novelties that sat next to pinball machines in bowling alleys, bars, and roller-skating rinks. With the arrival of *Asteroids* and *Space Invaders* in 1978, arcade video games came into their own. *Space Invaders*, a game in which the player shot row after row of advancing aliens, triggered a nationwide coin shortage in Japan so severe the Japanese government had to more than double yen production. Namco introduced the first color game in 1979 with the arrival of *Galaxian*, and then in 1980 the company released *Pac-Man*. The original name of the game was *Puckman*, derived from the Japanese *pakupaku*, which means "flapping open and closed" (e.g., the character's mouth). Despite the game's simple concept of guiding a yellow, dot-eating ball around a maze, over 100,000 arcade units were sold in the United States. The game inspired an entire line of merchandise from lunch boxes to stuffed toys. Between 1980 and 1983 many colorful, engaging video games were released, including *Defender*, *Donkey Kong*, *Centipede*, *Frogger*, and *Ms. Pac-Man*, which still holds the record for the most arcade games sold at 115,000, according to William Hunter, in "Player 2 Stage 4: Two Superstars" (2012, http://www.emuunlim.com/doteaters/play2sta4.htm). Video arcades sprang up in every mall and town in the United States. On January 18, 1982, the cover of *Time* magazine read: GRONK! FLASH! ZAP! VIDEO GAMES ARE BLITZING THE WORLD. The cover story, "Games That Play People" by John Skow, revealed that in 1981 nearly $5 billion in quarters (about $12.8 billion in 2012 dollars) was spent playing arcade games. By comparison, the U.S. film industry took in $2.8 billion that year (about $7.2 billion in 2012 dollars).

At the same time, game consoles were gaining popularity in living rooms across the United States. In 1977 Atari launched the Atari VCS (later named the Atari 2600) for $250 (about $959 in 2012 dollars). By Christmas 1979 sales were brisk as people realized that the system could support more than just *Pong*. With the release of *Space Invaders* on the system the following year, units flew off the shelves at $150 a piece (roughly $423 in 2012 dollars). Tekla E. Perry and Paul Wallich explain in "Design Case History: The Atari Video Computer System" (*IEEE Spectrum*, March 1983) that Atari sold over 12 million consoles between 1977 and 1983.

More than 200 games were made for the system. Other video systems such as Intellivision and Colecovision gained huge followings as well. Skow noted that 600,000 Intellivision units were sold in 1981. Overall, 1981 sales for home video games exceeded $1 billion (approximately $2.6 billion in 2012 dollars).

Video Game Industry Stumbles

By 1984 the Commodore 64 home computer had debuted at $1,000 ($2,236 in 2012 dollars), and the Apple IIc was introduced at the comparatively affordable price of $1,300 ($2,907 in 2012 dollars). Such computers not only offered better graphics than the contemporary video game consoles but also they were useful for practical applications such as spreadsheets and word processors. Consequently, people began to lose interest in video games and buy home computers instead. In 1983, faced with a collapsing video game market, losses of hundreds of millions of dollars, and far too much inventory, Atari loaded 14 tractor-trailer trucks with thousands of unsold cartridges and pieces of hardware. It drove the surplus out to a landfill site in Alamogordo, New Mexico, and buried the inventory in a concrete bunker under the desert. The following year Warner Communications, the owner of Atari, sold the game and computer divisions of Atari to Jack Tramiel (1928–2012), the founder of Commodore. Mattel, the maker of Intellivision, also shed its electronics division, and hundreds of arcades closed as well.

For several years gaming was relegated to the computer. Before 1983 computer games were low on graphics and heavy on text, but by 1984 a number of colorful and entertaining games became available for home computers, including the *Ultima* and *King's Quest* series. However, toy and electronics manufacturers in the United States were wary of investing in video game consoles after the Atari disaster.

Japanese companies were not nearly as pessimistic and continued to invest money into video console development. Nintendo, a company that originally manufactured Japanese playing cards, surprised the entire gaming market in 1986 when it released the Nintendo Entertainment System (NES). The games looked better than most arcade games from the early 1980s and took as long to play through as computer games. After two years on the market, the NES found its way into almost as many homes as the Atari 2600. As Pat Davies reported in "The Hottest Game in Town" (*Globe and Mail*, May 19, 1989), the sales of NES video games in 1988 reached $1.7 billion ($3.3 billion in 2012 dollars) in the United States alone. Arcades at the time also enjoyed a brief revival with the advent of complex fighting games such as *Mortal Kombat* and *Street Fighter II*. *Mortal Kombat*, which eventually made it onto the NES, inspired a congressional investigation into violence in video games and led to the establishment in 1994 of the Entertainment Software Rating Board, an industry self-regulatory organization that monitors the content of video games for depictions of violence, nudity, profanity, and other material that parents might find objectionable for young children.

Current and Future Gaming

Since the late 1980s the U.S. electronic gaming market has continued its rise, with the majority of the gaming industry's revenues coming from console systems and games. After the NES ran its course with estimated sales of 60 million units worldwide, the Sega Genesis video game system enjoyed a period of popularity. The electronics giant Sony entered the fray in 1995 when it released PlayStation in the United States. Nintendo answered Sony's challenge with Nintendo 64 in 1996, which sold 1.7 million units in the United States in the first three months, according to Michael Miller, in "A History of Home Video Game Consoles" (April 1, 2005, http://www.informit.com/articles/article.aspx?p=378141). In 2000 Sony PlayStation launched the PlayStation2. Taking note of the profits brought in by successful gaming systems, Microsoft, the largest software firm in the United States, launched the Xbox in 2001. Both Sony and Microsoft funded enormous advertising campaigns to promote their systems, and Microsoft sold its system at a loss to introduce it into more homes. Peter Lewis stated in "Should You Wait for the PS3?" (*Fortune*, November 22, 2005, http://money.cnn.com/2005/11/21/technology/playstation_fortune_1128 05/) that over 96 million PlayStation 2 consoles and 25 million Xbox systems had sold worldwide by the end of 2005. With the release of the Xbox 360 in 2005 and the PlayStation 3 and Nintendo Wii in 2006, the video game market enjoyed double-digit year-over-year growth.

By decade's end, however, overall sales began to slip. The marketing research firm NPD Group reports in the press release "2009 U.S. Video Game Industry and PC Game Software Retail Sales Reach $20.2 Billion" (January 14, 2010, http://www.npd.com/press/releases/press_100114.html) that retail video games produced roughly $19.7 billion in sales in 2009, an 8% drop from 2008 revenues of $21.4 billion. Sales of console hardware saw the biggest decline (13%), while console and portable software also saw sales decrease by approximately 10%. Sales fell even further in 2011, according to the NPD Group in "2011 Total Consumer Spending on All Games Content in the U.S. Estimated between $16.3 to $16.6 Billion" (January 12, 2012, https://www.npd.com/wps/portal/npd/us/news/press-releases/pr_120116/), as gaming revenues totaled between $16.3 and $16.6 billion, a decline of approximately 16% since 2009.

Overall, the computer game market has grown at a slower pace than the video game market. During the 1990s with the advent of Microsoft's Windows operating system, the computer game market split in two. Solitaire and countless other card and puzzle games found their way onto the desktops of every personal computer and provided a brief escape from work or schoolwork. At the same time, computers also became the platform for cutting-edge strategy and shooting games, which are generally played by a relatively small, devoted computer-gaming audience. Graphics-intensive games such as *Quake* and *Half Life 2* led to increased sales in computer components as gamers bought extra memory and bigger hard drives to boost computer performance to handle advanced graphic engines.

In the mid-1990s computer games began to go online. Hardcore fans of card games and battle and quest adventures found competitors on the Internet. The next generation of console systems also enabled gamers to go online and play against one another. In "The Future of Online Gaming" (*PC Magazine*, March 27, 2003), Cade Metz noted that by 2002 online gaming traffic made up nearly 9% of the overall traffic along the Internet backbone in the United States. The fastest growing segment of online gaming appeared to be in the console game market. Xbox Live, an online service for the Xbox, gained 350,000 subscriptions at the beginning of 2003. In 2005 Microsoft launched a more advanced version of the console, the Xbox 360. As Todd Bishop reports in "Xbox 360 Tops Wii and PS3 for 1st Time in Yearly Global Sales" (February 3, 2012, http://www.geekwire.com/2012/xbox-360-tops-wii-ps3-1st-time-yearly-global-sales/), by early 2012 Microsoft had sold 66 million Xbox 360 consoles worldwide.

By this time new technological innovations had created a rapidly expanding market for other gaming platforms. In *Teens, Kindness and Cruelty on Social Network Sites* (November 2011, http://pewinternet.org/~/media//Files/Reports/2011/PIP_Teens_Kindness_Cruelty_SNS_Report_Nov_2011_FINAL_110711.pdf), Amanda Lenhart et al. find that 50% of teens used social media sites such as Facebook or Twitter to play games in 2011. (See Table 5.1.) Younger teens were far more likely to seek gaming opportunities on social networking sites; as the report reveals, 69% of teens aged 12 to 13 played games on social media platforms, compared with 44% of teens between the ages of 14 and 17.

Gaming Violence and Addiction

Over the years games have grown exceedingly more complex and engaging. The *Sims* series by Electronic Arts Inc. has provided gamers with a "real-life" fantasy world where they can simulate alternate lives. Game series such as *Doom* and *Grand Theft Auto* allow people to take out their aggressions on virtual demons or rival gang members. Massively multiplayer online role-playing games (MMORPGs; in which a large number of players interact

TABLE 5.1

Teen activities on social networking sites, 2011

Send instant messages or chat with a friend through the social network site	88%
Post comments on something a friend has posted	87
Post a status update	86
Post a photo or video	80
Send private messages to a friend within the social network site	76
Tag people in posts, photos or videos	69
Play a game on a social network site	50
Median # of activities	6

Notes: Population = 799 for teens 12 to 17 years of age and parents, including oversample of minority families. Interviews were conducted in English and Spanish.

SOURCE: Amanda Lenhart et al., "How Teens Use Social Media Sites," in *Teens, Kindness and Cruelty on Social Network Sites*, Pew Internet & American Life Project, November 2011, http://pewinternet.org/~/media//Files/Reports/2011/PIP_Teens_Kindness_Cruelty_SNS_Report_Nov_2011_FINAL_110711.pdf (accessed October 8, 2012). Used by permission of the Pew Internet & American Life Project, which bears no responsibility for the interpretations presented or conclusions reached based on analysis of the data.

with each other in a virtual world that continues even when a player is offline), such as *World of Warcraft*, open up entire fantasy worlds where players are free to roam and embark on quests with other gamers.

As the complexity of games has grown, so, too, has the temptation for many to play video games in excess to escape their problems. Although still a relatively unstudied phenomenon, gaming addiction appears to be more and more commonplace. In "Video Game Addiction: A Medical Disorder?" (January 18, 2011, http://www.cbsnews.com/2100-204_162-2965003.html), CBS News cites an American Medical Association (AMA) report claiming that by 2011 up to five million American children were addicted to video games. Many psychologists believe games provide a means of escape for people with stressful lives or mental problems in much the same way as drugs and alcohol. A number of symptoms that accompany gaming addiction are similar to those of other impulse control disorders, including alcoholism and drug abuse. These include preoccupation with gaming life over real-life events, failed attempts to stem gaming behavior, having a sense of well-being while playing games, craving more game time as well as feeling irritable when not playing, neglecting family and friends, lying about the amount of time spent gaming, and denying the adverse effects of too much gaming. In June 2007 the Council on Science and Public Health urged the AMA to classify excessive gaming an addiction. Lindsey Tanner reports in "Is Video-Game Addiction a Mental Disorder?" (Associated Press, June 22, 2007, http://www.msnbc.msn.com/id/19354827/) that advocates of this classification hope the move will bring attention to the plight of those whose lives are affected by excessive gaming and will enable affected families to gain insurance coverage for treatment. As Nicholas K. Geranios reports in "Internet Addiction Center Opens in U.S."

(Associated Press, September 4, 2009, http://usatoday30.usatoday.com/tech/news/2009-09-03-internet-addiction_N.htm), the first residential Internet addiction treatment facility in the United States was founded in Fall City, Washington, in July 2009. Dubbed ReSTART, the center offers a 45-day treatment program, at a cost of $14,000. In response to mounting concerns about gaming and other forms of online addiction, in 2012 the American Psychiatric Association decided to list "Internet use disorder" as a subject "recommended for further study" in the fifth edition of the *Diagnostic and Statistical Manual for Mental Disorders*, due to be published in May 2013.

Another problem people have with video games is violence. Parents and teachers have always been concerned that violent games may lead to violent aggressive behavior. Fears were fueled in 1999 by the shootings at Columbine High School in Littleton, Colorado, where two teenage students killed 15 people. In their suicide note, the murderers said they drew inspiration from the video game *Doom*. In *Grand Theft of Innocence? Teens and Video Games* (September 16, 2003, http://www.gallup.com/poll/9253/Grand-Theft-Innocence-Teens-Video-Games.aspx), Steve Crabtree of the Gallup Organization indicates that many parents and educators are concerned about the violence in video games such as *Grand Theft Auto*. Crabtree states that the concern is perhaps justified. Nearly three-quarters (74%) of teens played video games at least one hour per week in 2003, and 60% of teens had at some point played a game in the *Grand Theft Auto* series. Not only do such violent games give teens a false impression of adult life, but also studies show that the games may hinder social development in some teens. According to Crabtree, a 2001 study at Tokyo University revealed that violent games stunt the development of the brain's frontal lobe, which is the part of the brain that controls antisocial behavior.

The ease with which young teens were able to obtain violent video games was also a cause for concern. As the Nielsen Company reports in *Grand Theft Auto: The Brand That Hits (and Injures and Steals and ... Sells)* (August 2008, http://www.mediainsight.nl/media/grandtheftauto4_final_8_11_08.pdf), 17% of all video gamers who purchased *Grand Theft Auto IV* in 2008 were between the ages of seven and 16. Sixty-one percent of these reported having purchased the games themselves. Of those who had someone else purchase the game for them, 80% acquired it through a parent or guardian. To confront this trend, some state governments began to craft legislation aimed at keeping violent video games out of the hands of children. In 2005 the state of California passed a law making it illegal to sell violent video games to minors. The ESA challenged the legislation in federal court, and in 2009 the U.S. Ninth Court of Appeals declared the law unconstitutional. As Bill Mears reports in "California Ban on Sale of 'Violent' Video Games to Children Rejected" (June 27, 2011, http://articles.cnn.com/2011-06-27/us/scotus.video.games_1_violent-video-games-game-makers-interactive-games?_s=PM:US), in June 2011 the Supreme Court of the United States ruled the California law unconstitutional by a 7 to 2 vote.

In spite of the negative consequences sometimes associated with video games, several studies examining the positive effects of gaming have emerged over the years. In *Video Games and Your Family* (2010), the Media Awareness Network outlined numerous benefits that video games offered children. According to the report, video games had the potential to teach reading and other learning skills, promote socialization with other game players, and help young people feel more comfortable with technology. At the same time, the report cautions that the violent images found in some video games can have a negative impact on a young child's development, and that parents should play a role in steering their children away from potentially traumatizing games. Other researchers have questioned the link between violent video games and aggressive behavior altogether. In "The Hitman Study: Violent Video Game Exposure Effects on Aggressive Behavior, Hostile Feelings, and Depression" (*European Psychologist*, 2010), Christopher J. Ferguson and Stephanie M. Rueda of Texas A&M International University find that there is no proven connection between violent games and aggression, while suggesting that in some cases violent games can actually help individuals suffering from depression or other mood disorders. In "Violent Video Games Not So Bad When Players Cooperate" (September 4, 2012, http://www.sciencedaily.com/releases/2012/09/120904170724.htm), the website ScienceDaily cites a pair of 2012 studies suggesting that college students who team up with their peers to play violent video games exhibit less aggression than individuals who play video games by themselves; at the same time, students who collaborate while playing violent video games demonstrate improved abilities to work with others cooperatively. "Most of the studies finding links between violent games and aggression were done with people playing alone," David Ewoldsen, a communications professor at Ohio State University and co-author of the studies, told Science-Daily. "The social aspect of today's video games can change things quite a bit."

Online Gambling

There is no doubt inside or outside the scientific community that gambling can be addictive. One troubling development on the Internet in the early 2000s was the continued rise in online gambling. According to a congressional statement by the U.S. deputy assistant attorney general John G. Malcolm (March 18, 2003, http://banking.senate.gov/03_03hrg/031803/malcolm.htm), 700 Internet gambling sites existed in 1999. By 2003 the U.S. Department of Justice estimated that 1,800 gambling sites were in place, bringing in roughly $4.2 billion. As Enjoli Francis of ABC News reports in "Online Gambling, Casinos to 'Sweep' U.S. in 2012" (December 28, 2011, http://abcnews.go.com/blogs/headlines/2011/12/winning-online-gambling-casinos-to-sweep-u-s-in-2012/), by 2011 online gambling was generating between $60 and $70 billion in revenues worldwide.

Many of these sites allow gamblers to wire money from their checking accounts into a gambling account run by the casino. When the player wishes to gamble, he or she simply goes online and begins a session. Because most of these big online gambling operations are based in foreign nations in the Caribbean or South America, the U.S. government cannot regulate them. Malcolm pointed to instances in which the online houses manipulated the software so that the odds of games such as blackjack are skewed heavily in the house's favor. Other fly-by-night gambling operations had simply run off with people's money. Even when these gambling houses are honest, they are still perceived as a threat to society by many lawmakers. People addicted to gambling, for example, might log in and gamble unfettered for hours at a time from work or home. They might lose hundreds or thousands of dollars with a few clicks of the mouse.

Malcolm also addressed the issue of money laundering through online casinos. Criminals who make their money from illegal activities such as drugs are known to use online casino accounts to stash their profits. Once the money is in the casino, the crooks use the games themselves to transfer money to their associates. Some criminals set up private tables at online casino sites and then intentionally lose their money to business associates at the table. In other instances, the casino is part of the crime organization. All the criminal has to do in these cases is to lose money to the casino.

In October 2006 Congress approved the Unlawful Internet Gambling Enforcement Act (Title VIII of the Security and Accountability for Every Port Act of 2006), which made it illegal for banks and credit card companies in the United States to make payments to Internet gambling sites, effectively ending online gambling nationwide. The prohibition was rooted in the Federal Wire Act of 1961, which outlawed the use of wire communication to transmit bets or wagers. As Michael McCarthy and Jon Swartz report in "New Legislation May Pull the Plug on Online Gambling" (October 3, 2006, http://usatoday30.usatoday.com/news/washington/2006-10-02-internet-gambling-usat_x.htm), PartyGaming, the world's largest online gambling company, generated 80% of its $1 billion revenue in 2005 from 920,000 active customers in the United States. At the time of the ban, the U.S. market accounted for an estimated 50% to 60% of online gambling worldwide.

After the passage of the act, several bills came under consideration to review and revise the regulation of online gaming. Among the items introduced were the Skill Game Protection Act, a bill sponsored by U.S. Representative Robert Wexler (1961–; D-FL) in 2007, which set out to exempt such games as poker, backgammon, and other games requiring skill from regulation under the Unlawful Internet Gambling Enforcement Act; the Internet Gambling Regulation, Consumer Protection, and Enforcement Act, sponsored by Barney Frank (1940–; D-MA) in 2009, which proposed legalizing online gambling under a new system of federal oversight and regulation; and the Internet Gambling Regulation and Tax Enforcement Act, a bill sponsored by Jim McDermott (1936–; D-WA) in 2010, which proposed licensing operators of Internet gambling sites and imposing taxes and fees on both gamers and site operators. A turning point in the legal struggle over online gambling came in December 2011, when the U.S. Justice Department declared that the 1961 Wire Act applied solely to sports-related gambling. As Nathan Vardi reports in "Department of Justice Flip-Flops on Internet Gambling" (December 23, 2011, http://www.forbes.com/sites/nathan vardi/2011/12/23/department-of-justice-flip-flops-on-internet-gambling/), the decision enabled states to begin selling lottery tickets online, while also creating a legal opening for Internet poker and other forms of casino gambling sites.

RECORDED MUSIC

The conversion from analog recordings to digital music during the 1980s changed the way Americans listened to music. Humans talk and listen in analog. When people speak, they create vibrations in their throats that then travel through the air around them like ripples in a pond. A membrane in the ear, known as an eardrum, picks up these vibrations, allowing people to hear. Patterns in these vibrations enable people to differentiate sounds from one another. Before compact discs (CDs) and MP3 files, all music was recorded in analog form. On a record player, the vibrations that create music are impressed into grooves on a vinyl disc. A needle passing over this impression vibrates in the same way, turning those vibrations into electrical waveforms that travel along a wire to an amplifier and into a speaker. With tape players, the analog waveforms are recorded in electronic form nearly verbatim on a magnetic tape.

The biggest problem with analog recordings is that each time the music is recorded or copied, the waveform degrades in quality much like a photocopy of an image. Digitizing the music resolves this problem of fidelity. To record and play music digitally, an analog-to-digital converter (ADC) and a digital-to-analog converter (DAC) are needed. In the recording process, the analog music is fed through the ADC, which samples the analog waveforms and then breaks them down into a series of binary numbers represented by zeros and ones. The numbers are then stored on a disc or a memory chip like any other type of digital information. To play the music back, these numbers are fed through a DAC. The DAC reads the numbers and reproduces the original analog waveform that then travels to the headphones or speakers. Because the numbers always reproduce a high-quality version of the original recording, no quality (fidelity) is lost, regardless of how many times the song is transferred or recorded.

Compact Discs

Digital music was first introduced into the U.S. mainstream in 1983 in the form of CDs. Klaas Compaan, a Dutch physicist, originally came up with the idea for the CD in 1969 and developed a glass prototype a year later at Philips Corporation. Over the next nine years both Philips and Sony worked on various prototypes of a CD player. In 1979 the two companies came together to create a final version and set the standards for the CD. The first CD players were sold in Japan and Europe in 1982 and then in the United States in 1983.

With a standard CD, music is recorded digitally on the surface of a polycarbonate plastic disc in a long spiral track 0.00002 inches (0.00005 cm) wide that winds from the center of the disk to the outer edges. A space 0.00006 inches (0.00015 cm) wide separates each ring of the spiral track from the one next to it. Tiny divots, or pits, a minimum of 0.00003 inches (0.00008 cm) long, are engraved into the surface of the track. The polycarbonate disc is then covered by a layer of aluminum, followed by a layer of clear acrylic. (See Figure 5.2.) As the disc spins in the disc drive, a laser follows this tiny track counterclockwise, and a light sensor, sitting next to the laser, tracks the changes in the laser light as it reflects off the CD. The laser strikes a nondivoted section of track, which causes the laser light to bounce off the aluminum and then back to the light sensor uninterrupted. However, each time the laser hits one of the divots along the CD track, the light is scattered. These flashes of light represent the binary code that makes up the music. Electronics

FIGURE 5.2

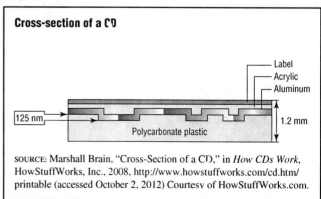

Cross-section of a CD

SOURCE: Marshall Brain, "Cross-Section of a CD," in *How CDs Work*, HowStuffWorks, Inc., 2008, http://www.howstuffworks.com/cd.htm/printable (accessed October 2, 2012) Courtesy of HowStuffWorks.com.

n the disc player read this code. The ones and zeros are then fed into a digital signal processor, which acts as a DAC, and the analog waveform for the music moves to the headphones or speakers.

When CD players were first released in the United States by both Sony and Philips in 1983, they were priced close to $900 a piece ($2,100 in 2012 dollars). The CDs themselves, which occupied a small section of the music store at the time, went for close to $20 a piece ($47 in 2012 dollars). Despite the high costs, the Census Bureau indicated in *Statistical Abstract of the United States: 2003* (2004, http://www.census.gov/prod/2004pubs/03statab/inforcomm.pdf) that 22.6 million CDs were sold in 1985. By 1990, 286.5 million CDs were sold. In *Statistical Abstract of the United States: 2012* (2012, http://www.census.gov/compendia/statab/2012/tables/12s1140.pdf), the Census Bureau reports that by 2000 this number peaked at 942.5 million, before plummeting to 225.8 million by 2010 due to competition from MP3 players and other digital and online music formats. Over the years CD players have become much more compact and have been equipped with many more features, often designed to increase sound quality. By 2013 personal CD players and portable CD stereo units were widely available for less than $50.

Rise of the MP3 Format

In 1985 the first CD read-only memory (CD-ROM) players were released for computers, again by Sony and Philips. CD-ROM players can read computer data from CD-ROMs as well as music from CDs. Even though people with early CD-ROMs were able to listen to CD music, downloading it onto a computer was difficult. A three-minute song on a CD consisted roughly of 32 megabytes. (Each byte consists of a string of eight ones and zeros that can be used to represent binary numbers from 0 to 255. In binary, which is a base-two number system, 1 is 00000001, 2 is 00000010, 3 is 00000011, and so on up to 255, which is represented as 11111111.) During the late 1980s and early 1990s most computer hard drives were only big enough to hold a few songs straight from an audio CD. In 1987 researchers at the Fraunhofer Institute for Integrated Circuits in Germany began to look into ways to compress digital video and sound data into smaller sizes for broadcasting purposes. Out of this work, the MP2 (MPEG-1 Audio Layer II) and then the MP3 (MPEG-1 Audio Layer III) audio file formats emerged. Other compression formats, such as Windows Media Audio and Advanced Audio Coding, have come onto the market since then but are not nearly as well known.

Using such compression formats and encoding software, digital songs can be compressed from 32 megabytes per song to as little as 3 megabytes per song.

CD recordings pick up any and every sound in a studio or concert. Compression systems, such as MP3, work by cutting out sounds in CD recordings that people do not pay attention to or do not hear. This may include sounds drowned out by louder instruments. In classical music, an MP3 encoder might cut out a nearly indiscernible note from a flautist or the sound of a faint cough in the audience. It then condenses the recording to one-tenth its previous size. When played back, the encoder reconstructs the song. The compressed files sound nearly as good as CD tracks and much better than audiotapes.

At first, these compression formats and encoding software existed only on home computers. In February 1999 Diamond Multimedia released the first hard drive–based music player. Because early players mainly played MP3 formats, all hard drive–based music players, such as the Apple iPod, became known as MP3 players. All MP3 players consist of a hard drive (many were available in 60 to 500 gigabyte range in 2013) and all the electronic circuitry necessary to transform MP3 and other compressed music files into analog music. Using a cable, these players can be hooked up directly to a home computer. Once connected, the user can download thousands of songs onto the hard drive of the MP3 device. When the user selects a song, a microprocessor in the player pulls the song from the hard drive. A built-in signal processor decompresses the MP3 file (or other type of compressed music file) into a digital CD format, converts the digital signal to an analog signal, and then sends the analog waveform to the headphones. Though compressed music files do not sound quite as good as CD tracks, people can place their entire music collection on a player smaller than the palm of their hand. Since 1999 significant advances in technology have led to major improvements in iPods and other MP3 players. By 2010, 47% of all American adults owned some form of MP3 device. (See Figure 5.3.) In 2013 most new players had color screens and the ability to play video files, which were typically compressed using a MPEG-4 video compression format.

MP3 and Peer-to-Peer File Sharing

The widespread use of MP3 files and the increased size of hard drives in the late 1990s caused a transformation in the music industry almost as big as the advent of digital music. People suddenly had the ability to store entire music libraries on their computers and swap music for free over peer-to-peer file-sharing networks. According to Michael Gowan, in "Requiem for Napster" (*PC World*, May 17, 2002), the Napster file-sharing service had approximately 80 million subscribers at its peak. However, the availability of free music cut deeply into the recording industry's sales. The Census Bureau states in *Statistical Abstract of the United States: 2012* that the recording industry had revenues of $14.3 billion in 2000. Sales then fell steadily over the next eight years, eventually dropping to $6.9 billion by 2010.

FIGURE 5.3

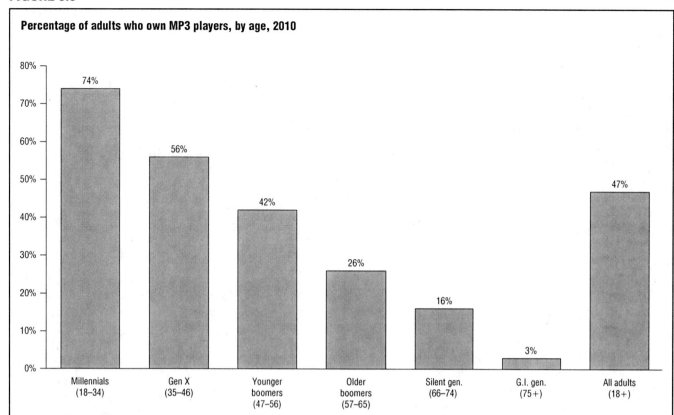

Percentage of adults who own MP3 players, by age, 2010

SOURCE: Kathryn Zickuhr, "Do You Own an iPod or Other MP3 Player?" in *Generations and Their Gadgets*, Pew Internet & American Life Project, February 3, 2011, http://www.pewinternet.org/~/media//Files/Reports/2011/PIP_Generations_and_Gadgets.pdf (accessed October 8, 2012). Used by permission of the Pew Internet & American Life Project, which bears no responsibility for the interpretations presented or conclusions reached based on analysis of the data.

Seeing diminishing profits at the turn of the 21st century, the Recording Industry Association of America (RIAA) sued Napster and the users of other peer-to-peer networks who shared music files (see Chapter 4). Some high-profile bands at the time, such as Metallica and Creed, joined the RIAA in its attempt to close down Napster. Other musicians, however, did not seem fazed by Internet file sharing. Radiohead released its 2000 album *Kid A* on the Internet three weeks before it was released in stores. The buzz generated by the Internet prerelease catapulted the album to number one in the United States after it hit record stores. Before *Kid A*, Radiohead had never had a number-one album in the United States.

The lawsuits brought on by the RIAA succeeded in putting an end to much of the free file-swapping on the Internet. The free Napster website shut down in July 2001 and reopened later as a pay music service where users could buy songs. After the RIAA began going after private citizens, traffic on many of the remaining peer-to-peer sites diminished greatly. The number of people using noncentralized peer-to-peer networks such as Kazaa dropped precipitously after the RIAA became litigious with file swappers in 2003. Lee Rainie et al.

of Pew/Internet reported in the data memo *The Impact of Music Industry Suits against Music File Swappers* (January 2004, http://www.pewinternet.org/~/media//Files/Reports/2004/PIP_File_Swapping_Memo_0104.pdf.pdf) that only 14% of American adults downloaded music from the Internet in the last two months of 2003, compared with 29% only six months earlier. Meanwhile, sales of digital music downloads increased rapidly over the remainder of the decade. According to *Statistical Abstract of the United States: 2012*, Americans purchased 139.4 million digital singles in 2004, along with 4.6 million digital albums. By 2010 Americans purchased nearly 1.2 billion singles online, and more than 83 million digital albums. According to Apple (2010, http://www.apple.com/pr/products/ipodhistory/), by June 2008 the company had sold five billion songs through its iTunes service. By February 2010 the total number of songs sold on iTunes had climbed to 10 billion. During this time, more and more Americans were also turning to online music streaming services, such as Pandora and Spotify, to gain personalized access to extensive digital music libraries. As Don Sears reports in "Why the Online Music Industry Is Such a Mess" (August 30, 2012, http://tech.fortune.cnn.com/2012/08/30/online-music-spotify-pandora-itunes/), by 2011

Spotify had 33 million registered users, four million of whom were paid subscribers.

TELEVISION

Although inventors had been trying to create a television as early as 1877, many people consider Philo Farnsworth (1906–1971) to be the father of the first modern, electronic television. He demonstrated his device for the first time in San Francisco in 1927, when he transmitted an image of a dollar sign. Using Farnsworth's design, Radio Corporation of America (RCA; then the owner of the National Broadcasting Company [NBC] network) began work on the first commercial television system in the late 1930s. In 1939 the first commercial televisions were introduced. Early televisions had tiny screens and were as big as small dressers. The pictures were in black and white, and at first the major networks only broadcast in the largest cities. Full-scale broadcasting began nationwide in 1947.

Since the early 1960s television has been the most popular medium of entertainment for Americans. In *There's No Place Like Home to Spend an Evening, Say Most Americans* (January 10, 2002, http://www.gallup.com/poll/5164/theres-place-like-home-spend-evening-say-most-americans.aspx), Lydia Saad of the Gallup Organization reported that 27% of Americans in a December 1960 poll said their favorite way of spending their evening was in front of a television. Resting, reading, and entertaining and visiting friends were ranked second, third, and fourth, respectively. Television appeared to hit its peak between the mid-1960s and early 1970s. A full 46% of people polled in February 1974 rated watching television as their favorite evening activity, followed by reading (14%), dining out (12%), and the somewhat ambiguous response of "staying at home with the family" (10%).

A survey reported in the *Statistical Abstract of the United States: 2012* (2012, http://www.census.gov/compendia/statab/2012/tables/12s1133.pdf) finds that in 2010 just under 93% of adults had watched television within the week prior to participating in the survey. Of those, nearly 83% had viewed cable television during that period. Among age groups, seniors watched more television than any other demographic, with 97.1% of those 65 and older watching TV during the previous week. By comparison, 89.6% of those aged 18 to 24 had watched television over that same span. Indeed, by 2012 many younger media users had begun turning to the Internet and mobile technology as their preferred source for video content. In "Ownership of TV Sets Falls in U.S." (May 3, 2011, http://www.nytimes.com/2011/05/03/business/media/03television.html), Brian Stelter reports that U.S. television ownership fell to 96.7% in 2011, down from 98.9% the previous year; according to the Nielsen Company, it marked the first time in 20 years that TV ownership fell in the United States. As Stelter reveals, one key reason for the decline was the increasing popularity of alternative video-viewing platforms.

Cable Television

Since the 1970s steady advances in cable, satellite, and digital technology have changed the way Americans watch television. According to the *Statistical Abstract of the United States: 2010* (2010, http://www.census.gov/compendia/statab/2010/tables/10s1095.pdf), cable television was installed in 19.9% of U.S. households with a television in 1980 (about 15.2 million homes); by 2007, nearly 70% of American households had cable television. In 2009 there were 65.8 million cable subscribers in the United States. By comparison, 80.7 million Americans had broadband Internet in their homes in 2009, while 52.5 million had mobile broadband service. (See Table 5.2.)

Cable television began in 1948 in Mahanoy City, Pennsylvania. John Walson (1915–1993), the owner of an electronics shop, began selling televisions in 1947. However, few customers in the local area wanted to buy a television because of the bad reception caused by the surrounding mountains. To increase sales potential, Walson erected an antenna on a nearby mountaintop, ran a cable from the antenna to his store, and connected it to his television. He then agreed to attach cables from his antenna to the houses of those who bought televisions from him. From then until the early 1970s, cable networks were generally only used in rural or mountainous areas. At most, early cable television programming included local broadcasts and a broadcast or two from a nearby region.

As early as 1965 the U.S. government and various contractors began putting up a communications satellite network. A satellite network remedied the biggest obstacle faced by broadcasters during the 1960s, which was the curvature of the earth. If the earth was flat, televisions could receive broadcast signals from thousands of miles away. However, because of the curvature of the earth, these broadcast signals escape into space after traveling about 100 miles (161 km). With a satellite system in place, a transmitter on the East Coast can beam a signal to a satellite above Kansas. The satellite then relays the signal to the West Coast without interruption.

Home Box Office (HBO) became the first pay cable station in 1972 and was the first television broadcaster to take advantage of a satellite communications network. HBO began in Wilkes-Barre, Pennsylvania, and broadcast its movies and shows to a limited number of cable networks in and around the state. In 1975, to expand the subscription television market, HBO leased the right to use one of the uplinks on RCA's *Satcom I* communications satellite. Once HBO was on the satellite network, any cable network provider around the United States

TABLE 5.2

Utilization of media, 2000–09

[100.2 represents 100,200,000]

Media	Unit	2000	2002	2003	2004	2005	2006	2007	2008	2009
Households with—										
Telephones[a]	Millions	100.2	104.0	107.1	106.4	107.0	108.8	112.2	112.7	114.0
Telephone service[a]	Percent	94.1	95.3	94.7	93.5	92.9	93.4	94.9	95.0	95.7
Land line households with wireless telephone[b]	Percent	X	X	X	X	42.4	45.6	58.9	58.5	59.4
Wireless-only[b]	Percent	X	X	X	X	7.3	10.5	13.6	17.5	22.7
Radio	Millions	100.5	105.1	106.7	108.3	109.9	110.5	110.5	115.6	114.0
Percent of total households	Percent	99.0	99.0	99.0	99.0	99.0	99.0	99.0	99.0	99.0
Average number of sets	Number	5.6	5.6	8.0	8.0	8.0	8.0	8.0	8.0	8.0
Total broadcast stations[c, d]	Number	NA	26,319	26,613	26,254	27,354	27,807	29,591	29,832	30,503
Radio stations	Number	NA	13,331	13,563	13,525	13,660	13,837	13,977	14,253	14,420
AM stations	Number	4,685	4,804	4,794	4,774	4,757	4,754	4,776	4,786	4,790
FM commercial	Number	5,892	6,173	6,217	6,218	6,231	6,266	6,309	6,427	6,479
FM educational	Number	NA	2,354	2,552	2,533	2,672	2,817	2,892	3,040	3,151
Television stations[c]	Number	1,663	1,719	1,733	1,748	1,750	1,756	1,759	1,759	1,782
Commercial	Number	1,288	1,338	1,352	1,366	1,370	1,376	1,379	1,378	1,392
VHF TV band	Number	567	583	585	589	588	587	583	582	373
UHF TV band	Number	721	755	767	777	782	789	796	796	1,019
Educational	Number	NA	381	381	382	380	380	380	381	390
VHF TV band	Number	NA	127	127	125	126	128	128	129	107
UHF TV band	Number	NA	254	254	257	254	252	252	252	283
Cable television systems[e]	Number	10,400	9,900	9,400	8,875	7,926	7,090	6,635	6,101	6,203
Cable subscribers	Millions	66.1	64.6	64.8	65.3	65.3	64.9	65.9	66.2	65.8
Cable availability (passed by cable)	Millions	91.7	90.7	90.8	91.6	92.6	94.1	95.1	95.4	95.5
Broadband subscribers[f]										
Total fixed broadband[g]	Millions	6.8	19.4	27.7	37.4	47.8	60.2	70.2	75.7	80.7
Mobile broadband	Millions	NA	NA	NA	NA	NA	NA	NA	25.0	52.5

NA = Not available.

[a]As of November. Based on Current Population Survey. For occupied housing units.

[b]From January to June. A "family" can be an individual or a group of two or more related persons living together in the same housing unit (a "household").

[c]As of December, 31.

[d]Includes Class A, Low Power TV, UHF and VHF Translators; FM Translators and Boosters; and Low Power FM stations.

[e]As of January 1.

[f]As of December. Connections over 200 kbps in at least one direction.

FCC Form 477 gathers standardized information about subscribership to high-speed Internet access services from telephone companies, cable system operators, terrestrial wireless service providers, satellite service providers, and any other facilities-based providers of advanced telecommunications capability Includes wireline, cable modem, and satelite and fixed wireless.

[g]Includes aDSI, sDSL, cable modem, FTTP, satelite, fixed wireless, power line, and other.

SOURCE: "Table 1132. Utilization and Number of Selected Media: 2000 to 2009," in *Statistical Abstract of the United States: 2012*, 131st ed., U.S. Department of Commerce, U.S. Census Bureau, 2011, http://www.census.gov/compendia/statab/2012/tables/12s1132.pdf (accessed October 2, 2012)

could buy a 9.8-foot (3-m) satellite dish and provide HBO for any house on the network. By 1978 HBO had one million customers. Ted Turner (1938–), who put his Atlanta-based station, WTBS, on the satellite network in 1976, created the Cable News Network (CNN) in 1980. The Music Television Network (MTV) and a number of other stations followed in 1981 and launched an era of exponential growth for the cable industry. Table 5.3 summarizes the growth in the cable and pay television industry between 1980 and 2010. In 1980, the cable television industry generated annual revenues of $2.6 billion; by 2010, this figure had grown to $93.4 billion a year.

The early 1980s also saw the emergence of video-cassette recorders (VCRs). As the Nielsen Company reports in *Television Audience 2010 & 2011* (2011, http://www.nielsen.com/content/dam/corporate/us/en/reports-downloads/2011-Reports/2010-2011-nielsen-television-audience-report.pdf), the percentage of television households with VCRs rose from 14% in 1985 to 66% in 1990, eventually climbing to 90% by 2005. As the market turned from videotape to digital video discs (DVDs), however, the percent of homes with a VCR began to fall steadily; according to Nielsen, VCR ownership declined to 65% in 2010, and was projected to drop to 57% by 2012.

Closed Captioning and the V-Chip

By the mid-1970s television had become the predominant medium not only for entertainment but also for news and emergency information. Recognizing this, the Federal Communications Commission (FCC) set aside part of the television broadcast spectrum for closed captioning for the hearing impaired. Closed captioning consists of scrolling text at the bottom of a television screen that spells out what is being said on television. Four years after the FCC action, the American Broadcasting Company (ABC), the Public Broadcasting Service (PBS), and NBC ran their first closed-captioned programs, which

TABLE 5.3

Cable and premium television subscriptions, monthly rates, and revenues, 1980–2010

[17,500 represents 17,500,000. Cable TV for calendar year. Premium TV as of December 31 of year shown]

| | Cable TV | | | | Premium TV | | | | | |
| | | | Revenue[a] | | Units[b] | | | Monthly rate[d] | | |
Year	Average basic subscribers (1,000)	Average monthly basic rate (dollars)	Total (million dollars)	Basic (million dollars)	Total premium[c] (1,000)	Premium cable (1,000)	Non-cable delivered premium (1,000)	All premium weighted average[e] (dollars)	Premium cable (dollars)	Non-cable delivered premium (dollars)
1980	17,500	7.69	2,609	1,615	8,581	7,336	(NA)	8.91	8.62	(NA)
1985	35,440	9.73	8,831	4,138	29,885	29,418	(NA)	10.29	10.25	(NA)
1990	50,520	16.78	17,582	10,174	39,902	39,751	(NA)	10.35	10.30	(NA)
1995	60,550	23.07	24,137	16,763	60,098	46,600	8,725	8.32	8.54	6.99
1997	63,600	26.48	28,931	20,213	72,910	51,450	17,500	8.33	8.43	8.00
1998	64,650	27.81	31,191	21,574	79,483	54,410	21,355	8.60	8.74	8.22
1999	65,500	28.92	34,095	22,732	84,234	56,985	25,532	8.75	8.85	8.50
2000	66,250	30.37	36,427	24,142	94,100	62,618	30,158	8.72	8.81	8.48
2001	66,732	32.87	41,847	26,324	101,676	68,353	32,780	8.97	9.10	8.66
2002	66,472	34.71	47,989	27,690	109,046	71,637	37,024	9.19	9.29	9.00
2003	66,050	36.59	53,242	29,000	108,522	71,740	36,364	9.38	9.45	9.23
2004	65,727	38.14	58,586	30,080	118,151	76,844	40,892	9.91	9.92	9.88
2005	65,337	39.63	64,891	31,075	126,067	81,790	43,780	9.95	9.97	9.93
2006	65,319	41.17	71,887	32,274	132,951	85,055	47,514	10.01	10.02	9.98
2007	65,141	42.72	78,937	33,393	143,009	90,878	51,595	10.05	10.06	10.02
2008	64,274	44.28	85,232	34,151	149,749	92,364	56,825	10.08	10.10	10.06
2009	62,874	46.13	89,479	34,804	150,111	85,818	64,293	10.12	10.13	10.09
2010	60,958	47.89	93,368	35,031	166,241	88,359	77,882	10.15	10.17	10.13

NA = Not available.

[a]Includes installation revenue, subscriber revenue, and nonsubscriber revenue; excludes telephony and high-speed access.

[b]Individual program services sold to subscribers.

[c]Includes multipoint distribution service (MDS), satellite TV (STV), multipoint multichannel distribution service (MMDS), satellite master antenna TV (SMATV), C-band satellite, DBS satellite and Telco Video for full- and mini-premium services.

[d]Weighted average representing 8 months of unregulated basic rate and 4 months of FCC rolled-back rate.

[e]Includes average premium unit price based on data for major premium movie services.

SOURCE: "Table 1142. Cable and Premium TV—Summary: 1980 to 2010," in *Statistical Abstract of the United States: 2012*, 131st ed., U.S. Department of Commerce, U.S. Census Bureau, 2011, http://www.census.gov/compendia/statab/2012/tables/12s1142.pdf (accessed October 2, 2012)

included the *Wonderful World of Disney* and the *ABC Sunday Night Movie*. At first, closed captioning was scripted, but then the National Captioning Institute developed a keyboard interface that could be used to create captioning for live television shows, sporting events, and newscasts. A stenographer listened to the audio portion of a broadcast and typed it into the broadcast in real time. In 1990 Congress required that all television receivers contain decoders that display closed captioning, and in the 1996 Telecommunications Act Congress insisted that closed captioning be included in all shows by the turn of the 21st century.

As part of this act, Congress also requested that broadcasters rate their shows. The industry heeded the request and developed the TV Parental Guidelines. At the start of every television show, a rating is shown in the corner of the screen for 15 seconds. TV-G designates general audiences, whereas TV-MA warns of content not suitable for anyone under 17. Even with the ratings system in place, parents across the country found they still could not monitor all the shows on cable as well as on broadcast television. Gloria Tristani (1953–), an FCC commissioner, said in a speech delivered at the 1999 Columbia/Barnard May luncheon (May 25, 1999, http://www.fcc.gov/Speeches/Tristani/spgt910.html) that the average child spent 25 hours per week in front of the television. In response, the FCC mandated in 2000 that all television sets 13 inches or larger contain a V-chip. The V-chip worked in conjunction with the ratings system. If a parent set the V-chip to allow only TV-G shows, the microchip would simply block every show not rated TV-G.

Advances in Broadcasting Technology

In 1994 a new way of broadcasting movies and television shows became available when RCA released its Direct Satellite System (DSS). The DSS was the first affordable satellite receiver available to the American public. By installing an 18-inch (46-cm) satellite dish on their houses, Americans could receive nearly 200 channels in their living rooms. To squeeze so many channels into a stream of data small enough to travel through space and back, the direct broadcasting satellite provider had to use a form of digital compression known as MPEG-1. The MPEG-1 compression format works much like an MP3 format. (The MP3 format in fact was developed from the audio portion of MPEG-1 format.) To employ the MPEG-1 format, all television shows recorded in analog must first be transformed by ADCs into a digital format. MPEG-1 encoders, owned by the direct broadcasting satellite provider, then compress the digital data largely by removing redundant scenery between frames. For example, if a character's face movement is the only discernible change between two frames in a movie, then the background from the first frame is applied to both frames, cutting out the redundant information in the second frame. The compressed signal is then beamed to the satellite network. On receiving the signal, the satellite network broadcasts the signal to homes all across the country. A DSS box in the home decompresses the signal and delivers it to the viewer.

Several years after the first direct broadcast satellites were released, cable companies introduced digital cable. Digital cable works in much the same way as direct broadcast satellites, but uses a slightly more advanced MPEG-2 format for compression. By digitally compressing their programming, cable providers found they could transmit 10 times more television stations than before along their cables. Many cable providers added music stations, pay-per-view movies, and multiple movie channels to their services. The only drawback with both the digital cable and satellite systems is that the decoder can only work on one television at a time, and it is usually bulky.

In terms of television accessories, the big development during the late 1990s was the DVD. DVDs work almost exactly in the same way as CDs, but the standard DVD can hold up to seven times more information per disc, which allows the DVD to carry the data needed for much larger video files. After its release in 1997, the DVD quickly rose to become the preferred format for watching recorded movies. In *Television Audience 2010 & 2011* the Nielsen Company reveals that 76% of TV households owned a DVD player in 2006, compared with 89% that owned a VCR. By 2010 the percentage of TV households with a DVD player climbed to 88%, whereas VCR ownership dropped to 65%.

The design and quality of TV sets also experienced a radical evolution during the 1990s and 2000s. Among the most significant innovations was the development of flat screen (or flat panel) televisions. Flat screen televisions offered numerous advantages over traditional television sets. For one, flat screens were more streamlined and energy efficient than traditional televisions, which used bulky cathode ray tubes to generate images. At the same time, flat screens offered the potential for a higher-resolution picture quality. The two principal technologies behind the emergence of flat screens were liquid crystal display (LCD) and plasma. Already widely used in calculators and laptop computers, LCD screens are composed of two polarized panels containing millions of liquid crystals, each of which controls a particular aspect of the light being projected through the screen. Plasma screens, on the other hand, contain tubes of gases that emit light when charged with electricity. By manipulating light in this way, LCD and plasma technologies are able to project images onto a television screen. The first flat-screen plasma televisions became widely available to consumers in 1997, and cost more than $7,000 ($10,000 in 2012 dollars). While LCD technology developed more gradually, by the early part of the new century LCD TVs began to compete with plasma models. Many higher-quality LCD televisions also began to use Light Emitting Diode (LED) backlighting technology, which produced a sharper picture quality while requiring less energy.

THE DEVELOPMENT OF 3-D TELEVISION. By 2012 a number of television manufacturers had introduced three-dimensional (3-D) television sets. Most of the new models projected 3-D images to viewers wearing special glasses, but in late 2010 Toshiba debuted the Regza GL1, a flat-panel 3-D television that required no glasses. Instead, as Dan Reisinger reports in "Digital Home" (October 4, 2010, http://news.cnet.com/8301-13506_3-20018421-17 .html), the Regza presented multiple images of each 2D frame that viewers' brains "superimposed ... to create a three-dimensional impression of the image." At the time of the product release, the sets were available only in 12- and 20-inch models, and the 3-D effect was viewable only within a limited area two to three feet (0.61 to 0.91 meters) from the screen. Two years later, Toshiba released its 55ZL2 3-D television. As John Archer reports (May 17, 2012, http://www.techradar.com/us/reviews/audio-visual/televisions/plasma-and-lcd-tvs/toshiba-55zl2-1080745/ review), the 55ZL2 boasted a 55-inch, ultra high-definition (HD) screen. During this time, Sarah Jacobsson Purewal writes in *PC World* (November 4, 2010, http://www .pcworld.com/article/209772/holographic_tv_coming_your _way_in_2017.html), researchers at the University of Arizona developed a holographic television system "that can render an image in near real-time and update the image every two seconds." With improvements in the capture, refresh rate, and projection speed of holographic images, Purewal notes, true 3-D television projection could be commercially available by 2017 and is expected by 2022.

Television and the Internet

As higher connection speeds and faster computers became more widespread, the Internet became a popular source of video entertainment. By the early 21st century, several video-sharing websites had been established, enabling Internet users from around the world to post videos and other recorded content online. Of these sites, YouTube quickly emerged as one of the most popular. Created in February 2005, YouTube allowed visitors to view and upload videos free of charge, while also enabling users to create their own accounts and video libraries. In "Video Websites Pop Up, Invite Postings" (*USA Today*, November 22, 2005, http://www.usatoday.com/tech/news/techinnovations/2005-11-21-video-websites_x.htm), Jefferson

Graham reports that the site had more than 200,000 registered users by late 2005. Traditional media outlets quickly recognized the marketing potential of YouTube, and soon clips from television programs, movie trailers, news features, and other mainstream content became available on the video site. YouTube's rapidly increasing popularity soon attracted the attention of major media and technology corporations, who regarded the site as a means of reaching new audiences of younger consumers. Indeed, the site's growth was staggering; as Andrew Ross Sorkin reports in the *New York Times* (October 10, 2006, http://www.nytimes.com/2006/10/10/technology/10deal.html), by October 2006 YouTube visitors were watching more than 100 million videos a day, a 4,900% increase in less than a year. A month later, Google acquired YouTube for $1.65 billion.

The success of YouTube inspired a wide range of other online outlets for video content. Prominent among these was Hulu, a streaming video site that airs shows and movies produced by major studios and TV networks. A number of other sites, particularly news and sports outlets, began to use video as a way of augmenting or supplementing their written content. At the same time, sites like YouTube enabled anyone to post videos online, making a broader and more diverse range of content available for viewing. According to Kathleen Moore of Pew/Internet in *71% of Online Adults Now Use Video Sharing Sites* (July 25, 2011, http://pewinternet.org/Reports/2011/Video-sharing-sites/Report.aspx), by 2011, 71% of adults reported had viewed content on an online video-sharing site. Young adults between the ages of 18 and 29 (92%) were most likely to view content on a video sharing site in 2011, while seniors aged 65 and older (31%) were the least likely. Sharing videos also became popular among teens during this time. As Amanda Lenhart estimates in *Teens & Online Video* (May 3, 2012, http://www.pewinternet.org/~/media//Files/Reports/2012/PIP_Teens_and_online_video.pdf), 27% of all Internet users between the ages of 12 and 17 recorded and uploaded video content onto the Internet in 2011.

Digital Television

Many confuse the concept of digital cable with digital television. Digital cable simply uses digital technology to compress the size of broadcasts so the customer has more channels. The digital signal also does not degrade as it travels across miles of coaxial cable. Most of the programming fed through the digital cable systems is not digitally recorded. Digital television, however, is digital from start to finish. Digital cameras are used to record the broadcast; cables, satellite systems, and broadcast towers send a digital signal; and digital televisions play the broadcast. The result is a television picture that more closely resembles an image on a computer monitor than an image on a television set. The FCC established a number of standards for digital television, which became mandatory for full-power stations on June 12, 2009. (See Table 5.4.) Standard-definition television (SDTV) has the resolution of an analog television, which is roughly 480 by 440 dots per inch (dpi) or 210,000 pixels in total. The next step up in visual quality is enhanced-definition television (EDTV), which generally has the same overall resolution as SDTV but features a wider screen. Finally, high-definition television (HDTV) is the highest quality television format with resolutions up to 1,920 dpi horizontally and 1,080 dpi vertically. Overall, HDTV has more than 2 million pixels to display each image, which provides the viewer with 10 times the detail of SDTV. For a television to meet HDTV standard, it also has to have the ability to play the latest versions of Dolby stereo.

As HDTV became more widespread, electronics manufacturers began to develop a higher quality DVD format known as Blu-ray. Capable of storing between 25 and 50 gigabytes of data, Blu-ray discs produced a picture definition that was far sharper than that offered by conventional DVDs. The first Blu-ray player was released by Sony in 2006. According to data compiled by the Digital Entertainment Group (DEG; June 29, 2012, http://degonline.org/pressreleases/2012/DEG_2Q12%20cover%20note_7.29.12_FINAL.pdf), by mid-2012 more than 42 million American households owned Blu-ray players.

TABLE 5.4

Digital television standards

Analog	Digital television (DTV)	High definition television (HDTV)
Date for final transition to digital was June 12, 2009. Since June 13, 2009, all full-power U.S. stations have broadcast digital-only signals. Consumers will always be able to connect an inexpensive receiver (a digital-to-analog converter box) to their existing analog TV to decode DTV broadcast signals. Digital-to-analog converter boxes will not convert your analog TV to High Definition (HD). Analog TV sets will continue to work with cable, satellite, videocassette recorders (VCR), DVD players, camcorders, video game consoles and other devices for many years.	Digital cable or digital satellite does not mean a program is in High Definition (HD). Multicasting is available. HDTV is available. Data streaming is available.	High-definition broadcasts offered. Best available picture resolution, clarity and color. Dolby theatre Surround Sound. Dolby Surround Sound. Widescreen "movie-like" format.

SOURCE: Adapted from "What Is DTV?" in *DTV.gov: What You Need to Know about the Digital Television Transition*, Federal Communications Commission, 2009, http://www.dtv.gov/whatisdtv.html (accessed October 2, 2012)

The digital television standards were adopted by the FCC after Congress passed the 1996 Telecommunications Act. The act called for a full conversion to digital television across the United States within 10 years. By 2006 every television station serving every market in the United States would be required to air digital programming. In addition, broadcasters would no longer have to air analog content. Americans with an analog television set would be required to buy either a digital television or a $50 to $100 ADC device to watch television. In 2005, however, only a small percentage of Americans had HDTV or even EDTV. Consequently, in 2005 Congress pushed the deadline for the digitization of television to February 17, 2009. This deadline, too, was later extended to June 2009.

On January 1, 2008, the National Telecommunications and Information Administration of the U.S. Department of Commerce began issuing $40 coupons that defrayed the cost of converter boxes, allowing consumers to continue using older, analog television sets after the conversion to digital broadcasting. Households were eligible to receive two coupons and were required to redeem them toward the purchase of converter boxes within 90 days. In December 2009 the TV Converter Box Coupon Program (December 9, 2009, http://www.ntia.doc.gov/legacy/dtvcoupon/reports/NTIA_DTVWeekly_120909.pdf) released the final number of coupon requests that had been received, processed, and redeemed. As of December 9, 2009, the program had received 64.1 million requests, and had approved coupons for 34.8 million households.

JOURNALISM AND NEW MEDIA

The many advances in new media have fundamentally changed the manner in which Americans get their news. As the Pew Research Center reports in "In Changing News Landscape, Even Television Is Vulnerable" (September 27, 2012, http://www.people-press.org/2012/09/27/in-changing-news-landscape-even-television-is-vulnerable/), during the early 1990s more than 70% of Americans said they had watched television news the day before; by 2012 this number had fallen to 55%. Over this same span, daily newspaper readership dropped from 56% to 29%, while the proportion of Americans who received news regularly over the radio fell from 54% to 33%. By contrast, the percentage of Americans who claimed to have regularly gotten news either online or on a mobile device climbed from 24% in 2004 to 39% in 2012; when including e-mail, podcast, social networking sites, and other electronic formats, this number rose to roughly half (50%) of Americans. This trend coincided with a steady erosion of consumer confidence toward mainstream news outlets between the 1990s and 2012. (See Figure 5.4.) Besides gaining popularity among Internet users, online news and information sources have also experienced increasing revenue. Online publishers generated approximately $19.5 billion in 2009, a 9.8% increase over 2008 ($17.8 billion). (See Table 5.5.)

High technology has not only changed how news and information are sold but also how reporters and writers do their jobs. Advanced communications and video technology have allowed reporters with established organizations to report from anywhere in the world in real time,

FIGURE 5.4

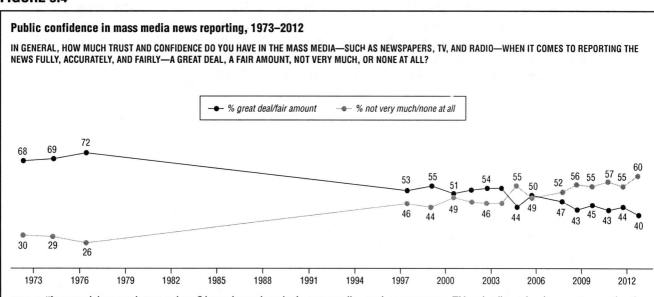

Public confidence in mass media news reporting, 1973–2012

IN GENERAL, HOW MUCH TRUST AND CONFIDENCE DO YOU HAVE IN THE MASS MEDIA—SUCH AS NEWSPAPERS, TV, AND RADIO—WHEN IT COMES TO REPORTING THE NEWS FULLY, ACCURATELY, AND FAIRLY—A GREAT DEAL, A FAIR AMOUNT, NOT VERY MUCH, OR NONE AT ALL?

SOURCE: "In general, how much trust and confidence do you have in the mass media—such as newspapers, TV, and radio—when it comes to reporting the news fully, accurately, and fairly—a great deal, a fair amount, not very much, or none at all?" in *Media Use and Evaluation*, the Gallup Organization, 2012, http://www.gallup.com/poll/1663/media-use-evaluation.aspx (accessed December 8, 2012). Copyright © 2012 by Gallup, Inc. All rights reserved. The content is used with permission; however, Gallup retains all rights of republication.

TABLE 5.5

Internet publishing and broadcasting—estimated revenues and expenses, 2005–09

In millions of dollars (9,378 represents $9,378,000,000). For taxable and tax-exempt employer firms. Covers NAICS 516. Establishments engaged in publishing and/or broadcasting on the Internet exclusively. Estimates have been adjusted to the results of the 2002 Economic Census. Based on the North American Industry Classification System (NAICS), 2002.]

Item	2005	2006	2007	2008	2009
Operating revenue	**9,378**	**11,510**	**15,035**	**17,760**	**19,504**
Source of revenue:					
Publishing and broadcasting of content on the internet	5,498	6,316	7,576	8,894	(S)
Online advertising space	1,812	2,579	3,469	4,298	4,957
Licensing of rights to use intellectual property	372	442	486	495	560
All other operating revenue	1,696	(S)	(S)	4,073	3,710
Breakdown of revenue by type of customer:					
Government	(S)	(S)	(S)	(S)	(S)
Business firms and not-for-profit organizations	6,615	7,894	9,784	12,061	13,454
Household consumers and individual users	2,227	2,991	4,344	4,527	4,825
Operating expenses	**8,202**	**10,102**	**13,211**	**15,453**	**17,080**
Personnel	3,563	4,398	5,648	6,790	6,855
Gross annual payroll	2,842	3,513	4,189	5,094	5,085
Employer's cost for fringe benefits	507	636	892	(S)	(S)
Temporary staff and leased employee expense	214	249	(S)	(S)	(S)
Expensed materials, parts and supplies (not for resale)	286	322	(S)	(S)	(S)
Expensed equipment	121	123	(S)	(S)	(S)
Expensed purchase of other materials, parts and supplies	165	199	(S)	235	388
Expensed purchased services	1,396	1,789	(S)	2,774	3,387
Expensed purchases of software	176	245	(S)	307	(S)
Purchased electricity and fuels (except motor fuel)	14	22	(S)	(S)	(S)
Lease and rental payments	310	343	(S)	537	(S)
Purchased repair and maintenance	90	96	(S)	(S)	(S)
Purchased advertising and promotional services	806	1,083	1,366	1,757	(S)
Other operating expenses	2,957	3,593	(S)	5,449	6,192
Depreciation and amortization charges	716	811	(S)	1,272	(S)
Government taxes and license fees	56	66	(S)	83	111

(S) Data do not meet publication standards.

SOURCE: "Table 1144. Internet Publishing and Broadcasting—Estimated Revenue and Expenses: 2005 to 2009," in *Statistical Abstract of the United States: 2012*, 131st ed., U.S. Department of Commerce, U.S. Census Bureau, 2011, http://www.census.gov/compendia/statab/2012/tables/12s1144.pdf (accessed October 2, 2012)

something that most modern viewers take for granted. With the Internet, anyone can report on current events or start a publication or web log (blog) and begin writing commentary. No longer do reporters and writers have to work for a large publishing house or magazine to build a reputation. Some blogs have grown so popular that they have a readership bigger than some major newspapers and magazines. For example, Matt Drudge (1967–) began the Drudge Report website/blog in 1997 to report on current events. He was largely responsible for breaking the story of President Bill Clinton's (1946–) relationship with the former White House intern Monica Lewinsky (1973–) in 1998. By December 2012 the website (December 20, 2012, http://www.drudgereport.com/) reported more than 11.4 billion visits in the previous 12 months and a daily tally of 35 million.

CHAPTER 6
HIGH TECHNOLOGY AND EDUCATION

Knowing how to use a computer or Internet browser has become as important a skill in modern life as knowing multiplication tables. Not having exposure to information technology restricts a person's access to job listings, e-mail communication, and dozens of convenient, efficient computer applications that make work and life easier. Aware of this, high schools and colleges in the late 1990s increased efforts to expose students to computers and the Internet before graduation. Most elementary and secondary schools installed computers with Internet access in classrooms and libraries. Many schools set up programs wherein their students could borrow laptops and handheld computers for extended periods of time. College administrations provided widespread broadband access to students on campus, and many professors required the use of the Internet and computer programs in college courses.

Due in part to these actions, high school and college students were among the most tech-savvy Americans at the turn of the 21st century. Kristin Purcell of the Pew Internet & American Life Project (Pew/Internet) reports in "Teens 2012: Truth, Trends, and Myths about Teen Online Behavior" (July 11, 2012, http://pewinternet.org/~/media//Files/Presentations/2012/July/KPurcell%20ACT%20Conf_PDF.pdf) that 95% of teenagers aged 12 to 17 years went online in 2011, compared with 82% of adults aged 18 years and older. Purcell also reveals that 80% of online teens used social media sites in 2011; of these, 93% maintained Facebook accounts and 24% had MySpace pages. Forty percent of teens who used social networking sites in 2011 checked their online status multiple times a day.

Providing students with access to high technology, however, has not been without problems. The Internet, computers, and cell phones have introduced a great deal of distraction into the life of many young people. They allow teenagers access to illicit material, such as pornography, that they normally could not obtain so easily.

In addition, these technologies open up avenues for cheating and plagiarism. Largely because of the Internet, academic cheating and plagiarism skyrocketed around the turn of the 21st century. Students appeared to have no qualms about copying text from the Internet and pasting it verbatim into reports and papers.

TECHNOLOGY AT SCHOOL

In February 1996 President Bill Clinton (1946–) signed the Telecommunications Act into law. This legislation ushered in the E-Rate Program, which provided elementary and secondary public schools with discounts of between 20% and 90% when purchasing computers for classrooms and libraries. The program had a tremendous impact on computer and Internet accessibility in public schools. By the 2008–09 school year, 99% of American public school teachers had computers in their classrooms; 95% of these computers had Internet access. (See Table 6.1.)

Technology and Instruction

Table 6.2 presents a breakdown of how frequently teachers used computers during class time in 2009, by school size, community type, and other factors. Forty-four percent of elementary school teachers reported using a computer in the classroom "often" in 2009, compared with only 34% of high school teachers. Teachers engaged in general instruction were the most likely to use a computer for teaching purposes often (47%), followed by special needs and English as a second language (ESL) teachers (44%). Teachers working in schools where 75% or more of the student body qualified for free or reduced-price lunch programs were the most likely to use computers in the classroom often, at 48%. In contrast, in schools where 35% or less of the student body was eligible for free or reduced-price lunch programs, only 36% of teachers reported using computers in the classroom with the same frequency.

TABLE 6.1

Percentage of public school teachers with computers in their classrooms, ratio of students to these computers, and percentage of these computers with Internet access, by selected characteristics, 2009

Characteristic	Computers in the classroom every day			Computers that can be brought into the classroom			Total computers (in or can be brought into the classroom)		
	Percent of teachers[a]	Ratio of students in the classroom to computers[b]	Percent of computers with Internet access	Percent of teachers[a]	Ratio of students in the classroom to computers[b]	Percent of computers with Internet access	Percent of teachers[a]	Ratio of students in the classroom to computers[b]	Percent of computers with Internet access
All public school teachers	**97**	**5.3**	**93**	**54**	**2.4**	**96**	**99**	**1.7**	**95**
School instructional level[c]									
Elementary	98	5.4	92	52	2.6	96	99	1.7	95
Secondary	95	5.2	94	57	2.3	96	98	1.6	96
School enrollment size									
Less than 300	97	4.5	92	53	2.4	98	99	1.6	96
300 to 999	97	5.4	94	53	2.5	96	99	1.7	95
1,000 or more	96	5.3	92	56	2.3	96	99	1.6	95
Community type									
City	96	5.2	92	54	2.7	95	99	1.8	94
Suburban	98	5.4	93	56	2.3	97	99	1.6	96
Town	96	5.2	93	52	2.7	96	99	1.8	95
Rural	97	5.3	95	52	2.4	95	99	1.6	95
Percent of students in the school eligible for free or reduced-price lunch									
Less than 35 percent	96	5.9	93	61	2.1	97	99	1.5	96
35 to 49 percent	98	5.4	92	52	2.5	96	99	1.7	94
50 to 74 percent	97	4.9	94	47	2.9	96	98	1.8	95
75 percent or more	97	4.7	93	50	3.0	94	100[d]	1.8	94
Main teaching assignment									
General education in self-contained classroom	99	5.5	91	49	3.1	96	99	2.0	94
Mathematics/computer science, science	95	6.6	92	61	2.0	96	99	1.5	95
Other academic subject[e]	96	7.7	97	60	2.2	97	99	1.7	97
Special education, English as a second language	99	3.1	92	49	1.7	96	99	1.1	95
Other assignment[f]	94	3.4	93	53	3.0	96	97	1.6	95
Elementary/secondary teaching experience									
3 or fewer years	95	5.5	95	53	2.6	93	99	1.8	94
4 to 9 years	97	5.4	94	57	2.2	97	99	1.6	96
10 to 19 years	97	5.6	91	53	2.5	97	99	1.7	95
20 or more years	97	4.8	93	52	2.5	96	99	1.6	95

[a]Percent of teachers with one or more computers with the characteristic.
[b]Ratio computed by dividing the number of students in all teachers' classrooms by the number of computers with the characteristic.
[c]Data for combined schools (those with both elementary and secondary grades) are included in the totals and in analyses by other school characteristics but are not shown separately.
[d]Rounds to 100 percent.
[e]Other academic subjects include English/language arts, foreign languages, and social sciences/social studies.
[f]Other assignments include arts and music; health/physical education; vocational, career, or technical education; and other (respondent asked to specify).

SOURCE: Lucinda Gray, Nina Thomas, and Laurie Lewis, "Table 1. Percent of Teachers with Computers in the Classroom Every Day and Percent That Can Bring Computers into the Classroom, Ratio of Students in the Classroom to These Computers, and Percent of These Computers with Internet Access, by School and Teacher Characteristics: 2009," in *Teachers' Use of Educational Technology in U.S. Public Schools: 2009*, U.S. Department of Education, Institute of Education Sciences, National Center for Education Statistics, May 2010, http://nces.ed.gov/pubs2010/2010040.pdf (accessed October 9, 2012).

TABLE 6.2

Frequency with which public school teachers or students use computers during instructional time, in the classroom and other school locations, by selected school and teacher characteristics, 2009

Characteristic	In the classroom					In other locations in the school				
	Not available	Never	Rarely	Some-times	Often	Not available	Never	Rarely	Some-times	Often
All public school teachers	1	10	19	29	40	2	8	19	43	29
School instructional level[a]										
Elementary	1	8	17	31	44	2	7	16	44	31
Secondary	2	16	23	25	34	2	10	25	40	24
School enrollment size										
Less than 300	1	9	23	28	39	3	6	18	47	27
300 to 999	1	9	18	30	43	2	7	16	44	32
1,000 or more	1	15	19	28	36	2	9	26	41	22
Community type										
City	1	10	19	30	40	2	8	20	44	26
Suburban	1	11	18	30	40	2	8	19	39	31
Town	1	9	19	25	46	1	7	18	51	24
Rural	1	11	18	31	38	1	7	18	44	30
Percent of students in the school eligible for free or reduced-price lunch										
Less than 35 percent	1	12	21	29	36	1	7	20	43	29
35 to 49 percent	1!	14	17	31	37	1	8	19	45	26
50 to 74 percent	2	8	18	28	44	3	8	18	44	27
75 percent or more	#	9	15	28	48	2	7	17	41	34
Main teaching assignment										
General education in self-contained classroom	1	6	13	33	47	2	6	12	46	34
Mathematics/computer science, science	1	15	22	26	36	3	11	25	40	21
Other academic subject[b]	1	14	24	29	32	1!	3	21	46	29
Special education, English as a second language	‡	5	21	29	44	‡	7	22	44	26
Other assignment[c]	3	14	19	24	41	1	15	21	35	27
Elementary/secondary teaching experience										
3 or fewer years	1	13	22	25	39	3	8	24	37	28
4 to 9 years	1	11	21	28	40	2	8	23	42	26
10 to 19 years	1	10	19	32	38	1	6	16	46	31
20 or more years	1	10	14	31	44	2	9	15	44	30

#Rounds to zero.
!Interpret data with caution; the coefficient of variation is greater than 50 percent.
‡Reporting standards not met.
[a]Data for combined schools (those with both elementary and secondary grades) are included in the totals and in analyses by other school characteristics but are not shown separately.
[b]Other academic subjects include English/language arts, foreign languages, and social sciences/social studies.
[c]Other assignments include arts and music; health/physical education; vocational, career, or technical education; and other (respondent asked to specify).
Note: Detail may not sum to totals due to rounding.

SOURCE: Lucinda Gray, Nina Thomas, and Laurie Lewis, "Table 2. Percentage Distribution of Teachers Reporting How Frequently They or Their Students Use Computers during Instructional Time in the Classroom and in Other Locations in the School, by School and Teacher Characteristics: 2009," in *Teachers' Use of Educational Technology in U.S. Public Schools: 2009*, U.S. Department of Education, Institute of Education Sciences, National Center for Education Statistics, May 2010, http://nces.ed.gov/pubs2010/2010040.pdf (accessed October 9, 2012)

Other advanced technologies are playing an increasingly important role in public school education. Table 6.3 shows the range of electronic devices that were available to public school teachers for use in the classroom. Digital cameras were the device most commonly available in U.S. public schools in 2009, with nearly two-thirds (64%) of teachers having access to them as needed. Other devices used in public schools in 2009 included liquid crystal display or digital light processing projectors (36%), interactive white boards (28%), and document cameras (22%). Of all the devices that were available in public school classrooms, videoconferencing units were used with the least frequency, with only 13% of teachers reporting using videoconferencing technology either often or sometimes.

Students are becoming active participants in the use of classroom technology in the 21st century. Table 6.4 shows the frequency with which public school students used various forms of advanced technology under the supervision of their teachers. Elementary school students were more likely to use technology to learn or practice basic skills (76%), whereas high school students used technology predominantly for conducting research (69%) or completing writing assignments (67%). Math and science students were the most likely to use technology to solve problems, perform calculations, or assess data in the classroom (61%), and students in English, social studies, and foreign language classes were the most likely to use technology to prepare and present multimedia presentations of their work (56%). Among all public school

TABLE 6.3

Availability and use of various technological devices in public schools, by selected school, student, and teacher characteristics, 2009

Characteristic	LCD or DLP projector			Videoconference unit			Interactive whiteboard			Classroom response system[a]		
	Availability			Availability			Availability			Availability		
	Available as needed	In classroom every day	Use sometimes or often	Available as needed	In classroom every day	Use sometimes or often	Available as needed	In classroom every day	Use sometimes or often	Available as needed	In classroom every day	Use sometimes or often
All public school teachers[b]	36	48	72	21	1	13	28	23	57	22	6	35
School instructional level[b]												
Elementary	37	44	68	19	1	12	31	23	58	21	7	35
Secondary	33	56	78	23	2	15	23	23	58	24	6	34
School enrollment size												
Less than 300	39	41	64	24	*	13	23	31	64	16	7	41
300 to 999	36	46	71	20	1	12	30	23	58	22	6	35
1,000 or more	34	55	77	21	2	15	26	22	54	24	7	33
Community type												
City	36	45	71	19	3	11	30	18	52	22	6	30
Suburban	36	49	73	19	1	15	30	22	59	21	6	37
Town	33	50	71	24	1!	8	22	29	65	22	7	37
Rural	36	48	72	23	1	15	28	27	56	24	7	35
Percent of students in the school eligible for free or reduced-price lunch												
Less than 35 percent	38	50	71	22	1	10	32	23	55	24	6	32
35 to 49 percent	39	44	69	19	1!	17	26	18	56	22	4	30
50 to 74 percent	30	51	75	20	2	12	26	27	63	21	8	39
75 percent or more	35	42	73	20	1	18	26	23	57	19	7	39
Main teaching assignment												
General education in self-contained classroom	39	39	67	17	1	11	32	20	57	19	5	37
Mathematics/computer science, science	25	66	80	23	1	11	22	36	66	33	9	34
Other academic subject[c]	34	54	78	22	2	11	27	23	57	24	6	32
Special education, English as a second language	47	33	59	24	*	18	32	15	47	20	5	33
Other assignment[d]	37	49	71	23	2	19	26	20	54	16	6	39
Elementary/secondary teaching experience												
3 or fewer years	33	51	76	18	2	12	20	24	69	22	6	29
4 to 9 years	35	52	77	20	2	12	30	22	55	21	5	38
10 to 19 years	36	48	71	22	1	14	30	24	54	24	7	35
20 or more years	38	42	66	22	1	15	30	23	58	22	7	35

TABLE 6.3

Availability and use of various technological devices in public schools, by selected school, student, and teacher characteristics, 2009 [CONTINUED]

Characteristic	Digital camera — Available as needed	In classroom every day	Use sometimes or often	MP3 player/iPod — Available as needed	In classroom every day	Use sometimes or often	Document camera[a] — Available as needed	In classroom every day	Use sometimes or often	Handheld device — Available as needed	In classroom every day	Use sometimes or often
All public school teachers[b]	64	14	49	18	5	36	22	17	56	8	4	50
School instructional level[b]												
Elementary	67	14	53	14	4	34	23	19	60	8	5	60
Secondary	57	13	41	24	6	37	23	13	48	8	2	28
School enrollment size												
Less than 300	65	17	56	14	5	35	18	13	54	9	3	50
300 to 999	67	14	51	16	4	32	22	18	59	8	5	55
1,000 or more	56	13	40	22	6	43	24	17	51	9	2	35
Community type												
City	61	11	48	17	5	39	20	20	64	10	4	47
Suburban	63	14	49	19	6	36	25	19	54	8	4	54
Town	65	16	54	18	3	35	22	14	50	9	4	45
Rural	68	15	47	16	4	32	20	14	54	7	3	49
Percent of students in the school eligible for free or reduced-price lunch												
Less than 35 percent	67	16	48	22	6	35	25	17	54	8	2	36
35 to 49 percent	66	13	49	20	4	34	21	16	50	7	5	46
50 to 74 percent	60	15	51	13	4	41	19	18	61	8	4	44
75 percent or more	61	9	49	14	4	33	23	17	58	10	7	72
Main teaching assignment												
General education in self-contained classroom	68	15	58	10	3	31	20	20	66	7	7	72
Mathematics/computer science, science	62	12	32	23	4	22	24	22	53	7	2	30
Other academic subject[c]	63	9	39	21	6	42	23	15	55	9	3	35
Special education, English as a second language	65	9	46	22	5	36	28	9	41	10	2	23
Other assignment[d]	56	27	62	22	8	48	23	13	45	10	4	45
Elementary/secondary teaching experience												
3 or fewer years	62	10	38	20	5	34	21	15	50	7	3	58
4 to 9 years	62	13	47	19	5	37	22	19	56	8	4	47
10 to 19 years	65	16	52	17	5	37	22	17	57	8	4	51
20 or more years	65	16	53	17	4	34	24	17	58	9	4	47

!Interpret data with caution; the coefficient of variation is greater than 50 percent.

*Reporting standards not met.

[a]Wireless systems allowing teachers to pose questions and students to respond using "clickers" or hand-held response pads, with responses compiled on a computer.

[b]Data for combined schools (those with both elementary and secondary grades) are included in the totals and in analyses by other school characteristics but are not shown separately.

[c]Other academic subjects include English/language arts, foreign languages, and social sciences/social studies.

[d]Other assignments include arts and music; health/physical education; vocational, career, or technical education; and other (respondent ask to specify).

[e]Devices that transmit images of 2- or 3-dimensional objects, text, or graphics to a computer monitor or LCD projector.

Note: For availability, the questionnaire included a response option of not available. For frequency of use, the response options were never, rarely, sometimes, and often. Responses for sometimes and often were combined in the table. Percents for use are based on the teachers who had the device available.

SOURCE: Lucinda Gray, Nina Thomas, and Laurie Lewis, "Table 3. Percent of Teachers Reporting the Availability of Various Technology Devices, and of Those with the Devices Available, Percent of Those Who Reported Using the Devices Sometimes or Often during their Classes, by School and Teacher Characteristics: 2009," in *Teachers' Use of Educational Technology in U.S. Public Schools: 2009*, U.S. Department of Education, Institute of Education Sciences, National Center for Education Statistics, May 2010, http://nces.ed.gov/pubs2010/2010040.pdf (accessed October 9, 2012)

TABLE 6.4

Frequency with which public school students use technology to perform various types of class work, by selected school, student, and teacher characteristics, 2009

Characteristic	Prepare written text		Create or use graphics or visual displays		Learn or practice basic skills		Conduct research		Correspond with others		Contribute to blogs or wikis		Use social networking websites	
	Rarely	Some-times or often	Rarely	Some-times or often	Rarely	Some-times or often	Rarely	Some-times or often	Rarely	Some-times or often	Rarely	Some-times or often	Rarely	Some-times or often
All public school teachers[a]	24	61	27	53	17	69	22	66	21	31	12	9	9	7
School instructional level[a]														
Elementary	27	57	29	49	15	76	23	64	20	26	10	7	7	6
Secondary	20	67	24	59	21	53	20	69	24	40	16	13	12	9
School enrollment size														
Less than 300	23	63	31	48	20	70	22	64	18	29	11	7	9	4
300 to 999	26	59	28	52	16	73	22	65	21	28	12	8	7	8
1,000 or more	21	64	24	56	20	57	21	67	23	40	15	12	12	8
Community type														
City	24	59	25	52	14	72	21	66	23	32	14	6	10	7
Suburban	24	61	27	53	16	70	23	64	20	32	10	12	7	7
Town	26	61	30	54	20	63	19	69	21	32	14	9	7	9
Rural	24	61	28	52	20	65	21	66	23	29	13	8	11	7
Percent of students in the school eligible for free or reduced-price lunch														
Less than 35 percent	21	66	27	56	21	61	21	67	22	33	12	11	8	6
35 to 49 percent	23	62	29	52	20	63	22	65	21	30	11	8	7	6
50 to 74 percent	27	55	28	49	15	73	21	65	21	30	13	7	8	8
75 percent or more	28	56	26	50	10	83	24	64	20	31	13	9	11	10
Main teaching assignment														
General education in self-contained classroom	28	54	30	45	12	83	24	59	18	22	8	6	7	5
Mathematics/computer science, science	26	52	26	53	20	59	27	56	23	32	11	7	7	7
Other academic subject[b]	21	70	30	56	24	54	18	76	21	40	15	16	10	9
Special education, English as a second language	21	70	23	59	13	80	19	73	24	31	16	8	10	8
Other assignment[c]	21	65	21	62	22	54	18	72	24	39	16	9	12	13
Elementary/secondary teaching experience														
3 or fewer years	28	53	27	49	16	67	26	58	21	30	11	10	8	8
4 to 9 years	27	58	27	52	19	67	23	65	21	33	13	10	10	5
10 to 19 years	22	63	30	51	16	70	21	67	22	29	12	9	7	7
20 or more years	22	64	25	57	16	70	18	69	21	33	13	8	9	10

TABLE 6.4

Frequency with which public school students use technology to perform various types of class work, by selected school, student, and teacher characteristics, 2009 [CONTINUED]

Characteristic	Solve problems, analyze data, or perform calculations		Conduct experiments or perform measurements		Develop and present multimedia presentations		Create art, music, movies, or webcasts		Develop or run demonstrations, models, or simulations		Design and produce a product	
	Rarely	Sometimes or often	Rarely	Sometimes or often	Rarely	Sometimes or often	Rarely	Sometimes or often	Rarely	Sometimes or often	Rarely	Sometimes or often
All public school teachers	23	45	25	25	25	42	24	25	23	17	17	13
School instructional level [a]												
Elementary	21	45	24	23	26	35	25	21	21	14	15	11
Secondary	25	46	27	30	24	53	24	32	26	25	20	17
School enrollment size												
Less than 300	23	44	28	21	22	37	22	23	22	15	15	16
300 to 999	22	46	24	25	25	40	25	23	23	15	17	12
1,000 or more	23	44	27	28	27	47	23	30	24	24	18	16
Community type												
City	21	45	22	26	25	41	24	21	24	16	18	12
Suburban	21	46	25	26	25	40	23	28	21	18	14	12
Town	26	45	29	25	25	46	26	26	27	19	22	18
Rural	24	45	27	25	25	43	25	23	23	17	18	14
Percent of students in the school eligible for free or reduced-price lunch												
Less than 35 percent	24	43	25	24	25	47	25	30	23	18	17	14
35 to 49 percent	24	42	26	23	28	38	24	18	22	17	17	13
50 to 74 percent	19	47	26	27	24	40	24	22	24	17	15	14
75 percent or more	22	52	25	28	24	36	22	22	22	18	20	11
Main teaching assignment												
General education in self-contained classroom	19	43	24	18	25	28	23	17	17	10	12	8
Mathematics/computer science, science [b]	20	61	27	45	29	40	23	17	27	25	17	11
Other academic subject [b]	26	35	24	17	24	56	29	32	26	18	22	19
Special education, English as a second language	29	40	28	23	27	38	25	25	26	13	21	8
Other assignment [c]	26	45	27	27	21	55	21	42	23	26	19	25
Elementary/secondary teaching experience												
3 or fewer years	23	45	25	27	23	41	24	23	20	16	13	9
4 to 9 years	22	46	25	28	24	44	24	28	21	19	17	14
10 to 19 years	23	44	26	23	26	41	23	26	25	17	18	13
20 or more years	26	46	25	25	26	41	26	22	24	17	19	15

[a]Data for combined schools (those with both elementary and secondary grades) are included in the totals and in analyses by other school characteristics but are not shown separately.

[b]Other academic subjects include English/language arts, foreign languages, and social sciences/social studies.

[c]Other assignments include arts and music; health/physical education; vocational, career, or technical education; and other (respondent asked to specify).

Note: Response options in the questionnaire were not applicable, never, rarely, sometimes, and often. Responses for sometimes and often were combined in the table. Percents are based on the teachers reporting that the activity applied to their students.

SOURCE: Lucinda Gray, Nina Thomas, and Laurie Lewis, "Table 7. Percent of Teachers Reporting How Frequently Their Students Performed Various Activities Using Educational Technology during Their Classes, Based on Teachers Reporting that the Activity Applied to Their Students, by School and Teacher Characteristics: 2009," in Teachers' Use of Educational Technology in U.S. Public Schools: 2009, U.S. Department of Education, Institute of Education Sciences, National Center for Education Statistics, May 2010, http://nces.ed.gov/pubs2010/2010040.pdf (accessed October 9, 2012)

teachers, only 7% reported using social media either sometimes or often for instructional purposes.

The Internet also enables teachers to communicate more effectively with students and their parents outside of the classroom. Among all public school teachers, conducting e-mail correspondence with parents concerning specific issues was the most preferred method of communication in 2009, with 79% of all teachers reporting they engaged in one-on-one e-mail communication with parents either sometimes or often. (See Table 6.5.) Table 6.5 also shows a correlation between household income levels and the extent to which teachers communicate with parents and students outside the classroom. In schools where 35% or less of the student body was eligible for free or reduced-price lunch programs, 92% of teachers corresponded with parents via e-mail either sometimes or often; in schools where 75% or more of the students qualified for lunch assistance programs, that number dropped to 48%.

Technology and Student Engagement

The use of technology to expand and improve educational opportunities for students has become a major priority for educators nationwide. Technology offers students a wide range of tools, from the Internet to interactive software, that are designed to boost academic performance and increase individual engagement with school subject matter. The Office of Educational Technology in the U.S. Department of Education outlines in *Transforming American Education: Learning Powered by Technology* (November 2010, http://www.ed.gov/sites/default/files/netp2010.pdf) a new model of instruction that uses technology to "provide engaging and powerful learning experiences and content, as well as resources and assessments that measure student achievement in more complete, authentic, and meaningful ways." The agency also asserts that "technology-based learning and assessment systems will be pivotal in improving student learning and generating data that can be used to continuously improve the education system at all levels."

The Office of Educational Technology cites numerous ways that technology provides new learning opportunities for students. The use of diverse learning tools such as graphics, animation, video, and other media can help facilitate a student's engagement with a wide variety of subjects. For example, in the area of mathematics, the use of statistical and graphing software enables younger learners to develop a basic understanding of complex concepts. For science teachers, introducing professional methods and investigative tools into the classroom can help students develop a sense of what it means to work in the field. In areas such as history, literature, and the social sciences, the online availability of digitalized original documents, whether through institutions such as the Smithsonian or on the World Wide Web, can help enhance a student's research in these fields. In these ways, many educators believe, technology can make students feel more invested in their learning experiences. At the same time, the ability to accumulate and analyze past academic results enables teachers to customize instruction to suit the needs of individual students, addressing problem areas in a more timely and effective manner.

Indeed, some studies indicate that many students express greater enthusiasm for technology-based learning than for more traditional educational methods. In *Charting the Path from Engagement to Achievement: A Report on the 2009 High School Survey of Student Engagement* (June 2010, http://ceep.indiana.edu/hssse/images/HSSSE_2010_Report.pdf), Ethan Yazzie-Mintz of the Center for Evaluation and Education Policy at Indiana University examines the attitudes of high school students toward a range of educational methods. Yazzie-Mintz finds that more than half (55%) of the students surveyed expressed either some or a high degree of excitement for lessons and class projects that involved some form of technology; only discussion and debate (61%) and group projects (60%) ranked higher. On the other end of the spectrum, only a quarter (26%) of students expressed any notable level of enthusiasm for teacher lectures. Several other conventional learning techniques, including art and drama activities (49%), presentations (46%), and role-playing exercises (43%), also elicited less enthusiasm from students overall.

PREVENTING ACCESS TO INAPPROPRIATE MATERIAL

In 2000 Congress passed the Children's Internet Protection Act (CIPA). Under CIPA, public schools and libraries that could not prove they use filtering or blocking technology to keep children from viewing pornographic or sexually explicit websites were no longer eligible for the E-Rate Program. Signed into law in April 2001, CIPA promptly became the target of a legal challenge launched by the American Library Association (ALA) and the American Civil Liberties Union (ACLU). In the lawsuit, the ALA and the ACLU argued that CIPA violated free speech rights guaranteed in the First Amendment. In June 2003 the U.S. Supreme Court upheld the legality of CIPA in *United States v. American Library Association* (539 U.S. 194). By 2005, 100% of U.S. public schools were in compliance with the law. In spite of this widespread acceptance of CIPA, some educators have raised questions about the law's potential to prevent students from engaging in legitimate research. Paul T. Jaeger and Zheng Yan suggest in "One Law with Two Outcomes: Comparing the Implementation of CIPA in Public Libraries and Schools" (*Information Technology & Libraries*, vol. 28, no. 1, March 2009) that even though opposition to CIPA in schools has been "very small," there are still some concerns that "filters in schools may create two classes of

TABLE 6.5

Frequency with which public school teachers use various forms of technology to communicate with students or their parents, by selected school, student, and teacher characteristics, 2009

Characteristic	Email or list-serve to send out group updates or information				Email to address individual concerns				Online bulletin board for class discussion			
	Parents		Students		Parents		Students		Parents		Students	
	Rarely	Some-times or often	Rarely	Some-times or often	Rarely	Some-times or often	Rarely	Some-times or often	Rarely	Some-times or often	Rarely	Some-times or often
All public school teachers	14	59	13	24	10	79	13	30	11	14	7	11
School instructional level[a]												
Elementary	14	58	10	18	11	75	10	20	10	13	6	8
Secondary	14	61	17	36	8	86	19	48	13	16	10	14
School enrollment size												
Less than 300	16	52	11	17	14	71	10	19	9	9	6	5
300 to 999	14	59	12	20	11	77	12	24	10	13	7	9
1,000 or more	13	62	15	36	6	86	17	48	13	18	10	16
Community type												
City	13	53	13	25	11	69	16	29	12	13	7	11
Suburban	15	60	13	25	9	82	13	32	10	16	7	12
Town	14	62	12	23	8	82	14	27	11	14	8	9
Rural	14	62	13	22	11	81	12	27	11	12	8	9
Percent of students in the school eligible for free or reduced-price lunch												
Less than 35 percent	10	69	14	30	4	92	14	38	11	16	8	13
35 to 49 percent	18	61	14	24	9	86	15	31	11	13	9	9
50 to 74 percent	15	58	13	20	12	77	13	25	10	13	6	8
75 percent or more	18	39	10	17	20	48	11	19	13	12	7	9
Main teaching assignment												
General education in self-contained classroom	15	53	8	13	12	70	7	13	8	9	5	5
Mathematics/computer science, science	14	61	17	30	7	88	19	41	12	18	8	17
Other academic subject[b]	13	66	14	34	7	87	16	44	12	15	8	14
Special education, English as a second language	11	58	17	17	9	71	15	22	12	15	8	9
Other assignment[c]	13	65	16	35	12	81	16	41	15	16	12	14
Elementary/secondary teaching experience												
3 or fewer years	15	50	9	19	9	74	11	26	11	15	8	13
4 to 9 years	16	59	14	23	10	79	14	27	9	14	6	12
10 to 19 years	12	62	14	25	9	81	14	29	11	14	7	9
20 or more years	13	61	13	27	11	79	13	35	14	12	8	10

TABLE 6.5

Frequency with which public school teachers use various forms of technology to communicate with students or their parents, by selected school, student, and teacher characteristics, 2009 [CONTINUED]

| Characteristic | Course or teacher web page | | | | Course or teacher blog | | | | Instant messaging | | | |
| | Parents | | Students | | Parents | | Students | | Parents | | Students | |
	Rarely	Some-times or often	Rarely	Some-times or often	Rarely	Some-times or often	Rarely	Some-times or often	Rarely	Some-times or often	Rarely	Some-times or often
All public school teachers	14	39	11	28	8	8	6	5	7	7	4	3
School instructional level[a]												
Elementary	14	39	9	25	8	7	5	4	6	7	3	2
Secondary	14	41	13	33	10	9	8	7	8	7	5	5
School enrollment size												
Less than 300	14	34	10	20	8	5	5	3	7	6	3	1
300 to 999	14	38	10	26	8	8	5	4	6	7	4	3
1,000 or more	14	43	12	35	9	11	7	8	8	7	4	5
Community type												
City	16	32	11	22	8	8	6	4	8	8	5	4
Suburban	13	43	10	32	8	9	6	6	6	5	3	3
Town	12	39	12	26	9	8	5	5	6	11	5	3
Rural	14	40	11	28	9	7	6	5	7	8	4	4
Percent of students in the school eligible for free or reduced-price lunch												
Less than 35 percent	13	47	10	36	8	9	5	7	6	5	4	3
35 to 49 percent	14	38	14	26	10	6	7	4	6	8	4	3
50 to 74 percent	14	35	10	24	8	8	6	5	7	8	4	4
75 percent or more	14	30	10	18	8	8	6	4	9	10	5	4
Main teaching assignment												
General education in self-contained classroom	12	35	8	20	7	6	4	2	6	7	3	2
Mathematics/computer science, science	13	45	12	38	8	8	6	6	7	7	4	4
Other academic subject[b]	14	41	11	35	9	11	6	9	7	5	4	3
Special education, English as a second language	15	35	13	20	10	9	7	4	9	6	5	3
Other assignment[c]	17	43	15	31	12	8	8	7	8	11	7	5
Elementary/secondary teaching experience												
3 or fewer years	12	34	10	23	7	8	4	5	6	4	2	3
4 to 9 years	13	38	11	27	7	8	5	6	6	6	4	3
10 to 19 years	13	41	10	30	7	9	6	5	7	8	4	3
20 or more years	16	41	12	29	11	8	8	5	8	9	6	4

[a]Data for combined schools (those with both elementary and secondary grades) are included in the totals and in analyses by other school characteristics but are not shown separately.

[b]Other academic subjects include English/language arts, foreign languages, and social sciences/social studies.

[c]Other assignments include arts and music; health/physical education; vocational, career, or technical education; and other (respondent asked to specify).

Note: Response options in the questionnaire were never, rarely, sometimes, and often. Responses for sometimes and often were combined in the table.

SOURCE: Lucinda Gray, Nina Thomas, and Laurie Lewis, "Table 8. Percent of Teachers Reporting How Frequently They Used Various Modes of Technology to Communicate with Parents or Students, by School and Teacher Characteristics: 2009," in *Teachers' Use of Educational Technology in U.S. Public Schools: 2009*, U.S. Department of Education, Institute of Education Sciences, National Center for Education Statistics, May 2010, http://nces.ed.gov/pubs2010/2010040.pdf (accessed October 9, 2012)

students—ones with only filtered access at school and ones who also can get unfiltered access at home." In "Minors' First Amendment Rights: CIPA and School Libraries" (*Knowledge Quest*, vol. 31, no. 1, September–October 2010), Theresa Chmara raises questions concerning the impact of CIPA on the first amendment rights of children, suggesting that the scope of the law has the potential to restrict students' access to legitimate educational material.

COLLEGES AND UNIVERSITIES

College students are among the most wired Americans and are typically the first to embrace new technologies. The marketing research firm Student Monitor (December 2012, http://www.studentmonitor.com/computing.php) reports that in 2012, 86% of full-time undergraduate college students owned their own computers before starting college and 17% planned to buy a new computer within the next year. The firm also reports that 88% of college students accessed the Internet at least once per day. With a weekly average of 19 hours, students spent twice as much time online in 2012 as those interviewed in 2000. Student Monitor also reveals that nearly nine out of 10 (88%) full-time undergraduate students had a cell phone.

By 2012 Internet use had become a dominant feature of college life. In "The Impact of Internet and Television Use on the Reading Habits and Practices of College Students" (*Journal of Adolescent and Adult Literacy*, vol. 52, no. 7, April 2009), Kouider Mokhtari, Carla A. Reichard, and Anne Gardner examine the ways in which the Internet has become integrated into the daily activities of college students. According to the researchers, college students spent an average of 2.5 hours per day online. By comparison, the average student devoted just about 2.2 hours per day to academic reading, 1.9 hours per day watching television, and 1.1 hours per day reading for pleasure. About 95% of students used the Internet every day, compared with 64% who read for school, 58.4% who watched television, and 31.8% who read for pleasure. Because college students are spending more time online, experts are beginning to explore how the Internet affects their academic and social lives. Dimitri A. Christakis et al. examine in "Problematic Internet Usage in US College Students: A Pilot Study" (*BMC Medicine*, vol. 9, June 22, 2011) the Internet habits of 224 American college students. The researchers find that 92% of the students reported staying online longer than they intended at least "occasionally" and 10% reported they "always" stayed on the Internet longer than they wanted. In spite of this trend, a minority (43%) of the students reported that their Internet habits had any real negative impact on their academics, whereas only 10.5% admitted they sometimes preferred the Internet to socializing with friends.

Technology and College Academics

The Internet has transformed college life from beginning to end, from the selection process undertaken by high school students considering different institutions to the employment and career services offered online to recent college graduates. In the 21st century high school students research prospective colleges and universities online, take virtual campus and dormitory tours, and download recruitment materials and application forms. College students enroll for classes, pay fees, order books and course materials, and may even take classes and tests online. For some professors, electronic textbooks (e-textbooks) have supplanted traditional textbooks as a primary means of assigning reading to their students. (See Figure 6.1.) The Internet has also become a vital mode of communication between students and faculty. I. Elaine Allen and Jeff Seaman note in *Digital Faculty: Professors, Teaching and Technology, 2012* (August 2012, http://www.insidehighered.com/download/?file=DigitalFaculty.pdf) that more than three-quarters (75.1%) of professors reported that digital communication had increased their overall level of communication with their students. As Figure 6.2 shows, female faculty members were somewhat more likely to report increased digital communication with their students than male faculty members.

The Internet has also radically transformed the ways that university libraries allocate their financial resources. According to the Association of Research Libraries (October 24, 2012, http://www.arl.org/stats/annualsurveys/arlstats/arlstats11.shtml), in 2000–01 university libraries spent $132.7 million on electronic resources, a figure that accounted for 16% of the $828.8 million spent on all library materials. By 2010–11 spending on electronic resources by university libraries increased to $856.2 million, or 63% of the total $1.4 billion that was devoted to library materials. That same year the average university spent $12.1 million on library materials, of which $7.6 million was dedicated to electronic resources. Of all the money that was spent on online and digital resources in 2010–11, the vast majority ($764.5 million) of funds went toward electronic serial publications.

The Internet and College Social Life

Since the 1990s technology has had a profound impact on everyday campus life. E-mail, the Internet, and mobile phones have transformed the way that college students communicate with each other, whether they are discussing academic coursework or simply making plans for the weekend. In particular, social networking sites such as Facebook and MySpace have played an important role in shaping the social relationships of college students in the 21st century. College students create social networking profiles for a variety of reasons. Many students view social networking sites as a way to maintain contact

FIGURE 6.1

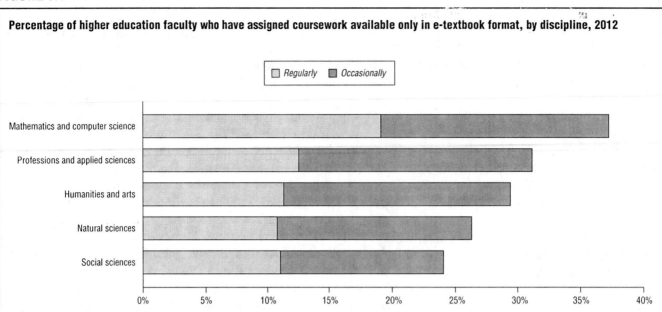

Percentage of higher education faculty who have assigned coursework available only in e-textbook format, by discipline, 2012

Regularly   Occasionally

- Mathematics and computer science
- Professions and applied sciences
- Humanities and arts
- Natural sciences
- Social sciences

0%   5%   10%   15%   20%   25%   30%   35%   40%

SOURCE: I. Elaine Allen and Jeff Seaman, "Assigned Material Available only in E-Textbook Format by Discipline—Faculty," in *Digital Faculty: Professors, Teaching and Technology, 2012*, Babson Survey Research Group in conjunction with *Inside Higher Ed*, August 2012, www.insidehighered.com/download/?file=DigitalFaculty.pdf (accessed October 9, 2012)

FIGURE 6.2

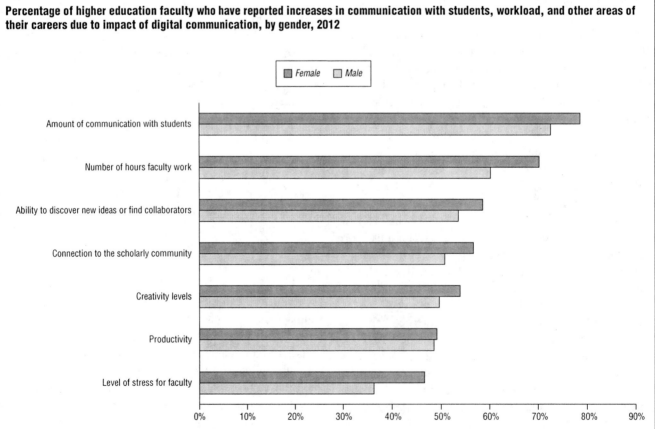

Percentage of higher education faculty who have reported increases in communication with students, workload, and other areas of their careers due to impact of digital communication, by gender, 2012

Female   Male

- Amount of communication with students
- Number of hours faculty work
- Ability to discover new ideas or find collaborators
- Connection to the scholarly community
- Creativity levels
- Productivity
- Level of stress for faculty

0%   10%   20%   30%   40%   50%   60%   70%   80%   90%

SOURCE: I. Elaine Allen and Jeff Seaman, "The Impact of Digital Communication—Gender Differences (Percent Reporting an Increase)—Faculty," in *Digital Faculty: Professors, Teaching and Technology, 2012*, Babson Survey Research Group in conjunction with *Inside Higher Ed*, August 2012, www.insidehighered.com/download/?file=DigitalFaculty.pdf (accessed October 9, 2012)

with old friends and meet new people. Reynol Junco of Lock Haven University finds in "In-class Multitasking and Academic Performance" (*Computers in Human Behavior*, vol. 28, no. 6, November 2012) that in 2012 between 87% and 92% of college undergraduates used Facebook every day, compared with 73% who sent or received text messages daily. On average, students who used Facebook spent more than an hour and 40 minutes on the site each day. Whereas 34% of college students reported texting during class at least sometimes, only 13% reported using Facebook 50% or more of the time they were in class. Social networking is not limited to university students. According to Kim Parker, Amanda Lenhart, and Kathleen Moore of Pew/Internet, in *The Digital Revolution and Higher Education: College Presidents, Public Differ on Value of Online Learning* (August 28, 2011, http://www.pewsocialtrends.org/2011/08/28/the-digital-revolution-and-higher-education/), 50% of U.S. college presidents had Facebook accounts in 2011.

Social networking profiles also provide students with a space for self-expression. In "Image and Video Disclosure of Substance Use on Social Media Websites" (*Computers in Human Behavior*, vol. 26, no. 6, November 2010), Elizabeth M. Morgan, Chareen Snelson, and Patt Elison-Bowers of Boise State University find that students typically view social networking pages as a way to describe their interests, upload pictures of themselves and their friends, and share other aspects of their personalities in a public forum. Although social networking can play a valuable role in helping students explore their own identity, as well as establish and sustain healthy social connections, it can also lead to negative behaviors. The researchers reveal that students often use social networking sites to post images or videos of themselves consuming alcohol or drugs, often without any consideration of who might see them. Morgan, Snelson, and Elison-Bowers indicate that 26% of the college students surveyed had posted images of themselves drinking alcohol on MySpace, compared with 17% who had posted such images on Facebook. Thirty percent had pictures of themselves drinking posted on MySpace by their friends, whereas 75% had such images posted by a friend of a friend; 29% had such images posted on Facebook by friends, and 67% by a friend of friend. Fewer than 1% of college students had posted images of themselves smoking marijuana online, or had images of themselves using marijuana posted by friends; however, a far higher percentage of students report having had such images posted by a friend of a friend on either MySpace (33%) or Facebook (25%). Morgan, Snelson, and Elison-Bowers find that a majority (55%) of the students surveyed believe it is "the right of the individual" to post pictures of themselves using alcohol online. In contrast, 78% objected to having images of themselves smoking marijuana on the Internet.

DISTANCE LEARNING

Besides providing students with a host of valuable new research tools, the Internet has also made education more widely available to a greater portion of the population. In the past, people who lived in remote areas of the country, had limited access to transportation, suffered from illness or other disabilities, or were constrained by work or other obligations struggled to pursue educational opportunities. With the emergence of distance learning programs, however, students were able to take classes online, from their own home. As Table 6.6 shows, during the 2009–10 academic year 55% of all public school districts in the United States offered distance learning programs for their students. Larger school districts were the most likely to offer online classes, with nearly three-quarters (74%) of districts with 10,000 students or more providing distance learning opportunities in 2009–10, compared with 51% of districts with fewer than 2,500 students. In 2009–10 nearly one-quarter (22%) of school districts allowed students to take a full course load consisting of only distance learning courses and 12% of districts allowed students to complete all graduation requirements taking only distance education classes. (See Table 6.7.) As Table 6.8 shows, school districts offered online courses to meet a wide range of student needs. Of school districts with students enrolled in distance learning classes, 64% cited the ability of students to take courses not otherwise available in school as a "very important" criteria for providing distance education opportunities; another 57% of school districts saw providing distance learning to students who had missed or failed classes as "very important." By comparison, only 5% of school districts cited overcrowding as a "very important" factor in providing distance learning courses.

Thomas A. Snyder and Sally A. Dillow report in *Digest of Education Statistics 2011* (June 2012, http://nces.ed.gov/pubs2012/2012001.pdf) that in 2002–03 a total of 317,070 students in kindergarten to 12th grade were enrolled in distance learning courses nationwide; by 2009–10 this number had risen to 1.8 million, an increase of 473%. High school students (1.3 million) accounted for the large majority of distance learning enrollments in 2009–10, followed by combined elementary and high school students (234,460), middle school students (154,970), and elementary school students (78,040). By region, the highest proportion of school districts offering distance learning in 2009–10 was in the Southeast, where 78% of all schools offered distance education courses; by comparison, only 39% of school districts in the Northeast offered distance learning opportunities to their students.

Distance learning programs also became widespread at colleges and universities in the early 21st century. In *Digital Revolution and Higher Education*, Taylor et al. indicate that in 2011, 89% of four-year public colleges and universities and 91% of two-year colleges offered

TABLE 6.6

Percentage of school districts with students enrolled in distance learning courses, by grade level and selected district characteristics, 2009–10

District characteristic	Districts with any students enrolled in distance education courses[a]	Districts with students enrolled in distance education courses at that instructional level[b]			
		Elementary schools	Middle or junior high schools	High schools	Combined or ungraded schools[c]
All public school districts	55	6	19	96	4
District enrollment size					
Less than 2,500	51	5	16	95	3
2,500 to 9,999	66	8	26	98	5
10,000 or more	74	11	34	98	5
Community type					
City	37	7	22	98	3!
Suburban	47	8	23	96	6
Town	67	9	25	98	4!
Rural	59	4	16	95	3
Region					
Northeast	39	4!	22	97	‡
Southeast	78	7	28	97	4
Central	62	6	17	97	4
West	51	7	17	94	5
Poverty concentration					
Less than 10 percent	54	5	20	96	2!
10 to 19 percent	56	6	20	96	5
20 percent or more	56	7	18	96	4

!Interpret data with caution; the coefficient of variation is greater than or equal to 30 percent.
‡Reporting standards not met. The coefficient of variation for this estimate is 50 percent or greater.
[a]Based on all public school districts.
[b]Based on the 55 percent of districts with students enrolled in distance education courses in the 12-month 2009–10 school year.
[c]Combined or ungraded schools are those in which the grades offered in the school span both elementary and secondary grades or that are not divided into grade levels. In survey questions that asked respondents to report by instructional level, the grade ranges were not defined for district respondents.
Note: Data are for the 12-month 2009–10 school year. Poverty estimates for school districts were based on Title I data provided to the U.S. Department of Education by the U.S. Census Bureau.

SOURCE: Barbara Queen and Laurie Lewis, "Table 1. Percent of Public School Districts with Any Students Enrolled in Distance Education Courses, and the Percent of Those Districts with Students Enrolled in Distance Education Courses at Various Instructional Levels, by District Characteristics: School Year 2009–10," in *Distance Education Courses for Public Elementary and Secondary School Students: 2009–10*, U.S. Department of Education, Institute of Education Sciences, National Center for Education Statistics, November 2011, http://nces.ed.gov/pubs2012/2012008.pdf (accessed October 9, 2012)

online classes to their students. In contrast, only 60% of private colleges and universities offered online classes as part of their curriculum. As Figure 6.3 shows, 82% of community colleges offered online classes in 2011, compared with 79% of research universities and 61% of liberal arts colleges. Schools categorized as "least selective" were the most likely to offer online courses (86%); by comparison, just over half (51%) of highly selective institutions provided online learning opportunities to students. In 2011 a slim majority (51%) of all college and university presidents believed online classes provide students with an educational experience comparable to that found in traditional classrooms. (See Figure 6.4.) Presidents of two-year colleges (66%) were the most likely to view online course offerings as having equal value as courses taught in person, whereas presidents of private four-year institutions (36%) were the least likely to find the two forms of learning to have equal value. Meanwhile, the digital age saw the rise of so-called online universities, such as the University of Phoenix and Kaplan University, that catered exclusively to students seeking to take classes over the Internet.

Faculty members at colleges and institutions offering online classes also recognize the benefits of online education to their students. As Figure 6.5 shows, support for online courses among faculty varied between academic disciplines in 2012. Nearly 75% of professors and instructors teaching courses in professions and applied sciences had recommended online classes to their students, compared with roughly 60% each of faculty in mathematics and computer science and in the social sciences. Just over half of instructors and professors in the humanities and arts and the natural sciences recommended online courses to their students.

Allen and Seaman explain in *Digital Faculty* that faculty and administrators at colleges and universities identified numerous positive benefits that are associated with online education. Figure 6.6 exhibits responses of higher education faculty and administrators in 2012 to various aspects of online courses. Roughly 90% of administrators and nearly 75% of faculty reported feeling more excitement than fear about the potential of online courses to increase the amount of data related to teaching and learning. A majority of both administrators and

TABLE 6.7

Percentage of school districts that allow students to take only distance learning courses during an academic term, or that allow students to fulfill all high school graduation requirements by taking only distance learning courses, by selected district characteristics, 2009–10

District characteristic	Students can take a full course load using only distance education courses	Students can fulfill all high school graduation requirements using only distance education courses
All public school districts with students enrolled in distance education courses	22	12
District enrollment size		
Less than 2,500	20	12
2,500 to 9,999	28	15
10,000 or more	24	13
Community type		
City	32	20
Suburban	25	15
Town	29	18
Rural	17	8
Region		
Northeast	22	11
Southeast	22	9
Central	24	15
West	21	11
Poverty concentration		
Less than 10 percent	23	13
10 to 19 percent	25	14
20 percent or more	19	9

Note: Percentages are based on districts with students enrolled in distance education courses and with high schools. Of the 55 percent of public school districts with students enrolled in distance education courses in the 12-month 2009–10 school year, 98 percent had high schools. Poverty estimates for school districts were based on Title I data provided to the U.S. Department of Education by the U.S. Census Bureau.

SOURCE: Barbara Queen and Laurie Lewis, "Table 7. Percent of Public School Districts with Students Enrolled in Distance Education Courses Indicating that Students Who Were Enrolled in Regular High School Programs Were Able to Take a Full Course Load in an Academic Term Using only Distance Education Courses, and the Percent Indicating that Students Can Fulfill All High School Graduation Requirements Using Only Distance Education Courses, by District Characteristics: School Year 2009–10," in *Distance Education Courses for Public Elementary and Secondary School Students: 2009–10*, U.S. Department of Education, Institute of Education Sciences, National Center for Education Statistics, November 2011, http://nces.ed.gov/pubs2012/2012008.pdf (accessed October 9, 2012)

faculty also felt more excitement than fear about the expansion of hybrid models of education that incorporate both in-class and online coursework (92.9% and 71.1%, respectively), about the prospect of libraries focusing on digital rather than on print collections (87.7% and 70.6%), and about the potential of online instruction to allow faculty to devote more time to coaching students individually (89% and 68.7%). However, a small minority of administrators and faculty members (19.3% and 12%, respectively) expressed excitement about the prospect of expanding for-profit education through online course offerings.

Still, Allen and Seaman reveal in *Conflicted: Faculty and Online Education, 2012* (June 2012, http://www.insidehighered.com/sites/default/server_files/files/IHE-BSRG-Conflict.pdf) that faculty at institutions of higher learning

also feel some degree of anxiety at the prospect of online education's continued growth in the 21st century. Figure 6.7 shows attitudes of higher education faculty toward the expansion of online education, separated according to academic discipline, tenure status, part-time or full-time status, and experience. Among academic disciplines, only the professions and applied sciences contained a majority (55.5%) of faculty members who expressed more excitement than fear about the growth of online learning in the 21st century. According to Allen and Seaman, instructors in the social sciences (36.2%) and the humanities and arts (34.5%) were the least likely to feel more excitement than fear about online education's future growth. A slim majority (50.7%) of nontenure track professors expressed more excitement than fear about the expansion of online education, compared with 35.4% of faculty who were tenure-tracked but not yet tenured and 34.8% of tenured faculty members.

CHEATING AND HIGH TECHNOLOGY

Cheating is one of the biggest problems facing academia and includes any instance in which a student breaks the rules for an assignment or test to gain an advantage over fellow classmates. A specific type of cheating known as plagiarism occurs when a student submits someone else's work as his or her own. Plagiarism itself has several forms, including purchasing a previously written paper, copying sentences or ideas from an original source document without proper attribution, or paying someone else to complete the work. In June 2005 Donald L. McCabe of Rutgers University, the founder of the Center for Academic Integrity (http://www.academicintegrity.org/), published the results of a three-year survey of 50,000 college students at 60 campuses across the country. Of those who admitted cheating in 2005, a quarter said they had cheated seriously on a test and half said they had cheated seriously on a written assignment. The Josephson Institute of Ethics states in *2012 Report Card on the Ethics of American Youth, Installment 1: Honesty and Integrity* (November 20, 2012, http://charactercounts.org/pdf/reportcard/2012/ReportCard-2012-DataTables-HonestyIntegrityCheating.pdf) that nearly one-third (32%) of high school students had copied a document from the Internet for a class assignment in 2012. The institute shows that male students (37%) were more likely to have plagiarized from the Internet than female students (27%). Of those surveyed, 52% admitted to having cheated on a test at least once.

The Internet and other types of information technology have only served to fuel the cheating epidemic in the United States. Phones with text messaging allow students the opportunity to communicate with outsiders or others in class during a test. Companies that specialize in writing papers for students, commonly known as "paper mills," can now deliver papers discreetly to students via

TABLE 6.8

Criteria for public school districts offering distance learning courses, ranked by relative importance, by selected district characteristics, 2009–10

District characteristic	Providing courses not otherwise available at school			Offering advanced placement or college-level courses			Reducing scheduling conflicts for students			Providing opportunities for students to recover course credits from classes missed or failed		
	Not important	Somewhat important	Very important	Not important	Somewhat important	Very important	Not important	Somewhat important	Very important	Not important	Somewhat important	Very important
All public school districts with students enrolled in distance education courses	18	17	64	35	20	41	30	38	30	24	15	57
District enrollment size												
Less than 2,500	15	14	69	33	18	45	31	39	28	29	18	49
2,500 to 9,999	24	22	53	41	23	33	30	37	31	15	11	72
10,000 or more	25	27	47	40	30	29	21	31	47	7	10	81
Community type												
City	31	30	37	52	22	23	40	27	30	7	6	81
Suburban	27	19	52	42	25	30	31	31	36	21	12	66
Town	22	16	60	38	19	40	32	42	26	20	15	60
Rural	11	15	73	29	19	48	28	41	30	30	18	49
Region												
Northeast	13	11	75	36	22	39	31	32	36	34	17	46
Southeast	7	18	74	25	23	51	22	35	42	16	15	65
Central	20	17	61	41	16	38	33	38	27	24	14	59
West	23	20	56	32	23	42	31	43	26	24	17	56
Poverty concentration												
Less than 10 percent	19	15	64	40	21	36	30	37	31	28	11	60
10 to 19 percent	18	18	62	34	18	43	29	40	29	24	16	55
20 percent or more	16	17	65	33	22	42	32	36	31	22	18	57

TABLE 6.8

Criteria for public school districts offering distance learning courses, ranked by relative importance, by selected district characteristics, 2009–10 [CONTINUED]

District characteristic	Providing opportunities for students to accelerate credit accumulation for early graduation			Providing opportunities for students who are homebound or have special needs			Addressing school space limitations			Generating more district revenues		
	Not important	Somewhat important	Very important	Not important	Somewhat important	Very important	Not important	Somewhat important	Very important	Not important	Somewhat important	Very important
All public school districts with students enrolled in distance education courses	55	27	15	40	30	25	82	11	5	82	8	5
District enrollment size												
Less than 2,500	58	26	12	46	27	22	84	10	4	82	7	5
2,500 to 9,999	50	26	20	29	36	30	80	11	6	82	9	4
10,000 or more	36	36	25	18	37	41	69	22	7	73	15	8
Community type												
City	41	23	29	18	35	41	69	15!	12!	69	12	11!
Suburban	54	26	19	30	32	35	79	13	6	84	10	3!
Town	55	25	18	35	31	30	83	11	3	78	10	5!
Rural	57	29	11	49	29	17	84	9	4	84	6	5
Region												
Northeast	61	26	11	47	26	24	78	15	5!	87	4!	4!
Southeast	50	27	18	35	35	25	71	17	8	85	5	2!
Central	62	23	11	39	30	26	88	6	3	82	10	4!
West	44	33	22	41	30	25	81	12	6!	76	10	9
Poverty concentration												
Less than 10 percent	59	24	15	44	27	24	82	11	4	86	8	3!
10 to 19 percent	53	30	14	38	32	26	83	10	4	80	9	5
20 percent or more	54	24	18	41	30	24	79	12	6	81	7	7

!Interpret data with caution; the coefficient of variation is greater than or equal to 30 percent.

Note: Response options in the questionnaire were "not important," "somewhat important," "very important," and "don't know." The "don't know" responses are not shown in the table. Percentages are based on the 55 percent of public school districts with students enrolled in distance education courses in the 12-month 2009-10 school year. Poverty estimates for school districts were based on Title I data provided to the U.S. Department of Education by the U.S. Census Bureau.

SOURCE: Barbara Queen and Laurie Lewis, "Table 10. Percent of Public School Districts with Students Enrolled in Distance Education Courses Indicating How Important Various Reasons Were for Having Distance Education Courses in Their District, by District Characteristics: School Year 2009–10," in *Distance Education Courses for Public Elementary and Secondary School Students: 2009–10*, U.S. Department of Education, Institute of Education Sciences, National Center for Education Statistics, November 2011, http://nces.ed.gov/pubs2012/2012008.pdf (accessed October 9, 2012)

FIGURE 6.3

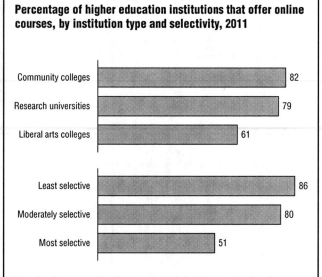

Percentage of higher education institutions that offer online courses, by institution type and selectivity, 2011

Community colleges	82
Research universities	79
Liberal arts colleges	61
Least selective	86
Moderately selective	80
Most selective	51

Note: Based on survey of college presidents. Selectivity categories based on Barron's Profile of American Colleges 2011.

SOURCE: Kim Parker, Amanda Lenhart, and Kathleen Moore, "Online Learning by Type of Institution, Selectivity," in *The Digital Revolution and Higher Education: College Presidents, Public Differ on Value of Online Learning,* Pew Internet & American Life Project, August 28, 2011, http://www.pewsocialtrends.org/2011/08/28/the-digital-revolution-and-higher-education/(accessed October 9, 2012). Used by permission of the Pew Internet & American Life Project, which bears no responsibility for the interpretations presented or conclusions reached based on analysis of the data.

FIGURE 6.4

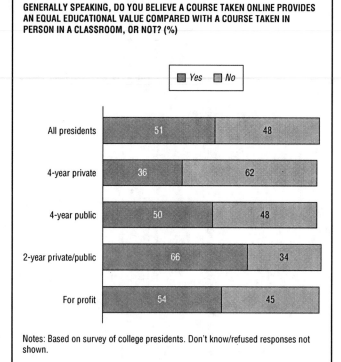

Percentage of college presidents who believe online courses provide educational value equal to that of courses taught in the classroom, by institution type, 2011

GENERALLY SPEAKING, DO YOU BELIEVE A COURSE TAKEN ONLINE PROVIDES AN EQUAL EDUCATIONAL VALUE COMPARED WITH A COURSE TAKEN IN PERSON IN A CLASSROOM, OR NOT? (%)

Legend: ■ Yes ■ No

	Yes	No
All presidents	51	48
4-year private	36	62
4-year public	50	48
2-year private/public	66	34
For profit	54	45

Notes: Based on survey of college presidents. Don't know/refused responses not shown.

SOURCE: Kim Parker, Amanda Lenhart, and Kathleen Moore, "Presidents' Views on Learning Online vs. in the Classroom," in *The Digital Revolution and Higher Education: College Presidents, Public Differ on Value of Online Learning,* Pew Internet & American Life Project, August 28, 2011, http://www.pewsocialtrends.org/2011/08/28/the-digital-revolution-and-higher-education/ (accessed October 9, 2012). Used by permission of the Pew Internet & American Life Project, which bears no responsibility for the interpretations presented or conclusions reached based on analysis of the data.

e-mail. In general, the Internet provides an endless source of documents and papers from which students might copy material. Catching plagiarism on the Internet, however, involves combing through countless articles and websites. The issue of plagiarism from web sources is further complicated by the fact that the Internet has obscured the distinction between what information requires attribution and what is public knowledge. In 2011 more than half (55%) of college presidents in the United States believed that plagiarism had increased over the previous decade; of these, an overwhelming majority (89%) believed that technology had played a key role in this rise. (See Figure 6.8 and Figure 6.9.)

To catch plagiarizers, some schools are using high-technology online services such as Turnitin.com. This online service receives papers from students and teachers and scans them into a database. The papers are then checked against more than 9 billion web pages, previously submitted student papers, and a number of books and encyclopedias. Turnitin.com (2012, http://turn itin.com/en_us/about-us/our-company) indicates that it handled over 60 million papers in 2011; on a single day in December of that year the service processed 300,000 papers, at one point receiving 500 submissions per minute.

As of 2012, Princeton University and many other leading schools were still not using antiplagiarism services, holding to the belief that their campuses did not foster a culture in which cheating is acceptable. Paul Craft writes in "Some Schools Resist Anti-cheating Software" (*Washington Monthly College Guide,* July 13, 2010) that Emily Aronson, a spokesperson for Princeton, asserted that even though the university had considered implementing Turnitin software as recently as 2006, it ultimately decided that "adopting this kind of software sends a message to our students that is not one that we want to send. We don't want to presume that they aren't approaching their work honestly. We want to presume that they're behaving with integrity." Regardless, cheating remains a serious problem even at the nation's most elite institutions. This adherence to principles suffered a serious challenge in 2012, after details concerning a major plagiarism scandal at Harvard University emerged. According to Hana N. Rouse and Justin C. Worland, in "Faust Addresses Cheating Scandal" (*Harvard Crimson,*

FIGURE 6.5

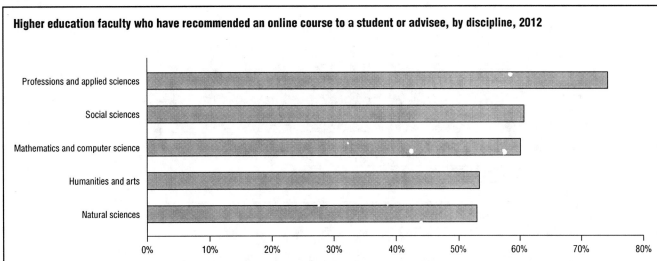

Higher education faculty who have recommended an online course to a student or advisee, by discipline, 2012

SOURCE: I. Elaine Allen and Jeff Seaman, "Recommended an Online Course to a Student or Advisee—Faculty at Institutions with Online Offerings," in *Conflicted: Faculty and Online Education, 2012*, Babson Survey Research Group in conjunction with *Inside Higher Ed*, June 2012, http://www .insidehighered.com/sites/default/server_files/files/IHE-BSRG-Conflict.pdf (accessed October 9, 2012)

FIGURE 6.6

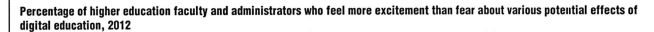

Percentage of higher education faculty and administrators who feel more excitement than fear about various potential effects of digital education, 2012

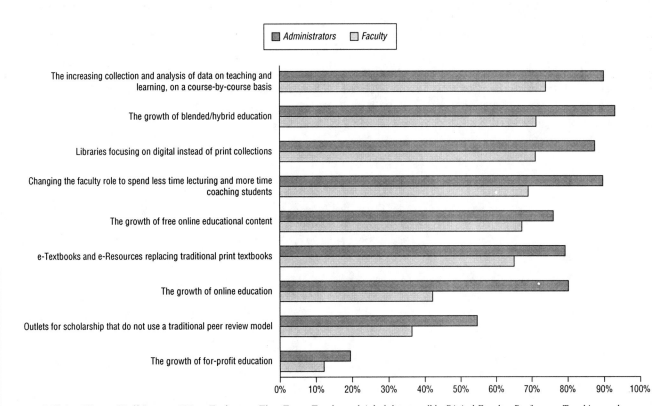

SOURCE: I. Elaine Allen and Jeff Seaman, "More Excitement Than Fear—Faculty and Administrators," in *Digital Faculty: Professors, Teaching and Technology, 2012*, Babson Survey Research Group in conjunction with *Inside Higher Ed*, August 2012, www.insidehighered.com/download/? file=DigitalFaculty.pdf (accessed October 9, 2012)

FIGURE 6.7

Higher education faculty who feel more excitement than fear concerning the growth of online education, by discipline, 2012

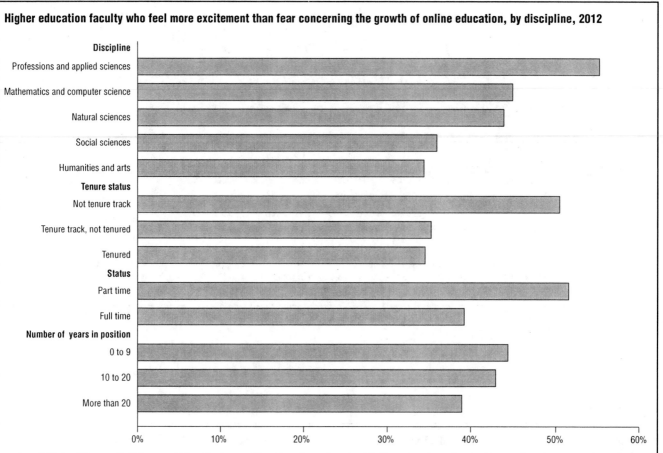

SOURCE: I. Elaine Allen and Jeff Seaman, "More Excitement Than Fear about Growth of Online Education—Faculty," in *Conflicted: Faculty and Online Education, 2012*, Babson Survey Research Group in conjunction with *Inside Higher Ed*, June 2012, http://www.insidehighered.com/sites/default/server_files/files/IHE-BSRG-Conflict.pdf (accessed October 9, 2012)

October 4, 2012), 125 students enrolled in a government course entitled "Introduction to Congress" were accused of plagiarizing or illegally collaborating on a take-home exam. Citing the university president Drew Faust's response to the incident, Rouse and Worland report that the scandal "sparked an important discussion about cheating in higher education" during the fall of 2012, both at Harvard and other Ivy League institutions.

FIGURE 6.8

Percentage of college presidents who believe that plagiarism among college students has increased in the past decade, 2011

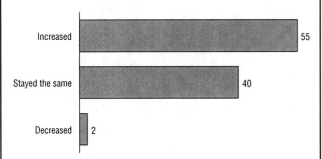

Note: Based on survey of college presidents. Don't know/refused responses not shown.

SOURCE: Kim Parker, Amanda Lenhart, and Kathleen Moore, "Plagiarism in Papers among College Students," in *The Digital Revolution and Higher Education: College Presidents, Public Differ on Value of Online Learning*, Pew Internet & American Life Project, August 28, 2011, http://www.pewsocialtrends.org/2011/08/28/the-digital-revolution-and-higher-education/ (accessed October 9, 2012). Used by permission of the Pew Internet & American Life Project, which bears no responsibility for the interpretations presented or conclusions reached based on analysis of the data.

FIGURE 6.9

Among college presidents who believe incidences of plagiarism have risen in the past decade, percent who believe technology has played a major role in the increase, 2011

HOW MUCH OF A ROLE HAVE COMPUTERS AND THE INTERNET PLAYED IN THE INCREASE IN PLAGIARISM? (%)

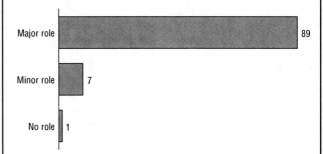

Note: Based on college presidents who said plagiarism in papers among students has increased over past decade (sample size = 556). Don't know/refused responses not shown.

SOURCE: Kim Parker, Amanda Lenhart, and Kathleen Moore, "Plagiarism and Technology," in *The Digital Revolution and Higher Education: College Presidents, Public Differ on Value of Online Learning*, Pew Internet & American Life Project, August 28, 2011, http://www.pewsocialtrends.org/2011/08/28/the-digital-revolution-and-higher-education/ (accessed October 9, 2012). Used by permission of the Pew Internet & American Life Project, which bears no responsibility for the interpretations presented or conclusions reached based on analysis of the data.

CHAPTER 7
INFORMATION TECHNOLOGY AND GOVERNMENT

Since the 1990s government bodies in the United States at the local, state, and federal levels have made a concerted effort to use the Internet and other types of information technology (IT) to streamline their operations and dealings with the public. Much of this effort has been focused on making information available via the Internet. Local and municipal governments now post meeting minutes and agendas online. States have erected websites that allow citizens to renew registrations, obtain licenses, and track legislation online. The federal government has brought myriad services and information to the Internet, allowing Americans to do everything from applying for a patent online to reviewing the holdings of the Smithsonian Institution. The American public has taken advantage of these services in large numbers. Aaron Smith of the Pew Internet & American Life Project (Pew/Internet) reports in *Government Online* (April 27, 2010, http://pewinternet .org/~/media//Files/Reports/2010/PIP_Government_Online _2010_with_topline.pdf) that in 2010, 82% of all Internet users had visited a government website in the previous 12 months; 48% had looked for information about a specific policy or issue and 46% had visited government websites to learn what sort of services a particular agency provides.

Various government entities have employed other forms of IT to streamline services outside of cyberspace. After the hotly contested 2000 presidential race between Governor George W. Bush (1946–) of Texas and Vice President Albert Gore Jr. (1948–), state election commissions replaced many of the aging mechanical voting systems with electronic touch screen and optical scanning systems. These systems made the voting booth accessible for many disabled people and presumably led to more accurate ballot totals in elections. Advances in communications and detection systems have also given rise to networks along U.S. highways that monitor traffic and weather conditions on a real-time basis. For example, in 1999 the federal government designated 511 as the

universal phone number by which people can access these systems to obtain details on traffic and weather in their area. In addition, technology has enabled the federal government to undertake ambitious and far-reaching improvements to the nation's infrastructure. For example, the Energy Independence and Security Act of 2007 included a provision calling for the creation of a smart grid, with the aim of streamlining the transmission and distribution of electricity throughout the United States.

COMMUNICATING WITH GOVFRNMENT

American citizens are constantly interacting with their government online. According to the government IT firm MeriTalk, in *Uncle Sam at Your Service: The 2011 Federal Customer Experience Study* (August 29, 2011, http://www.meritalk.com/pdfs/MeriTalk_2011_Federal _Customer_Experience_Report_082911_Final.pdf), 44% of Americans surveyed had visited a federal government website to find information about government programs or benefits between 2010 and 2011, and 41% had gone online to download a government form. By comparison, 34% of respondents had contacted a federal agency by phone, and 24% had visited a federal office in person. Of those Americans who interacted with the federal government via a website in 2011, more than two-thirds (67%) described the experience as either "good" or "excellent." Meanwhile, roughly half of Americans who interacted with federal agencies in person (52%), via e-mail (51%), or over the phone (51%) reported their experience as being "good" or "excellent." Elizabeth Montalbano reports in "Internet Tops for Communicating with Government" (*InformationWeek*, September 12, 2011) that in 2011 roughly one out of five (18.7%) Americans wanted the government to facilitate social networking between citizens with similar interests and needs.

FEDERAL GOVERNMENT AND INTERNET TECHNOLOGIES

Since the early 1990s hundreds of federal government websites have been established on the Internet. In the beginning each agency or division developed its website in a unique way, offering varying levels of accessibility to the user. Some were useful and informative. For example, in 1994 the U.S. Census Bureau launched the first U.S. government World Wide Web portal. From the start, hundreds of U.S. census records from decades past could be easily viewed on the website.

The Internal Revenue Service (IRS) also maintained a useful site. In 1997 the IRS began allowing people to download tax forms and file their taxes electronically. Nearly a million tax returns were filed from home computers that first year. Filing taxes online quickly became one of the most popular forms of Internet contact with the federal government. The IRS (June 8, 2012, http://www.irs.gov/uac/Filing-Season-Statistics-for-Week-Ending-June-8,-2012) reports that as of June 8, 2012, it had received 113.1 million individual tax returns online. This was a 6.2% increase over the number of e-filings during the same period in the previous year (106.4 million) and represented 82% of the total number of individual returns received in 2012.

However, many other government websites, such as the National Oceanic and Atmospheric Administration website, offered citizens little in the way of practical information or accessibility. By the late 1990s profit-driven commercial websites far outshone most government websites in both appearance and functionality. Seeing the untapped potential of many government websites, Congress and the White House put through a series of initiatives and laws to make federal government websites and services more accessible to the American people.

Government Paperwork Elimination Act

One of the first major congressional acts designed to improve the functionality of government websites was the Government Paperwork Elimination Act (GPEA) of 1998. The GPEA required that by October 2003 each government agency should provide people, wherever possible, with the option of submitting information or transacting business electronically. The act mandated that forms and documents involved in government transactions be placed online and that electronic signature systems be put in place to replace paper signatures. For example, companies that made electronic components for the National Aeronautics and Space Administration (NASA) were required to have the option to bid for contracts, complete all paperwork with regard to sale of the merchandise, and receive payment without having to use paper. Similarly, individuals were to have the option to apply for a patent online or to fill out a U.S. census survey on the Internet. FedForms.gov

was created as a portal to all electronic forms that are available from the federal government, and by 2012 it cataloged thousands of forms for more than 170 agencies.

E-Government Act

In 2001 President Bush initiated the President's Management Agenda, which contained a number of initiatives that were intended to expand the role of the Internet in the federal government beyond the scope of the GPEA. Many of these initiatives were made law in 2002, when Congress passed the E-Government Act. The E-Government Act was a broad-reaching piece of legislation that was designed to streamline government websites and provide a wide range of services to the American people via the Internet. The act established the E-Government Fund to provide money for agencies that could not afford IT and website development. In *FY 2011 Report to Congress on the Implementation of the E-Government Act of 2002* (March 7, 2012, http://www.whitehouse.gov/sites/default/files/omb/assets/egov_docs/fy11__e-gov_act_report.pdf), the Office of Management and Budget (OMB) notes that in 2011, $7.2 million of the fund was dedicated to promoting greater transparency, primarily through the implementation of the Federal Funding Accountability and Transparency Act (FFATA) of 2006. Among the online services funded by this initiative are USASpending.gov, which provides citizens with information concerning federal spending and contracts, and Performance.gov, a site dedicated to promoting federal initiatives that are aimed at improving government accountability and efficiency. In addition, $740,000 of the fund was devoted to promoting further innovation within the federal IT system.

Many of these goals established standards for government websites that were already in operation. Existing government websites were required to provide links to organization policy and hierarchy on the front page and to present their information in a way that was easily searchable. Many agencies with multiple websites, such as NASA or the U.S. Environmental Protection Agency, were asked to consolidate their sites so that all the information for the public could be reached within a few clicks of the agency's main page. The E-Government Act also supported new websites that were designed to provide basic services for American citizens. The site FirstGov.gov was deemed the official portal for all federal government websites. FirstGov.gov, which began operating in February 2000, provided links to more than 22,000 federal and state websites as well as a hierarchical index of all government organizations. In January 2007 FirstGov.gov was renamed USA.gov; three years later the administration of President Barack Obama (1961–) launched an updated version of USA.gov that featured a new design and a wider range of applications. The article "USA.gov's Redesign Includes Apps for Mobile Users" (*Washington Post*, July 6, 2010) notes that by July 2010 USA.gov was receiving an average of 4.2 million visitors per month.

Another website that the E-Government Act officially authorized was Regulations.gov, which was launched in January 2003. Regulations.gov lists pending regulations that are proposed by government agencies and allows citizens and nongovernmental agencies to comment on the regulations. The government agencies are then required to review the comments on Regulations.gov before putting a regulation into effect. This process provides the American people with the ability to influence government regulation—a privilege that was previously available primarily to organized lobbyists.

As a result of these White House initiatives and congressional acts supporting e-government, federal agencies have come to offer many valuable online services to Americans. For example, the Environmental Protection Agency oversees the web portal My Environment (http://www.epa.gov/myenvironment) that enables citizens to search for information about environmental issues such as air quality and water conditions, report violations, and find ways to communicate and collaborate with other environmental activists in their area. It has also been used to save the government money. For example, in December 2008 the Social Security Administration launched iClaim, an online application system for retirees. According to the OMB, in *FY 2011 Report to Congress on the Implementation of the E-Government Act of 2002*, 41% of retirement claims were made over the Internet in 2010, resulting in estimated savings of $16 million. According to projections, the iClaim system was expected to save an additional $100 million between fiscal years (FYs) 2011 and 2019.

In January 2011 President Obama signed the GPRA Modernization Act. The law effectively updated the 1993 Government Performance and Results Act, which attempted to make the management of government programs more efficient. Overseen by the director of the Office of Management and Budget, the GPRA Modernization Act requires government agencies to make information about programs, strategic objectives, and other aspects of their work more accessible to Congress and the public, both by improving their websites and by publishing all plans and reports in "searchable, machine-readable" formats.

In April 2011, in recognition of the increasing importance of the Internet as a means for American citizens to interact with the federal government, President Obama issued Executive Order 13571, "Streamlining Service Delivery and Improving Customer Service" (April 27, 2011, http://www.whitehouse.gov/the-press-office/2011/04/27/executive-order-streamlining-service-delivery-and-improving-customer-ser), in which he called on government agencies to focus on developing "lower-cost, self-service options accessed by the Internet or mobile phone and improved processes that deliver services faster and more responsively."

SATISFACTION WITH GOVERNMENT WEBSITES. Even though some dissatisfaction exists with federal government websites, the American people seem to be happy with the improvements in e-government. Since 2003 the U.S. government has tracked websites in its annual American Customer Service Index. This index measures how satisfied the American people are with various aspects of the federal government. Table 7.1 reveals that, out of the websites on the survey that facilitated transactions or e-commerce with the government during the second quarter of 2012, users were happiest with two Social Security Administration sites: iClaim (http://www.socialsecurity.gov/applyonline), which helps facilitate the Social Security application process, and the Retirement Estimator (http://www.ssa.gov/estimator/), a site that is designed to help retirees calculate their potential benefits. Among departmental portals or main sites, the U.S. Citizenship and Immigration Services Resource Center (http://www.uscis.gov/portal/site/uscis/citizenship) was the top scorer, with a satisfaction rating of 89 out of a possible 100 points. The lowest score in the survey, a 45, was received by TreasuryDirect (http://treasurydirect.gov/), the financial services portal of the U.S. Department of the Treasury. Overall satisfaction with government websites rose steadily between 2003 and 2012, from a low of 69 points during the fourth quarter in 2003 to 75.6 points during the second quarter in 2012. (See Figure 7.1.) Websites relating to e-commerce and other government-related transactions (78 points) ranked slightly higher than federal information and news sites (76 points) and primary department sites (74 points). (See Table 7.2.)

Government Regulation

The federal government has passed few laws that are designed to control Internet commerce or content compared with other broadcasting media. The Federal Communications Commission (FCC), which regulates all television and radio content, treats the Internet more like print media than like broadcast media. Unless a major law is being violated, people can publish all manner of pornography, illicit writing, and misleading information on the Internet without fear of repercussion. Activities that are illegal in many states or the United States as a whole, such as purchasing Cuban cigars, can be done online with little fear of prosecution. In addition, most purchases made on the Internet were not subject to local sales tax as of 2012, and states and municipalities were forbidden by the Internet Tax Freedom Act of 1998 to tax Internet use.

For the most part, Congress has been reluctant to place restrictions or taxes on the Internet. In 2005 a bill to make spyware illegal was rejected in the U.S. Senate, and in November 2007 Congress extended the tax ban on both interstate Internet commerce and Internet service to 2014. As for content, Congress is wary of potential public

TABLE 7.1

American Consumer Satisfaction Index (ACSI) scores for e-government websites, first two quarters 2012

Dept	Website	Q1 2012	Q2 2012	Score change
SSA	SSA iClaim—socialsecurity.gov/applyonline	92	92	0
SSA	SSA retirement estimator—ssa.gov/estimator	91	90	−1
SSA	Extra help with medicare prescription drug plan costs—socialsecurity.gov/i1020	89	90	1
DHS	U.S. citizenship and immigration services resource center—uscis.gov/portal/site/uscis/citizenship	89	89	0
SSA	SSA electronic access/online statement—ssa.gov/mystatement	NM	88	NA
HHS	National Heart, Lung, and Blood Institute website—nhlbi.nih.gov	NM	87	NA
HHS	MedlinePlus en español—medlineplus.gov/esp	86	86	0
HHS	MedlinePlus—medlineplus.gov	86	86	0
HHS	National Library of Medicine AIDS Information—aidsinfo.nih.gov	83	86	3
HHS	HHS Healthy People—healthypeople.gov	84	85	1
HHS	Girls health—girlshealth.gov	81	84	3
DHS	U.S. citizenship and immigration services español—uscis.gov/portal/site/uscis-es	86	84	−2
SSA	Social Security Business Services online—ssa.gov/bso/bsowelcome.htm	83	83	0
DOC	National Geodetic Society, National Oceanic and Atmospheric Administration website—ngs.noaa.gov	83	83	0
SSA	Social Security internet disability report—ssa.gov/applyfordisability	83	83	0
HHS	National Cancer Institute main website—cancer.gov	82	83	1
HHS	National Women's Health Information Center (NWHIC) main website—womenshealth.gov	84	83	−1
PBGC	MyPAA—https://egov.pbgc.gov/mypaa	79	83	4
PBGC	MyPBA—https://egov.pbgc.gov/mypba	84	83	−1
CIA	Recruitment website—cia.gov/careers	82	83	1
HHS	National Cancer Institute Site en Español—cancer.gov/espanol	82	83	1
NASA	NASA main website—nasa.gov	82	82	0
HHS	SAMHSA Store—store.samhsa.gov	81	82	1
HHS	CDC main website—cdc.gov	82	82	0
DHS	Federal Emergency Management Agency Ready Campaign—ready.gov	79	82	3
DOS	Recruitment website—careers.state.gov	80	82	2
HHS	NIAMS public website—niams.nih.gov	81	82	1
FTC	FTC complaint assistant website—ftccomplaintassistant.gov	NM	81	NA
DHS	U.S. citizenship and immigration services—uscis.gov/portal/site/uscis	82	81	−1
Treasury	U.S. Mint online catalog and main website—usmint.gov	78	81	3
DOD	DoD Navy—navy.mil	83	81	−2
HHS	AHRQ Health Care Innovations Exchange—innovations.ahrq.gov	80	81	1
DOJ	FBI main website—fbi.gov	79	81	2
HHS	National Institute of Child Health and Human Development—nichd.nih.gov	80	81	1
HHS	NIDDK—www2.niddk.nih.gov	82	81	−1
DOJ	NIJ main website—ojp.gov/nij	81	81	0
DOD	DoD Air Force—af.mil	80	81	1
DOD	Pentagon channel—pentagonchannel.mil	80	80	0
FTC	FTC OnGuardOnline—onguardonline.gov	82	80	−2
HHS	AHRQ National Guideline Clearinghouse—guideline.gov	75	79	4
DOD	Department of Defense portal—defense.gov	75	79	4
HHS	National Institute of Dental and Craniofacial Research—nidcr.nih.gov	80	79	−1
HHS	Agency for Healthcare Research and Quality—ahrq.gov	76	79	3
DOL	Department of Labor Job Listings—doors.dol.gov	78	78	0
HHS	AHRQ Effective Health Care program—effectivehealthcare.ahrq.gov	79	78	−1
HHS	National Library of Medicine main website—nlm.nih.gov	77	78	1
DHS	U.S. citizenship and immigration services—uscis.gov/e-verify	80	77	−3
GAO	GAO main public website—gao.gov	75	77	2
DOS	U.S. Department of State Bureau of Educational and Cultural Affairs alumni website—exchanges.state.gov	74	77	3
DOT	Federal Aviation Administration—faa.gov	76	77	1
DOI	National Park Service main website—nps.gov	80	77	−3
DOS	Bureau of Consular Affairs—travel.state.gov	77	77	0
HHS	HHS National Health Information Center—Healthfinder.gov	78	76	−2
HHS	National Institute of Allergy and Infectious Diseases—www3.niaid.nih.gov	76	76	0
DOL	Bureau of Labor Statistics—bls.gov	74	76	2
DOS	U.S. Department of State Bureau of Educational and Cultural Affairs alumni website—https://alumni.state.gov	76	75	−1
DOS	Department of State blog website—blogs.state.gov	76	75	−1
USDA	FAS main website—fas.usda.gov	75	75	0
NRC	U.S. Nuclear Regulatory Commission website—nrc.gov	73	75	2
SBA	SBA main website—sba.gov	72	74	2
USDA	Recreation One-Stop—recreation.gov	71	74	3
NIST	National Institute for Standards and Technology main website—nist.gov	75	74	−1
DOS	Department of State main website—state.gov	74	74	0
FDIC	FDIC main website—fdic.gov	75	74	−1
GSA	GSA main website—gsa.gov	74	73	−1
HHS	SAMHSA website—samhsa.gov	74	73	−1
HHS	AHRQ CAHPS—cahps.ahrq.gov	74	73	−1
HHS	Health Resources and Services Administration main website—hrsa.gov	74	73	−1
Treasury	Making Home Affordable—makinghomeaffordable.gov	72	73	1

TABLE 7.1

American Consumer Satisfaction Index (ACSI) scores for e-government websites, first two quarters 2012 [CONTINUED]

Dept	Website	Q1 2012	Q2 2012	Score change
DOT	U.S. Department of Transportation—fhwa.dot.gov	73	72	−1
ITC	U.S. International Trade Commission main website—usitc.gov	74	72	−2
HHS	National Library of Medicine Clinical Trials website—clinicaltrials.gov	73	72	−1
SSA	Social Security online: Frequently asked questions—ssa-custhelp.ssa.gov	69	71	2
PBGC	U.S. PBGC main website—pbgc.gov	72	71	−1
USDA	ERS main website—ers.usda.gov	73	71	−2
FDIC	FDIC Applications—www2.fdic.gov	68	71	3
VA	VA Main website—va.gov and myhealthva.gov	70	71	1
SSA	Social Security online (main website)—socialsecurity.gov	68	71	3
OPM	Recruitment website—usajobs.gov	68	70	2
DHS	Department of Homeland Security main website—dhs.gov	70	70	0
GSA	GSA Auctions—gsaauctions.gov	71	69	−2
HHS	U.S. Food and Drug Administration main website—fda.gov	68	69	1
DOI	U.S. geological survey—usgs.gov	71	68	−3
USDA	FSIS main website—fsis.usda.gov	69	68	−1
DOC	BEA main website—bea.gov	69	68	−1
Treasury	IRS main website—irs.gov	70	68	−2
EPA	U.S. Environmental Protection Agency—epa.gov	69	67	−2
OPM	OPM Veterans Employment website—fedshirevets.gov	66	67	1
NARA	NARA main public website—archives.gov	73	67	−6
DOT	DOT Research and Innovative Technology Administration website—rita.dot.gov	66	66	0
DOT	Federal Railroad Administration main website—fra.dot.gov	66	66	0
USDA	NRCS website—nrcs.usda.gov	61	64	3
DOD	TRICARE—tricare.mil	63	64	1
GSA	General Services Administration GSAXcess—gsaxcess.gov	64	64	0
DOL	Disability—Disability.gov	64	63	−1
Treasury	Treasury main website—treasury.gov	61	63	2
DOT	Federal Motor Carrier Safety Administration main website—fmcsa.dot.gov	65	63	−2
GSA	Official site to buy U.S. government property—govsales.gov	66	63	−3
Treasury	USTTB website—ttb.gov	66	63	−3
HHS	HHS—grants.gov	61	62	1
USDA	Forest Service main website—fs.usda.gov	61	60	−1
DHS	Federal Emergency Management Agency main website—fema.gov	65	59	−6
Treasury	TreasuryDirect—treasurydirect.gov	40	45	5

SOURCE: Larry Freed and Rhonda Berg, "Q2 2012 ACSI E-Government Satisfaction Index," in *Satisfying the 21st Century Citizen in a Multi-Device, Multi-Channel World: American Consumer Satisfaction Index (ACSI) E-Government Satisfaction Index (Q2 2012)*, ForeSee, July 24, 2012, http://www.foresee.com/research-white-papers/_downloads/acsi-egov-q2-2012-foresee.pdf?utm_source=Social%2BMedia&utm_medium=8.22Egov%2BBlog%2BPost&utm_campaign=Blog%2B (accessed October 9, 2012)

backlash that it would encounter if it regulates activities such as Internet pornography. Furthermore, enforcing strict regulations would be difficult. Unlike radio or television, publishing content on the web is exceedingly easy. Anyone, provided he or she has willing participants, can set up a web server for several thousand dollars, take pornographic pictures, and post them on the Internet. If the U.S. government did make Internet pornography illegal altogether, such sites could easily be moved offshore, where U.S. laws would not apply. Another option the government has is to place restrictions and controls on all computers and web browsers in the United States. Such a plan may have been feasible back in the early 1990s, when Internet backbones and browsers were still in the development phase. However, placing such controls on the tens of millions of current computers and web browsers now in use would neither be well received nor easily implemented.

NETWORK NEUTRALITY. During the first decade of the 21st century the issue of network neutrality became the subject of fierce debate among policymakers, private corporations, and consumer advocates. Network neutrality, or net neutrality, is a legal principle aimed at guaranteeing open and unlimited access to all legal content, applications, and other products and services on the Internet, without regulation or other forms of interference from Internet Service Providers (ISPs) or the government.

The concept of net neutrality first became widespread in 2003, with the publication of Tim Wu's "Network Neutrality, Broadband Discrimination" (*Journal of Telecommunications and High Technology Law*, vol. 2, 2003). In this influential paper, Wu, a law professor at the University of Virginia, argues that legislation guaranteeing net neutrality is the best way to ensure that all online content and applications remain equally available to Internet users. Wu's position arose partly in response to an emerging tendency among some telecommunications companies to privilege some online content or applications over others. Specifically, some cable providers had begun blocking certain applications or content or transmitting some data faster than other data, typically by establishing unique contracts with individual companies. In doing so,

FIGURE 7.1

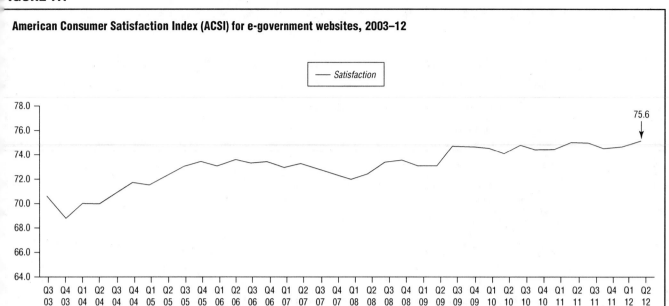

American Consumer Satisfaction Index (ACSI) for e-government websites, 2003–12

SOURCE: Larry Freed and Rhonda Berg, "ACSI E-Government Satisfaction Index (Satisfaction by Quarter) 2003–2012," in *Satisfying the 21st Century Citizen in a Multi-Device, Multi-Channel World: American Consumer Satisfaction Index (ACSI) E-Government Satisfaction Index (Q2 2012)*, ForeSee, July 24, 2012, http://www.foresee.com/research-white-papers/_downloads/acsi-egov-q2-2012-foresee.pdf?utm_source=Social%2BMedia&utm_medium=8.22Egov%2BBlog%2BPost&utm_campaign=Blog%2B (accessed October 9, 2012)

TABLE 7.2

American Consumer Satisfaction Index (ACSI) scores by category, 2006–12

Category	Satisfaction scores by category							
	Q2 2006	Q2 2007	Q2 2008	Q2 2009	Q2 2010	Q2 2011	Q2 2012	Q2 2012
E-commerce/transactional	75	77	77	78	82	77	78	78
News/information	73	73	72	73	74	75	75	76
Portals/department main sites	75	73	74	74	74	75	74	74

SOURCE: Larry Freed and Rhonda Berg, "Agency/Department/Program Satisfaction Scores by Category," in *Satisfying the 21st Century Citizen in a Multi-Device, Multi-Channel World: American Consumer Satisfaction Index (ACSI) E-Government Satisfaction Index (Q2 2012)*, ForeSee, July 24, 2012, http://www.foresee.com/research-white-papers/_downloads/acsi-egov-q2-2012-foresee.pdf?utm_source=Social%2BMedia&utm_medium=8.22Egov%2BBlog%2BPost&utm_campaign=Blog%2B (accessed October 9, 2012)

cable providers granted companies that were willing to pay additional charges a clear advantage over their competitors, while simultaneously denying consumers equal access to rival information or products.

Two years after Wu's paper appeared, the FCC released its "Broadband Policy Statement" (September 23, 2005, http://www.publicknowledge.org/pdf/FCC-05-151A1.pdf), in which it outlined four basic principles that were intended to guarantee the right to unlimited Internet access for all U.S. citizens: "*To encourage broadband deployment and preserve and promote the open and interconnected nature of the public Internet*, consumers are entitled to access the lawful Internet content of their choice.... [To] run applications and use services of their choice, subject to the needs of law enforcement.... [To] connect their choice of legal devices that do not harm the network.... [To] competition among network providers, application and service providers, and content providers."

Also known as the "Internet Policy Statement," the FCC's position was largely aimed at preventing telecommunications companies from unfairly controlling the flow of information online.

Proponents of net neutrality generally believe that free, unregulated access to online information and services is vital to guaranteeing the rights of all citizens to view the Internet content of their choice. Furthermore, supporters of net neutrality have argued that maintaining an open Internet is the best way to ensure continued technological innovation in the digital age. A number of major corporations, notably Microsoft and Google, have been outspoken in their support of net neutrality. Opponents of net neutrality, such as cable providers and network hardware manufacturers, have insisted that the right to offer tiered services (in other words, different levels of service based on different fees) is guaranteed by law. Opponents have also asserted that tiered service plans ultimately promote free market competition on the Internet. The question of net neutrality has also sparked a wide range of opinions among lawmakers. Some members of Congress have attempted to grant the federal government additional powers to oversee and regulate telecommunications companies, with the specific aim of safeguarding net neutrality. Notable among these was the Internet Freedom Preservation Act of 2009, introduced by Representative Edward Markey (1946–: D-MA). That same year the FCC introduced two additional principles to its original "Broadband Policy Statement" that were aimed at preventing ISPs from discriminating against certain Internet content, while also granting consumers the right to total access to all ISP policies.

The battle between the federal government and the telecommunications companies became more intense in 2008. That year the FCC ruled that the telecommunications firm Comcast had illegally blocked its subscribers from using certain Internet software applications. In March 2010 a federal court overturned the FCC's judgment against Comcast, throwing the agency's power to ensure net neutrality into doubt. In response to the ruling, the FCC began exploring other means of guaranteeing the right to neutral broadband use. Joe Nocera reports in "The Struggle for What We Already Have" (New York Times, September 3, 2010) that the commission hoped to use a broader interpretation of the Telecommunications Act of 1996 to impose tighter controls over ISPs.

The FCC attempted to reach a compromise in December 2010, when it voted 3–2 to prohibit telecommunications companies from controlling Internet traffic in ways that favored certain subscribers over others; however, the new restriction did not apply to smart phones or tablets. According to David Lieberman, in "Net Neutrality Vote Irks Many" (USA Today, December 21, 2010), the FCC ruling provoked harsh criticism from supporters on both sides of the issue. Net neutrality advocates complained that the regulation contained loopholes that would enable telecommunications companies to continue manipulating certain forms of web traffic. On the contrary, John Boehner (1949–; R-OH), the Speaker of the U.S. House of Representatives, asserted that the ruling represented a "power grab" on the part of the federal government and promised to fight it in Congress. Indeed, the FCC decision remained the subject of intense debate over the next two years. In "No Neutrality on Net" (Daily Variety, October 13, 2012), Ted Johnson reveals that opposition to the government's net neutrality rules prompted a legal challenge from the telecommunications

giant Verizon, while also forming a key component of the Republican Party's presidential election platform in 2012. Although President Obama's reelection ultimately stalled Republican opposition, as of December 2012 the question of the rule's legality remained unresolved.

CONTROLLING THE ASSAULT OF NON-SOLICITED PORNOGRAPHY AND MARKETING ACT. What little Internet regulation the federal government has enacted has been met with mixed results. On January 1, 2004, the Controlling the Assault of Non-Solicited Pornography and Marketing (CAN-SPAM) Act went into effect. The act required that all unsolicited commercial e-mail contain a legitimate return address as well as instructions on how to opt out of receiving additional solicitations from the sender. Spam must also state in the subject line if the e-mail is pornographic in nature. Violators of these rules were to be subject to heavy fines. As of 2012, the largest fine ever imposed under the CAN-SPAM Act was an $873 million judgment awarded to the social networking site Facebook in 2008. Jessica Guynn reports in "Facebook Wins $873-Million Judgment against Spammer" (Los Angeles Times, November 24, 2008) that the Canadian citizen Adam Guerbuez was found guilty of sending more than 4 million spam messages to Facebook users over a two-month period. The judgment was nearly four times greater than the $230 million won by the rival social networking site MySpace in a similar case the previous May.

CHILDREN'S INTERNET PROTECTION ACT. A more successful regulation is the Children's Internet Protection Act of 2000 (CIPA). Under the act, public schools and libraries were required to keep minors from viewing explicitly sexual content on public school and library computers. If these organizations did not comply, they would no longer receive government assistance in buying IT equipment. Public school systems throughout the country were quick to adapt to the new law, and by 2005, 100% of U.S. public schools had complied with CIPA. Regulations involving children's welfare have always been warmly received by the public, so this fact may account for CIPA's success.

ADAM WALSH CHILD PROTECTION AND SAFETY ACT. Another effort using IT and the Internet in an attempt to protect the innocence and safety of children is the Adam Walsh Child Protection and Safety Act of 2006. It established a tiered-system of sexual offenses and required that convicted sexual offenders register and update their whereabouts with local law enforcement agencies for designated periods of time based on the seriousness of their offenses. The act established the National Sex Offender Public Registry Website (http://www.nsopr.gov/; the site was renamed the Dru Sjodin National Sex Offender Public Website in 2006), a national database of registered sex offenders that is searchable by name, state, county, town, or zip code. Table 7.3 shows the information

TABLE 7.3

Required registration information under the Sex Offender Registration and Notification Act

- Criminal history
- Date of birth
- DNA sample
- Driver's license or identification card
- Employer address
- Fingerprints
- Internet identifiers
- Name
- Palm prints
- Passport and immigration documents
- Phone numbers
- Photograph
- Physical description
- Professional licensing information
- Resident address
- School address
- Social Security number(s)
- Temporary lodging information
- Text of registration offense
- Vehicle license plate number and description

SOURCE: Laura L. Rogers, "VI. Required Registration Information: SORNA, §114," in *The Adam Walsh Act: A National Endeavor to Protect Children and Families*, U.S. Department of Justice, Office of Justice Programs, SMART Office, July 2008, http://www.search.org/files/ppt/SMARTOfficeUpdate0708.ppt (accessed October 3, 2012)

TABLE 7.4

Public website information required under the Sex Offender Registration and Notification Act

- Name
- Photograph
- Physical description
- Current offense & prior sex offenses
- Employer address
- Resident address
- School address
- Vehicle(s) license plate number and description

SOURCE: Laura L. Rogers, "VII. Disclosure and Sharing of Information: Public Website Required Information," in *The Adam Walsh Act: A National Endeavor to Protect Children and Families*, U.S. Department of Justice, Office of Justice Programs, SMART Office, July 2008, http://www.search.org/files/ppt/SMARTOfficeUpdate0708.ppt (accessed October 3, 2012)

that convicted offenders are required to provide to law enforcement agencies under the Adam Walsh Child Protection and Safety Act, Title I, which is known as the Sex Offender Registration and Notification Act. However, the public website discloses only the personal data that is presented in Table 7.4. According to the National Center for Missing and Exploited Children (July 11, 2012, http://www.missingkids.com/en_US/documents/sex-offender-map.pdf), by 2012 there were 722,499 registered sex offenders in the United States. In "Department of Justice Releases First National Strategy for Child Exploitation Prevention and Interdiction" (August 2, 2010, http://www.justice.gov/opa/pr/2010/August/10-opa-887.html), the U.S. Department of Justice announced that it was launching a nationwide law enforcement operation aimed at apprehending the 500 most dangerous sex offenders who were not in compliance with registry requirements.

TECHNOLOGY AND NATIONAL SECURITY

The use of IT has become central to issues of national security in the 21st century. The speed at which information in the modern age can be retrieved has played a key role in the War on Terror. Identifying the terrorists who were responsible for the events of September 11, 2001 (9/11), would have been an arduous if not impossible task were it not for electronic records of the terrorists' credit card and rental car use. The Federal Bureau of Investigation was able to post a full list of the suspected terrorists within three days of the attacks, giving the White House the necessary information it needed to plan retaliatory measures.

Since 9/11 many new technologies have been designed to catch terrorists before they strike. Data mining is by far the most controversial and perhaps the most powerful of the new technologies that are being developed. Since 2001 the U.S. Department of Homeland Security has spent a tremendous amount of time and money trying to create a database and database-searching techniques that enable authorities to view records of millions of citizens within seconds and determine if they have a link to terrorism. According to John Borland, in "A Global Assault on Anonymity" (CNET.com, October 20, 2004), one attempt at such a system was called the Multistate Anti-Terrorism Information Exchange (MATRIX). The system contained the data from five state law enforcement centers as well as nationwide financial and commercial data of millions of Americans. Before its termination, the system was reportedly able to match criminal records with financial records to assess whether or not a person was a terrorist threat. The database held much more information than a typical criminal database and could be used, for instance, to do a background check on someone applying for a license to drive hazardous materials across the country. The project was canceled in April 2005 after many complaints from concerned citizens and civil rights organizations such as the American Civil Liberties Union (ACLU).

Many believed that other data mining systems were still being developed by the federal government following the cancellation of MATRIX. In "Pentagon Sets Its Sights on Social Networking Websites" (*New Scientist*, June 9, 2006), Paul Marks explains that the National Security Agency (NSA) was funding a program called the Disruptive Technology Office (DTO) in 2006. The reported role of the DTO was to combine data on people from many different sources, including phone records and online social networks such as MySpace. The existence of the program was not beyond the realm of reason. Leslie Cauley reports in "NSA Has Massive Database of Americans'

Phone Calls" (*USA Today*, May 11, 2006) that in 2006 the NSA was already secretly analyzing billions of phone records in an effort to find potential terrorists in the United States. The NSA did not obtain a court's approval before searching the phone records, which many considered to be an illegal act. In August 2006 Judge Anna Diggs-Taylor (1932–) of the U.S. District Court declared the program unconstitutional and ordered it to stop. However, the program continued while the case was appealed and Congress worked to develop a modified system of surveillance.

In July 2008 President Bush signed into law the Foreign Intelligence Surveillance Act of 1978 Amendments Act of 2008. Besides broadening the ability of the federal government to conduct high-tech investigations that are aimed at identifying foreign terrorist activity, the act shields U.S. telecommunications firms from lawsuits that stem from their cooperation in government wiretap investigations of their customers. On the day the new law was passed, the ACLU filed a lawsuit in federal court contending that the new law violated the U.S. Constitution on numerous grounds, including the right to privacy. The ACLU reports in "Amnesty et al. v. Clapper: FISA Amendments Act Challenge" (December 2012, http://www.aclu.org/national-security/amnesty-et-al-v-clapper) that the case was dismissed by a district court judge in August 2009. Two years later, in March 2011, a federal appeals court reversed the district judge's decision, reinstating the ACLU's lawsuit against the government. In May 2012 the U.S. Supreme Court agreed to hear the case, and oral arguments were heard that October. As of December 2012, the Court had not given its ruling.

Even as IT serves as a vital tool in the War on Terror, it can also pose a serious challenge to the government's control of classified information. The extent to which government secrets were vulnerable in the information age was exposed in April 2010, when WikiLeaks, an activist media website, released a classified video that showed a U.S. Apache helicopter killing 11 unarmed civilians in Iraq in 2007. The following month Private First Class Bradley Manning (1987–), a U.S. Army intelligence analyst, was arrested on charges of illegally copying the video, along with more than 250,000 classified diplomatic cables, and sending them to the website. David Dishneau and Ben Nuckols report in "Prosecutors to Question Manning in WikiLeaks Case" (Yahoo! News, November 30, 2012) that Manning's actions represented "the biggest leak of classified material in U.S. history." Even though many politicians and U.S. officials saw Manning as a traitor, a number of free-speech advocates and political activists considered him to be a hero. Eventually, his supporters established the website BradleyManning.org to help promote his legal defense and to protest reports of his harsh treatment while in prison awaiting trial. In "WikiLeaks' Julian Assange Suffering from Chronic Lung Condition" (Time.com, November 29, 2012), Sorcha Pollak indicates that Julian Assange (1971–), the founder of WikiLeaks, also faced the possibility of extradition to the United States for his role in making the classified documents public.

IT also has the capacity to inflict damage that goes beyond the exchange of classified data. With the emergence of increasingly complex computer systems within both government agencies and private industry, terrorists, hackers, and governments soon developed the power to disrupt, and even destroy, real physical targets. The extent of this threat first achieved widespread attention in 2010, when cybersecurity experts became aware of a new form of malware that had the capacity to infiltrate massive industrial control systems and seize control of the systems' functions. Dubbed Stuxnet, this highly sophisticated cyber worm had the potential to trigger a catastrophic chain of events at a high-security site, such as a nuclear power plant. Indeed, Mark Clayton reports in "Stuxnet Malware Is 'Weapon' out to Destroy ... Iran's Bushehr Nuclear Plant?" (*Christian Science Monitor*, September 21, 2010) that in 2010 many cybersecurity experts believed Stuxnet had infected the Bushehr nuclear power plant in Iran, which is one of the most sensitive, high-risk nuclear sites in the world. According to Ellen Nakashima and Joby Warrick, in "Stuxnet Was Work of U.S. and Israeli Experts, Officials Say" (*Washington Post*, June 1, 2012), the operation against the Iranian nuclear program was later discovered to have been launched as a joint mission between the United States and Israel and authorized by President Obama. In the end, the Stuxnet attack destroyed roughly one-sixth of Iran's uranium centrifuges.

By 2012 the potential for other sophisticated forms of cyberwarfare had emerged as a new type of threat to U.S. national security. In *Occupying the Information High Ground: Chinese Capabilities for Computer Network Operations and Cyber Espionage* (March 7, 2012, http://www.uscc.gov/RFP/2012/USCC%20Report_Chinese_CapabilitiesforComputer_NetworkOperationsandCyberEspionage.pdf), Bryan Krekel, Patton Adams, and George Bakos assert that in 2012 China was in the process of developing a strategy known as "information confrontation," while making "the ability to exert control over an adversary's information and information systems" one of its key defense priorities in the early 21st century. The article "How to Survive a Cyberwar" (Bloomberg.com, August 2, 2012) notes that according to General Keith Alexander, the head of the U.S. Cyber Command, electronic breaches of U.S. targets resulted in the loss of roughly $1 trillion in intellectual property losses between 2009 and 2011. In the face of these burgeoning threats, President Obama issued in October 2012 "Presidential Policy Directive 20" (https://www.hsdl.org/?abstract&

TABLE 7.5

Principal sources for news coverage of political campaigns, 2002, 2006, and 2010

	2002	2006	2010
Television	66%	69%	67%
Newspapers	33	34	27
Internet	7	15	24
Radio	13	17	14
Magazines	1	2	2

SOURCE: Aaron Smith, "Main Sources of Campaign News, 2002–2010," in *The Internet and Campaign 2010*, Pew Internet & American Life Project, March 17, 2011, http://www.pewinternet.org/~/media//Files/Reports/2011/Internet%20and%20Campaign%202010.pdf (accessed October 9, 2012). Used by permission of the Pew Internet & American Life Project, which bears no responsibility for the interpretations presented or conclusions reached based on analysis of the data.

did=725668), a classified order that established new guidelines for the "cyber-operations of military and federal agencies."

ELECTIONS AND POLITICS

The Internet has not only influenced how people interact with the government but also how people approach politics. The number of people who read political news online increased dramatically between 2002 and 2010. In *The Internet and Campaign 2010* (March 17, 2011, http://www.pewinternet.org/~/media//Files/Reports/2011/Internet%20and%20Campaign%202010.pdf), Smith finds that nearly a quarter (24%) of American adults turned to the Internet as their primary source of political news in 2010, compared with only 7% in 2002 and 15% in 2006. (See Table 7.5.) Table 7.6 offers an overview of online political involvement along demographic lines. In November 2010, 54% of all American adults used the Internet to find information about political issues. In general, men (56%) were somewhat more likely than women (52%) to use the Internet to learn about politics. Online political activities were far more prevalent among younger adults. Sixty-seven percent of American adults aged 18 to 29 years used the Internet to engage in political activities online, compared with 61% of adults aged 30 to 49 years, 53% of those aged 50 to 64 years, and 26% of those aged 65 years and older. Non-Hispanic white Americans (57%) used the Internet for political purposes more than non-Hispanic African-Americans (45%) and Hispanics (39%), and college graduates (76%) used the Internet for political purposes at a far higher rate than people who did not graduate from high school (17%).

Online Participation in the 2012 Presidential Race

During the 2012 presidential campaign people engaged in a wide range of political activities over the Internet. Aaron Smith and Maeve Duggan of Pew/Internet indicate in *Online Political Videos and Campaign 2012*

TABLE 7.6

Percentage of adults who went online to find political news, participate in political activities, or engage in social networking for political purposes, by selected characteristics, November 2010

All adults	54%
Gender	
Men	56
Women	52
Age	
18–29	67
30–49	61
50–64	53
65+	26
Race/ethnicity	
White, non-Hispanic	57
Black, non-Hispanic	45
Hispanic	39
Household income	
Less than $30,000	36
$30,000–$49,999	60
$50,000–$74,999	66
$75,000+	77
Education level	
Some high school	17
High school graduate	43
Some college	65
College+	76
Congressional vote	
Republican voters	69
Democratic voters	56
Non-voters	42
Attitude towards Tea Party	
Agree	70
Disagree	66
No opinion	52
Have not heard of	30

SOURCE: Aaron Smith, "Online Political Users," in *The Internet and Campaign 2010*, Pew Internet & American Life Project, March 17, 2011, http://www.pewinternet.org/~/media//Files/Reports/2011/Internet%20and%20Campaign%202010.pdf (accessed October 9, 2012). Used by permission of the Pew Internet & American Life Project, which bears no responsibility for the interpretations presented or conclusions reached based on analysis of the data.

(November 2, 2012, http://pewinternet.org/~/media//Files/Reports/2012/PIP_State_of_the_2012_race_online_video_final.pdf) that 55% of all registered voters and 66% of all registered voters who go online watched political videos on the Internet during the 2012 campaign. Nearly half (48%) of online registered voters watched political news on the Internet in 2012, while more than a quarter (28%) watched live events, including campaign speeches and debates.

Social networking sites also played an increasingly central role in the way Internet users learned about politics in 2012. Overall, online adults with liberal (74%) or moderate (70%) political views were more likely than conservatives (60%) to use social networking sites. (See Figure 7.2.) A comparable percentage of very conservative (52%) and very

FIGURE 7.2

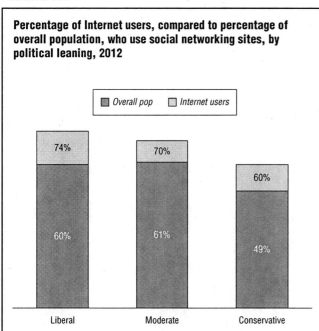

Percentage of Internet users, compared to percentage of overall population, who use social networking sites, by political leaning, 2012

Notes: Sample size for overall survey = 2,253. Sample size for internet users = 1,729. Survey was conducted on landline and cell phones and in English and Spanish.

SOURCE: Lee Rainie and Aaron Smith, "Who Uses Social Networking Sites," in *Social Networking Sites and Politics*, Pew Internet & American Life Project, March 12, 2012, http://www.pewinternet .org/~/media//Files/Reports/2012/PIP_SNS_and_politics.pdf (accessed October 10, 2012). Used by permission of the Pew Internet & American Life Project, which bears no responsibility for the interpretations presented or conclusions reached based on analysis of the data.

liberal (54%) social networking site users reported discovering that a friend had political views that were different than what they expected, based on that friend's posts on a social networking site. (See Figure 7.3.) By comparison, only 33% of social networking users with moderate views reported being surprised by a friend's political affiliation. According to Figure 7.4, very conservative and very liberal social networking users were also the most likely to "like" a political post online (64% and 66%, respectively), to respond with positive comments to political posts (49% and 52%, respectively), or "friend" someone who shared their political views (25% and 24%, respectively). Furthermore, very liberal (29%) and liberal (30%) social networking site users were slightly more likely to refrain from posting a political comment out of fear of offending others, compared with very conservative (27%) and conservative (24%) social networking site users. (See Figure 7.5.)

Mobile devices were another important tool for finding political news and information during the 2012 campaign. According to Smith and Duggan, in *The State of the 2012 Election—Mobile Politics* (October 9, 2012, http://www.pewinternet.org/~/media//Files/Reports/2012/ PIP_State_of_the_2012_race_mobile.pdf), 88% of registered voters owned a cell phone in 2012, more than a quarter (27%) of whom used their phone to keep up with campaign news; another 19% sent campaign-related texts to friends or family members. Liberals (37%) were more likely than either moderates (28%) or conservatives (25%) to use their phone to stay informed of political news in 2012. (See Table 7.7.) Among smart phone users, 45% used their mobile device to read political comments on social networking sites and 35% used their phone to research whether a statement they had just heard about a candidate or campaign was accurate. Whereas Republicans (90%) were more likely than Democrats (85%) to own a cell phone, a larger proportion of Democrats (47%) than Republicans (45%) owned a smart phone during the 2012 campaign. (See Table 7.8.) As Table 7.9 shows, 20% each of Democrats, Republicans, and Independents reported sending political texts in 2012.

Political Websites

Extensive use of the Internet by political campaigns did not really begin until the 2004 presidential election. Before that time most campaign websites simply contained a series of news releases and lists of endorsements for the candidate. In *Untuned Keyboards: Online Campaigners, Citizens, and Portals in the 2002 Elections* (March 21, 2003, http://www.pewinternet.org/~/media/ Files/Reports/2003/PIP_IPDI_Politics_Report.pdf.pdf), Michael Cornfield, Lee Rainie, and John B. Horrigan indicate that a large percentage of campaign managers believed that Internet fund-raising was neither effective nor easy to implement and that the Internet was not considered to be a useful way to mobilize volunteers. The fact that most campaign offices did not maintain or know how to maintain a secure website compounded the problem. Without such security in place, constituents were reluctant to provide any personal information or make online contributions.

Although some state and national politicians in the past had employed the Internet piecemeal to raise money or to organize rallies, most analysts agree that the 2004 Howard Dean (1948–) Democratic presidential primary campaign was the first to use the Internet to its potential. The Dean campaign established a website that provided a number of services for supporters. The site contained a link to Meetup.com, where supporters could log in, find like-minded Dean supporters in close proximity, and arrange a meeting. The matchmaking site brought together people all over the country and led to hundreds of ad hoc campaign centers for Dean. The website also supported an official blog where supporters could read opinions from campaign staffers and comment on the campaign and political issues. By reading the blogs and responses, campaign strategists gained insight into what supporters wanted from Dean. Perhaps the most important feature on the Dean site was the Contribute button. According to Grant Gross, in "Election 2004: Howard Dean Profits

FIGURE 7.3

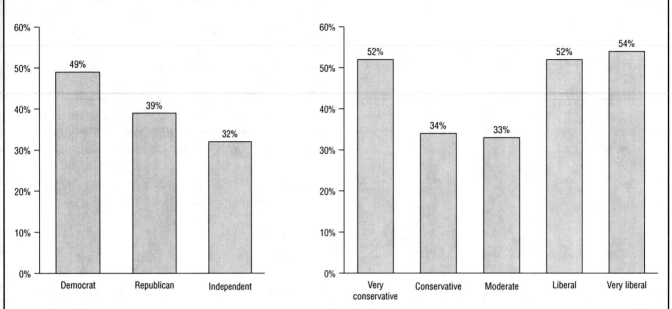

Percentage of social networking site users who discovered a friend's political views were different than they expected, by party affiliation and political leaning, 2012

Notes: Population for social networking site users = 1,047. Survey was conducted on landline and cell phones and in English and Spanish.

SOURCE: Lee Rainie and Aaron Smith, "Social Networking Site Users Learned via Someone's Posts That a Friend Had Different Political Views Than They Thought," in *Social Networking Sites and Politics*, Pew Internet & American Life Project, March 12, 2012, http://www.pewinternet.org/~/media//Files/Reports/2012/PIP_SNS_and_politics.pdf (accessed October 10, 2012). Used by permission of the Pew Internet & American Life Project, which bears no responsibility for the interpretations presented or conclusions reached based on analysis of the data.

from Web Campaign" (*CIO Magazine*, January 15, 2004), Dean collected $7.4 million in online donations between April 1 and September 30, 2003, from 110,786 separate online contributors. All told, by the end of September 2003 Dean had raised $25.4 million, which was $5 million more than John Kerry (1943–), who ended up winning the Democratic nomination.

The campaign and the Internet donations also worked within the confines that were established by the Bipartisan Campaign Reform Act of 2002, commonly known as the McCain-Feingold Act. This legislation was designed to prevent a relatively small number of organizations and individuals from having disproportionate influence in politics. The law banned soft money campaign contributions (large donations by corporations, labor unions, wealthy individuals, and special interest groups that skirted federal campaign regulations by supporting political parties rather than individual candidates). The bill also set a maximum political party contribution of $25,000 in hard money per individual. As the Dean campaign revealed, the Internet provided a way for many Americans to contribute smaller sums of money to their favorite candidate, thus making campaign finance more democratic. Many of the other 2004 presidential candidates implemented similar Internet strategies when they saw Dean's success.

Dean's use of the Internet and technology was utilized and improved on by Obama during the 2008 Democratic presidential campaign. Obama broke all previous campaign contribution records, raising a total of $750 million over the course of his campaign, $600 million of which came from Internet-based contributions, as reported by his campaign in December 2008. The total surpassed the combined contributions of both John Kerry and George W. Bush during the 2004 presidential race and far exceeded the contributions raised by Obama's Republican rival, the U.S. senator John McCain (1936–).

Even though Obama spent an estimated $240 million on traditional television ads during the campaign, he also used website ads, e-mail, text messages, and more than a dozen different social networking sites, such as Facebook and MySpace, as well as his own website, BarackObama.com, to raise awareness of his campaign, ask for contributions, and allow fellow supporters to connect with each other. The use of such technology was especially appealing to a younger, tech-savvy demographic. Obama's strategy was to create an online grassroots movement that encouraged small contributions of $100 or less from many voters, a strategy that turned out to be very effective. The strategy did not come without controversy, however, as contributors giving less than $200 do not need to be publicly reported. This opened the door to allegations that some of the donors used fictitious names or gave

FIGURE 7.4

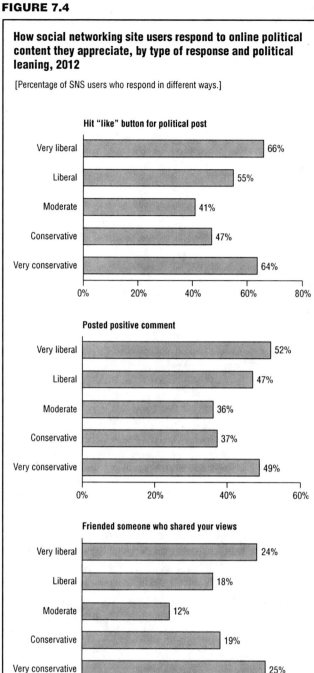

How social networking site users respond to online political content they appreciate, by type of response and political leaning, 2012

[Percentage of SNS users who respond in different ways.]

Hit "like" button for political post

Very liberal	66%
Liberal	55%
Moderate	41%
Conservative	47%
Very conservative	64%

Posted positive comment

Very liberal	52%
Liberal	47%
Moderate	36%
Conservative	37%
Very conservative	49%

Friended someone who shared your views

Very liberal	24%
Liberal	18%
Moderate	12%
Conservative	19%
Very conservative	25%

Notes: SNS = Social networking sites. Population for social networking site users = 1,047. Population for very conservative SNS users is 56. Survey was conducted on landline and cell phones and in English and Spanish.

SOURCE: Lee Rainie and Aaron Smith, "What SNS Users Do about Political Content on the Sites That They Appreciate," in *Social Networking Sites and Politics*, Pew Internet & American Life Project, March 12, 2012, http://www.pewinternet.org/~/media//Files/Reports/2012/PIP_SNS_and_politics.pdf (accessed October 10, 2012). Used by permission of the Pew Internet & American Life Project, which bears no responsibility for the interpretations presented or conclusions reached based on analysis of the data.

FIGURE 7.5

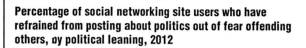

Percentage of social networking site users who have refrained from posting about politics out of fear offending others, by political leaning, 2012

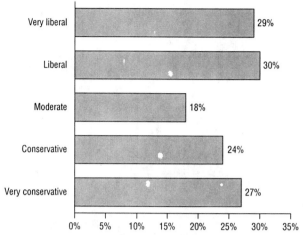

Very liberal	29%
Liberal	30%
Moderate	18%
Conservative	24%
Very conservative	27%

SOURCE: Lee Rainie and Aaron Smith, "Those Who Have Not Made SNS Posts about Politics for Fear of offending Others," in *Social Networking Sites and Politics*, Pew Internet & American Life Project, March 12, 2012, http://www.pewinternet.org/~/media//Files/Reports/2012/PIP_SNS_and_politics.pdf (accessed October 10, 2012). Used by permission of the Pew Internet & American Life Project, which bears no responsibility for the interpretations presented or conclusions reached based on analysis of the data.

After Obama was elected on November 4, 2008, with Joe Biden (1942–) as vice president, the campaign continued using online technology to keep Americans informed about the transition to power. Its Change.gov website presented information about the processes leading up to the inauguration on January 20, 2009. It also featured a blog and other information, with president-elect Obama giving weekly video addresses discussing the transition. Once in office, Obama made information about his policies available on BarackObama.com and allowed supporters to continue making financial contributions to Organizing for America, a movement aimed at helping communities throughout the United States become politically organized. During his presidency, Obama made his weekly video addresses available on the official White House website (http://www.whitehouse.gov/briefing-room/weekly-address). Obama, Biden, and various members of his administration also e-mailed supporters on occasion to describe pieces of legislation, such as the health care bill.

During his successful 2012 reelection bid, President Obama continued to use the Internet as a means of organizing campaign volunteers, while also promoting voting drives in individual states. Ari Melber notes in "For Election Day, Obama Bests Romney in Online Mobilization" (*Nation*, November 5, 2012) that in 2012 the Obama campaign launched the website GottaVote.org, which

more than the $2,300-per-person allowed by federal law for general elections. The campaign stated that it had safeguards in place and returned money from such donors.

TABLE 7.7

Percentage of registered voters who use their cell phones to follow campaign coverage or receive other political news, by party affiliation and political leaning, 2012

Based on registered voters who own a cell phone	
Total (sample size = 731)	27%
Party ID	
Republicans (sample size = 200)	26
Democrats (sample size = 240)	27
Independents (sample size = 253)	30
Party ID (w/leaners)	
Republicans + Rep-leaning Independents (sample size = 328)	26
Democrats + Dem-leaning Independents (sample size = 333)	30
Ideology	
Liberal (sample size = 126)	37*
Moderate (sample size = 254)	28
Conservative (sample size = 307)	25

*Represents significant difference between rows.
Notes: Population = 1,005 adults ages 18 and older, including 400 interviews conducted on respondent's cell phone. The survey was conducted in English. Margin of error is +/−4.3 percentage points for cell phone users who are registered voters (sample size = 731).

SOURCE: Aaron Smith and Maeve Duggan, "Cell Phones and Campaign News," in *The State of the 2012 Election—Mobile Politics*, Pew Internet & American Life Project, October 9, 2012, http://www.pewinternet. org/~/media//Files/Reports/2012/PIP_State_of_the_2012_race_mobile.pdf (accessed October 10, 2012). Used by permission of the Pew Internet & American Life Project, which bears no responsibility for the interpretations presented or conclusions reached based on analysis of the data.

TABLE 7.8

Percentage of registered voters who own cell phones or smart phones, use text messaging, or use or download apps, by party affiliation and political leaning, 2012

	% of cell owners in each group who...			
	Own cell Phone	Own a smartphone	Use text messaging	Use or download apps
All registered voters	88%	48%	74%	45%
Party ID				
Republicans	90	45	67	44
Democrats	85	47	75	43
Independents	89	49	77	45
Party ID (w/leaners)				
Republicans + Rep-leaning Independents	91	47	71	42
Democrats + Dem-leaning Independents	85	48	77	46
Ideology				
Liberal	87	56*	81*	49
Moderate	90	55*	78	50
Conservative	87	40	68	39

*Represents significant difference between rows.
Notes: Population = 1,005 adults ages 18 and older, including 400 interviews conducted on respondent's cell phone. The survey was conducted in English. Margin of error is +/−4.3 percentage points for cell phone users who are registered voters (sample size = 731).

SOURCE: Aaron Smith and Maeve Duggan, "Cell Phone Ownership and Usage," in *The State of the 2012 Election—Mobile Politics*, Pew Internet & American Life Project, October 9, 2012, http://www.pewinternet.org/~/media//Files/Reports/2012/ PIP_State_of_the_2012_race_mobile.pdf (accessed October 10, 2012). Used by permission of the Pew Internet & American Life Project, which bears no responsibility for the interpretations presented or conclusions reached based on analysis of the data.

was aimed at providing potential voters with important information about polling places, voting hours, and information about regulations concerning local voting laws.

IT and the Voting Booth

To help bring IT into voting booths, in 2002 Congress passed and the president signed the Help America Vote Act (HAVA). The act was a direct response to the hotly contested 2000 presidential campaign in which disputes over punch-card ballots in Florida contributed to a month-long delay of nationwide presidential election results. The punch-card ballots were prone to human error in that people would sometimes punch out the wrong perforated circle or not punch the card all the way through. HAVA required states to upgrade to electronic voting systems by the 2006 national election. The bill allotted $3.9 billion to help states replace old punch-card and lever systems with new voting machines. Even though HAVA did not specify precisely which voting machines states were required to use, the act did provide a list of features the machines should have. Among other things, the machines should keep an electronic and paper record of the votes, be accessible to those with disabilities, allow voters to review their ballots before they are cast, and notify voters if they misvote (e.g., vote twice for the same office).

The two types of machines that came closest to meeting HAVA's requirements were used heavily in subsequent elections. The first type is the optical scanning (Marksense) voting system. This system operates much like the paper-based standardized tests given in high schools and colleges. Using a dark lead pencil or black ink pen, voters darken ovals next to the names of candidates for whom they wish to vote. With the sheet in front of them, voters can review their ballots before casting them. The sheet is then fed into a scanner. If an error or misvote occurs on the ballot, the scanner spits the ballot out. It is then discarded and the voter votes again. If the ballot is acceptable, the machine scans the ballot using lasers and the votes are registered in the machine. The problem with optical scanning systems, however, is that they are not accessible to disabled people who have trouble seeing or do not have complete control of their fine motor skills.

The second type of machine, known as a direct recording electronic (DRE) voting system, covers all the requirements laid down by HAVA. DRE systems are akin to touch-screen automated teller machines. The voter stands in front of the touch screen and a list of candidates for a given political contest is displayed on the screen.

TABLE 7.9

Percentage of registered voters who send political texts, sign up for political text updates, or receive unwanted political text messages, by party affiliation and political leaning, 2012

	Send political texts to others	Sign up to receive text updates from candidate/group	Receive unwanted political texts
Total for RV's who use text messaging (sample size = 476)	19%	5%	5%
Party ID			
Republicans (sample size = 116)	20	6	3
Democrats (sample size = 160)	20	8	4
Independents (sample size = 172)	20	3	5
Party ID (w/leaners)			
Republicans + Rep-leaning Independents (sample size = 202)	22	5	5
Democrats + Dem-leaning Independents (sample size = 227)	20	7	3
Ideology			
Liberal (sample size = 92)	23	5	7
Moderate (sample size = 176)	18	7	3
Conservative (sample size = 183)	20	5	6

*Represents significant difference between rows.
Notes: Population = 1,005 adults ages 18 and older, including 400 interviews conducted on respondent's cell phone. The survey was conducted in English. Margin of error is +/−4.3 percentage points for cell phone users who are registered voters (sample size = 731).

SOURCE: Aaron Smith and Maeve Duggan, "Political Text Messages," in *The State of the 2012 Election—Mobile Politics,* Pew Internet & American Life Project, October 9, 2012, http://www.pewinternet.org/~/media//Files/Reports/2012/PIP_State_of_the_2012_race_mobile.pdf (accessed October 10, 2012). Used by permission of the Pew Internet & American Life Project, which bears no responsibility for the interpretations presented or conclusions reached based on analysis of the data.

The voter simply touches the candidate's name to vote for that person, and the machine displays the next list of candidates. DRE systems can be equipped with Braille keyboards and headsets for the blind, and voting choices can be made larger on the screen for those who lack fine motor skills. The machine notifies the voter if he or she has misvoted and allows for a review of votes on a final checkout screen before they are cast. The machine prints out a paper record resembling a spreadsheet at the end of the voting day. Proponents claim that the DRE system is better than the optical system because the DRE system eliminates the potential human error involved in coloring in circles and is easier for the disabled.

Even though DRE systems meet HAVA's requirements, controversy still surrounds their use. Many people are concerned that hackers can somehow tap into these systems and change the votes. A second and perhaps more realistic concern is that the complicated computer hardware and software in these systems can malfunction. In "Is E-Voting Safe?" (*PC World*, April 28, 2004), Paul Boutin discusses a study on DRE systems that was conducted by computer scientists at the California Institute of Technology and the Massachusetts Institute of Technology (MIT) in 2001. The study concluded that touch-screen machines were slightly more accurate than punch-card machines. The residual margin of error for the DRE machines, which equates to the percentage of votes that are thrown out because of error, was 2.3%. This was only marginally better than the 2.5% error rate generated by punch-card systems. By contrast, optically scanned paper ballots had an error rate of only 1.5%. One

possible solution for the DRE systems that some states have implemented is the use of redundant paper ballots. In this instance, receipt printers are attached to the DRE machines. When the person is done voting, the printer prints a version of the person's vote. This paper can then be reviewed and placed into a ballot box for later review if necessary.

The new voting machines did appear to make some difference in the 2004 presidential election. Charles Stewart III of MIT states in "Measuring the Improvement (or Lack of Improvement) in Voting since 2000 in the U.S." (January 14, 2006, http://web.mit.edu/cstewart/www/papers/measuring_2.pdf) that the number of votes that had to be thrown out because of error between the 2000 and 2004 presidential elections dropped from 1.9% to 1.1% among those states and counties where the statistics were available. (It should be noted that the reported/detected error from election officials may have been lower than the actual error.) Even though many factors could have contributed to this reduction, those counties that updated to optical scanning voting machines or DRE systems showed some of the most significant drops in voting error.

In spite of these promising signs, by 2008 a number of states, notably Florida, were compelled to replace many of the voting machines they had installed only six years earlier, amid concerns that the machines were vulnerable to error or security risks. The article "Voting Shouldn't Be a Game of Chance" (*Washington Post*, November 2, 2008) reports numerous problems that were related to early electronic voting in the weeks preceding the 2008 presidential election, including instances where voters were unable to select the candidates they wanted on touch-screen voting systems. Even with a record turnout of 132.6 million voters for the November 4 election, incidences of problems with electronic voting machines were relatively minor. Still, the question of the reliability of e-voting remained a subject of debate, particularly as one-third of all states did not require paper records of electronic ballots. In August 2010 a number of lawmakers, led by Representative Rush Holt (1948–; D-NJ), submitted a letter to the U.S. attorney general Eric Holder Jr. (1951–) recommending that the Department of Justice require all states to generate paper voting records during the November 2010 elections.

Even though the reliability of voting machines remained a source of concern during the 2012 presidential campaign, no serious issues emerged that affected the outcome of the election. However, Clayton reports in "Voting-Machine Glitches: How Bad Was It on Election Day around the Country?" (*Christian Science Monitor*, November 7, 2012) that on election day 2012 problems with voting machines resulted in long delays at polling places, as instances of machine breakdowns and "vote flipping" (poorly calibrated machines that mistakenly turn a vote for one candidate into a vote for another candidate) were reported from several states throughout the country.

VOTING AND THE INTERNET. As the normalcy of conducting many personal transactions over the Internet became more widespread during the early 21st century, some observers began anticipating online voting and suggested that the convenience of voting online would increase voter participation in elections. However, Susannah Fox, Janna Quitney Anderson, and Lee Rainie reveal in *The Future of the Internet* (January 9, 2005, http://www.pewinternet.org/~/media//Files/Reports/2005/PIP_Future_of_Internet.pdf.pdf) that a survey of 1,286 technology experts found only 32% of those interviewed agreed that network security concerns would be solved to the point that more than half of American votes would be cast online by 2014. Among those who disagreed with this prediction, Peter Denning of the Naval Postgraduate School in Monterey, California, wrote, "There's a good chance that ... [by 2014] we will have learned to design robust, trustworthy voting systems. But voter apathy is related not to the voting system but to the perception that the vote counts." Ted Eytan of Group Health Cooperative in Maryland maintained, "Voting security is likely unobtainable, regardless of the technology. There is too much at stake, and there are too many incentives to corrupt the process. There will need to be a physical representation of a vote in the future."

A turning point in the evolution of online voting came in October 2009, with the passage of the Military and Overseas Voter Empowerment Act. Under the new law, states were empowered to send electronic voter registration forms, election information, and even blank ballots to Americans living overseas, thereby saving the time and money associated with sending materials through conventional mail. Perhaps more significantly, the new system made it possible for the votes of military personnel and other overseas Americans to be counted in a timely manner, eliminating the lag time that was traditionally associated with counting absentee voting ballots. A month after the law passed, Massachusetts became the first state to adopt the new procedures. In "States Move to Allow Overseas and Military Voters to Cast Ballots by Internet" (*New York Times*, May 8. 2010), Ian Urbina notes that by May 2010, 33 states had instituted laws allowing Americans abroad to vote via e-mail or fax. The shift to Internet voting caused a great deal of concern among Internet security experts and other voting advocates. Urbina quotes John Bonifaz of the voting rights organization Voter Action as saying that the move toward online voting "basically takes the hazards we've seen with electronic voting and puts them on steroids."

GOVERNMENT IMPROVEMENTS IN DAILY LIFE
511 Travel Information System

Using advanced technology, the federal and state governments have begun to put into place a nationwide travel information system known as 511. The 511 system is an attempt to unify the many automated information systems that were already operated by state and local governments. Dozens of cities and states set up these systems during the 1990s, when cell phones and advanced communications became affordable. Callers and Internet users could retrieve information on traffic jams and road conditions over the phone or on the Internet. For example, the Advanced Regional Traffic Interactive Management and Information System (ARTIMIS) was set up in 1995 to monitor traffic and alert people to traffic problems on 88 miles (142 km) of freeway in the Cincinnati, Ohio, metropolitan area. ARTIMIS used cameras and hundreds of detectors to monitor the flow of traffic along these freeways. People could dial into the system at any time to retrieve the information.

However, most of these systems had one big flaw. To access them by phone, drivers typically had to remember an unfamiliar, seven-digit number. Consequently, these services were rarely used. Noticing this problem, the U.S. Department of Transportation (DOT) approached the FCC and asked that a three-digit number be established to connect users to local travel information anywhere in the country. The FCC chose 511. The number was short and would automatically be associated with the more widely used 411 and 911. Ultimately, the DOT wanted all driver information systems to adopt the 511 number so that any driver in the country could receive information by simply dialing 511.

With the support of the DOT, the 511 Deployment Coalition was formed in 2001 by a number of federal and state agencies to establish guidelines and procedures for implementing local 511 travel information systems. The coalition explains in *America's Travel Information Number: Implementation and Operational Guidelines for 511 Services* (September 2005, http://www.ops.fhwa.dot.gov/511/resources/publications/511guide_ver3/511guide3.htm) that 511 services should allow a driver to access automated recordings on travel conditions through a series of voice commands or touch-tone commands on the phone. At bare minimum, the system should provide conditions for major arteries in the designated region.

Many previously developed systems such as the TravInfo service in San Francisco, California, quickly adopted the number for their travel services. The DOT also awarded $100,000 grants to states or cities without traffic advisory systems to fund implementation plans. Figure 7.6 displays the states that used the 511 number and those that received funding to implement a system as of August 2011.

National Do Not Call Registry

Another attempt by the federal government to respond to the everyday concerns of the American public is the National Do Not Call Registry (https://www.donotcall.gov/default.aspx), which is managed by the Federal Trade Commission (FTC). Launched in June 2003, the registry was established with the simple goal of reducing the number of unwanted telemarketing calls received by consumers. Under the Telemarketing Sales Rule that outlined the program, commercial telemarketers were allowed to access the list for a fee to continue making

FIGURE 7.6

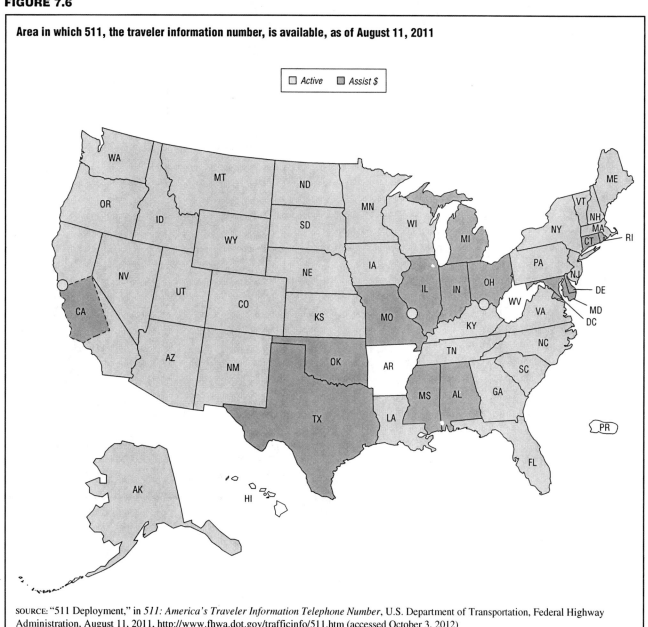

Area in which 511, the traveler information number, is available, as of August 11, 2011

☐ Active   ■ Assist $

SOURCE: "511 Deployment," in *511: America's Traveler Information Telephone Number*, U.S. Department of Transportation, Federal Highway Administration, August 11, 2011, http://www.fhwa.dot.gov/trafficinfo/511.htm (accessed October 3, 2012)

unsolicited calls to numbers in their area that were not registered. In addition, telemarketers could continue to call those on the list with whom they had an established business relationship within the preceding 18 months. The Do Not Call Registry contained more than 10 million phone numbers by the end of its first four days of operation, according to the FTC in *Annual Report to Congress for FY 2006* (April 2007, http://www.ftc.gov/os/2007/04/P034305FY2006RptOnDNC.pdf). The FTC indicates in *National Do Not Call Registry Data Book FY 2012* (October 2012, http://www.ftc.gov/os/2012/10/1210dnc-databook.pdf) that in 2012, 217.6 million phone numbers had been submitted to the service, which covered all U.S. states and territories. (See Table 7.10.) As Figure 7.7 shows, the number of complaints received annually by the National Do Not Call Registry rose steadily during the previous decade, from 579,838 in 2004 to 3.8 million in 2012, an increase of 562%.

TABLE 7.10

Do Not Call Registrations, 2012

Active registrations

Consumer state	Active registrations
Alabama	3,207,509
Alaska	330,754
Arizona	4,498,144
Arkansas	1,917,890
California	24,524,648
Colorado	4,342,049
Connecticut	3,013,067
Delaware	717,216
District of Columbia	576,471
Florida	14,010,491
Georgia	6,794,716
Hawaii	725,779
Idaho	1,088,730
Illinois	9,428,321
Indiana	3,745,232
Iowa	2,367,584
Kansas	2,267,642
Kentucky	3,134,519
Louisiana	2,687,052
Maine	1,005,478
Maryland	4,528,061
Massachusetts	5,558,073
Michigan	7,573,033
Minnesota	4,168,083
Mississippi	1,549,358
Missouri	3,849,290
Montana	742,721
Nebraska	1,430,058
Nevada	1,822,122
New Hampshire	1,147,287
New Jersey	6,951,831
New Mexico	1,350,760
New York	13,295,784
North Carolina	6,460,030
North Dakota	486,759
Ohio	8,557,707
Oklahoma	2,536,997
Oregon	2,791,116
Pennsylvania	9,651,242
Rhode Island	797,350
South Carolina	2,913,765
South Dakota	599,111
Tennessee	4,309,124
Texas	14,789,360
Utah	1,823,554
Vermont	456,279
Virginia	6,004,720
Washington	4,924,897
West Virginia	1,129,341
Wisconsin	3,872,916
Wyoming	428,013

*"Active Registrations" reflect the total number of phone numbers registered on the National Do Not Call Registry as of September 30, 2012.

SOURCE: Adapted from "Fiscal Year 2012 National Do Not Call Registry Registration and Complaint Figures by State Population," in *National Do Not Call Registry Data Book: FY 2012*, Federal Trade Commission, October 2012, http://www.ftc.gov/os/2012/10/1210dnc-databook.pdf (accessed December 6, 2012)

FIGURE 7.7

Do Not Call registrations and complaints, 2003–12

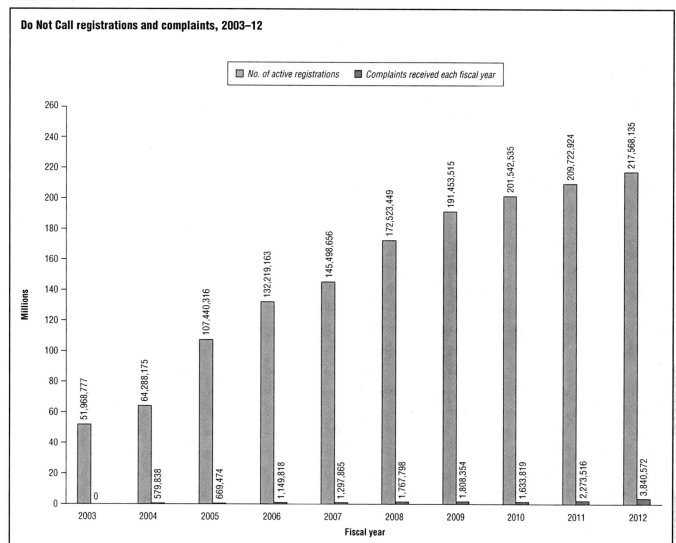

Note: Active registration and complaint figures reflect the total number of phone numbers registered and the total number of National Do Not Call Registry complaints submitted to the FTC as of September 30, 2012.

SOURCE: "National Do Not Call Registry Active Registration and Complaint Figures," in *National Do Not Call Registry Data Book: FY 2012*, Federal Trade Commission, October 2012, http://www.ftc.gov/os/2012/10/1210dnc-databook.pdf (accessed December 6, 2012)

CHAPTER 8
HEALTH RESOURCES IN THE INFORMATION AGE

Before the Internet, finding the latest information on a health issue typically required access to a university or medical library. Most medical studies and information existed in expensive books and journals, which were generally written for those with formal training. The Internet gave rise to a plethora of accessible, informative websites that average consumers could comprehend. The rise of online pharmacies also allowed people the convenience of ordering and receiving prescription drugs and medical supplies at home. Despite some problems such as the online sale of counterfeit medications and the existence of faulty medical information on the web, a majority of Americans still used the Internet to research health-related matters in 2012. Susannah Fox of the Pew Internet & America Life Project (Pew/Internet) reports in *Health Topics* (February 1, 2011, http://pewinternet.org/~/media//Files/Reports/2011/PIP_Health_Topics.pdf) that in 2010, 59% of all American adults went online to learn about medical or health issues. (See Table 8.1.) At the same, an increasing number of Americans were using their cell phone to seek information on health-related topics. In *Mobile Health 2012* (November 8, 2012, http://www.pewinternet.org/~/media//Files/Reports/2012/PIP_Mobile-Health2012.pdf), Susannah Fox and Maeve Duggan of Pew/Internet note that 31% of all cell phone owners used their phone to research health or medical issues in 2012, up from only 17% in 2010.

The Internet has also benefited those who work in the health care fields. The Internet allows medical researchers to share information as never before. Enormous databases accessible on the Internet contain references to nearly all published medical papers, sparing researchers the frustration of hunting through print indexes. The Internet also provides the perfect medium for posting health care research data, such as statistics on disease prevalence, and research organizations can post data from thousands of disease studies. The availability of research data has fostered a new era of scientific cooperation

wherein medical results from labs halfway around the world can be brought together with a click of a mouse.

HEALTH CARE ON THE INTERNET

Table 8.1 offers a glimpse into some demographic trends behind online health research. In 2010 more women (65%) than men (53%) used the Internet to learn about medical or health-related issues. Among ethnic groups, whites (63%) were considerably more likely to research health issues online than African-Americans (47%) or Hispanics (45%). In addition, age played a major factor in determining whether or not someone was likely to view the Internet as a potential health resource. According to Table 8.1, 71% of adults aged 18 to 29 years and 66% of those aged 30 to 49 years used the Internet to find health or medical information. Roughly three-fifths (58%) of adults aged 50 to 64 years went online for health information, while less than one-third (29%) of those aged 65 years and older did so.

Education and income also helped determine whether or not someone went online to learn about health or medical matters. Adults who had pursued higher education were the most likely to use the Internet for medical-related searches, with 81% of college graduates and 70% of adults who had attended some college going online to learn about health issues. (See Table 8.1.) By comparison, less than a quarter (24%) of adults who did not graduate from high school viewed the Internet as a useful health resource. Adults with higher incomes were also more likely to search for health information online than those from lower-income households. As Table 8.1 reveals, 83% of adults with household incomes of $75,000 or more per year and 71% of adults with household incomes of between $50,000 and $74,999 per year went online for health or medical information. This is compared with 66% of those with household incomes of between $30,000 and $49,999 per year and 41% of those with household incomes of below $30,000 per year.

TABLE 8.1

Percentage of people who search for health information online, compared to percentage of all adults who go online, by selected characteristics, 2010

	Percentage of all adults who go online	Percentage of all adults who look online for health information
All adults in the U.S.	74%	59%
Gender		
Male	73	53
Female	75	65
Race		
White	77	63
African American	66	47
Latino	62	45
Age		
18–29	92	71
30–49	79	66
50–64	71	58
65+	40	29
Education		
Some high school	38	24
High school	64	45
Some college	84	70
College graduate	91	81
Household income		
<$30,000	57	41
$30,000–$49,999	80	66
$50,000–$74,999	86	71
$75,000+	95	83

SOURCE: Susannah Fox, "Looking Online for Health Information: Demographics," in *Health Topics: 80% of Internet Users Look for Health Information Online*, Pew Internet & American Life Project, February 1, 2011, http://pewinternet.org/~/media//Files/Reports/2011/PIP_Health_ Topics.pdf (accessed October 3, 2012). Used by permission of the Pew Internet & American Life Project, which bears no responsibility for the interpretations presented or conclusions reached based on analysis of the data.

Types of Health-Related Searches Made by Americans

Americans use the Internet to search for information on a wide range of health-related issues. Table 8.2 shows the various types of medical and health topics that were researched by online adults in 2010. Eighty percent of all Internet users researched at least one health-related subject in 2010. Online college graduates (89%) were the most likely to research health or medical issues on the Internet, compared with only 62% of adult Internet users who never finished high school. Roughly two-thirds (66%) of Internet users searched for information on a specific health problem or disease, the highest percentage of any category; while 56% went online to find information relating to particular treatments or procedures. Half (50%) of women Internet users used the Internet to find information about doctors, compared with just over one-third (36%) of online men. Women (24%) were nearly twice as likely as men (13%) to go online to find information relating to pregnancy and childbirth. In contrast, men (23%) were slightly more likely than women (22%) to go online to research environmental health issues.

Only 7% of all adult Internet users in 2010 went online to find information relating to end-of-life care.

Factors such as race, ethnicity, and age also determine the likelihood of an Internet user researching health-related issues online. In 2010 more white Internet users (82%) looked online for health and medical information than online Hispanics (73%) or African-Americans (71%). (See Table 8.3.) On the whole, majorities of white Internet users searched for information relating to a particular disease or medical problem (70%) or for information concerning a specific medical procedure or treatment (60%). Roughly a quarter (23%) of online Hispanics went online to find information about pregnancy and childbirth, compared with 21% of African-Americans and 17% of whites. African-Americans were slightly more likely to look for information relating to food safety, with 31% of online African-Americans using the Internet to learn about food safety or recalls, compared with 29% each of online whites and online Hispanics. According to Table 8.3, 84% of adult Internet users aged 30 to 49 years went online to search for information related to health or medical issues, which was more than any other age group; people aged 65 years and older (72%) were the least likely to research health-related topics on the Internet. Online adults aged 18 to 29 years (28%) and 30 to 49 years (25%) were far more likely to search the Internet for information relating to pregnancy and childbirth, compared with only 4% each of adults aged 50 to 54 years and 65 years and older.

Adults who are responsible for caring for a child, parent, friend, or other loved one also take advantage of the Internet as a health resource. Indeed, among all online adults, caregivers (79%) were more likely than noncaregivers (71%) to go online to research health-related issues in 2010. (See Table 8.4.) As Table 8.5 shows, online caregivers were far more likely than online noncaregivers to research a particular disease or medical problem on the Internet (76% and 61%, respectively) or to look for information about specific procedures or treatments (69% and 50%, respectively). Online caregivers (38%) were also more than twice as likely as online noncaregivers (18%) to consult the Internet for reviews of particular medical treatments or medications. (See Table 8.6.) Likewise, online caregivers took greater advantage of social media to learn about health-related subjects in 2010. One out of five (20%) online caregivers consulted a social networking site to find information about health issues in 2010, compared with only 12% of online noncaregivers. (See Table 8.7.)

In 2010, 15% of all adults used a mobile device to find heath information. (See Table 8.8.) More than a quarter (28%) of adults aged 18 to 29 years used a cell phone to find out about health-related subjects, the highest percentage of any age demographic; by comparison, only 5% of adults aged 65 years and older learned about

TABLE 8.2

Types of health topics online adults research on the Internet, by gender and educational level, 2010

Health topic	All Internet users N = 2,065	Sex		Education level			
		Women N = 1,198	Men N = 867	Some high school N = 122	High school graduate N = 552	Some college N = 563	College graduate N = 813
Specific disease or medical problem	66	74	57	45	54	70	77
Certain medical treatment or procedure	56	63	48	32	44	60	67
Doctors or other health professionals	44	50	36	26	31	43	58
Hospitals or other medical facilities	36	41	30	21	27	35	47
Health insurance, including private insurance, Medicare or Medicaid	33	34	32	13	27	34	42
Food safety or recalls	29	32	26	17	21	33	36
Drug safety or recalls	24	28	19	15	17	26	30
Environmental health hazards	22	22	23	21	15	23	28
Pregnancy and childbirth	19	24	13	19	15	21	19
Memory loss, dementia, or Alzheimer's	17	19	14	14	12	20	18
Medical test results	16	18	14	7	11	16	23
How to manage chronic pain	14	15	13	12	10	18	16
Long-term care for an elderly or disabled person	12	13	9	13	7	13	14
End-of-life decisions	7	7	7	2	5	9	9
Another health topic not included in the survey	28	31	25	10	17	33	37
At least one of the above topics	**80**	**86**	**73**	**62**	**70**	**83**	**89**

SOURCE: Adapted from Susannah Fox, "Section Four: Summary Charts," in *Health Topics: 80% of Internet Users Look for Health Information Online*, Pew Internet & American Life Project, February 1, 2011, http://pewinternet.org/~/media//Files/Reports/2011/PIP_Health_Topics.pdf (accessed October 10, 2012). Used by permission of the Pew Internet & American Life Project, which bears no responsibility for the interpretations presented or conclusions reached based on analysis of the data.

TABLE 8.3

Types of health topics online adults research on the Internet, by race and age, 2010

Health topic	All Internet users N = 2,065	Race/ethnicity			Age			
		White N = 1,267	Black N = 356	Latino N = 285	18–29 N = 499	30–49 N = 666	50–64 N = 581	65+ N = 274
Specific disease or medical problem	66	70	54	58	60	70	69	62
Certain medical treatment or procedure	56	60	42	47	48	60	59	55
Doctors or other health professionals	44	45	41	36	37	53	41	30
Hospitals or other medical facilities	36	35	38	34	34	43	29	25
Health insurance, including private insurance, Medicare or Medicaid	33	33	31	33	32	36	32	30
Food safety or recalls	29	29	31	29	27	33	28	25
Drug safety or recalls	24	25	22	19	21	29	21	19
Environmental health hazards	22	23	22	18	24	23	19	23
Pregnancy and childbirth	19	17	21	23	28	25	4	4
Memory loss, dementia, or Alzheimer's	17	17	18	14	16	14	19	14
Medical test results	16	17	11	17	15	19	14	17
How to manage chronic pain	14	14	14	13	14	16	12	14
Long-term care for an elderly or disabled person	12	12	12	9	10	10	16	10
End-of-life decisions	7	6	9	8	6	8	8	2
Another health topic not included in the survey	28	30	22	24	25	33	26	19
At least one of the above topics	**80**	**82**	**71**	**73**	**77**	**84**	**81**	**72**

SOURCE: Adapted from Susannah Fox, "Section Four: Summary Charts," in *Health Topics: 80% of Internet Users Look for Health Information Online*, Pew Internet & American Life Project, February 1, 2011, http://pewinternet.org/~/media//Files/Reports/2011/PIP_Health_Topics.pdf (accessed October 10, 2012). Used by permission of the Pew Internet & American Life Project, which bears no responsibility for the interpretations presented or conclusions reached based on analysis of the data.

health or medical issues with a mobile device. Hispanics (21%) were more likely than African-Americans (15%) or whites (13%) to learn about health matters using their cell phone. Among cell phone owners, nearly one out of 10 (9%) downloaded health-related software applications (apps) in 2010. (See Table 8.9.) Cell phone owners 18 to 29 years were the most likely to download health-related apps, at 15%; this percentage was nearly double

that of cell phone owners aged 30 to 49 years (8%) who downloaded health-related apps to their mobile phone.

As more and more adults go online for health information, many health care officials have begun to worry that Americans are using the Internet to diagnose their own ailments in the hope of avoiding time-consuming but necessary visits to the doctor's office. The biggest

TABLE 8.4

Percentage of all caregivers and non-caregivers who search for health information on the Internet, compared to percentage of all adults who go online, by health status, 2010

	Percentage of all adults who go online	Percentage of all adults who look online for health information
All adults in the U.S.	74%	59%
Caregiver status		
Currently caring for a loved one (population = 860)	79	70
Not a caregiver	71	54
Recent medical crisis		
Experienced within past year-self or someone close (population = 982)	76	65
No recent experience	72	55
Recent personal health change		
Experienced within past year (population = 499)	68	56
No recent experience	75	59
Chronic disease status		
One or more chronic conditions (population = 1,488)	64	53
No conditions	81	62
Disability status		
One or more disabilities (population = 906)	54	42
No disabilities	81	65

SOURCE: Susannah Fox, "Looking Online for Health Information: Health Status," in *Health Topics: 80% of Internet Users Look for Health Information Online*, Pew Internet & American Life Project, February 1, 2011, http://pewinternet.org/~/media//Files/Reports/2011/PIP_Health_Topics.pdf (accessed October 10, 2012). Used by permission of the Pew Internet & American Life Project, which bears no responsibility for the interpretations presented or conclusions reached based on analysis of the data.

TABLE 8.5

Percentage of online caregivers and non-caregivers who have researched specific health topics on the Internet, 2010

The % of online caregivers vs. other Internet users who have looked online for information about each of the following topics

Have you ever looked online for information about...	Caregivers	Non-caregivers
A specific disease or medical problem	76%*	61%
A certain medical treatment or procedure	69*	50
Doctors or other health professionals	51*	40
Hospitals or other medical facilities	44*	31
Health insurance, including private insurance, Medicare or Medicaid	39*	30
Food safety or recalls	35*	27
Drug safety or recalls	32*	20
Environmental health hazards	30*	19
Medical test results	27*	12
Memory loss, dementia, or Alzheimer's	26*	12
Pregnancy and childbirth	23*	16
Long-term care for an elderly or disabled person	20*	7
How to manage chronic pain	20*	11
End-of-life decisions	11*	5
Any other health issue	40*	22
Yes to any of the above topics	**88***	**76**

*Denotes statistically significant difference.

SOURCE: Susannah Fox and Joanna Brenner, "Health Topics," in *Family Caregivers Online*, Pew Internet & American Life Project, July 12, 2012, http://pewinternet.org/~/media//Files/Reports/2012/PIP_Family_Caregivers_Online.pdf (accessed October 10, 2012). Used by permission of the Pew Internet & American Life Project, which bears no responsibility for the interpretations presented or conclusions reached based on analysis of the data.

problem with self-diagnosis is that it is rarely objective. Using advice from online websites is especially problematic in that it is often incomplete. In "A User's Guide to Finding and Evaluating Health Information on the Web" (May 9, 2012, http://www.mlanet.org/resources/userguide.html), the Medical Library Association (MLA) provides a list of recommendations that those seeking health information on the Internet should follow. These recommendations include identifying each site's sponsor, checking the date of information on the site, and verifying that the material is rooted in fact, as opposed to opinion.

Top Websites for Health Information

According to the MLA, in "A User's Guide to Finding and Evaluating Health Information on the Web," the most useful medical websites in 2012 were:

- Cancer.gov, National Cancer Institute (http://www.cancer.gov/)

- CDC.gov, Centers for Disease Control and Prevention (http://www.cdc.gov/)

- Familydoctor.org, American Academy of Family Physicians (http://familydoctor.org/)

- Healthfinder, National Health Information Center (http://www.healthfinder.gov/)

- HIVInsite.com, University of California, San Francisco Center for HIV Information (http://hivinsite.ucsf.edu/)

- KidsHealth.org, Nemours Foundation (http://www.kidshealth.org/)

- Mayo Clinic (http://www.mayoclinic.com/)

- MedlinePlus.gov, U.S. National Library of Medicine (http://www.medlineplus.gov/)

- NOAH: New York Online Access to Health (http://www.noah-health.org/)

These websites were evaluated in part on their credibility, content, sponsorship/authorship, purpose, and design. The general medicine websites noted by the MLA include Healthfinder.gov, Familydoctor.org, MedlinePlus.gov, Noah-health.org, and Mayoclinic.com. Like MedlinePlus, these sites contain information on many medical diseases and conditions. The not-for-profit Kidshealth.org (2012, http://www.kidshealth.org/parent/kh_misc/about.html) focuses on health care for children from prenatal care through adolescence. This website maintains separate areas for kids, teenagers, and parents, and in 2012 it received more than 750,000 visitors per day.

TABLE 8.6

Percentage of online caregivers and non-caregivers who have read reviews of healthcare-related topics on the Internet, or posted reviews of healthcare-related topics, 2010

Have you ever...	Caregivers	Non-caregivers
Consulted online reviews of particular drugs or medical treatments	38%*	18%
Consulted online rankings or reviews of doctors or other providers	21*	13
Consulted online rankings or reviews of hospitals or other medical facilities	20*	12
Posted your experiences with a particular drug or medical treatment online	7*	2
Posted a review online of a doctor	6*	4
Posted a review online of a hospital	5	3
Have used the Internet to do any of these	47*	28

*Denotes statistically significant difference.

SOURCE: Susannah Fox and Joanna Brenner, "Health Care Reviews Online," in *Family Caregivers Online*, Pew Internet & American Life Project, July 12, 2012, http://pewinternet.org/~/media//Files/Reports/2012/PIP_Family_Caregivers_Online.pdf (accessed October 10, 2012). Used by permission of the Pew Internet & American Life Project, which bears no responsibility for the interpretations presented or conclusions reached based on analysis of the data.

TABLE 8.7

Percentage of online caregivers and non-caregivers who use social networking to discuss or research various health-related issues, 2010

Have you ever used social networking sites like Facebook and MySpace to...	Caregivers	Non-caregivers
Follow your friends' personal health experiences or health updates	28%*	21%
Remember or memorialize others who suffered from a certain health condition	21	16
Get health information	20*	12
Raise money or draw attention to a health-related issue or cause	17	13
Start or join a health-related group	9	8

*Denotes statistically significant difference.

SOURCE: Susannah Fox and Joanna Brenner, "Social Networking Site Use," in *Family Caregivers Online*, Pew Internet & American Life Project, July 12, 2012, http://pewinternet.org/~/media//Files/Reports/2012/PIP_Family_Caregivers_Online.pdf (accessed October 10, 2012). Used by permission of the Pew Internet & American Life Project, which bears no responsibility for the interpretations presented or conclusions reached based on analysis of the data.

Facts on the human immunodeficiency virus (HIV) are available at HIVInsite.com, and Cancer.gov presents information on cancer types, causes, and treatments. Cancer.gov also maintains a database of clinical trials that are being conducted all over the country for those who seek information on alternative treatments. Finally, CDC.gov, which is operated by the Centers for Disease Control and Prevention (CDC), contains information on communicable diseases, immunization, and disease prevention.

MedlinePlus, the most comprehensive general medicine site, made its debut on the Internet in October 1998

TABLE 8.8

Percentage of cell phone users who use their phones to research health information, by selected characteristics, 2010

	Percentage who own a cell phone	Percentage who use a cell phone to look for health info
All adults in the U.S.	85%	15%
Gender		
Male	88	15
Female	82	13
Race		
White	85	13
African American	79	15
Latino	84	21
Age		
18–29	96	28
30–49	90	16
50–64	85	6
65+	58	5
Education		
Some high school	69	16
High school	82	10
Some college	91	19
College graduate	90	18
Household income		
<$30,000	75	11
$30,000–$49,999	90	15
$50,000–$74,999	93	16
$75,000+	95	18
Language		
English	85	15
Spanish (population = 197)	74	10
Community type		
Rural	77	9
Suburban	86	14
Urban	84	18

Notes: Population = 3,001 adults and the margin of error is +/−3 percentage points for the full sample. Margins of error for sub-populations are higher.

SOURCE: Susannah Fox, "Health Information Is Going Mobile," in *The Social Life of Health Information, 2011*, Pew Internet & American Life Project, May 12, 2011, http://pewinternet.org/~/media//Files/Reports/2011/PIP_Social_Life_of_Health_Info.pdf (accessed October 10, 2012). Used by permission of the Pew Internet & American Life Project, which bears no responsibility for the interpretations presented or conclusions reached based on analysis of the data.

with 22 health topics in its library. The site received over 682,000 page hits during its first three months. By 2012 the site held information on more than 900 diseases and conditions. A search on MedlinePlus for a disease typically yields definitions, fact sheets, drug information, the latest news on the disease, and links to places where further information can be found. During the second quarter of fiscal year (FY) 2007 the site recorded 245 million page views, an all-time high. (See Figure 8.1.) Traffic dropped considerably over the next year and a half, however, falling to 161 million views during the fourth quarter of FY 2008. Traffic to MedlinePlus rose steadily between 2008 and the first quarter of 2012, when the site received 198 million page views, while attracting a record 55.5 million unique visitors.

TABLE 8.9

Percentage of cell phone users who have downloaded health-related apps, by selected characteristics, 2010

Total cell phone users	9%
Gender	
Male	10
Female	8
Race	
White	7
African American	15*
Hispanic	11
Age (at time of survey)	
18–29	15*
30–49	8
50–64	6
65+	5
Education	
Some high school	9
High school graduate	6
Some college	13*
College graduate or more	9
Household Income	
<$30,000	7
$30,000–$49,999	8
$50,000–$74,999	12
$75,000+	11
Language	
English	9*
Spanish	1
Community type	
Rural	4
Suburban	9
Urban	12*

*Indicates a significant difference.

Notes: Population = 3,001 adults and population for cell phone users = 2,485. The margin of error is +/−2.5 percentage points for all adults and 3 points for cell phone users.

SOURCE: Susannah Fox, "Mobile Health Apps," in *The Social Life of Health Information, 2011*, Pew Internet & American Life Project, May 12, 2011, http://pewinternet.org/~/media//Files/Reports/2011/PIP_Social_Life_of_Health_Info.pdf (accessed October 10, 2012). Used by permission of the Pew Internet & American Life Project, which bears no responsibility for the interpretations presented or conclusions reached based on analysis of the data.

MEDICATION ONLINE

The Internet also contains a wealth of information about prescription and nonprescription drugs. Since the late 1990s the online pharmacy business has been growing at a steady rate. Most major online pharmacies, such as Drugstore.com and Walgreen's online pharmacy, are legitimate. They carry the Verified Internet Pharmacy Practice Sites seal of approval (VIPPS, issued by the National Association of Boards of Pharmacy [NABP]), meaning that they comply with all state and federal laws. Much like traditional pharmacies, these online drug stores require that a prescription be faxed or called in by a doctor. Such pharmacies also send the drug to the patient complete with dosage and warning information on the bottle. According to the NABP, in "Buying Medicine Online" (2012, http://www.nabp.net/programs/consumer-protection/buying-medicine-online/), as of December 2012

there were 50 VIPPS-certified pharmaceutical websites, working in collaboration with over 12,000 online pharmacies, operating in the United States.

However, unlawful virtual pharmacies, which do not follow U.S. state and federal regulations, have begun operating on the Internet as well. In some cases, online pharmacies are operating illegally simply because they are based overseas. For example, even though many Canadian pharmacies follow strict standards that are comparable to those imposed on legitimate U.S. pharmacies, it is still illegal for individuals in the United States to buy pharmaceuticals from Canadian pharmacies. Of greater concern to health and law enforcement officials, however, is the rise of illegitimate online pharmacies. Although many online pharmacies that cater to the U.S. market claim to be located in Canada, research shows that many of them are actually located in other countries, including the United States. Many of these pharmacies will sell patients prescription drugs without a prescription, provide counterfeit or contaminated drugs, or send medications in the wrong dosages. Furthermore, a number of online pharmacies are either fronts for other businesses, or else conceal phishing scams or other harmful online activities. Brian Krebs reports in "Few Online 'Canadian Pharmacies' Based in Canada, FDA Says" (*Washington Post*, June 14, 2005) that a U.S. Food and Drug Administration (FDA) investigation of 11,000 online pharmacies in 2005 revealed that fewer than 1,000 actually sold prescription drugs. In addition, two-thirds of these online pharmacies did not require customers to have a prescription to buy medications.

For many patients in the United States, the lure of online pharmacies is their convenience and low cost. In 2012 millions of Americans were without health insurance, and millions more had limited prescription drug benefits. In some cases, cheaper online pharmacies represented the difference between obtaining much-needed medications and going without them. PharmacyChecker.com notes in the press release "Savings on Brand Name Drugs Rise to 85% Using Verified Online Pharmacies Outside the U.S., According to PharmacyChecker.com" (November 20, 2012, http://www.pharmacychecker.com/news/online_pharmacy_prescription_savings_2012.asp) that brand-name medications purchased from "verified online pharmacies" in 2012 cost an average of 85% less than drugs that were sold at traditional pharmacies. For example, a consumer who needed a 90-day supply of the acid reflux and ulcer drug Nexium could expect to pay $737.97 at a local drugstore, while the same prescription purchased through an international online pharmacy cost only $67.50, a savings of 91%.

Online Pharmacies, Safety, and the Law

Regardless, purchasing drugs online carries substantial risks. Illegitimate online pharmacies have generated a great deal of concern among health care professionals

FIGURE 8.1

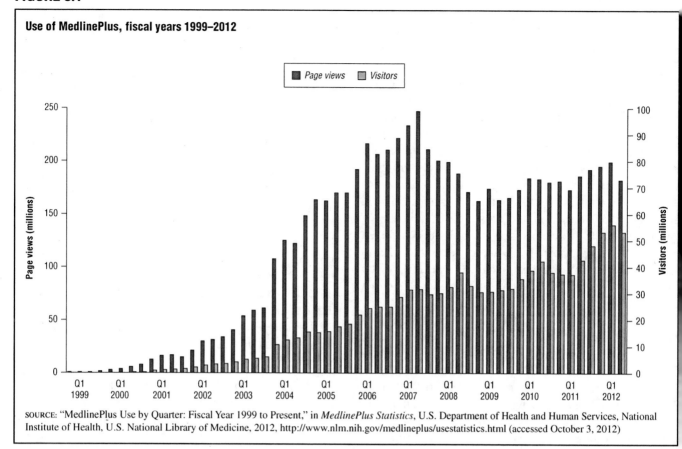

Use of MedlinePlus, fiscal years 1999–2012

SOURCE: "MedlinePlus Use by Quarter: Fiscal Year 1999 to Present," in *MedlinePlus Statistics*, U.S. Department of Health and Human Services, National Institute of Health, U.S. National Library of Medicine, 2012, http://www.nlm.nih.gov/medlineplus/usestatistics.html (accessed October 3, 2012)

and government lawmakers in the United States. One problem is that state medical boards, which typically oversee brick-and-mortar operations, have difficulty monitoring pharmaceutical websites. Even though some of these pharmacies follow many of the same standards as legitimate operations, others disregard them altogether. Besides providing drugs without a prescription, many send patients drugs without warning labels or dosage information. In an investigation of approximately 10,000 online pharmacies marketing to patients in the United States, the NABP (October 2012, http://www.nabp.net/programs/consumer-protection/buying-medicine-online/) finds that only 3% adhered to standard pharmacy regulations and practices. Of the online pharmacies labeled "not recommended" by the NAPB, 23% were operating outside of the United States and 50% sold drugs that were either foreign or had not received official FDA approval. Furthermore, 87% of online pharmacies that failed to comply with U.S. law offered to sell drugs without a prescription. In spite of these dangers, many Americans continued to seek lower drug prices on the Internet. In "FDA Warns of Rising Risks of Online Pharmacies" (NBC News, September 28, 2012), Linda A. Johnson indicates that 25% of all adults who shopped online in 2012 had purchased prescription medication through an online pharmacy. An even higher proportion of online shoppers (30%), however, felt uncertain about the safety of buying drugs over the Internet.

In the face of this trend, Congress has crafted legislation aimed at controlling the rapidly expanding trade in illegal online drugs. In 2008 President George W. Bush (1946–) signed the Ryan Haight Online Pharmacy Consumer Protection Act, a law that imposed several new restrictions on the sale of online pharmaceuticals. The law was named for Ryan Haight (1982–2001), a California teenager who died after overdosing on painkillers he had purchased illegally over the Internet. Among the law's key provisions included the requirement that all prescriptions be accompanied by a physical consultation between a doctor and a patient. Furthermore, the law imposed a ban on all online advertisements for illegal prescription medications. In spite of these new regulations, some in the pharmaceutical industry maintained that the law did not go far enough to curb the traffic in illegal pharmaceuticals online. In "Internet Search Engines Promote Illegal Online Pharmacies" (September 18, 2009, http://www.safemedicines.org/2009/09/internet-search-engines-promote-illegal-online-pharmacies.html), the Partnership for Safe Medicines and the Pharmaceutical Institute note their fear that illegal prescription drug traffic will continue to proliferate until search engines such as Google and Yahoo! are held liable for hosting and facilitating access to illegal online pharmacies.

When federal and state agencies become aware of illegitimate pharmacies in the United States, they attempt o shut them down. However, government regulators can do little about controlling pharmacies that are outside of U.S. borders. In the eyes of law enforcement officials, global cooperation is critical to controlling traffic in illegal online drugs. According to the World Health Organization (WHO), in "Growing Threat from Counterfeit Medicines" (*Bulletin of the World Health Organization*, vol. 88, no. 4, April 2010), in 2009 the International Criminal Police Organization (Interpol) helped coordinate a series of international law enforcement operations throughout the world. In one series of raids, officials seized more than 20 million illegal pharmaceutical products throughout China and Southeast Asia and closed down 100 illicit prescription drug storefronts. In Europe law enforcement officers seized 34 million counterfeit pills in a two-month span, while another operation uncovered 1,200 illegal online pharmacies. Overall, the WHO finds that of all the medications sold by illegal Internet pharmacies that fail to reveal a physical address, roughly 50% are counterfeit. The Partnership for Safe Medicines reports in "Global Sting Operation Shuts down 18,000 Illegal Online Pharmacies, Seizes 3.75 Million Counterfeit Medicines Worth over $10.5 Million" (October 4, 2012, http://www.safemedicines.org/) that in September 2012 Interpol launched a wide-reaching operation that was aimed at disrupting the global traffic in illegal online prescription drugs. Called Pangea V, the operation was the "largest internet-based sting operation of its kind" and led to the seizure of 3.8 million units of counterfeit prescription drugs and successfully shut down 18,000 rogue websites.

In spite of continued efforts by domestic and international law enforcement agencies, the problem of illegal online prescription drugs remained pervasive in 2012. Mike Harvey reports in "Cyber-Criminals Cashing in with Online Pharmacies" (*Times* [London], November 28, 2009) that one Russia-based criminal network, known as Glavmed, was affiliated with more than 120,000 illicit online pharmacies. Harvey notes that organizations such as Glavmed are also responsible for billions of spam e-mail messages that market illegal online pharmacies. In addition, many lawmakers in the United States believe that illegal prescription drugs will remain a threat for as long as the costs of legal pharmaceutical products remain prohibitively high. In January 2009 Senator David Vitter (1961–; R-LA) introduced the Pharmaceutical Market Access Act, a bill proposing to allow for the importation of prescription drugs from select overseas markets into the United States. The proposed law was primarily aimed at increasing competition among drug companies to drive down prices. According to estimates provided by the Congressional Budget Office, the law had the potential to reduce prescription drug costs by approximately $50 billion over a 10-year period. In 2011 a similar bill, the Pharmaceutical Market Access and Drug Safety Act, was introduced by Senator Olympia Snowe (1947–; R-ME). As of December 2012, the bill remained in committee.

Meanwhile, U.S. law enforcement efforts to curb the traffic in illegal online pharmaceuticals remained aggressive. In a speech delivered to the Opiate Abuse Conference in September 2010, the U.S. attorney general Eric Holder Jr. (1951–; http://www.justice.gov/ag/speeches/2010/ag-speech-100910.html) asserted that, during the first nine months of 2010, the Drug Enforcement Agency had seized "more than $62 million in proceeds and assets and … helped to shut down 'pill mill' pain clinics, prescription forgery rings, and illegal online pharmacies." Holder also claimed that the Ryan Haight Online Pharmacy Consumer Protection Act had already played a major role in reducing the number of illegal online pharmacies selling prescription drugs in the United States. In "Two Indicted in Phila. in Illegal Online Drug Sales" (*Philadelphia Inquirer*, May 13, 2010), Nathan Gorenstein reports that the first prosecution under the Ryan Haight Act was initiated in May 2010, when federal prosecutors indicted two individuals, one American and one from the Bahamas, in association with an illegal online diet pill ring.

Because of the many unethical and illegal practices that are encountered by consumers making pharmaceutical purchases online, the FDA provides the guide "Buying Prescription Medicine Online: A Consumer Safety Guide" (October 4, 2012, http://www.fda.gov/Drugs/Resources ForYou/ucm080588.htm) to reduce or eliminate many issues surrounding Internet pharmacies. The FDA recommends that patients use only sites that require a prescription, have pharmacists available to answer questions, and adequately protect the privacy of customers. It also suggests that online consumers use only state-licensed U.S. pharmacies. In 2012 the FDA launched the BeSafeRx initiative (http://www.fda.gov/besaferx), which is aimed at providing the public with vital information concerning the dangers that are involved with purchasing drugs over the Internet.

MEDICAL DATA REVOLUTION

Since the 1980s information technology (IT) and the Internet have transformed the field of medical research. Before launching a medical research project, a scientist must first know what has been done in the area he or she plans to study. For example, the initial step for a researcher who wants to find a cure for Alzheimer's would be to analyze previous data on the subject. Only then could the researcher formulate new theories and design experiments that advance the field. Before the Internet and the widespread use of computer databases, researchers seeking such information were required to spend days at medical libraries, sifting through thick journal indexes that cataloged thousands upon thousands of past journal articles by subject. The advent of computer databases changed all that. Huge medical indexes were put in digital form, which allowed researchers to compile a full list of research articles in minutes instead of days. MEDLINE/PubMed, which is maintained by the National Library of Medicine, is one of the most comprehensive and widely used of these databases. The National Library of Medicine (April 9, 2010, http://www.nlm.nih.gov/pubs/factsheets/dif_med_pub.html) states that in 2010 MEDLINE contained citations and abstracts summarizing papers that were published in nearly 5,400 biomedical journals in the United States and more than 80 other countries. By simply going online to MEDLINE and typing a query, a researcher can track down every published paper on most medical topics.

The ability of computers and the Internet to store and transmit scientific data has also transformed the way medical research is conducted. The Internet allows scientists from all over the world to share data on diseases and patient attributes. Computers can then perform statistical analyses on disease data in relation to various aspects of patient histories, such as age, geographic location, and even the presence of other diseases.

The CDC's National Center for Health Statistics (NCHS, http://www.cdc.gov/nchs/) database contains statistics on a variety of diseases including arthritis, heart disease, HIV, and even tooth decay. All this information is freely available for scientists to use in their research. The NCHS also provides valuable data to other government agencies. For example, in 2010 the NCHS worked with the Federal Interagency Forum on Child and Family Statistics, a group of government agencies that is dedicated to collecting and sharing data on children and families, to create *America's Children in Brief: Key National Indicators of Well-Being, 2010* (July 2010, http://childstats.gov/pdf/ac2010/ac_10.pdf). Among the contributions provided by the NCHS to the report were data measuring premature births and low birthrates, blood-lead levels in children between the ages of one and five years, and statistics evaluating the link between poverty and dental care in school-age children.

Computer databases and the Internet have also become invaluable resources for organ and tissue donor programs. For example, treatments for leukemia (a type of cancer) sometimes destroy the bone marrow, which produces red and white blood cells and platelets. To replace the bone marrow, a transplant from another person is needed. However, finding compatible bone marrow is difficult. Typically, a match may not even exist within the same family. The National Bone Marrow Donor Registry is a computer database of people who have agreed to donate their bone marrow to those in need. A doctor with a patient in need of a transplant can simply log onto the registry via the Internet and pull up all possible matches in the country. The Organ Procurement and Transplantation

Network (OPTN) maintains a similar database for internal organ transplants, including kidney, pancreas, heart, lung, and intestine. The OPTN's secure transplant information database keeps track of exactly which patients are in need of a transplant. Table 8.10 displays the number of candidates who were waiting on the OPTN in October 2012. All necessary forms and patient histories are also included in the database. Should a donor's heart become available in a medical facility anywhere in the United States, the attending physician can access the database to find patients who are waiting for a new heart.

HEALTH IT

IT is changing the way patients interact with their health care providers and the way health care providers interact with one another to ensure prompt, safe, and effective treatments. Electronic health records are expected to improve health care by keeping all information about a patient's health history, including medications, immunizations, laboratory and test results, allergies, and family history in one accessible online location. As U.S. health care systems become networked, information about a patient will be immediately available regardless of the treatment location. Even though electronic medical records provide enormous benefits to both patients and health care professionals, they also pose a number of new challenges. Alicia Gallegos indicates in "Legal Risks of Going Paperless" (*American Medical News*, March 5, 2012) that the potential for data breaches, system errors, and other problems relating to the transmission of data online leave health care professionals vulnerable to new forms of legal action. In "Benefits and Drawbacks of Electronic Health Record Systems" (*Journal of Risk Management and Healthcare Policy*, vol. 4, May 11, 2012), Nir Menachemi and Taleah H. Collum cite a number of financial disadvantages involved with implementing electronic health records, including the high costs that are related

TABLE 8.10

Number of organ-transplant candidates registered with the Organ Procurement and Transplantation Network, October 2012

All*	115,919
Kidney	93,801
Liver	16,046
Heart	3,300
Kidney/pancreas	2,150
Lung	1,635
Pancreas	1,238
Intestine	261
Heart/lung	52

*All candidates will be less than the sum due to candidates waiting for multiple organs.

SOURCE: Adapted from "Waiting List Candidates," U.S. Department of Health & Human Services, Health Resources and Services Administration, Organ Procurement and Transplantation Network, October 3, 2012, http://optn.transplant.hrsa.gov/data/ (accessed October 3, 2012)

to launching and maintaining medical information online and the problems of lost productivity that are involved with the transition from paper to electronic data-keeping systems.

The Agency for Healthcare Research and Quality (AHRQ) of the U.S. Department of Health and Human Services (HHS) maintains a website (http://www.ahrq .gov/qual/patientsafetyix.htm#online) that provides information and resources aimed at reducing incidences of medical error. The AHRQ believes that by using IT to integrate health history with medication information many deaths and injuries stemming from medical errors can be prevented. Computerized health record systems would provide attending doctors with dosage information about medications already prescribed for each patient, check for potential interactions with other medications, and alert physicians to patient allergies. Anticipated benefits of integrated health IT include electronic health records for patients that can be easily shared by health care providers; electronic transmittal of medical test results; and electronic prescription messaging, which will improve efficiency and reduce human errors in reading paper prescriptions.

To facilitate the development of a nationwide electronic health system, President Bush established in April 2004 the Office of the National Coordinator for Health Information Technology (ONC) within the HHS. This office provides leadership in developing standards, policies, and the necessary infrastructure that will allow the flow of health information nationwide. *Healthcare IT News* (http://www.healthcareitnews.com/), an online journal examining the role of IT in the medical profession, maintains a website that is dedicated to providing regular updates on the development of the Nationwide Health Information Network (NHIN). Known as NHIN-Watch (http://www.nhinwatch.com/), the site reports on various federal, state, and local health care IT initiatives, analyzes critical surveys and studies, and provides other news relating to the NHIN project.

The Health Information Technology for Economic and Clinical Health (HITECH) Act, which was part of the Economic Recovery and Reinvestment Act of 2009, was designed to improve and expand IT systems across the U.S. health care industry. HITECH provided the HHS with approximately $2 billion to help fund regional health care IT networks, with the aim of helping medical professionals coordinate patient care more quickly and efficiently, while reducing cases of medical errors. Supervised by the ONC, HITECH was also dedicated to maintaining online security to safeguard patient privacy. In January 2012 the ONC presented the status report *Update on the Adoption of Health Information Technology and Related Efforts to Facilitate the Electronic Use and Exchange of Health Information* (http://healthit.hhs.gov/) to Congress. As

Figure 8.2 shows, 39% of nonhospital-based primary physicians had adopted electronic health record systems in 2011, up from 20% in 2008. The ONC notes an even more dramatic rise in the use of electronic prescription technology; whereas 0.8% of nonhospital-based physicians wrote electronic prescriptions in December 2006, by December 2011 this figure had risen to 44.4%. (See Figure 8.3.) As Figure 8.4 shows, by December 2011 the vast majority of retail pharmacists (93%) were using electronic prescription technology. During this same period the ONC also launched the Challenge Grants program, which was aimed at helping states develop and implement electronic record-sharing technology. By 2011 the program had awarded more than $547.7 million to state and local health services agencies throughout the country. (See Table 8.11.)

FIGURE 8.2

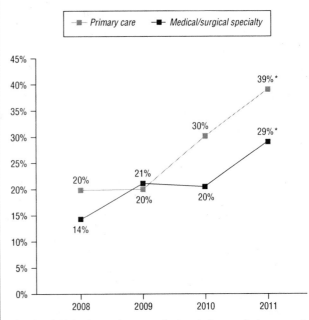

Adoption of electronic health records among nonhospital-based primary care physicians and specialists, 2008–11

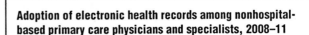

*Significantly higher than previous year estimate, or in the case of primary care all other physicians, at p < 0.05.

SOURCE: "Figure 1. Adoption of 'Basic' Electronic Health Records among Non-Hospital-Based Physicians," in *Update on the Adoption of Health Information Technology and Related Efforts to Facilitate the Electronic Use and Exchange of Health Information: A Report to Congress*, U.S. Department of Health and Human Services, Office of the National Coordinator for Health Information Technology (ONC), January 2012, http://healthit.hhs.gov/portal/server.pt/gateway/ PTARGS_0_0_4383_1239_15610_43/http%3B/wci-pu bcontent/ publish/onc/public_communities/p_t/resources_and_public_affairs/ reports/reports_portlet/files/january2012__update_on_hit_adoption_ report_to_congress.pdf (accessed October 10, 2012)

FIGURE 8.3

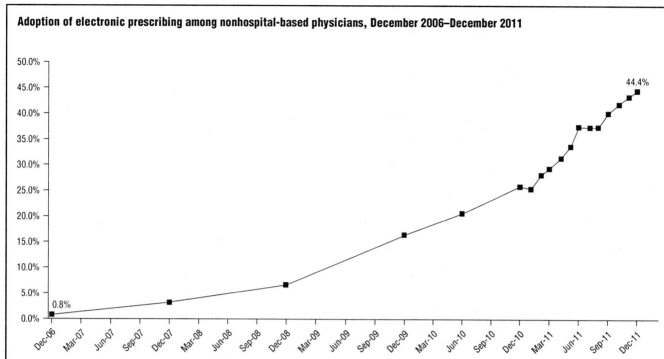

Adoption of electronic prescribing among nonhospital-based physicians, December 2006–December 2011

SOURCE: "Figure 3. Adoption of Electronic Prescribing through an Electronic Health Record among Non-Hospital-Based Physicians," in *Update on the Adoption of Health Information Technology and Related Efforts to Facilitate the Electronic Use and Exchange of Health Information: A Report to Congress*, U.S. Department of Health and Human Services, Office of the National Coordinator for Health Information Technology (ONC), January 2012, http://healthit.hhs.gov/portal/server.pt/gateway/PTARGS_0_0_4383_1239_15610_43/http%3B/wci-pubcontent/publish/onc/public_communities/p_t/resources_and_public_affairs/reports/reports_portlet/files/january2012__update_on_hit_adoption_report_to_congress.pdf (accessed October 10, 2012)

FIGURE 8.4

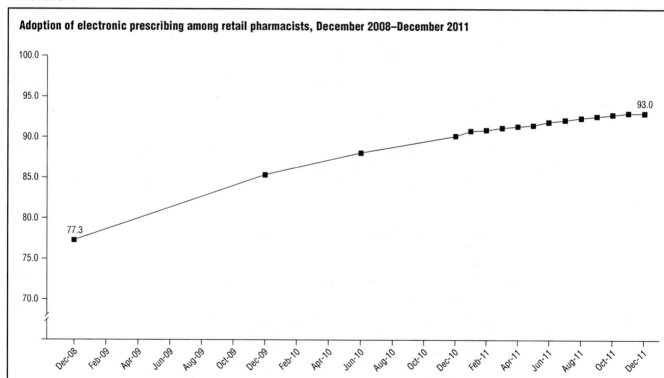

Adoption of electronic prescribing among retail pharmacists, December 2008–December 2011

SOURCE: "Figure 4. Adoption of Electronic Prescribing among Retail Community Pharmacies," in *Update on the Adoption of Health Information Technology and Related Efforts to Facilitate the Electronic Use and Exchange of Health Information: A Report to Congress*, U.S. Department of Health and Human Services, Office of the National Coordinator for Health Information Technology (ONC), January 2012, http://healthit.hhs.gov/portal/server.pt/gateway/PTARGS_0_0_4383_1239_15610_43/http%3B/wci-pubcontent/publish/onc/public_communities/p_t/resources_and_public_affairs/reports/reports_portlet/files/january2012__update_on_hit_adoption_report_to_congress.pdf (accessed October 10, 2012)

TABLE 8.11

Funds awarded through State Health Information Exchange (HIE) Cooperative Agreement Program, 2010 and 2011

State/SDE	Award amount
Alabama Medicaid Agency	$10,564,789
State of Alaska	$4,963,063
Arizona Governor's Office of Economic Recovery	$9,377,000
Arkansas Dept of Finance and Administration	$7,909,401
California Health and Human Services Agency	$38,752,536
Colorado Regional Health Information Organization*	$9,175,777
Department of Public Health, State of CT	$7,297,930
Delaware Health Information Network	$4,680,284
Government of the District of Columbia	$5,189,709
Agency of Health Care Administration (FL)	$20,738,582
Georgia Department of Community Health*	$13,003,003
The Hawaii Health Information Exchange	$5,602,318
Idaho Health Data Exchange	$5,940,500
Illinois Department of Health Care and Family Services	$18,837,639
Indiana Health Information Technology, Inc.*	$10,300,000
Iowa Department of Public Health	$8,375,000
Kansas Health Information Exchange Project	$9,010,066
Cabinet for Health and Family Services (Kentucky)	$9,750,000
Louisiana Health Care Quality Forum	$10,583,000
Maine Department of Health and Human Services	$6,599,401
The Maryland Department of Health and Mental Hygiene*	$9,313,924
Massachusetts Technology Park Corporation*	$10,599,719
Michigan Department of Health	$14,993,085
Minnesota Department of Health	$9,622,000
State of Mississippi	$10,387,000
Missouri Depart of Social Services	$13,765,040
HealthShare Montana*	$5,767,926
Nebraska Department of Administrative Services	$6,837,180
Nevada Department of Health and Human Services	$6,133,426
New Hampshire Department of Health and Human Services	$5,457,856
New Jersey Health Care Facilities Financing Authority	$11,408,594
LCF Research, New Mexico	$7,070,441
New York eHealth Collaborative Inc.	$22,364,782
North Carolina Health Information Exchange*	$12,950,860
State of North Dakota, Information Technology Department	$5,343,733
Ohio Health Information Partnership LLC	$14,872,199
Oklahoma Health Care Authority*	$8,883,741
State of Oregon	$8,579,992
Governor's Office of Health Care Reform Commonwealth of Pennsylvania	$17,140,446
Rhode Island Quality Institute	$5,280,000
South Carolina Department of Health & Human Services	$9,576,408
South Dakota Department of Health	$6,081,750
State of Tennessee	$11,664,580
Texas Health and Human Services Commission	$28,810,208
Utah Department of Health	$6,296,705
Vermont Department of Human Services	$5,034,328
Virginia Department of Health	$11,613,537
Health Care Authority (Washington)	$11,300,000
West Virginia Department of Health and Human Resources	$7,819,000
Wisconsin Department of Health and Family Services	$9,441,000
Office of the Governor (Wyoming)	$4,873,000
Pacific Ecommerce Development Corporation (American Samoa)	$600,000
Office of the Governor (Guam)	$1,600,000
Commonwealth of the NMI, Department of Public Health	$800,000
Oficina del Gobernador La Fortaeza (Puerto Rico)	$7,770,980
Virgin Islands Department of Health	$1,000,000
Total	**$547,703,438**

*Existing State HIEs that received new funding through the HIE Challenge Grant Program on January 27, 2011.

SOURCE: "Untitled," in *State Health Information Exchange Cooperative Agreement Program*, U.S. Department of Health and Human Services, Office of the National Coordinator for Health Information Technology, August 11, 2012, http://healthit.hhs.gov/portal/server.pt/community/healthit_hhs_gov__ state_health_information_exchange_program/1488 (accessed October 4, 2012)

CHAPTER 9
HIGH TECHNOLOGY AND DAILY LIFE

Since the early 1980s high technology (high tech) has crept into every aspect of American life and has become in some instances as mundane as running water or refrigeration. Many Americans think nothing of going online to check the weather, purchase movie tickets, watch videos, or read up on their favorite hobbies. The Internet also contains an endless list of resources that most people would never have room for on their bookshelf but now take for granted nonetheless, including maps, dictionaries, phone books, and even manuals on most products. The Internet has become a great way to communicate with others as well, and millions have used it to make a date, schedule appointments, or find old friends. Over time, innovations in computing have also allowed Americans to become more mobile. Kathryn Zickuhr and Aaron Smith of the Pew Internet & American Life Project (Pew/Internet) report in *Digital Differences* (April 13, 2012, http://pewinternet.org/~/media//Files/Reports/2012/PIP_Digital_differences_041312.pdf) that 63% of all adults used wireless Internet in 2011. Furthermore, a new generation of mobile devices, notably tablet computers such as the Apple iPad and e-book readers such as the Amazon Kindle, were becoming increasingly popular. As Figure 9.1 shows, in 2010 only 4% of all American adults owned tablet computers. A similar proportion (5%) owned e-readers. (See Figure 9.2.) By 2012, 19% of all American adults owned tablet computers and 19% owned e-book readers. (See Figure 9.3.)

The Internet and mobile devices are not the only new technology to have become ubiquitous in everyday American life. Microchips, sensors, and display screens can be found on or in just about every appliance in the home. They allow people to do everything from control the home thermostat from a remote computer to heat water with microwave radiation. Most American automobiles have dozens of complex sensors that monitor engine performance, regulate gas flow, sense obstacles, and pinpoint the vehicle's

location. As of 2012, robots were making their way into U.S. homes to complete time-consuming tasks such as mowing the lawn and vacuuming the living room.

EVERYDAY ACTIVITIES AND THE INTERNET

In *Search Engine Use 2012* (March 9, 2012, http://www.pewinternet.org/~/media//Files/Reports/2012/PIP_Search_Engine_Use_2012.pdf), Kristin Purcell, Joanna Brenner, and Lee Rainie of Pew/Internet indicate that searching for information on the Internet remains one of the most prevalent activities among American adults. In 2002 just over half (52%) of all Americans used search engines; by February 2012 this percentage had grown to 73%. Furthermore, by 2012, 91% of online adults used search engines, which made searching for information the second-most popular Internet activity after sending and receiving e-mails (92%). As Table 9.1 reveals, 96% of online adults aged 18 to 29 years had used a search engine by 2012. White Internet users (93%) were more likely than online African-Americans (89%) or Hispanics (79%) to search for something online. In addition, online adults from high-income households were far more likely to have conducted an Internet search in the past day than those from middle- or lower-income brackets. For example, more than three-quarters (76%) of online adults with household incomes of $75,000 or more per year responded that they had used a search engine in the previous day, compared with 66% of adults with household incomes of between $50,000 and $74,999 per year, 54% of adults with household incomes of between $30,000 and $49,999 per year, and 45% of adults with household incomes of less than $30,000 per year. The discrepancy in search engine use was even starker when accounting for education level. In 2012, 74% of college graduates had used a search engine in the previous day; by comparison, only one-third (34%) of Internet adults without a high school diploma had searched for something online within the past day.

FIGURE 9.1

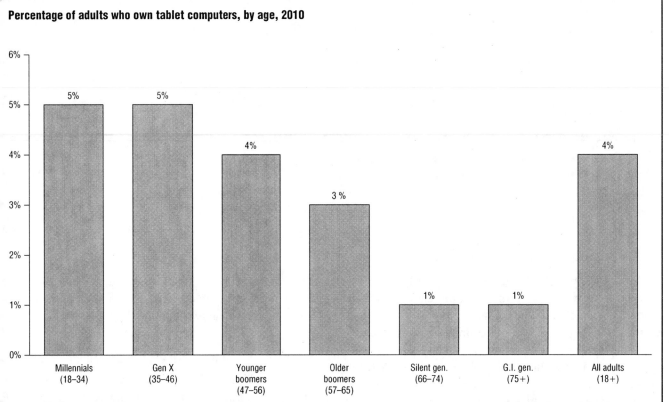

Percentage of adults who own tablet computers, by age, 2010

SOURCE: Kathryn Zickuhr, "Do You Own a Tablet Computer, Like an iPad?" in *Generations and Their Gadgets*, Pew Internet & American Life Project, February 3, 2011, http://www.pewinternet.org/~/media//Files/Reports/2011/PIP_Generations_and_Gadgets.pdf (accessed October 8, 2012). Used by permission of the Pew Internet & American Life Project, which bears no responsibility for the interpretations presented or conclusions reached based on analysis of the data.

FIGURE 9.2

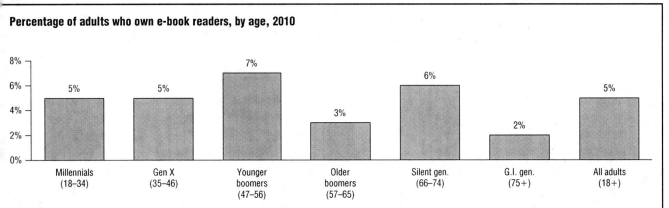

Percentage of adults who own e-book readers, by age, 2010

SOURCE: Kathryn Zickuhr, "Do You Own an Electronic Book Device or E-Book Reader, Such as a Kindle or Sony Digital Book?" in *Generations and Their Gadgets*, Pew Internet & American Life Project, February 3, 2011, http://www.pewinternet.org/~/media//Files/Reports/2011/PIP_Generations_and_Gadgets.pdf (accessed October 8, 2012). Used by permission of the Pew Internet & American Life Project, which bears no responsibility for the interpretations presented or conclusions reached based on analysis of the data.

With more and more Americans exploring the World Wide Web, protecting personal privacy became one of the central challenges of online life in the 21st century. Purcell, Brenner, and Rainie note that by 2012 search engines such as Google were systematically collecting and storing the online habits of their users; these habits were compiled into individual "profiles," which were then made accessible to online marketers. As companies gathered information about the interests and activities of Internet users, they were able to tailor their marketing

FIGURE 9.3

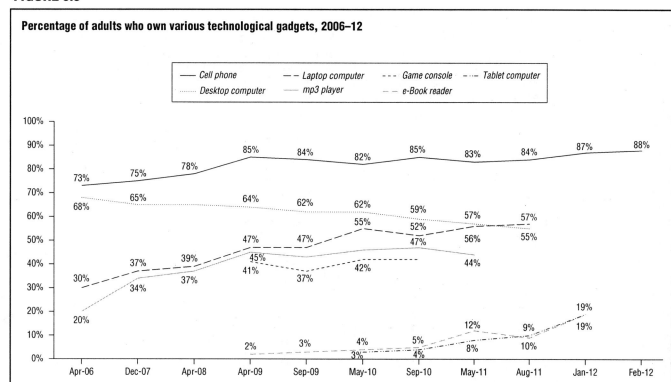

Percentage of adults who own various technological gadgets, 2006–12

SOURCE: Kathryn Zickuhr and Aaron Smith, "Adult Gadget Ownership over Time (2006–2012)," in *Digital Differences*, Pew Internet & American Life Project, April 13, 2012, http://pewinternet.org/Reports/2012/Digital-differences/Overview/Digital-differences.aspx (accessed October 4, 2012). Used by permission of the Pew Internet & American Life Project, which bears no responsibility for the interpretations presented or conclusions reached based on analysis of the data.

efforts in very precise ways. Indeed, as Table 9.2 shows, 59% of online adults experienced some form of targeted advertising in 2012. Most Internet users viewed this form of marketing as an invasion of privacy, as well as an unwelcome nuisance. According to Purcell, Brenner, and Rainie, nearly three-quarters (73%) of search engine users disapproved of the practice of using an individual's online activities for marketing purposes. Even though a vast majority of Americans disapproved of targeted advertising, relatively few knew how to protect their personal data on the Internet. In 2012 only 38% of online adults knew how to take steps to prevent websites from accessing their personal information online. (See Table 9.3.)

Communications

Communications have become a big part of people's everyday Internet experiences. E-mail, instant messaging, blogging, social networking sites, and Twitter offer multiple opportunities for staying in touch with family, friends, and associates, as well as for contacting organizations, becoming acquainted with others who share similar interests, or simply meeting new people. The increasingly interactive concept of the Internet is commonly referred to as Web 2.0, a term that was first coined by Darcy DiNucci in her 1999 essay "Fragmented Future" (*Print*, July–August 1999). In this landmark work, DiNucci predicted that in the future the web "will be understood not as screenfuls of text and graphics but as a transport mechanism, the ether through which interactivity happens."

With its fundamental reliance on consumer participation, the Internet has inspired a high level of creativity among its users. Nowhere has this phenomenon been more prevalent than in the realm of content creation. According to Rainie, Brenner, and Purcell, in *Photos and Videos as Social Currency Online* (September 13, 2012, http://pewinternet.org/~/media//Files/Reports/2012/PIP_Online LifeinPictures_PDF.pdf), 45% of all adult Internet users posted original photographs online in 2012. More than two-thirds (67%) of Internet users aged 18 to 29 years posted their pictures online, compared with only 50% of online adults aged 30 to 49 years. In addition, 18% of online adults posted original videos on the Internet in 2012. Teens were even more likely to post original videos on the Internet. In 2011 more than a quarter (27%) of online teens aged 12 to 17 years were recording and uploading their own videos to the Internet. (See Table 9.4.) Overall, visits to video-sharing sites increased considerably between 2006 and 2011. Nowhere was this growth more prominent than among online adults living in rural areas. In December

TABLE 9.1

Percentage of online adults who use search engines, by selcted characteristics, 2012

	% of each group who ever use search engines	% of each group who used a search engine yesterday
All online adults	91%	59%
Gender		
Male	90	59
Female	92	60
Race/ethnicity		
White	93*	63*
African American	89*	44
Hispanic	79	44
Age		
18–29	96	66*
30–49	91	65*
50–64	92	52*
65+	80	38
Education		
Some high school	78	34
High school	88*	45*
Some college	94*	65*
College graduate	95*	74*
Household income		
<$30,000	84	45
$30,000–$49,999	93*	54*
$50,000–$74,999	97*	66*
$75,000+	95*	76*

*Denotes statistically significant difference with other rows in that category.

SOURCE: Kristen Purcell, Joanna Brenner, and Lee Rainie, "Who Uses Search?" in *Search Engine Use 2012*, Pew Internet & American Life Project, March 9, 2012, http://www.pewinternet.org/~/media//Files/Reports/2012/PIP_Search_Engine_Use_2012.pdf (accessed October 10, 2012). Used by permission of the Pew Internet & American Life Project, which bears no responsibility for the interpretations presented or conclusions reached based on analysis of the data.

TABLE 9.2

Percentage of online adults who have experienced targeted Internet advertising, by selected characteristics, 2012

HAVE YOU, PERSONALLY, EVER NOTICED ADVERTISEMENTS ONLINE THAT ARE DIRECTLY RELATED TO THINGS YOU HAVE RECENTLY SEARCHED FOR OR SITES YOU HAVE RECENTLY VISITED, OR HAS THIS NEVER HAPPENED TO YOU?

	% of each group answering "yes"
All online adults (sample size = 1,729)	59%
Gender	
Male (sample size = 804)	62
Female (sample size = 925)	56
Race/ethnicity	
White (sample size = 1,229)	62
African American (sample size = 172)	51
Hispanic (sample size = 184)	46
Age	
18–29 (sample size = 316)	62
30–49 (sample size = 532)	62
50–64 (sample size = 521)	56
65+ (sample size = 320)	47
Education	
Some high school (sample size = 108)	38
High school (sample size = 465)	44
Some college (sample size = 447)	64
College graduate (sample size = 698)	73
Household income	
<$30,000 (sample size = 390)	48
$30,000–$49,999 (sample size = 290)	57
$50,000–$74,999 (sample size = 250)	67
$75,000+ (sample size = 523)	69

SOURCE: Kristen Purcell, Joanna Brenner, and Lee Rainie, "Who Experiences Targeted Advertising Online?" in *Search Engine Use 2012*, Pew Internet & American Life Project, March 9, 2012, http://www.pewinternet.org/~/media//Files/Reports/2012/PIP_Search_Engine_Use_2012.pdf (accessed October 10, 2012). Used by permission of the Pew Internet & American Life Project, which bears no responsibility for the interpretations presented or conclusions reached based on analysis of the data.

2006 only 21% of rural Internet adults used online video sharing sites; by April 2011 this percentage had risen to 68%. (See Figure 9.4.)

With the proliferation of images on the Internet, a number of online adults also began sharing other people's photographs on social networking sites, photo sharing sites, or other web pages that were accessible to the general public. Rainie, Brenner, and Purcell note that in 2012 more than one-third (35%) of all adult Internet users reposted images they found online and 25% reposted videos. This trend was more prevalent among younger Internet users, with over half (52%) of online adults aged 18 to 29 years reposting images they found on the web and 44% sharing videos originally posted elsewhere.

BLOGGING. Among the forms of Internet communication that have rapidly gained acceptance is the web log (blog), in which individuals publish their personal experiences and views on topics such as entertainment, politics, sports, and religion. In *Generations 2010*

(December 16, 2010, http://pewinternet.org/~/media//Files/Reports/2010/PIP_Generations_and_Tech10.pdf), Kathryn Zickuhr of Pew/Internet notes that 32% of all online adults read some kind of blog in 2010. Younger Internet users were the most likely to visit blog sites. Forty-three percent of adults aged 18 to 33 years read blogs in 2010, compared with 34% of online adults aged 34 to 45 years and 27% of those aged 46 to 55 years. In addition, 14% of all adult Internet users maintained their own blog in 2010.

John Rampton reports in "Blogging Stats 2012" (July 13, 2012, http://blogging.org/blog/blogging-stats-2012-infographic/) that in 2012 there were approximately 31 million bloggers in the United States, who provided content for roughly 42 million individual blogs. Nearly half (48%) of the bloggers in 2012 were white, and African-Americans accounted for another 38% of all bloggers. Rampton reveals that the audience for blogs was also considerable in 2012. That year 329 million people viewed blogs. On average, 25 billion blog pages

TABLE 9.3

Percentage of online adults who know how to limit outside access to their personal information on the Internet, by selected characteristics, 2012

ARE YOU AWARE OF ANY WAYS INTERNET USERS LIKE YOURSELF CAN LIMIT HOW MUCH PERSONAL INFORMATION WEBSITES COLLECT ABOUT YOU, OR ARE YOU NOT AWARE OF ANY WAYS TO DO THIS?

	% of each group answering "yes"
All online adults (sample size = 1,729)	38%
Gender	
Male (sample size = 804)	42
Female (sample size = 925)	35
Race/ethnicity	
White (sample size = 1,229)	41
African American (sample size = 172)	34
Hispanic (sample size = 184)	27
Age	
18–29 (sample size = 316)	41
30–49 (sample size = 532)	42
50–64 (sample size = 521)	34
65+ (sample size = 320)	27
Education	
Some high school (sample size = 108)	28
High school (sample size = 465)	31
Some college (sample size = 447)	43
College graduate (sample size = 698)	44
Household income	
<$30,000 (sample size = 390)	34
$30,000–$49,999 (sample size = 290)	41
$50,000–$74,999 (sample size = 250)	32
$75,000+ (sample size = 523)	44

SOURCE: Kristen Purcell, Joanna Brenner, and Lee Rainie, "Who Knows How to Limit Websites' Access to Their Personal Information Online?" in *Search Engine Use 2012*, Pew Internet & American Life Project, March 9, 2012, http://www.pewinternet.org/~/media//Files/Reports/2012/PIP_Search_Engine_Use_2012.pdf (accessed October 10, 2012). Used by permission of the Pew Internet & American Life Project, which bears no responsibility for the interpretations presented or conclusions reached based on analysis of the data.

TABLE 9.4

Percentage of online teens who have recorded and uploaded videos to the Internet, by selected characteristics, 2011

All Internet users	27%
Gender	
Boys	28
Girls	26
Age	
12–13	21*
14–17	30
Race/ethnicity	
White, non-Hispanic	27
Black, non-Hispanic	29
Hispanic (English- and Spanish-speaking)	26
Household income	
Less than $30,000	24
$30,000–$49,999	30
$50,000–$74,999	30
$75,000+	27
Education level of parents	
Less than high school	23
High school graduate	22
Some college	28
College+	32
Community type	
Urban	29
Suburban	27
Rural	23

*Indicates statistically significant difference between rows.
Notes: Population = 799 teens ages 12–17 and a parent or guardian. Interviews were conducted in English and Spanish on landlines and cell phones.

SOURCE: Amanda Lenhart, "Who Records and Uploads Video?" in *Teens & Online Video*, Pew Internet & American Life Project, May 3, 2012, http://www.pewinternet.org/~/media/Files/Reports/2012/PIP_Teens_and_online_video.pdf (accessed October 10, 2012). Used by permission of the Pew Internet & American Life Project, which bears no responsibility for the interpretations presented or conclusions reached based on analysis of the data.

were viewed each month. There were an average of 500,000 new blog posts and 400,000 new comments on blogs each day. In addition, 60% of U.S. businesses maintained a company blog in 2012.

TWITTER. One important new form of online communication that emerged during the first decade of the 21st century was Twitter. Launched by the small San Francisco, California, start-up Obvious in 2006, Twitter provides online users with a platform for sending brief messages to friends or other individuals who have chosen to receive updates from a particular Twitter page. Known as "tweets," these messages must be 140 characters or fewer and are used to convey a wide range of information to large numbers of people simultaneously. In *Twitter Use 2012* (May 31, 2012, http://www.pewinternet.org/~/media//Files/Reports/2012/PIP_Twitter_Use_2012.pdf), Aaron Smith and Joanna Brenner of Pew/Internet indicate that 8% of all online adults used Twitter in November 2010. (See Figure 9.5.) By February 2012 this number had risen to 15%. This span

also saw a substantial increase in the proportion of online adults who used Twitter on a daily basis, from 2% in November 2010 to 8% in February 2012.

Overall, women who use the Internet are slightly more likely to use Twitter than online men. As Table 9.5 shows, 15% of online women used Twitter in 2012, compared with 14% of online men. Among ethnic groups, non-Hispanic African-American Internet users (28%) were more likely to use Twitter than online non-Hispanic whites (12%) or Hispanics (14%). Online adults with college degrees (17%) were more inclined to use Twitter than those who only graduated from high school (12%); however, more than one out of five (22%) online adults who never completed high school used Twitter in 2012, the most of any education level. In addition, low-income adult Internet users were more likely to use Twitter than high-income online adults. Nearly one-fifth (19%) of online adults with household incomes of less than $30,000 per year used Twitter in 2012, followed by

FIGURE 9.4

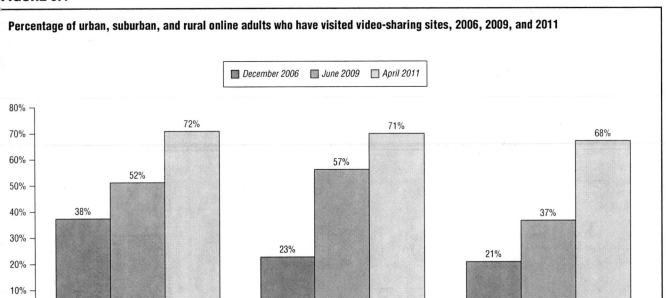

Percentage of urban, suburban, and rural online adults who have visited video-sharing sites, 2006, 2009, and 2011

December 2006 ▪ June 2009 ▪ April 2011

Notes: Sample size = 2,277 adult internet users ages 18 and older, including 755 cell phone interviews. Interviews were conducted in English and Spanish.

SOURCE: Kathleen Moore, "Visits to Online Video-Sharing Sites Increasing Most in Rural Areas," in *71% of Online Adults Now Use Video-Sharing Sites*, Pew Internet & American Life Project, July 25, 2011, http://pewinternet.org/~/media//Files/Reports/2011/Video%20sharing%202011.pdf (accessed October 10, 2012). Used by permission of the Pew Internet & American Life Project, which bears no responsibility for the interpretations presented or conclusions reached based on analysis of the data.

those with household incomes of $75,000 or more per year (17%), those with household incomes of between $50,000 and $74,999 per year (14%), and those with household incomes of between $30,000 and $49,999 per year (12%).

Smith and Brenner also chart the growth in Twitter use among various age groups between November 2010 and February 2012. Thirty-one percent of online adults aged 18 to 24 years used Twitter in 2012, the most of any age group; by comparison, only 17% of adult Internet users aged 25 to 34 years used Twitter that same year. The proportion of online adults aged 55 to 64 years who used Twitter more than doubled between 2010 and 2012, from 4% to 9%. The percentage of Twitter users aged 35 to 44 years also doubled during this span, from 8% to 16%.

SOCIAL NETWORKING. Arguably the most important development in online communication has been the rise of social networking during the early 21st century. Websites such as Facebook, MySpace, and Google+ allow members to create virtual profiles on the Internet, where they can upload pictures, share personal and professional information, post messages, and forge connections with other social network users (a process commonly known as "friending"). Of the three major social networking sites, Facebook has emerged as the most popular. According to Internet World Stats (2012, http://www.internetworldstats.com/

stats2.htm), by June 2012 there were over 166 million Facebook profiles in the United States alone, a figure accounting for more than half (53%) of the country's total population. Dominic Rushe reports in "Facebook Has 1Bn Users but Still Posts a Loss" (*Guardian* [London], October 24, 2012) that by October 2012 the social networking giant had amassed over 1 billion users worldwide.

Among online adults, social networking sites tend to be dominated by younger Internet users. In *Social Networking Sites and Our Lives* (June 16, 2011, http://www.pewinternet.org/~/media//Files/Reports/2011/PIP%20-%20Social%20networking%20sites%20and%20our%20lives.pdf), Keith N. Hampton et al. report that nearly half (48%) of all adult social networking users were under the age of 35 years in 2010; roughly three-quarters (74%) of all adult social networking site users were under the age of 50 years. Of all the major social networking sites, MySpace attracted the largest proportion of younger online adults. Over seven out of 10 (71%) MySpace users were aged 18 to 35 years in 2010; by comparison, less than half (49%) of all adult Facebook users were under the age of 35 years. In general, women outnumbered men by substantial margins on social networking sites, accounting for 57% of all MySpace users and 58% of all Facebook users in 2010. In contrast, male users of the professional social networking site LinkedIn outnumbered female users, 63% to 37%.

FIGURE 9.5

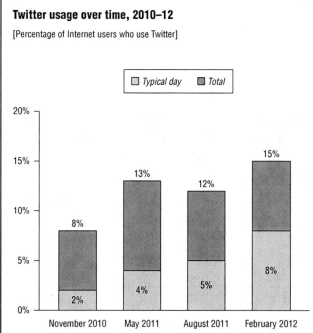

Twitter usage over time, 2010–12

[Percentage of Internet users who use Twitter]

Notes: Population = 2,253 adults age 18 and older, including 901 cell phone interviews conducted in English and Spanish. Margin of error is +/−2.7 percentage points for Internet users (sample size = 1,729).

SOURCE: Aaron Smith and Joanna Brenner, "Twitter Usage over Time," in *Twitter Use 2012*, Pew Internet & American Life Project, May 31, 2012, http://www.pewinternet.org/~/media//Files/Reports/2012/PIP_Twitter_Use_2012.pdf (accessed October 10, 2012). Used by permission of the Pew Internet & American Life Project, which bears no responsibility for the interpretations presented or conclusions reached based on analysis of the data.

TABLE 9.5

Percentage of online adults who use Twitter, by selected characteristics, 2012

All adult Internet users (sample size = 1,729)	**15%**
Men (sample size = 804)	14
Women (sample size = 925)	15
Age	
18–29 (sample size = 316)	26*
30–49 (sample size = 532)	14
50–64 (sample size = 521)	9
65+ (sample size = 320)	4
Race/ethnicity	
White, non-Hispanic (sample size = 1,229)	12
Black, non-Hispanic (sample size = 172)	28*
Hispanic (sample size = 184)	14
Annual household income	
Less than $30,000/yr (sample size = 390)	19
$30,000–$49,999 (sample size = 290)	12
$50,000–$74,999 (sample size = 250)	14
$75,000+ (sample size = 523)	17
Education level	
No high school diploma (sample size = 108)	22
High school graduate (sample size = 465)	12
Some college (sample size = 447)	14
College+ (sample size = 698)	17
Geographic location	
Urban (sample size = 520)	19*
Suburban (sample size = 842)	14*
Rural (sample size = 280)	8

*Represents significant difference compared with all other rows in group.
Notes: Population = 2,253 adults age 18 and older, including 901 cell phone interviews. Interviews conducted in English and Spanish. The margin of error is +/−2.7 percentage points for Internet users.

SOURCE: Aaron Smith and Joanna Brenner, "Who Uses Twitter?" in *Twitter Use 2012*, Pew Internet & American Life Project, May 31, 2012, http://www.pewinternet.org/~/media//Files/Reports/2012/ PIP_Twitter_Use_2012.pdf (accessed October 10, 2012). Used by permission of the Pew Internet & American Life Project, which bears no responsibility for the interpretations presented or conclusions reached based on analysis of the data.

Social media use among teens also grew rapidly during this period. Amanda Lenhart et al. of Pew/Internet report in *Teens, Kindness and Cruelty on Social Network Sites* (November 9, 2011, http://pewinternet.org/~/media//Files/Reports/2011/PIP_Teens_Kindness_Cruelty_SNS_Report_Nov_2011_FINAL_110711.pdf) that 55% of online teens used social networking sites in 2006; by 2011 this figure had grown to 80%. Facebook was by far the most popular social media platform among teen Internet users. Among online teens who maintained one social networking account, nearly nine out of 10 (89%) had Facebook profiles; among teens who kept more than one social media profile, 99% were on Facebook. In general, the experiences of online teens who used social networking sites were mostly positive. In 2011 nearly two-thirds (65%) of teen social networking users reported having experiences on social networking that made them feel good about themselves and 58% reported feeling closer to another person because of social media. (See Figure 9.6.) Lenhart et al. report that nearly seven out of 10 (69%) teen social media users felt that people were predominantly kind to one another on social networking sites. Regardless, 88% of teen social networking users claim to have witnessed at least one instance of someone being mean or cruel to someone else on a social media site in 2011.

ONLINE PRIVACY. The online behavior of teens sometimes renders them vulnerable to breaches of privacy. For example, 30% of online teens aged 12 to 17 years reported having shared one of their Internet passwords with a friend or significant other in 2011. (See Table 9.6.) Teenage girls (38%) were significantly more likely to trust a friend or significant other with an online password than teenage boys (23%). An even larger proportion (44%) of online teens falsified their age to access a website in 2011. As Internet use becomes a basic fact of life among younger Americans, the role of parents in monitoring the online activities of their teenage children has become more prevalent. As Figure 9.7 shows, roughly 61% of parents of online teens tracked the websites their teens visited in 2000; by 2011 this figure had grown to 77%.

Cyberbullying

Advances in communication have also led to new forms of negative online behavior, particularly among children and adolescents. One form of abuse that became

FIGURE 9.6

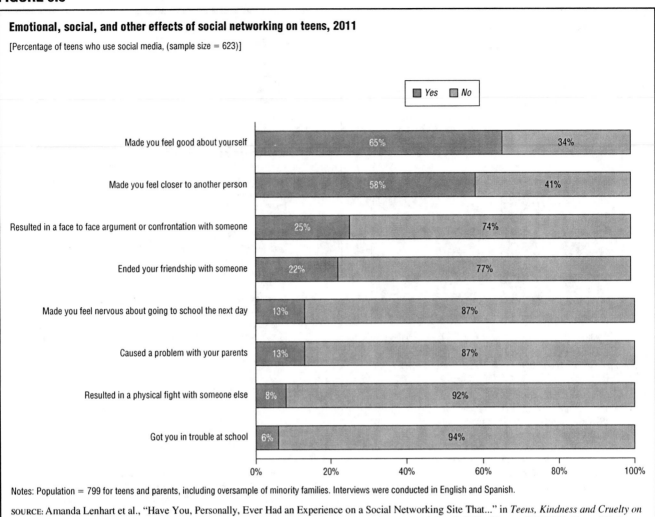

Emotional, social, and other effects of social networking on teens, 2011

[Percentage of teens who use social media, (sample size = 623)]

Notes: Population = 799 for teens and parents, including oversample of minority families. Interviews were conducted in English and Spanish.

SOURCE: Amanda Lenhart et al., "Have You, Personally, Ever Had an Experience on a Social Networking Site That…" in *Teens, Kindness and Cruelty on Social Network Sites*, Pew Internet & American Life Project, November 2011, http://pewinternet.org/~/media//Files/Reports/2011/PIP_Teens_Kindness_Cruelty_SNS_Report_Nov_2011_FINAL_110711.pdf (accessed October 10, 2012). Used by permission of the Pew Internet & American Life Project, which bears no responsibility for the interpretations presented or conclusions reached based on analysis of the data.

a concern during the early part of the 21st century was cyberbullying. Cyberbullying refers to situations in which a child or teenager is harassed, humiliated, or intimidated by other children, teens, or adults through the use of the Internet or other forms of interactive communication, notably cell phones. Cyberbullies torment their victims by sending them malicious, sometimes threatening e-mails or text messages, or by posting pernicious rumors about the victims on the Internet, typically on blogs or social networking sites. Figure 9.8 shows that 8% of all American teens had experienced some form of online bullying in 2011, while another 9% had been bullied via text messages. Cyberbullying is particularly damaging to the emotional health of children because of its potential to spread to wide audiences, as well as the relative ease with which it eludes the detection of parents and teachers. In addition, the physical distance separating the cyberbullies from the victims can desensitize antagonists to the harm they are inflicting, leading to behavior that is far more hateful and cruel than it would be if the perpetrators and victims were face to face. Because it uses technologies that have become omnipresent in the lives of most young people, cyberbullying also has the power to reach far beyond the school yard, following victims wherever they go, at any hour of the day.

In some cases, cyberbullying can have sexual overtones. In "Internet Gives Teenage Bullies Weapons to Wound from Afar" (*New York Times*, August 26, 2004), Amy Harmon reports that adolescent boys often use texting as a means of sharing sexually charged comments about their female classmates. Harmon also describes cases in which underage girls have sent sexual images or videos of themselves to others via some form of online communication (a practice commonly known as "sexting"), only to have those digital images disseminated over the Internet by the person for whom they were originally intended. In many such instances, unsuspecting girls are betrayed by their own boyfriends. Sometimes, cyberbullying can inflict fatal consequences. In one notorious case from 2006, Megan Meier (1992–2006), a 13-year-old girl

TABLE 9.6

Percentage of online teens who have falsified their age on the Internet, or shared an online password, by gender and age, 2011

	Said they were older to access a website	Shared a password with a friend or S.O.
All teen Internet users	44	30
Gender		
Boys[a]	43	23
Girls[b]	46	38[a]
Age groups		
12–13[a]	49	17
14–17[b]	42	36[a]
Age by year		
12[a]	45	13
13[b]	54[f]	21
14[c]	53[f]	29[a]
15[d]	47[f]	43[ab]
16[e]	38	33[a]
17[f]	30	41[ab]

Note: Columns marked with (a) or another letter indicates a statistically significant difference between rows. Statistical significance is determined within each column and section. Population = 770 for teen Internet users. Interviews were conducted in English and Spanish.

SOURCE: Amanda Lenhart et al., "Faslifying Age Information and Sharing Passwords," in *Teens, Kindness and Cruelty on Social Network Sites*, Pew Internet & American Life Project, November 2011, http://pewinternet.org/~/media//Files/Reports/2011/PIP_Teens_Kindness_Cruelty_SNS_Report_Nov_2011_FINAL_110711.pdf (accessed October 10, 2012). Used by permission of the Pew Internet & American Life Project, which bears no responsibility for the interpretations presented or conclusions reached based on analysis of the data.

FIGURE 9.7

Parents of online teens who check the websites their teens have visited, 2000–11

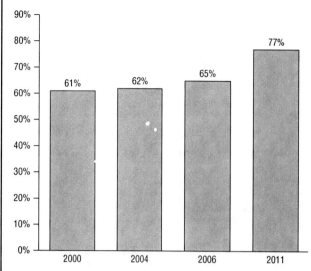

SOURCE: Amanda Lenhart et al., "Parents Who Check on the Websites Their Teens Have Visited," in *Teens, Kindness and Cruelty on Social Network Sites*, Pew Internet & American Life Project, November 2011, http://pewinternet.org/-/media//Files/Reports/2011/PIP_Teens_1 Kindness_Cruelty_SNS_Report_Nc/_2011_FIN \L_110711.pdf (accessed October 10, 2012). Used by permission of the Pew Internet & American Life Project, which bears no responsibility for the interpretations presented or conclusions reached based on analysis of the data.

from Missouri, committed suicide after receiving malicious communications from a teenage boy over MySpace. As it later turned out, the teenage boy was a fictitious character created by the mother of one of Megan's friends. The case prompted several states to pass anti-cyberbullying legislation the following year. In 2008 the state of Missouri passed its own statute, commonly known as Megan's Law, prohibiting malicious online communications between adults and children.

By 2012 legislation appeared to have some positive effect on curbing instances of cyberbullying. According to Sameer Hinduja and Justin W. Patchin of the Cyberbullying Research Center, in *State Cyberbullying Laws: A Brief Review of State Cyberbullying Laws and Policies* (November 2012, http://www.cyberbullying.us/Bullying_and_Cyberbullying_Laws.pdf), as of November 2012 every state in the country except Montana had passed some form of antibullying statute. Of these state laws, 47 included provisions outlawing electronic harassment, while 16 specifically prohibited cyberbullying. Regardless, the problem of cyberbullying remains a major concern to parents and school and law enforcement officials. Furthermore, as online communications continue to evolve, new platforms for online harassment emerge. For example, in 2009 a new social networking site, Formspring, was created, allowing users to create profiles where others can post comments about them. Because the comments are anonymous, many Formspring users soon became the victims of yet another form of cyberbullying.

THE IMPACT OF THE TYLER CLEMENTI CASE. Cyberbullying once again received national attention in September 2010, when Tyler Clementi (1992–2010), a freshman at Rutgers University, jumped to his death from New York's George Washington Bridge. The ensuing investigation revealed that Clementi's roommate, Dharun Ravi (1992–), had secretly shot a video of Clementi engaged in sexual activity with another male and posted the footage online; another resident of Clementi's dorm, Molly Wei, was also implicated in the incident. In a bitter irony, Clementi used his cell phone to post a brief suicide message on his Facebook page minutes before jumping off the bridge, writing simply: "Jumping off the gw bridge sorry." Ravi and Wei were subsequently charged with two counts of invasion of privacy; prosecutors also considered filing hate crime charges against the students.

In February 2012 Wei entered into a plea agreement with prosecutors. As part of the deal, she was sentenced to 300 hours of community service and ordered to undergo counseling, in exchange for testifying against Ravi in court. The following May, Ravi was convicted on multiple charges relating to Clementi's death, including bias intimidation and invasion of privacy, and

FIGURE 9.8

Percentage of teens who have been bullied in past 12 months, in person, online, by text, or by phone, 2011

IN THE PAST 12 MONTHS, HAVE YOU BEEN BULLIED ____?

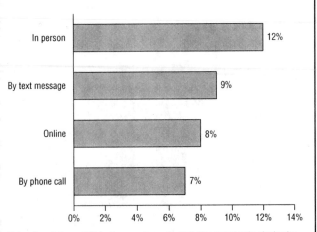

Notes: Population = 799 for teens and parents, including oversample of minority families. Interviews were conducted in English and Spanish.

SOURCE: Amanda Lenhart et al., "In the Past 12 Months, Have You Been Bullied...?" in *Teens, Kindness and Cruelty on Social Network Sites*, Pew Internet & American Life Project, November 2011, http://pewinternet.org/~/media//Files/Reports/2011/PIP_Teens_Kindness_Cruelty_SNS_Report_Nov_2011_FINAL_110711.pdf (accessed October 10, 2012). Used by permission of the Pew Internet & American Life Project, which bears no responsibility for the interpretations presented or conclusions reached based on analysis of the data.

sentenced to 30 days in jail. Michael Koenigs, Candace Smith, and Christina Ng report in "Rutgers Trial: Dharun Ravi Sentenced to 30 Days in Jail" (ABC News, May 21, 2012) that Judge Glenn Berman (1947–) told the courtroom, "I do not believe he hated Tyler Clementi. He had no reason to, but I do believe he acted out of colossal insensitivity." In response to the sentencing, prosecutors in the case, who had expected a longer sentence, announced that they would appeal Berman's decision. As of December 2012, the outcome of the appeal was still pending. Even though Ravi issued an apology shortly after the trial, it did little to reform his image. The article "Parents of Rutgers Spying Victim Reject Roommate's Apology" (Associated Press, May 29, 2012) notes that Clementi's parents, Joseph and Jane Clementi, rejected Ravi's overture, calling it nothing more than a "public relations piece."

Clementi's death coincided with a rash of suicides involving gay teens in 2010, and the Rutgers incident proved to be a watershed moment in the nationwide discourse on the issues of cyberbullying and hate crimes. Clementi's suicide inspired a flood of sympathy from celebrities and other public figures, who were outspoken in condemning bullying tactics against gays and lesbians. Nicole Santa Cruz reports in "Offering Hope to Gay Teens on YouTube" (*Los Angeles Times*, October 10, 2010) that Clementi's suicide prompted

the columnist Dan Savage (1964–) to launch the It Gets Better Project, an online video series aimed at reaching out to young gays and lesbians who feel isolated and stigmatized because of their sexuality. Within the first three weeks, more than 650 individuals had posted their own video testimonies that offered personal messages of moral support, and Savage's site had received more than 1.2 million visitors. In October 2010 President Barack Obama (1961–; http://www.whitehouse.gov/it-gets-better-transcript) filmed his own short address condemning acts of cyberbullying that targeted victims' sexual orientation. Obama spoke of his own struggles with discrimination as a child, while offering a message of hope to young victims of bullying: "You are not alone. You didn't do anything wrong. You didn't do anything to deserve being bullied. And there is a whole world waiting for you, filled with possibilities."

Work

Information technology has touched nearly every industry in the U.S. economy, and for many Americans communications technologies have provided the opportunity to work at home either in a home-based business or after hours for their primary employer. The U.S. Bureau of Labor Statistics (BLS) indicates in "Work-at-Home Patterns by Occupation" (March 2009, http://www.bls.gov/opub/ils/pdf/opbils72.pdf) that between 2003 and 2007 roughly 12.2% of all American workers did some portion of their job at home on an average day. Of these, self-employed individuals (34.3%) were significantly more likely to work at least part of the time at home than wage and salary earners (10%). Among wage and salary workers, those involved in the education, training, and library professions (28.1%) were the most likely to work at home, whereas production workers (2%) were the least likely. On average, more than half (54.9%) of all self-employed individuals involved in the fields of arts, design, entertainment, sports, and media worked at home between 2003 and 2007.

One development with the potential to revolutionize how Americans work was the rapid evolution of cloud computing technologies. Cloud computing refers to the use of software, tools, and other applications that are available on online servers, as opposed to being stored on the hard drive of a personal computer. For example, Google Docs enables users to create and save documents online, thereby allowing another user (such as a coworker) to access the information directly through his or her own Internet connection. Many popular forms of cloud computing had already gained widespread popularity by 2012, notably the file sharing site Dropbox, web-based e-mail services such as Hotmail and Gmail, social networking sites such as Facebook, and the status updating service Twitter. Furthermore, cloud computing has made it possible for businesses to form virtual offices, allowing workers at various remote locations to link up and collaborate with each other through a common web-based platform.

For example, Microsoft SharePoint enables partners in a business enterprise to exchange documents and other files, share tools and applications, and communicate with each other all within a common Internet platform. According to Janna Quitney Anderson and Lee Rainie, in *The Future of Cloud Computing* (June 11, 2010, http://www.pewinternet .org/~/media//Files/Reports/2010/PIP_Future_of_the _Internet_cloud_computing.pdf), a survey of technology experts reveals that 71% believe the majority of Americans who use computers for their jobs will work primarily via cloud computing by 2020.

Romance

Besides hosting a wide range of online dating sites such as eHarmony and Match.com, the Internet also plays a role in the way that Americans experience their romantic relationships. In "Online Dating Statistics" (June 20, 2012, http://www.statisticbrain.com/online-dating-statistics/), Statistic Brain reveals that 40 million American adults had tried an online dating service by 2012. That same year eHarmony had a total of 20 million members and Match.com had 15 million. Overall, 20% of all committed relationships in 2012 originated on the Internet; likewise, 17% of marriages that had taken place in the previous year began as an online relationship. On average, married couples who met online dated for 18.5 months before marrying; by comparison, couples who did not meet online dated for an average of 42 months before marrying. By 2012 the online dating industry was generating revenues of over $1 billion annually.

Social networking has also had a profound influence on the way people form and maintain romantic relationships in the digital age. According to the Zoosk Blog, in "Zoosk's Social Media Etiquette Survey & Findings" (September 18, 2012, http://blog.zoosk.com/2012/09/18/ zoosks-social-media-etiquette-survey-findings/), 81% of online U.S. couples communicated with each other via some form of technology on a daily basis in 2012, and 60% used Facebook or other social networking sites to post their feelings about their partner or spouse publicly. Overall, just over half (51%) of women appreciated the romantic social media posts of their family or friends, compared with 37% of men. However, even as people's relationship information became more public, the majority of online adults still strove to maintain some degree of privacy in their romantic lives. The Zoosk Blog finds that nearly four-fifths (78%) of respondents preferred receiving a romantic text to having their significant other post something about their personal feelings on a social media site such as Facebook or Twitter.

Shopping

Use of the Internet for making retail purchases has been rising steadily for several years. The U.S. Census Bureau states in *Quarterly Retail E-Commerce Sales: 3rd Quarter 2012* (November 16, 2012, http://www.census .gov/retail/mrts/www/data/pdf/ec_current.pdf) that retail e-commerce sales for the third quarter of 2012 amounted to $57 billion, or 5.2% of the $1.1 trillion total retail sales in the United States; the $57 billion figure represented an increase of 3.7% over e-commerce retail sales for the second quarter of 2012 and 17.3% over e-commerce retail sales for the third quarter of 2011.

In "Number of Online Buyers in the United States from 2010 to 2016" (2012, http://www.statista.com/statistics/ 197063/number-of-online-buyers-in-the-us/), the statistical data company Statista reveals that 136.9 million Americans aged 14 years and older had purchased something online in 2010; by 2012 this figure had risen to 149.8 million, an increase of 9%. According to Thad Rueter, in "More Holiday Shoppers Head Online" (October 16, 2012, http://www .internetretailer.com/2012/10/16/more-holiday-shoppers-head-online), during the 2012 holiday season an estimated 51.8% of American consumers were expected to do at least some of their shopping over the Internet, up from 46.7% the previous year. The e-commerce software company Fortune3 reports in "How People Shop Online—Ecommerce Statistics" (August 27, 2012, http:// www.fortune3.com/blog/2012/08/how-people-shop-online-ecommerce-statistics/) that among people who shop online, a significant majority (73%) do at least half of all their shopping over the Internet; another 66% prefer to shop online than at retail stores.

In addition, cell phones are becoming an important tool for consumers who still prefer to do their shopping in person. Aaron Smith of Pew/Internet notes in *The Rise of In-Store Mobile Commerce* (January 30, 2012, http://www.pewinternet.org/~/ media//Files/Reports/2012/In_Store_Mobile_Commerce.pdf) that 25% of all cell phone owners used their mobile device to conduct price comparisons while shopping at a retail store in 2012. Thirty-eight percent of cell phone owners called a friend for advice while shopping, while another 24% used their phone to search for product reviews online. (See Table 9.7.) Female cell phone owners (40%) were slightly more likely than men (37%) to call a friend for advice while shopping. In contrast, male cell phone owners (27%) were more likely than women (22%) to look up product reviews while at a retail store. Overall, younger cell phone owners were the most likely either to call a friend or to look up product reviews while shopping. Nearly half (49%) of cell phone owners aged 18 to 29 years called a friend for shopping advice, while another 41% researched product reviews while shopping. By comparison, cell phone owners aged 65 years and older were the least likely either to call a friend (22%) or to look up reviews of particular products (4%) while shopping at a retail store.

Alternate Realities

As time passed, many Internet users met, developed social relationships, or spent long periods of time online

TABLE 9.7

Percentage of adult cell phone owners who use their phones for real-time product reviews or advice, by selected characteristics, 2012

	Call a friend for advice about a purchase	Look up product reviews online	Total
All cell owners (n = 896)	38%	24%	48%
Gender			
Men (n = 437)	37	27	49
Women (n = 459)	40	22	46
Age			
18–29 (n = 128)	49*	41*	63*
30–49 (n = 221)	45*	34*	59*
50–64 (n = 245)	32	13	36
65+ (n = 251)	22	4	24
Race/ethnicity			
White (n = 686)	37	21	45
Non-white (n = 185)	42	33*	53
Household Income			
Less than $50,000 (n = 379)	41	23	48
$50,000+ (n = 373)	40	27	50
Education level			
High school graduate or less (n = 322)	35	17	40
Some college (n = 199)	47*	32*	56*
College+ (n = 362)	36	29*	50*
Geographic Location			
Urban (n = 237)	40	29*	52*
Suburban (n = 434)	38	24*	47*
Rural (n = 163)	32	12	36

*Indicates statistically significant difference between rows.

Notes: Population = 1,000 adults ages 18 and older, including 400 interviews conducted on respondent's cell phone. The survey was conducted in English. Margin of error is +/−3.9 percentage points.

SOURCE: Aaron Smith, "Who Uses Their Phones for Real-Time Product Reviews and Advice?" in *The Rise of In-Store Mobile Commerce*, Pew Internet & American Life Project, January 30, 2012, http://www.pewinternet .org/~/media//Files/Reports/2012/In_Store_Mobile_Commerce.pdf (accessed October 10, 2012). Used by permission of the Pew Internet & American Life Project, which bears no responsibility for the interpretations presented or conclusions reached based on analysis of the data.

in virtual worlds such as Second Life (http://secondlife .com/), Ultima Online (http://uo.com/), and other massively multiplayer online role-playing games. Even children took care of virtual pets online in WebKinz World (http://www.webkinz.com/), where among many other activities players could send their pets to school; earn money by working, growing crops, or playing games; and shop for virtual groceries, vacations, and home furnishings. According to Amanda Lenhart et al., in *Social Media & Mobile Internet Use among Teens and Young Adults* (February 3, 2010, http://www.pewinternet.org/~/media// Files/Reports/2010/PIP_Social_Media_and_Young_Adults _Report_Final_with_toplines.pdf), involvement with virtual worlds becomes increasingly less common as Internet users become older. Among online teens aged 12 to 13 years, 11% were engaged with virtual worlds in 2010, whereas among teens aged 14 to 17 years this proportion fell to 7%. Among online adults, only 4% used virtual worlds.

Nevertheless, in 2012 many in the technology industry were beginning to observe ways in which virtual and alternative realities were becoming incorporated into everyday life. One trend that was garnering some attention within tech circles was the concept of "gamification." Gamification describes a process through which aspects of game-playing—including the pleasure involved with confronting certain challenges, participating in interactive competitions, and receiving rewards for performing particular tasks—becomes incorporated into an increasing number of everyday activities. In *Gamification: Experts Expect Game Layers to Expand in the Future, with Positive and Negative Results* (May 18, 2012, http://www .pewinternet.org/~/media//Files/Reports/2012/PIP_Future_ of_Internet_2012_Gamification.pdf), Janna Quitney Anderson and Lee Rainie asked 1,021 technology experts and stakeholders their views on the extent to which gamification will impact American life in the coming decade. A majority (53%) of those surveyed said gamification will play a key role in transforming numerous facets of everyday life, including work, health, and education. Cathy Cavanagh, an associate professor of educational technology at the University of Florida, told Anderson and Rainie, "People will increasingly expect game elements in a wide range of activities. Game-development tools will enable most people to gamify many aspects of life and work, in digital, physical, and blended environments." However, for some experts the prospect of increased gamification of society also carries certain risks. Danah Boyd, a researcher for Microsoft, reported in the survey, "It's a modern-day form of manipulation. And like all cognitive manipulation, it can help people and it can hurt people. And we will see both." David Kirschner, a research assistant at the Nanyang Technological University in Singapore, expressed particular concern about the power of corporations to use gamification to exert greater control over individuals. "Companies should take responsibility for the tremendous power they wield in society. I fear they won't, but I hope they do," Kirschner argued. "We've all got to be very critical when fun can mask trouble."

Another major technological development in 2012 was in the field of augmented reality. Mez Breeze explains in "How Augmented Reality Will Change the Way We Live" (August 25, 2012, thenextweb.com/ insider/2012/08/25/how-augmented-reality-will-change- way-live/) that virtual reality immerses a user in a digital world, whereas augmented reality involves the incorporation of digital technology into an individual's experience of the "physical world," in a way that amplifies "actual/ physical reality to enhance information" by introducing "additional contexts and content" to a particular activity or event. For example, with augmented reality smart phone owners can view a shopping plaza through the lens of their mobile device and immediately learn which stores and businesses the plaza contains, what their hours of operation are, what menu specials the restaurants are offering that day, and so on.

HOME ELECTRONICS REVOLUTION

During the 1970s and early 1980s advances in circuit manufacturing lowered the price of integrated electronic components from hundreds of dollars to less than $10 in some instances. Since then, electronic chips, displays, and sensors have worked their way into everything from washing machines to hairdryers to coffeemakers. Overall, these electronics have given people more control over the settings on their appliances, lighting, and heating and cooling systems.

High-Tech Home Features

Many home appliances and systems have become fully programmable and even Internet accessible. For example, interactive, online thermostats come installed in many new homes. These thermostats, which can be connected to the Internet, give the homeowner the option of remotely setting and monitoring the temperature of the house from any computer or cell phone with Internet access. The thermostat also alerts the user of a malfunction or a gas leak in the system. Zone lighting systems contain electronics that enable homeowners to program lighting configurations for multiple areas of the same room. With the touch of a button, one side of a room can be illuminated for reading while the other side remains dark for watching television.

Another programmable fixture that is available in many newer homes is the electronic keypad locking system. The advantage of the keypad over the normal lock is that it can be easily reprogrammed. If a homeowner wants to keep someone out, this can be done by simply changing the lock code. The lock can also be set to let in certain people, such as a painter, only during certain times of the day. Some keypad locks contain circuit boards that can be plugged into a broadband connection, which gives the homeowner the option of remotely changing the lock codes or keeping a record of who comes and goes. By 2012 some companies offered automated home systems that tied the lights, door locks, thermostat, and home security system into one control center that could be accessed by the Internet. These systems can be placed in different modes for when the homeowner is awake, asleep, or away. For example, when the homeowner goes out of town, all he or she has to do is press a button and the lights are turned off, the alarm is set, and the thermostat is turned down. In addition, in the event a security alarm is activated, systems automatically send prerecorded messages to phone numbers that have been programmed into the system, including emergency services or the homeowner's work or cell phone.

Smart Appliances

As technology progresses and electronics become even more affordable, makers of appliances will likely continue to add additional electronic features. By 2012 many of these advances were aimed at making appliances more energy efficient. As part of the American Recovery and Reinvestment Act of 2009, the federal government offered cash rebates to consumers who traded in older appliances for new, more eco-friendly models. The law also provided $4 billion in funding to the U.S. Department of Energy toward improvements to the nation's smart grid, a system that will allow power suppliers to "communicate" with home appliances, through a system of sensors and other digital technologies, to regulate and reduce overall electricity usage. Richard Babyak notes in "Searching for Smart Standards" (*Appliance Design*, January 2010) that many advances in the manufacturing of environmentally friendly appliances are being undertaken to streamline interaction with the smart grid. Babyak also raises several of the key issues surrounding this process, including safety standards and the degree of control that consumers will maintain over their home appliances.

A number of technologies were emerging in 2012 that allowed people to operate every minor and major appliance via a remote control or telephone. One such protocol, known as ZigBee, was being developed by the ZigBee Alliance, a consortium of more than 250 companies that includes Motorola, Honeywell, Samsung, and Mitsubishi Electric. ZigBee is a networkable, low-power, two-way communication technology with a range of about 250 feet (76 m) that can receive and send data. ZigBee-enabled utilities and appliances can be operated and adjusted through a wireless remote. In this way, every appliance or entertainment system in the house can be monitored and activated via remote control. A base station capable of communicating with the ZigBee radio chips can be easily attached to a phone line as well. By calling into the base station via phone, the homeowner can check the status of an oven or a coffeemaker using the touch-tone commands.

Some technological innovations are designed to make basic everyday routines even easier. For example, the Nokia Lumia 920, which was launched in September 2012, was among the first smart phones to recharge using a wireless inductive charging pad rather than a traditional plug-in adapter. Two months later Konica Minolta unveiled a new light-emitting diode desk lamp that had a wireless phone charger built into its base. Meanwhile, advances in near field communication enable smart phone owners to conduct routine financial transactions, or even routine tasks, through their mobile devices. In "Sony's SmartTags Could Change Phone Habits" (CNET.com, January 16, 2012), Christopher MacManus reports that in 2012 Sony released a programmable token called the SmartTag, which allowed consumers to set an alarm, turn on a wireless connection, or even switch their phone to "silent" simply by swiping it over the SmartTag.

ROBOTS

Around the turn of the 21st century the first practical, automated robots went on sale for the consumer market. Far from the convenient marvels depicted in futuristic television shows, these robots performed only simple tasks. As of 2012, a number of models of robotic vacuum cleaners could be found on the market, and people were buying them. According to the iRobot Corporation (2012, http://www.irobot.com/en/us/Company/About/Our_History.aspx), the maker of Roomba robotic vacuums and Scooba floor washers, the company had sold more than 8 million home robots worldwide by 2012. Most robotic vacuum cleaners used various sensors to feel their way around the room, picking up dirt as they went. For example, the Electrolux Trilobite 2.0 uses ultrasound sensors to detect and avoid obstacles in its way as it goes back and forth across the room, sucking up dirt and recording where it has been.

Other devices available in 2012 included robotic mowers, pool cleaners, and gutter cleaners. The Robomow automatically zigzags back and forth over a lawn, cutting the grass as it goes. Sensors are imbedded in bumpers that surround the entire mower, and if it bangs into something bigger than a large piece of bark, it backs off. A low-voltage guide wire set up by the user around the perimeter of the yard lets the mower know if it is crossing the boundaries of the lawn, in which case it turns around. In addition, the mower can be programmed to leave its base station and mow the lawn at preset days and times, and then return to the base station to be recharged. Robomow models were priced at about $1,700 and up in 2012.

Programmable Robots

Another type of robot, which made its debut in 2005, was the PC-BOT by White Box Robotics. In "Plug-and-Play Robots" (*Scientific American*, March 22, 2004), W. Wayt Gibbs remarks that the knee-high robots "look like R2-D2 droids that have been redesigned by Cadillac." PC-BOTs are built from everyday computer components and accessories. Each one has a digital camera, speakers, slots for peripheral components such as a disc drive, and sensors mounted on the outside. A standard hard drive, microprocessor, drive motor, and stabilizer are contained within the chassis. The whole unit is mounted on wheels. The innovation behind the PC-BOTs, however, does not lie in its components, but in the fact that the machine is fully programmable. According to Gibbs, face and object recognition software can be installed on a PC-BOT, which allow it to recognize various people and objects in its environment and then act on that information. One useful application allows the robot to roam around the owner's house when the owner is out of town. If the robot spots a strange figure or detects a loud noise, it can e-mail or send a page to the owner. In 2012 PC-BOTs were available from about $5,600 and up.

Humanoid Robots

Several large companies and many academic laboratories have been experimenting with complex humanoid robots. The most famous of these is probably Honda's Advanced Step in Innovation Mobility (ASIMO) robot (http://world.honda.com/ASIMO/). Researchers at Honda have been working on the ASIMO design since 1986. As of 2012, the robot could recognize faces programmed into its memory, walk over uneven surfaces, hop on one leg, climb stairs, and run at a speed of 5.6 miles (9 km) per hour. Honda's goal is to create a robot that can be remotely controlled by a handicapped person to complete basic chores around the house such as retrieving the mail, doing the dishes, or moving items from one place to another. In November 2007 the Vietnamese robotics company TOSY introduced the TOSY Ping Pong Playing Robot (TOPIO) at the International Robot Exhibition in Tokyo, Japan. Capable of playing table tennis against a human opponent, the TOPIO used cameras and image recognition software to detect the precise location and movement of a ping pong ball. Within two years, the company introduced a lighter, more agile version of its robot, the TOPIO 3.0.

During the first decade of the 21st century the National Aeronautics and Space Administration (NASA) developed a humanoid robot that was designed to perform repairs and other basic operations on the outside of the *International Space Station*. A robotic torso modeled after the upper half of the human body, the Robonaut simulated the actions of an astronaut inside the space station using virtual reality technology. Whereas astronauts required several hours of preparation before entering the deadly vacuum outside the space station, the Robonaut could make the transition within a matter of minutes. By 2010 NASA, working together with engineers from General Motors (GM), had developed a faster, more dexterous version of its humanoid robot, the Robonaut 2 (R2), which employed a "touch sensitivity" technology to perform more complex tasks. The Robonaut 2 successfully joined the crew of the *International Space Station* in February 2011.

Many scientists and engineers worldwide have been working on ways to make robots even more anthropomorphic (having human characteristics) than ASIMO and other humanoid robots. In late 2009 researchers at the Campus Bio-Medico in Rome successfully tested a biomechanical hand. In the experiment, the robotic hand was linked with electrodes to the arm of an amputee, who was able to make the hand move and perform basic actions with his thoughts. In October 2010 researchers working at the National Institute of Advanced Industrial Science and Technology in Japan unveiled the HRP-4C, a robot that used voice and motion-capture software to simulate human singing, breathing patterns, facial expressions, and gestures.

HIGH-TECH AUTOMOBILES

Technological innovations for everyday life are not just occurring in the home. Many types of advanced information technology have made it into the automobile as well. Vehicle buyers in 2012 had the option to choose certain models of sedans and minivans that were equipped with night-vision cameras and proximity sensors in their bumpers. Night-vision cameras enable drivers to see obstacles in the road at night, and proximity sensors help prevent accidents by alerting the driver if something, such as a parked vehicle or a small child, is too close to the bumper. Global positioning systems (GPS) have been incorporated into many new vehicles. GPS continuously picks up signals that are broadcast from a network of stationary (nonorbiting) satellites positioned above the earth. By analyzing its proximity in relation to three of the satellites in the network, GPS can pinpoint its location on the earth's surface. Most systems that use GPS then combine this information with an up-to-date map of the local roads to display the vehicle's position on a street map.

Advances in Safety

In "Intelligence: Behold the All-Seeing, Self-Parking, Safety-Enforcing, Networked Automobile" (*Popular Science*, September 25, 2004), Paul Horrell suggests that vehicles will not only continue to become more fuel efficient but also more intelligent. Companies are employing external sensors to inform the driver and systems within the vehicle of impending danger. For example, the French automobile maker Peugeot Citroën installed a system of infrared sensors that scan painted road markings on each side of the vehicle and alert the driver if he or she strays out of the lane. If the blinker is not on and the driver strays to the left, the sensors perceive the vehicle crossing the line in the road and the left side of the driver's seat vibrates. If the driver strays to the right, the right side of the seat vibrates. In 2009 Peugeot Citroën introduced Snow Motion, an anti-skid system that was designed for extreme road conditions. Automobile makers have also developed systems that allow vehicles to communicate with one another to warn drivers of delays or of dangerous road conditions ahead. Sensor-equipped cars employing the wireless local area network (WLAN) send information via the WLAN to warn other cars in close proximity

when they encounter a traffic jam or black ice. These cars then relay the information to other cars and so on until every car and driver in the area is made aware of the traffic jam or the black ice.

Among the most promising new safety technologies are frontal radar and driver-state monitoring. Frontal radar is a collision-avoidance technology that works by informing drivers of obstacles in their path up to 660 feet (200 m) ahead. The technology is integrated into adaptive cruise control to automatically slow the vehicle to keep a safe distance behind other vehicles. Driver-state monitoring incorporates infrared cameras to assess the driver's fatigue level, issuing a warning if the driver seems too tired to drive safely. Another important advancement in automobile safety has been the development of the electronic stability control (ESC) system. Using smart-braking technology, ESC helps prevent collisions and rollovers in situations where the driver is losing control of the vehicle. According to the article "Electronic Stability Control 101" (*Consumer Reports*, April 15, 2010), ESC represents the "single most important safety advance since the development of the safety belt." In the press release "New NHTSA Report Shows Federal ESC Requirement Saving Lives" (November 30, 2012, http://www.nhtsa.gov/), the National Highway Traffic Safety Administration (NHTSA) indicates that ESC technology saved an estimated 2,202 lives between 2008 and 2010. The NHTSA has mandated that beginning in 2012 ESC will be a required standard feature in all new vehicles manufactured in the United States.

In-Vehicle Communications Systems

By combining GPS, cell phone, and sensor technology, several companies have developed in-vehicle communications systems. GM's OnStar (2012, https://www.onstar.com/web/portal/onstartechnology) is one of the most widely used of these in-vehicle systems, with more than 6 million subscribers. The OnStar Corporation, which is a subsidiary of GM, first offered the OnStar system on GM vehicles in 1996. The system is activated when the user presses either a blue button or a red button in the vehicle or when the vehicle's air bags are deployed. Pressing the blue button instructs the OnStar cellular unit to dial the main OnStar switchboard. A GPS then relays the vehicle's coordinates through the built-in mobile phone to the operator, telling him or her exactly where the vehicle is. Sensors planted on the vehicle's major systems let the operator know how it is functioning. The vehicle owner can then request roadside assistance, directions, or information on the status of the vehicle. In the event of a life-threatening emergency, the red button contacts an OnStar emergency service operator, who calls the nearest emergency service provider. The system is also triggered if the air bags are deployed. In this event, the OnStar emergency operator is called, and he or she notifies the nearest emergency service provider, telling it where the accident took place as well as the make and model of the vehicle. Furthermore, the user can call the OnStar operator from a phone outside the vehicle to open the door locks or to report a stolen vehicle. Finally, once each month owners of OnStar-equipped vehicles receive an e-mail containing a diagnostic analysis of their vehicle that covers everything from the condition of the engine and braking systems to the pressure in their tires and when they need to change their oil.

Automated Vehicles

In October 2010 the technology company Google announced that it had developed automated vehicles that had driven more than 140,000 miles (225,000 km) without human control during testing events on U.S. roads. To navigate the streets without human control, the vehicles used a combination of video cameras, radar sensors, laser range finders, and maps. The only reported accident that occurred during road testing was when a Google automated vehicle was hit from behind by a human-operated car that failed to stop at a traffic light.

Cy Ryan reports in "Nevada Issues Google First License for Self-Driving Car" (*Las Vegas Sun*, May 7, 2012) that in November 2011 Nevada became the first state in the union to allow driverless cars on public roads. In May 2012 the Nevada Department of Motor Vehicles issued the first official self-driving car license to Google, enabling the company to begin testing the vehicles on the state's streets and highways. In September 2012 Governor Jerry Brown (1938–) of California signed a similar law that allowed self-driving cars to travel on public roadways. In "Larry Page Finally Explains Why Google Is Working on Self-Driving Cars" (*San Francisco Chronicle*, December 11, 2012), in an interview with Nicholas Carlson, Larry Page, the co-founder and chief executive officer of Google, described the motivation behind the company's ambitious self-driving car project. "We want to do things that will motivate the most amazing people in the world to want to work on them," Page said. "You look at self-driving cars. You know a lot of people die, and there's a lot of wasted labor. The better transportation you have, the more choice in jobs. And that's social good. That's probably an economic good. I like it when we're picking problems like that: big things where technology can have a really big impact. And we're pretty sure we can do it."

IMPORTANT NAMES AND ADDRESSES

American Customer Satisfaction Index LLC
625 Avis Dr.
Ann Arbor, MI 48108
(734) 913-0788
FAX: (734) 913-0790
E-mail: info@theacsi.org
URL: http://www.theacsi.org/

Association of Public and Land-Grant Universities
1307 New York Ave. NW, Ste. 400
Washington, DC 20005-4722
(202) 478-6040
FAX: (202) 478-6046
URL: http://www.aplu.org/

Centers for Disease Control and Prevention
1600 Clifton Rd.
Atlanta, GA 30333
1-800-232-4636
URL: http://www.cdc.gov/

CERT Program
4500 Fifth Ave.
Pittsburgh, PA 15213-2612
(412) 268-7090
FAX: (412) 268-6989
E-mail: cert@cert.org
URL: http://www.cert.org/

Computer Security Institute
350 Hudson St., Ste. 300
New York, NY 10014
(610) 604-4604
E-mail: csi@ubm.com
URL: http://www.gocsi.com/

Economics and Statistics Administration U.S. Department of Commerce
1401 Constitution Ave. NW, Rm. 4848
Washington, DC 20230
(202) 482-6607
E-mail: ESAwebmaster@doc.gov
URL: http://www.esa.doc.gov/

Facebook, Inc.
1601 Willow Rd.
Menlo Park, CA 94025
(650) 618-7714
URL: http://www.facebook.com/

Federal Communications Commission
445 12th St. SW
Washington, DC 20554
1-888-225-5322
FAX: 1-866-418-0232
E-mail: fccinfo@fcc.gov
URL: http://www.fcc.gov/

Federal Deposit Insurance Corporation
550 17th St. NW
Washington, DC 20429
1-877-275-3342
URL: http://www.fdic.gov/

Federal Election Commission
999 E St. NW
Washington, DC 20463
(202) 694-1000
1-800-424-9530
URL: http://www.fec.gov/

Federal Trade Commission
600 Pennsylvania Ave. NW
Washington, DC 20580
(202) 326-2222
URL: http://www.ftc.gov/

Google Inc.
1600 Amphitheatre Pkwy.
Mountain View, CA 94043
(650) 253-0000
FAX: (650) 253-0001
URL: http://www.google.com/about/company/

Governors Highway Safety Association
444 N. Capitol St. NW, Ste. 722
Washington, DC 20001-1534
(202) 789-0942
FAX: (202) 789-0946

E-mail: headquarters@ghsa.org
URL: http://www.statehighwaysafety.org/

Honda Motor Company
1-1, 2-Chome, Minami-Aoyama, Minato-Ku
Tokyo, Japan 107-8556
(011-81-3) 3423-1111
URL: http://world.honda.com/ASIMO/

Intelligent Transportation Society of America
1100 17th St. NW, Ste. 1200
Washington, DC 20036
(202) 484-4847
1-800-374-8472
E-mail: info@itsa.org
URL: http://www.itsa.org/

Intelligent Transportation Systems U.S. Department of Transportation
1200 New Jersey Ave. SE
Washington, DC 20590
1-800-853-1351
E-mail: RITAInfo@dot.gov
URL: http://www.its.dot.gov/

International Center for Academic Integrity
126 Hardin Hall
Clemson University
Clemson, SC 29634-5138
(864) 656-1293
FAX: (864) 656-2858
E-mail: CAI-L@clemson.edu
URL: http://www.academicintegrity.org/

Internet Society
1775 Wiehle Ave., Ste. 201
Reston, VA 20190-5108
(703) 439-2120
FAX: (703) 326-9881
E-mail: isoc@isoc.org
URL: http://www.internetsociety.org/

Internet2
1000 Oakbrook Dr., Ste. 300
Ann Arbor, MI 48104

(734) 913-4250
FAX: (734) 913-4255
E-mail: info@internet2.edu
URL: http://www.internet2.edu/

iRobot Corporation
8 Crosby Dr.
Bedford, MA 01730
(781) 430-3000
FAX: (781) 430-3001
E-mail: contact@irobot.com
URL: http://www.irobot.com/

Kaspersky Lab US
500 Unicorn Park, Third Floor
Woburn, MA 01801
(781) 503-1800
1-866-328-5700
FAX: (781) 503-1818
URL: http://usa.kaspersky.com/

Medical Library Association
65 E. Wacker Place, Ste. 1900
Chicago, IL 60601-7246
(312) 419-9094
FAX: (312) 419-8950
E-mail: info@mlahq.org
URL: http://www.mlanet.org/

Motion Picture Association of America
1600 Eye St. NW
Washington, DC 20006
(202) 293-1966
FAX: (202) 296-7410
URL: http://www.mpaa.org/

National Aeronautics and Space Administration
NASA Headquarters, Ste. 5K39
Washington, DC 20546
(202) 358-0000
FAX: (202) 358-4338
E-mail: public-inquiries@hq.nasa.gov
URL: http://www.nasa.gov/

National Center for Education Statistics Institute of Education Sciences
1990 K St. NW, Eighth and Ninth Floors
Washington, DC 20006
(202) 502-7300
FAX: (202) 502-7466
URL: http://nces.ed.gov/

National Science Foundation
4201 Wilson Blvd.
Arlington, VA 22230
(703) 292-5111
1-800-877-8339
E-mail: info@nsf.gov
URL: http://www.nsf.gov/

The Nielsen Company
770 Broadway
New York, NY 10003-9595
(646) 654-5000
URL: http://www.nielsen.com/

Office of Management and Budget
725 17th St. NW
Washington, DC 20503
(202) 395-3080
FAX: (202) 395-3888
URL: http://www.whitehouse.gov/omb/

On-Line Gamers Anonymous World Services Inc.
104 Miller Ln.
Harrisburg, PA 17110
(612) 245-1115
URL: http://www.olganon.org/

Pew Internet & American Life Project
1615 L St. NW, Ste. 700
Washington, DC 20036
(202) 419-4500
FAX: (202) 419-4505
E-mail: data@pewinternet.org
URL: http://www.pewinternet.org/

Recording Industry Association of America
1025 F St. NW, 10th Floor
Washington, DC 20004
(202) 775-0101
URL: http://www.riaa.com/

The Spamhaus Project
18 Ave. Louis Casai
Geneva, Switzerland CH-1209
E-mail: media-int@spamhaus.org
URL: http://www.spamhaus.org/

TV Parental Guidelines Monitoring Board
PO Box 14097
Washington, DC 20004

(202) 879-9364
E-mail: tvomb@usa.net
URL: http://www.tvguidelines.org/

United Network for Organ Sharing
700 N. Fourth St.
Richmond, VA 23219
(804) 782-4800
FAX: (804) 782-4817
URL: http://www.unos.org/

U.S. Census Bureau
4600 Silver Hill Rd.
Washington, DC 20233
(301) 763-4636
1-800-923-8282
URL: http://www.census.gov/

US-CERT Security Operations Center U.S. Department of Homeland Security
245 Murray Ln. SW, Bldg. 410
Washington, DC 20598
(703) 235-5110
1-888-282-0870
E-mail: info@us-cert.gov
URL: http://www.us-cert.gov/

U.S. Department of Homeland Security
Washington, DC 20528
(202) 282-8000
URL: http://www.dhs.gov/

U.S. Department of Justice—Computer Crime and Intellectual Property Section
950 Pennsylvania Ave. NW
Washington, DC 20530-0001
(202) 514-2000
E-mail: AskDOJ@usdoj.gov
URL: http://www.usdoj.gov/

U.S. Department of Labor
200 Constitution Ave. NW
Washington, DC 20210
1-866-487-2365
URL: http://www.dol.gov/

U.S. Government Accountability Office
441 G St. NW
Washington, DC 20548
(202) 512-3000
E-mail: contact@gao.gov
URL: http://www.gao.gov/

RESOURCES

The Pew Charitable Trust established the Pew Internet & American Life Project (Pew/Internet) in 1999. Since then, Pew/Internet has conducted dozens of surveys to determine just who in the United States uses the Internet and how they use it. *Digital Differences* (Kathryn Zickuhr and Aaron Smith, April 13, 2012) and *Search Engine Use 2012* (Kristen Purcell, Joanna Brenner, and Lee Rainie, March 9, 2012) report Pew/Internet's findings on the adoption of Internet technology. *Teens, Kindness and Cruelty on Social Network Sites* (Amanda Lenhart et al., November 9, 2011), *Generations and Their Gadgets* (Kathryn Zickuhr, February 3, 2011), and *Teens & Online Video* (Amanda Lenhart, May 3, 2012) report on specific demographic groups. *Online Political Videos and Campaign 2012* (Aaron Smith and Maeve Duggan, November 2, 2012), *The State of the 2012 Election—Mobile Politics* (Aaron Smith and Maeve Duggan, October 9, 2012), and *Social Networking Sites and Politics* (Lee Rainie and Aaron Smith, March 12, 2012) illustrate how much the Internet influences the various ways that Americans engage with politics and the government. Pew/Internet publications that examine health care and the Internet include *Family Caregivers Online* (Susannah Fox and Joanna Brenner, July 12, 2012) and *The Social Life of Health Information, 2011* (Susannah Fox, May 12, 2011).

Other publications by Pew/Internet that were useful in preparing this volume include *Teens, Smartphones & Texting* (Amanda Lenhart, March 19, 2012), *The Rise of In-Store Mobile Commerce* (Aaron Smith, January 30, 2012), *Twitter Use 2012* (Aaron Smith and Joanna Brenner, May 31, 2012), *The Digital Revolution and Higher Education: College Presidents, Public Differ on Value of Online Learning* (Kim Parker, Amanda Lenhart, and Kathleen Moore, August 28, 2011), *Social Networking Sites and Our Lives* (Keith N. Hampton et al., June 16, 2011), and *17% of Cell Phone Owners Do Most of Their Browsing on Their Phone, Rather Than a Computer or Other Device* (Aaron Smith, June 26, 2012), among others.

The Gallup Organization provides valuable results from polls on topics such as Internet and cell phone use, e-crime, e-commerce, and entertainment, among others. Reports consulted for this book include *Computers and the Internet* (2012) and *Media Use and Evaluation* (2012).

A number of excellent accounts of Internet history can be found online, including Robert H. Zakon's *Hobbes' Internet Timeline 10.2* (December 30, 2011, http://www.zakon.org/robert/internet/timeline/). Most of these histories are listed in the Internet Society's *Histories of the Internet* (December 2012, http://www.isoc.org/internet/history/). *A Brief History of the Internet* (December 2003, http://www.isoc.org/internet/history/brief.shtml) was written by some of the people who gave rise to the Internet, including Vinton G. Cerf, the creator of TCP/IP. *An Atlas of Cyberspaces* (February 2007, http://personalpages.manchester.ac.uk/staff/m.dodge/cybergeography/atlas/atlas.html) by Martin Dodge and Rob Kitchin displays map after map of the Internet networks that have spanned the United States since the creation of ARPANET. The Internet2 website (http://www.internet2.edu/) contains a great deal of information on the Internet2 consortium as well as on the future of the Internet.

A number of magazines and websites report on the latest developments in technology. In print, *New Scientist*, *PC World*, *Popular Science*, *Scientific American*, and *Wired* contain articles on the most recent trends in electronics and software. On the Internet, CNET.com, eWeek.com, TechWeb.com, Wired.com, and ZDNet.com post the latest news in high tech daily.

The Federal Communications Commission (FCC) is the government agency responsible for regulating which devices can use the various portions of the electromagnetic spectrum. The agency also regulates television and radio programming. The FCC website (http://www.fcc.gov/) provides information on the Children's Internet Protection

Act, closed captioning, high-definition television, radio spectrum allocation, the transition to digital television, and the V-Chip.

The U.S. Census Bureau's *Statistical Abstract of the United States* contains a number of statistics illustrating the effects of technology on American life. These include the percentage of households with computer and Internet access, the amount of time and money Americans spend on various media and media systems (e.g., television and radio), and the number of Americans with credit and debit card accounts. The Census Bureau's *E-Stats* provides financial statistics on e-commerce in the United States.

The U.S. Department of Commerce compiles reports on Internet usage and on the effects of high tech on the economy. Its landmark study *Digital Economy 2003* (December 2003) reports on how high tech has transformed the U.S. economy. The Department of Commerce also publishes the serial publications *Industry Economic Accounts* and *Quarterly Retail E-Commerce Sales*, which provide information on the economic impact of the Internet and information technology. In addition, the U.S. Department of Labor tracks employment statistics and trends in publications such as *Mass Layoff Statistics* (2012) and "Work-at-Home Patterns by Occupation" (March 2009).

The Federal Trade Commission (FTC) hosts a website (http://www.ftc.gov/bcp/edu/microsites/idtheft) that houses a number of reports and informational brochures on identity theft and Internet fraud. The FTC publications consulted for this book include the *Consumer Sentinel Network Data Book for January–December 2011* (February 2012). The U.S. Department of Justice maintains a website on cybercrime (http://www.justice.gov/criminal/cybercrime/) that contains reports on identity theft and Internet fraud. The site also includes several reports on intellectual property theft, including the *2010 Joint Strategic Plan on Intellectual Property Enforcement* (June 2010).

The Internet Crime Complaint Center (IC3), a division of the Federal Bureau of Investigation, monitors and responds to major threats to the Internet such as large-scale hacking incidents and virus attacks. Each year, IC3, in conjunction with the Department of Justice, the Bureau of Justice Assistance, and the National White Collar Crime Center, publishes the *Internet Crime Report*, which outlines e-crime incidents reported by U.S. businesses. These crimes include anything from Internet fraud to hacking incidents to viruses. The U.S. Department of Homeland Security website (http://www.dhs.gov/) and the U.S. Computer Emergency Readiness Team website (http://www.us-cert.gov/) contain reports on how the government is using high tech to combat threats to national security.

To get more information on optical scan and digital recording electronic voting machines and about how national elections are conducted, visit the Federal Election Commission website (http://www.fec.gov/). The Intelligent Transportation Systems Joint Program Office, which is located within the U.S. Department of Transportation, contains reports on 511 deployment and operations. The American Customer Satisfaction Index scores for many of the federal government's most popular sites can be found at http://www.theacsi.org/. The Office of Management and Budget website (http://www.whitehouse.gov/omb/) provides information on President Barack Obama's e-government initiatives as well as on the E-Government Act of 2002.

The Centers for Disease Control and Prevention website (http://www.cdc.gov/) reports on how researchers are employing the Internet, global positioning systems, and other high-tech equipment to analyze the risks that are associated with major diseases. Information on the development of a nationwide health information network is presented by the U.S. Department of Health and Human Services in *The ONC-Coordinated Federal Health IT Strategic Plan: 2008–2012* (June 3, 2008). Additional information about technological developments in the health care field can be found in *U.S. Department of Health and Human Services Strategic Plan, Fiscal Years 2010–2015* (2011).

The National Center for Education Statistics provides a number of reports that detail the use of computers and the Internet in the classroom. The reports discussed in this book are *Digest of Education Statistics 2011* (Thomas A. Snyder and Sally A. Dillow, June 2012), *Distance Education Courses for Public Elementary and Secondary School Students: 2009–10* (Barbara Queen and Laurie Lewis, November 2011), and *Teachers' Use of Educational Technology in U.S. Public Schools: 2009* (Lucinda Gray, Nina Thomas, and Laurie Lewis, May 2010).

INDEX